POWER, PERSONALITIES AND POLICIES:
ESSAYS IN HONOUR OF
DONALD CAMERON WATT

# Power, Personalities and Policies:

## Essays in Honour of Donald Cameron Watt

edited by

MICHAEL GRAHAM FRY

*University of Southern California*

FRANK CASS

First published in 1992 in Great Britain by
FRANK CASS & CO. LTD.
Gainsborough House, Gainsborough Road,
London E11 1RS, England

and in the United States of America by
FRANK CASS
c/o International Specialized Book Services, Inc.
5602 N.E. Hassalo Street, Portland, Oregon 97213

British Library Cataloguing in Publication Data

Power, Personalities and Policies: Essays
in Honour of Donald Cameron Watt
I. Fry, Michael G.
907.202

ISBN 0-7146-3428-X

Library of Congress Cataloging-in-Publication Data

Power, personalities, and policies: essays in honour of Donald
    Cameron Watt / edited by Michael Graham Fry.
        p.   cm.
    "The writings of Donald Cameron Watt": p.
    Includes index.
    ISBN 0-7146-3428-X
    1. World politics—20th century.   2. Watt, Donald Cameron.
I. Watt, Donald Cameron.   II. Fry, Michael G.
D443.P676   1992
327'.09'04—dc20                                      92-13528
                                                           CIP


ISBN 0 7146 3428 X

Typeset by Vitaset, Paddock Wood, Kent
Printed in Great Britain by Bookcraft Ltd

# Contents

# Notes on Contributors

**Sidney Aster** is Professor of History, Erindale College, University of Toronto. His dissertation was entitled 'British Policy Towards the USSR and the Onset of the Second World War, March 1938–August 1939'. He is the author of *1939, The Making of the Second World War* (1973) and *British Foreign Policy, 1918–1945: A Guide to Research and Research Materials* (2nd ed., 1991).

**Uri Bialer** is Professor of International Relations, The Hebrew University of Jerusalem. His dissertation was entitled 'Some Aspects of the Fear of Bombardment from the Air and the Making of British Defense and Foreign Policy, 1932–1939'. He is the author of *The Shadow of the Bomber* (1980) and *Between East and West* (1990).

**Martin van Creveld** is Professor of History, The Hebrew University of Jerusalem. His dissertation was entitled 'Hitler's Strategy, 1940–41; the Balkan Clue'. He is the author of *Command in War* (1985) and *Technology and War* (1989).

**John P. Fox** was Maxwell Fellow in the Study and Teaching of the Holocaust, Oxford Centre for Postgraduate Hebrew Studies, 1990–91. His dissertation was entitled 'The Formulation of Germany's Far Eastern Policy, 1933–1936'. He is the author of *Germany and the Far Eastern Crisis, 1931–1938. A Study in Diplomacy and Ideology* (1982).

**Michael Graham Fry** is Professor of International Relations, University of Southern California. His dissertation was entitled 'Anglo-American-Canadian Relations, with Special Reference to Naval and Far Eastern Affairs, 1918–1922'. He is the author of *Lloyd George and Foreign Policy, Volume One. The Education of a Statesman, 1890–1916* (1977) and *History, the White House and the Kremlin. Statesmen as Historians* (1991).

**B.J.C. McKercher** is Associate Professor of History, Royal Military College of Canada, Kingston. His dissertation was entitled 'The British Foreign Policy-making elite and its attitudes towards the United States, November 1924–June 1929'. He is the author of *The Second Baldwin Government and the United States, 1924–1929: Attitudes and Diplomacy* (1984) and *Esme Howard: A Diplomatic Biography* (1989).

**Larry Pratt** is Professor of Political Science, University of Alberta. His dissertation was entitled 'The Strategic Elements in British Policy in the Eastern Mediterranean, 1936–1939'. He is the author of *East of Suez, West of Malta* (1976) and *Canada, NATO and the Bomb* (1988).

**Norman Rose** is Chaim Weizmann Professor of International Relations at the Hebrew University. His dissertation was entitled 'The Gentile Zionists. A Study in Anglo-Zionist Diplomacy, 1929–1939'. He is the author of *Vansittart. Study of a Diplomat* (1978) and *Chaim Weizmann. A Biography* (1987).

**Robert J. Young** is Professor of History, University of Winnipeg. His dissertation was entitled 'Strategy and Diplomacy in France: Some Aspects of the Military Factor in the Formulation of French Foreign Policy, 1934–1939'. He is the author of *In Command of France: French Foreign Policy and Military Planning, 1933–1940* (1978) and *Power and Pleasure: Louis Barthou and the Third French Republic, 1862–1934* (1991).

**Wesley K. Wark** is Associate Professor of History, University of Toronto. His dissertation was entitled 'British Military and Economic Intelligence on Nazi Germany 1933–1939'. He is the author of *The Ultimate Enemy. British Intelligence and Nazi Germany, 1933–1939* (1985) and editor of *Spy Fiction, Spy Films and Real Intelligence* (1991).

# Foreword

Donald Cameron Watt's *How War Came. The Immediate Origins of the Second World War* (1989), confirmed his reputation as one of the foremost historians of international relations of his generation.

Diplomatic history has become, in the course of the last 25 years or so, international history. The transformation has been welcomed almost universally, although much has remained as it was, and not every change has been particularly fruitful. Donald Watt was never a diplomatic historian in the narrow sense. He was always something more than that. *Personalities and Policies: Studies in the Formulation of British Foreign Policy in the Twentieth Century* (1965), marked his emergence in a definitive way as a scholar of the first rank. It moved his reputation well beyond that which he already enjoyed as editor of the *Documents on German Foreign Policy, 1918–1945*, because of his work at the Royal Institute for International Affairs, and his early contributions to the study of appeasement, the Suez crisis, Mediterranean diplomacy, German politics and foreign policy, Anglo-German and Italo-German relations, imperial and Commonwealth affairs, British foreign policy and Anglo-American relations. Many of his earlier essays, written before the archives were open, have, it should be emphasized, stood the test of time.

*Personalities and Policies* also heralded the role Donald Watt would play in shaping international history, giving it form and credibility intellectually, without a trace of destructive radicalism. Because his work was conceptual and implicitly theoretical, and sometimes explicitly so, he could joust with political scientists labouring in the field of enquiry that is international relations, and to some effect. In certain ways, Donald Watt led the methodological debate among historians of international relations, a debate not marked particularly either by enthusiasm or persistence on the part of his colleagues in the profession. The aversion of most historians to discussions of methodology continues without significant interruption. He wove together strategy and diplomacy, diplomatic theory and practice, the domestic and the international spheres, societies and foreign policy.

Recognizing that the study of international relations rested unsteadily somewhere between economics and psychology, Donald Watt opened up the examination of elite beliefs and perceptions, their creation and influence on behaviour, across generations, and their trans-national, that is trans-Atlantic, significance. Most recently, he has influenced, almost as much as any other single scholar, the methods and substance of intelligence studies. He has brought to that subject an innovative flair, a sophisticated technique of reasoning through inference, the instincts of a former intelligence officer, the intuitive gifts and scepticism of a great historian, and a sustained brilliance as an essayist.

Donald Watt is, above all else, a historian of the inter-war years. He has pushed on into the Second World War and well beyond, but has never ventured back before 1914. Britain, Germany and the United States, and their relations, are at the core of his work. But his reach beyond them is remarkable – to the other European great powers, the Middle East, the Empire and Commonwealth, and East Asia. He is very much the academic historian's historian, but not at the cost either of seeking to inform attentive publics about historical and contemporary issues, or of being indifferent to the need to provide discussion on contemporary issues with a historical perspective. And that concern, along with his interest in naval affairs, no doubt, led him to the seas, to oil, and to the issue of regimes to regulate use of the seas and the exploitation of maritime resources. In all this, Donald Watt could be challenging, even controversial. He is never afraid of controversy and is willing to confront established interpretations and opinions, and forthrightly so, but always with a regard for reputation that was entirely appropriate.

*Professor* Watt is best described as formidable but kind. He looked for merit in his graduate students, so that he could show them how promising they were, how accomplished they could become, if they worked hard. That was both comforting and challenging. He was, above all else, 'straight' with his students, guiding when necessary, leaving them alone when it was wise to do so, helping them to reason and write, commenting in great detail on what they wrote. Students rose to their respective levels of achievement, and beyond, and left his supervision self-reliant and confident, valuing his scholarship and his friendship. Some of them, predictably, have begun to make a mark in universities throughout the Western world. Canadians always received a warm and quizzical welcome, perhaps because his mother, a Canadian, the daughter of the bishop of Ontario, met his

father, who taught history at Queen's University, at the Christmas
Ball at the Royal Military College in Kingston in 1926. But so did
the rest of us who went to the London School of Economics to work
with him. And we acknowledge that Donald Watt set standards of
scholarship that few of us thought we could match. For the most part
we were right.

Michael Graham Fry

# Thucydides and International History

## LARRY PRATT

For the principal and proper work of history being to instruct and enable men, by the knowledge of actions past, to bear themselves prudently in the present and providently towards the future: there is not extant any other (merely human) that doth more naturally and fully perform it, than this of my author. . . . Thucydides is one, who, though he never digress to read a lecture, moral or political, upon his own text, nor enter into men's hearts further than the acts themselves evidently guide him: is yet accounted the most politick historiographer that ever writ.

Thomas Hobbes, 'To the Readers', of his seventeenth-century translation of Thucydides.[1]

This essay is about Thucydides and the origins of international history as a field of scholarly inquiry. The focus of the essay is the Athenian historian's treatment of power, particularly sea-power, and the development of hegemonies in the history of classical Greece's international relations. If Thucydides invented political history, as some have argued,[2] he did so by examining the behaviour of the state primarily in its *external* aspect, in the conduct of its relations with other states in peace and war. Unlike the philosophers whose interest was in the inner life of the ideal *polis* (city), Thucydides's subject was the real city in a state of war and revolution – the 'greatest *kinesis*' (motion), as he called the Peloponnesian War of 431–404 BC. Given what he knew of war's character and what it does to human psychology and conduct, how could he write of the ideal city? His analysis of civil strife – *stasis* – showed how war could bring out the worst instincts in individuals:

The sufferings which revolution entailed upon the cities were many and terrible, such as have occurred and always will occur, as long as the nature of mankind remains the same, though in severer or milder form, and varying in their symptoms, according to the variety of the particular cases. In peace and prosperity states and individuals have better sentiments, because they do not find themselves suddenly confronted with imperious necessities; but war takes away the easy supply of daily wants, and so proves a rough master that brings most men's characters to a level with their fortunes (3.82).[3]

That same rough master, war, which releases the ungovernable passions of men and brutally alters their judgement and behaviour, had prompted Thucydides to write the history of the war between the Athenians and the Peloponnesians, 'beginning at the moment that it broke out, and believing that it would be a great war, and more worthy of relation than any that had preceded it' (1.1). His preference for *contemporary* history as the only reliable history emerged from a conviction that, first, 'nothing on a great scale, either in war or in other matters' had happened in the remote past, and, second, that so many events of the distant past had been distorted by poets or the compositions of chroniclers 'that are attractive at truth's expense, the subjects they treat of being out of the reach of evidence, and time having robbed most of them of historical value by enthroning them in the region of legend' (1.1; 1.21).

War had to be understood as a social and political phenomenon, and its causes must be sought in the decisions of individuals and the actions and relationships of states – not in the legends and oracles circulated by poets and story-tellers. If superstition and religion played any role in Thucydides's account of the war, it was because most leaders lacked political knowledge and intelligence (*gnome*), and were prone to fall back on religious illusions and false conceptions of the world. Disasters occurred when some leading personalities, such as the indecisive Athenian statesman Nicias, allowed religious piety to govern their public duties; while others, like the leaders of Melos, literally denied the military power arrayed against them, taking refuge in the delusory hope that the gods would save them from destruction. Thucydides admired effective action, and effectiveness in war and politics required the abandonment of all dangerous, self-defeating illusions. In explicit contrast to the approach of Herodotus, his somewhat older contemporary and the chronicler of the Greek–Persian wars, Thucydides would relate his history of the Athenian–Spartan power struggle without describing a single intervention by the gods. Herodotus had written that the Trojan War occurred for reasons of divine requital (for every great wrongdoing, great also are the punishments of the gods). His account of the Persian Wars reflected his belief that the power that rules the world reveals itself through signs, visions and oracles; in these are to be found the origins of great empires and the causes of wars. But the gods and oracles are not implicated in Thucydides's account of the immediate and deeper causes of the Peloponnesian War; nowhere does he attribute to non-human forces the slightest responsibility for the terrible war and related disasters that befell Greece after 431.

Thucydides, like two later philosophers of war, Machiavelli and Clausewitz, wrote as one who had held high office but, after experiencing war's vicissitudes, had withdrawn to write about politics and military affairs. Elected as one of Athens' ten military commanders during the war, Thucydides had failed to relieve the strategically important town of Amphipolis after it fell to the great Spartan general, Brasidas. The Athenians had banished him for twenty years. Of the war, he wrote: 'I lived through the whole of it, being of an age to comprehend events, and giving my attention to them in order to know the exact truth about them' (5.26). In a famous programmatic chapter of the *History*, he said that the speeches in the book had been written so as to say 'what was in my opinion demanded of them [the speakers] by the various occasions, of course adhering as closely as possible to the general sense of what they really said'; but he also spoke of using 'the most severe and detailed tests possible' to check the accuracy of his narrative. He had not relied on a single source or even on his own impressions. 'My conclusions have cost me some labour from the want of agreement between accounts of the same occurrences by different eye-witnesses, arising sometimes from imperfect memory, sometimes from undue partiality for one side or the other.' His history of the war had not been written to please everyone's taste:

The absence of romance in my history will, I fear, detract somewhat from its interest; but if it be judged useful by those inquirers who desire an exact knowledge of the past as an aid to the interpretation of the future, which in the course of human things must resemble if it does not reflect it, I shall be content. In fine, I have written my work, not as an essay which is to win the applause of the moment, but as a possession for all time (1.22).

In other words, he saw this greatest war as a paradigm that could be usefully studied in order to discover the real causes and nature, of not just a specific conflict, but of all war.

Thucydides's treatment of two concepts – power and hegemony – is central to his analysis of international history. His psychological assumptions concerning the true (though often concealed) interests and motives that underlie human behaviour also require examination.

All men, say the Athenians at the first assembly at Sparta, are driven by fear, honour and profit (1.76), and it is upon these universal human motives – not sentiments of friendship, ties of race, or party ideology – that states are able to build coalitions and engage in great collective actions. Self-interest is the only reliable guide we have to assist us in the evaluation of such actions.

## A Consciousness of Power

There is a striking passage near the opening of the *History* in which Thucydides speaks of the difficulties involved in assessing the relative power of states and in distinguishing between the *appearance* and the *reality* of power. In this passage Thucydides cautions his readers against a contempt for the material power or armament of some older centres of civilization, an error that 'no exact observer' would make. Suppose, he says, the city of Sparta became desolate and only the remains of a few temples and public buildings were left. As time passed, future generations would find it hard to believe that this unimpressive place had really been as powerful as its fame reputed it to be. And yet, he notes, the Spartans of his day occupy two-fifths of the Peloponnese and also lead numerous allies outside the region. 'Still, as the city is neither built in a compact form nor adorned with magnificent temples and public edifices, but composed of villages after the old fashion of Hellas, there would be an impression of inadequacy.' On the other hand, if Athens were to suffer the same misfortune: 'I suppose that any inference from the appearance presented to the eye would make her power to have been twice as great as it is' (1.10). If we had only the material remains and no written histories to guide us, the appearance of Athens would lead us to conclude that it was several times more powerful than, not just Sparta, but cities as great as Argos, Thebes, and Corinth.[4] The archaeological remains alone would distract us from the ancient view that the strength of a state depends as much on the virtue of its citizens as on its wealth and numbers.

Thucydides argues that the assessment of power is subject to distortions of a psychological nature because the analyst makes inferences 'from the appearance presented to the eye', and what appears to posterity to be proof of great power (for example, the remains of temples and monuments) may in reality be only an illusion. The multiplicity of such distortions and illusions that mask reality and distract observers is part of the deep problem confronting those who seek truth in the remote past or even in contemporary history.

Thucydides is also cautioning that it can be a fatal mistake for a statesman merely to look at a state and its cultural achievements without taking its armaments and reputation for war into account; in particular, the adversaries of Sparta are warned that its power is far greater than mere appearances would indicate (the superficial brilliance and dynamism of Athens having led many to underestimate Sparta's true strengths). Political and military actions are the *erga* (deeds), by which we judge human greatness and assess the power of cities such as Sparta and Athens and their capacity to rule over others.[5]

Power (*dynamis*), is a central concept in the analysis of international politics, but, as Thucydides here cautions us, it is also elusive and hard to measure. The place to begin a discussion of what Thucydides means by power is in the 18 brief chapters of the so-called Archaeology (1.2-19) of the first book, the highly compressed opening of the *History* in which he sets out his views on the central role of *dynamis* – particularly seapower – in Greece's material progress up to the fifth century. His stated purpose in the Archaeology is to review the events of early Greece in order to show that no earlier wars or collective actions compared in greatness with the Peloponnesian War, and that the weaknesses of earlier times prevented the Greeks from achieving the power or material wealth attained by cities such as Athens in his own day. It is characteristic of his method that these few pages of the work also establish his sceptical, unsentimental stance toward the remote past, a past without romance or gods or supernatural heroes, while setting out a brilliant sweeping theory about how the accumulation of *dynamis* at sea and great collective actions brought progress to the Hellenic world. The Archaeology contains no Thucydidean speeches, and there can be no doubt that the voice and the ideas in this excursus are those of the historian himself. His method is to reconstruct the prehistory of Greece using bold inferences and hypotheses drawn from his close observation of human behaviour and power politics in his own time. Although he does not hold to a static view of human nature or reduce history to a set of abstract principles, he does assume that individuals and groups have always been moved by fear, greed and the desire to accumulate *dynamis*. In the words of a great classicist: 'Thucydides is looking at the past with the eyes of a fifth-century politician: he thinks only of *power*.'[6]

His theory is an attempt to explain how early Greece gradually overcame its insecurity and geographical disunity through the growth of seapower, commerce and capital; why it was that the Greeks, seeking an escape from backwardness, were compelled to conquer the sea and to make the Aegean Sea their true home. Without security and stability, there can be no material progress; without the accumulation of *dynamis* – resources, men and ships – and its consolidation under stable leadership, the development of civilized society, as epitomized in fifth-century Athens, would be impossible. Supernatural and religious factors have no role at all in Thucydides's realistic theory of power and progress. What he refers to as the 'absence of romance in my history' (1.22) is much in evidence throughout the Archaeology. Looking back into the remote past, he sees self-interest and the familiar elements in human nature always at play: fear, greed and the dominion of the powerful over the weak are the forces that drove the peoples of Hellas to overcome their frailty and division. He sketches an unromantic portrait of 'the weakness of ancient times'; people were uprooted, insecure, incapable of engaging in great concerted actions:

. . . it is evident that the country now called Hellas had in ancient times no settled population; on the contrary, migrations were of frequent occurrence, the several tribes readily abandoning their homes under the pressure of superior numbers. Without commerce, without freedom of communication either by land or sea, cultivating no more of their territory than the exigencies of life required, destitute of capital, never planting their land (for they could not tell when an invader might not come and take it all away, and when he did come they had no walls to stop him), thinking that the necessities of daily sustenance could be supplied at one place as well as another, they cared little for shifting their habitation, and consequently neither built great cities nor attained to any other form of greatness (1.2).

Factionalism within cities (*stasis*) is adduced as another barrier to collective action by the early Greeks, especially in fertile areas where 'the goodness of the land favoured the aggrandizement of particular individuals, and thus created faction which proved a fertile source of ruin. It also invited invasion' (1.2). Areas where the soil was poor, such as Attica – the region surrounding Athens – escaped internal polarization and foreign intervention, though not in Thucydides' own day. *Stasis* is represented throughout the *History* as the force that enfeebles cities by destroying their capacity to act in a concerted manner. If *dynamis* is created via collective actions, domestic polarization is what destroys or paralyses it.[7] During war, ideological conflict between states is often reproduced *within* the belligerent states, and this can cause a most violent faction or *stasis*, as Thucydides shows in his famous account of the debasement of Hellenic values during the revolution in Corcyra (3.81-83). Here in the Archaeology, which he uses to foreshadow so many themes developed in his analysis of the Peloponnesian War, internal disorder is already established as the violent companion of greed, envy and the fear that rules the Thucydidean universe.

Power involves concerted action; in isolation, neither cities nor citizens can realize their *dynamis*. Before the Trojan War, he argues, the Greeks lacked control of the sea and had no sense of their common identity; they were 'prevented by their want of strength and the absence of mutual intercourse from displaying any collective action' (1.3). There was no commerce and no accumulation of wealth. Piracy thrived – men were forced into it for their livelihood – and in the general disorder people were forced to carry arms for personal safety. 'The whole of Hellas used once to carry arms, their habitations being unprotected, and their communication with each other unsafe' (1.6). This situation only began to change when Minos, the legendary tyrant of Crete, formed a navy and began to clear the seas of pirates, 'a necessary step to secure the revenues for his own use'. Communication by sea became easier as he colonized many of the islands and expelled the pirates. This permitted seaborne commerce to grow, the coastal populations to acquire wealth and walls for their towns, and self-interest to divide the new settlements into rulers and ruled:

For the love of gain would reconcile the weaker to the dominion of the stronger, and the possession of capital enabled the more powerful to reduce the smaller towns to subjection (1.8).

Greece began to develop, then, only after mastery of the sea had been gained through the actions of a powerful leader, a *hegemon*. Use of the sea was for Thucydides a measure of the technical progress as well as the *dynamis* of a civilization. Even in early Greece, navies were 'an element of the greatest power to those who cultivated them, alike in revenue and dominion' (1.15). Naval supremacy – or thalassocracy – is the basis of all successful imperialism in Thucydides. The Athenian empire of the fifth century is only the latest stage in a process that stretches back to the Minoan period. Minos is the exemplar or model, the *paradeigma*, of an effective hegemony based upon seapower and financial resources. Thucydides uses the example to show that once the security problem was dealt with by Minos and surpluses of capital became available, the so-called 'law of the stronger' began to organize the Greeks into recognizable hierarchies – rulers and ruled; wealthy and poor; strong and weak. The essential idea here – it is arguably the fundamental concept of the Archaeology – is that the strong control the weak for their mutual advantage.[8] The supremacy of Minos succeeded because it served the interests of the weak as well as the powerful; the weak submitted voluntarily to the rule of the stronger because of fear – they needed protection – and the love of gain. The subjects were no less venal, no less motivated by profit than the imperialists. The latter, selfishly striving only for dominion and wealth, opened the seas for navigation and commerce and thereby made it feasible for Greece to begin to escape the fear and scarcity of early times.[9] The development of Hellas proceeded from the consolidation of power and wealth by the strongest states, and especially by those willing to lead the Greeks in concerted actions.

The first great collective enterprise of the Greeks, their first major coalition or hegemonial alliance, was the expedition against Troy under the leadership of Agamemnon of Mycenae. For Thucydides, the capacity to pool interests and to act in concert on international questions is evidence of *dynamis*, but it does not arise spontaneously. Men, ships and capital must be mobilized and deployed by experienced leaders who have the intelligence and judgement to use their power effectively, and who know how to practice self-restraint. Usually associated in Thucydides with the development and use of seapower, collective action involves leadership (or hegemony) and a common fear – the shared apprehension of some future danger or evil. From the standpoint of the classical realist, fear (or insecurity) is the force that sets international politics in motion; it is 'the prime motive of international politics. For all powers at all times are concerned primarily with their security, and most powers at most times find their security threatened'.[10] That fear rather than goodwill is the foundation of interstate coalitions and the motive for many of their joint actions is the moral of Thucydides's account of the Greek expedition to Troy, and one that foreshadows much of his analysis of the international politics before, as well as during, the Peloponnesian War. What caused the Greeks to unite and follow their *hegemon*, Agamemnon, 'was more, in my opinion, his superiority in strength than the oaths to Tyndareus, which bound the suitors of Helen to follow him'. Agamemnon inherited the vast wealth and power of Pelops, and what established his right to lead the Greeks was that:

He had also a navy far stronger than his contemporaries, so that, in my opinion, fear was quite as strong an element as love in the formation of the confederate expedition (1.9).

Reducing Homer's heroes to the status of ordinary mortals moved by fear and self-interest as much as by sentiments of loyalty and friendship, Thucydides strips the romantic element from the greatest of Greek epics in order to reveal the true causes of the action against Troy, and to show that the Trojan war was 'far from equalling' the Peloponnesian War of his own day. The other Greeks followed Agamemnon because they feared his superior power, not because they had sworn to do so: they submitted to his rule out of self-interest. It is implied that a single strong leader or *hegemon*, a Minos, an Agamemnon, or an Athens, superior at sea, is a prerequisite for effective collective action by states; concentrations of power and resources are required for the progressive development of any civilization, and mastery of the sea is the indispensable condition in the accumulation of power and wealth. Thucydides adds that it was the poverty of Greece and the insufficiency of its finances and supplies that prevented the expedition to Troy from attaining a quick success. For want of money, many of the Greeks abandoned the siege of Troy and took up subsistence agriculture and piracy out of necessity, thus prolonging the war for ten long years. Lacking financial reserves, the Greeks of Agamemnon's day could not attain the progress and greatness achieved in Periclean Athens in Thucydides's own time.

Naval power and financial capital are inextricably linked in Thucydides's conception of progress. Wealth alone cannot provide a city with safety and independence, it cannot keep a foreign army from invading its territory or an enemy's fleet from blockading its coasts. To have security and independence in a world in which war is always possible, a city must be strong enough to inspire fear in others, and therefore it needs armaments, allies and knowledge in war. However, unlike later realists such as Machiavelli, he does not disparage wealth or fear it unduly as a cause of a state's ruin.[11] On the contrary, Thucydides – who owned gold mines in Thrace and was himself a wealthy and influential man[12] – identifies material progress with expansion, flourishing trade, prosperous cities, and technical achievements within the framework of a great empire. The love of gain, the drive to acquire wealth, is a primary motive force in human behaviour and in Greek expansionism; greed is what led Minos to clear the seas of pirates, and then induced the weak to accept the hegemony of the stronger. Mastery of the sea involves great expenditures on harbours, ships, and manpower; an imperial power such as Athens could not hope to prevail in war without great financial reserves. And prosperity was also required to placate the Athenian *demos*, the people, and their expectations: without public wealth and the promise of a higher living standard, they were unlikely to support the ruling politicians.

The accumulation of wealth is the indispensable basis of any great civilization, but it cannot occur without the unification of power and a sense of stablity – what Thucydides calls 'the quiet which must precede growth' (1.12).[13] Material progress comes about when life is settled and people have enough security, and this can happen only after power has been centralized by some stronger progressive authority – for instance, Minos. In the conditions of shifting populations and decentralized power that prevailed in early Greece, people were always insecure and unwilling to make the longer-term commitments – whether cultivating the land or planting orchards – necessary for development. The Archaeology argues that the solution was not for each tiny Greek settlement to build economic as well as physical walls around itself, but for all to accept the supremacy of the strongest maritime power in return for its provision of protection, leadership, and the prospect of a better standard of life. Thus, Thucydides argues, the escape from the margins of existence into modernity – progress – occurs through the leadership of the strong – hegemony; the strong rule the weak for their mutual advantage.

The ancient Greeks thought of the history of their international relations as a succession of hegemonies. There is no conception of the balance of power in Thucydides or in other Greek writings on war and peace.[14] But after the foundation of the Spartan-led Peloponnesian League in the sixth century there is the idea of a leading power in the system, a power with recognized primacy and wide-ranging powers of initiative to look after the general welfare. Martin Wight observed in his *Systems of States* that the Greeks 'seem to have had a fundamentally *hegemonial* theory of the states-system. From the sixth century they seem to have thought of it as having a natural leader or "president", and they had several terms for this concept – *prostates tes Hellados, hegemon*'.[15] The acceptance by a dominant power of obligations to its allies and responsibilities toward the states-system was one side of hegemony; the duty of its allies to serve and follow the *hegemon* in peace and war was its other side. Thucydides conceived of international relations among the Greek cities very much in these terms. His archaeological review of power is basically an introduction to maritime supremacy, tracing the line of thalassocracies from Minos of Crete to the beginnings of the Athenian empire at the time of the great Persian expedition against Greece early in the fifth century. Indeed, Thucydides' entire *History* is (among other themes) an extended analysis of contested hegemony in peace and war.

After Troy, 'as the power of Hellas grew, and the acquisition of wealth became more of an object', the Greeks, as Thucydides puts it, applied themselves more closely to the sea. Tyrannies were established throughout Hellas. At the great commercial city of Corinth, the early Greek warship, the long, narrow fifty-oared vessel, was replaced by the much faster and larger 'trireme', propelled by 170 rowers seated on three levels. Those cities that acquired large navies used them to cultivate power, but Thucydides emphasizes once again the barriers to the growth of *dynamis* and Greek unity. There were no great wars or expeditions, and the tyrants, preoccupied with their own security, were incapable of anything prodigious:

Wars by land there were none, none at least by which power was acquired; we have the usual border contests, but of distant expeditions with conquest for object we hear nothing among the Hellenes. There was no union of subject cities round a great state, no spontaneous combination of equals for confederate expeditions. . . . Again, wherever there were tyrants, their habit of providing simply for themselves, of looking solely to their personal comfort and family aggrandizement, made safety the great aim of their policy, and prevented anything great from proceeding from them. . . . Thus for a long time everywhere in Hellas do we find causes which make the states alike incapable of combination for great and national ends, or of any vigorous action of their own (1.15–16).

In the final stages, two great political developments swept away the barriers to the centralization of power and the achievement of material progress in Greece. First, in the sixth century Sparta formed its hegemonial alliance-system, the Peloponnesian League, and, with cool deliberation, deposed the tyrants in a number of Greek cities, including Athens. Sparta, a land and military power with a notorious dislike of the sea, was none the less admired by conservatives for its political continuity and stable institutions and laws, advantages that enabled it 'to arrange the affairs of the other states'. Recognized by much of Greece as its natural leader, Sparta was the ideal *hoplite* state, proud of its anti-tyrant reputation and, particularly during the reign of its greatest king, Kleomenes (*c.*520–490), prepared to export its version of constitutional order, *eunomia*, beyond the Peloponnese. Sparta's overthrow of the Peisistratid tyranny at Athens *c.*510 – an intervention the Spartans later had cause to regret and failed to overturn – made the radical Athenian democracy possible; it also opened the way for the transformation of power in Greece.

The second great development that forced Greece to change and power to become unified was the external challenge to the Greek cities and states-system from Persia in the early fifth century. Neither Persia's punitive attack in 490 nor the great invasion by Xerxes a decade later unified Greece into a single 'nation': many Greek cities Medized, that is, submitted to Persia's rule, and the 31 Greek cities that fought did so for liberty, not for national pride. Moreover, the coalition that repulsed Xerxes at the naval battle of Salamis in 480 and the land battle of Plataea in 479 soon split into two blocs, one led by Athens, the other by Sparta. The crisis was none the less a turning point for the Greek city-states, for those that chose to resist the Persian invasion now saw the necessity of accepting the need for united action under Sparta's leadership. Fear, the agency of so much collective action in interstate relations, forced some of the Greek cities into their first great collaborative enterprise since the Trojan War. 'In the face of this great danger the command of the confederate Hellenes was assumed by the Lacedaemonians in virtue of their superior power, and the Athenians, having made up their minds to abandon their city, broke up their homes, threw themselves into their ships, and became a naval people' (1.18).

But this Hellenic alliance under Spartan hegemony lasted only as long as the fear seemed real, and at the moment of victory over Xerxes, the coalition split and the rivalry began between Sparta and Athens for supremacy over the Greek states-system. Thucydides concludes his anatomy of power with a brief contrast of the rival hegemonies before the outbreak of the Peloponnesian War.

The policy of Lacedaemon was not to exact tribute from her allies, but merely to secure their subservience to her interests by establishing oligarchies among them; Athens, on the contrary, had by degrees deprived hers of their ships, and imposed instead contributions in money on all except Chios and Lesbos (1.19).

Like many of Thucydides's antitheses this is highly compressed, but the meaning is clear: although Sparta interfered in the affairs of its allies in order to ensure the rule of the few, the Spartan policy of not exacting tribute meant that the freedom of its allies was less impaired than that of the allies of Athens, who by stages surrendered their liberty along with their means of defending themselves to imperial Athens.

Thucydides's analysis of the remote past discloses a number of his central assumptions about power and international history. The Archaeology also teaches us much about how Thucydides proposed to relate his findings about the past to his analysis of contemporary (fifth-century) international problems. Rather as we might use an introductory chapter to set out certain theoretical premises and hypotheses, the opening pages of the *History* are used, not merely to speculate about the remote past, but also to develop ideas, concepts and methods of analysis that resonate throughout the work as a whole. This echoing effect, which grows along with the reader's familiarity with the work, is produced by Thucydides' technique of using narrative and speeches to foreshadow events and establish patterns of behaviour: for instance, Minos of Crete, who founded a navy to clear the seas of pirates and raise revenues, is a precursor of the Athenian empire. Written ostensibly to prove that the Peloponnesian war was the 'greatest movement yet known in history' (1.1), the Archaeology analyses forces that have always operated, albeit on a lesser scale, in Greek history. It anticipates much of what Thucydides later relates about the role of naval power and financial wealth in interstate relations, the motives of fear, greed and self-interest in state behaviour, and of imperialism and war as great collective enterprises.

As noted, one fundamental idea of the Archaeology is that the stronger powers rule the weak for their mutual advantage: this right of the stronger, which Thucydides has the Athenians assert on several occasions before and during their war with Sparta, is an application of fifth-century Sophist teaching: that there are those who rule and those who are ruled, and that ruling others is an expression of freedom. A second key idea of the Archaeology is that collective action in international politics is difficult, and typically requires a common fear of a superior or of an external enemy. And, third, there is the idea of the sea itself as an escape route from the *stasis* and backwardness of mainland Greece. It was the lack of a territory to be exploited economically, combined with their fears, that pushed the Greeks out to sea. As they began to master it they discovered their own *dynamis*. The development and use of seapower is equated with technical achievement and the greatness of empire. This is unquestionably a pessimistic theory of human progress, but it is a theory of progress all the same.[16]

## Hegemony: Leaders and Followers

When the Greeks of the classical age thought about the organization of power in their system of city-states, they thought in terms of recognized leadership or *hegemonia*, the primacy of one powerful state in a confederacy or states-system over the others. Although they assumed war to be a natural and inevitable condition, a consequence of the nature of man,[17] the ancient Greeks also knew that a resort to force can be a costly, unpredictable way of using the state's *dynamis*. Empire, involving direct and coercive rule, was anathema to the Greek city-states. Because their first instinct was to preserve the freedom and autonomy of each individual *polis*, they preferred loosely organized hegemonial alliances to forcibly imposed, centralized empires; policy and psychological techniques of rule to outright coercion. Thucydides implies in the Archaeology and elsewhere in his *History* that leadership of the strongest power over a league of autonomous states is more expedient – and perhaps more just – than imperial rule, which several of his speakers, in reference to the Athenian empire, call tyrannical: forcible rule (*arche*) may excite envy and dislike as well as fear. Cities, like people, are stubborn and often resist being ruled by force, for it means they have forfeited their rights to freedom and self-government. The ancient Greeks equated freedom with the right of the stronger to rule others, to oppress and dominate; but they also believed that it is as much in man's nature to resist being conquered as it is to conquer.[18] To attempt to rule others with force and threats is thus to invite protracted, violent resistance; whereas a good policy – a prudent and moderate approach – can head off revolts before they occur. The Greek author Xenophon, writing a few years after Thucydides, stresses the intractability of human nature and the instability of all regimes, for 'men unite against none so readily as against those whom they see attempting to rule over them'. Anyone aspiring to an empire should emulate Cyrus, founder of the Persian empire, and 'cast a kind of spell' over those he would conquer: that is, use psychological means and an economy of force.[19]

From about the seventh century until their conquest by Philip of Macedon in 338 BC, the Greeks recognized the respective hegemonies of Argos, Sparta, Sparta and Athens, Sparta, and Thebes, much as the German confederacy conceded the hegemony to Prussia in the nineteenth century or the states of Western Europe acknowledged America's primacy after the Second World War. The expression of hegemony in these cases was roughly equivalent to what, according to Xenophon, the Achaeans told their leader, Sparta, in 389: 'We serve with you howsoever you direct and follow whithersoever you lead'.[20] A *hegemon* was a city with power enough to look after the general interests of its allies and of the Hellenic system as well as its own interests; one that had the obligation, as Corinth defined it, 'to show a special care for the common welfare in return for the special honours accorded to them by all in other ways' (1.120). The offer of protection was central to the obligation; a *hegemon* that abandoned its allies, as Sparta seemed to do, for example, at the end of the first ten years of the Peloponnesian War when it signed a treaty with Athens, risked losing its claim to the support of its allies and opened the way for a pretender to the supremacy, such as Argos, to attempt to seize 'the duty of consulting for the safety' of the allies (V.27-30).

Modern connotations of 'hegemony' are not always helpful in understanding what the ancient Greeks meant by *hegemonia*: that is, the acknowledged leadership or primacy of a single powerful state in a system of independent states. In classical Greece a hegemonial alliance contained a basic duality: it was between the *hegemon*, who took a sacred oath to protect and lead its allies and enjoyed sweeping powers of command and initiative, and the lesser allies, whose sworn duty was to follow the leading state in peace as in war. The Greeks thought of hegemony in terms of mutual advantage, believing that weaker powers not only consent to follow the leading state, but also that it may be in their interests actively to seek an alliance with a leading state which has the power to offer protection and material rewards. This is what happened in the immediate aftermath of the Greek victory over the Persians in 480/79, when, as Thucydides argued, the Athenians 'succeeded to the supremacy by the voluntary act of the allies' through the hatred of the latter for Sparta's violent regent, Pausanias. The scattered Ionian cities of the Aegean and the coast of Asia Minor, desiring protection and wanting to take revenge against Persia by 'ravaging the king's country', turned away from the traditional leader, Sparta (which was in any case reluctant to accept new commitments and 'desired to be rid of the Median war' [1.95]), and invited the Athenians to lead them. Sparta accepted the Athenian claim to share the hegemony, albeit with unspoken reservations. In the late summer of 478, the Athenians, full of self-confidence and ambition after their naval victories over Persia, acceded to the request of the Ionian Greeks to head a new maritime alliance, based initially on the island of Delos, the centre of Ionian religious activities; this Delian League or Confederacy was to be the precursor to the Athenian empire. But Thucydides is definite that the original initiative came from the Ionian Greeks, who were seeking protection as well as Persian booty (1.94-96). Fear and greed led the Ionians to Athens and its fleet in much the same way that the earlier Greeks found their *hegemones* in Minos and Agamemnon.

Perhaps because they are uncomfortable with the notion that small but independent states accept the primacy of the strong in their own self-interest, modern theorists have analysed hegemony in international politics as if it were imposed from above upon weaker states who were merely passive objects to be manipulated at will. For those who view international politics from the standpoint of the initiatives and interactions of great powers, such explanations will probably suffice. A modern formulation of hegemony, developed in Hedley Bull's *The Anarchical Society*, suggests that the relative absence of coercion in this type of international relationship stems from a preference of the dominant power for less costly 'instruments' than military action. Bull implies that the operation of hegemonial alliances is mostly a question of great power preferences.

Where a great power exercises hegemony over the lesser powers in a particular area or constellation, there is the resort to force and the threat of force, but this is not habitual and uninhibited but occasional and reluctant. The great power prefers to rely upon instruments other than the direct use or threat of force, and will employ the latter only in situations of extremity and with a sense that in doing so it is incurring a political cost.[21]

But this is incomplete. Like so much of contemporary theorizing about international politics, radical as well as mainstream, it is one-sided in that it tends to exaggerate the power of dominant states and to ignore the interests and motives of the lesser powers in supporting the primacy of the stronger states. In addition, we need to know why hegemonies come to be established, what interests and expectations of a hegemony the lesser members may hold, whether the *hegemon* or leading state is perceived to have duties as well as prerogatives, and under what circumstances a hegemonial alliance of independent states can be transformed into an empire by a dominant power; how *hegemonia* (leadership) can be made into *arche* (rule).

The hegemony of ancient Greece was won and lost in war. Sparta, the pre-eminent military power in continental Greece for nearly two centuries, was viewed as the 'natural' leader, 'president of Greece', *prostates tes Hellas*. The Spartan state was built on colonial wars and territorial conquest, especially the subjugation of the peoples of Messenia in the south-west Peloponnese in two ferocious wars before the sixth century. The Messenians were enslaved, and their political identity was extinguished. This conquered *helot* class henceforth produced, on pain of death, the agricultural harvests required by the individual Spartiates (as full citizens were called) to retain their rights of citizenship. Raised from a very young age according to a rigid discipline to be fit for warfare (but very little else), the Spartiates were in a permanent state of war with the Messenian *helots* – indeed, every year they formally declared war on them – and the security problem of keeping these slaves from rising up against the greatly outnumbered Spartiates shaped every aspect of Sparta's foreign and military policy. It was because they lived on top of an active human volcano that the Spartiates were driven to organize themselves as a community of professional soldiers, and to work only at military discipline and war. It was not the fear of an external enemy, such as Argos or Athens, that made Sparta into an armed camp without walls; walls would have been of little use in protecting the Spartiates from slave insurrections. Fear – not an abstract fear or a hypothetical fear, or a fear of a potential threat, but the real, palpable and all-pervading fear of being 'eaten raw' by the *helots*[22] – forced the Spartiates to act as the unpaid bodyguards of one another, and prompted its governors to seek and support external allies – particularly allies with oligarchic constitutions – as insurance against the threat of domestic upheaval. 'Sparta', Martin Wight has noted, 'affords perhaps the clearest example in history of the primacy of *domestic* policy, since her domestic policy was nothing but the conduct of a permanent war by the Spartiates against the subjugated majority of the population; and this preoccupation governed every other aspect of policy.'[23]

Sparta's power derived from its regime, which in turn stood on a foundation of fear. Its peculiar internal security problem was the source of much of its xenophobia, its secretiveness and exclusiveness, and its heavy emphasis on training its citizens in the arts of warfare. Sparta's policy was often isolationist, it was frequently slow to come to decisions, and sometimes indifferent to the plight of its allies. Sparta was capable of acting with ruthlessness for reasons of expediency and self-interest. Its society was rigid and unchanging, and this left Sparta extremely vulnerable to sudden changes in its external situation.

It is easy for modern-day observers, to whom Sparta seems but a brutal anachronism, to focus only on these negative traits and to forget Thucydides' admonition near the opening of the *History* that this seemingly unimpressive and old-fashioned state, though lacking in grandeur and pomp, was in reality far more powerful than it might 'look' to subsequent generations. Like some other fifth-century Athenian thinkers, such as Socrates, Thucydides esteemed certain Spartan ways and institutions. He was impressed by Sparta's continuity and effective action,[24] he admired the discipline and steadiness of its *hoplite* army,[25] and he contrasted the durability of its constitution with the instabilities of Greek democracy. Notwithstanding his historical views on the superiority of seapower and its role in Greek progress, there is evidence in the *History* to support the contention that Thucydides, an aristocratic and conservative man, identified with Sparta's oligarchy as opposed to the most likely alternative, Athenian democracy, and that the Athenian historian 'preferred the Spartan manner to the Athenian manner'.[26] As one who lamented the passing of the old Hellenic values during the Peloponnesian War, Thucydides admired Sparta's prudence, sobriety and *sophrosyne*, an aristocratic or oligarchic word that means stability, self-restraint, moderation – characteristics that were notably absent in democratic Athens following the death of its great leader, Pericles.[27] Although Sparta suffered from *stasis* for a long time, it 'still at a very early period obtained good laws, and enjoyed a freedom from tyrants which was unbroken; it has possessed the same form of government for more than four hundred years, reckoning to the end of the late war, and has thus been in a position to arrange the affairs of the other states'.

Note here that the power 'to arrange the affairs of other states' derives, not from arms, but from 'good laws' and constitutional stability. Sparta put down the tyrants, introduced *eunomia* (oligarchic government) in other Greek cities, and thereby opened the way for all of Hellas to develop (1.17-18). Thucydides also admired the self-control of the Spartans, their capacity – again, in sharp contrast to the Athenians – to resist the temptations of *pleonexia*, of greed, of always 'grasping for something more', and to moderate their power by exercising self-restraint and avoiding arrogance. The Athenian empire, like the people of Athens, always wanted more. The Spartans were one of the very few peoples who knew how to be wise in prosperity, whose heads were not turned by success (8.25).

Sparta's prowess in war and the reputation of its heavy infantry *hoplite*, army were legendary – the ancient histories are full of references to the terrors inspired in enemy soldiers by the sound of Spartan flutes and the sight of the scarlet tunics and long hair of the slow-marching *hoplites* of a Spartan phalanx.[28] Herodotus reports the exiled Spartan king, Demaratus, telling the Persian ruler, Xerxes, that, fighting individually, the Spartans are 'no worse' than any other people;

together, they are the most gallant men on earth. For they are free – but not altogether so. They have as the despot over them Law, and they fear him much more than your men fear you. At least they do whatever he bids them do; and he bids them always the same thing: not to flee from the fight before any multitude of men whatever but to stand firm in their ranks and either conquer or die.[29]

Although the Spartan army was small, even by Greek standards, and the number of Spartiates was probably no more than 8,000 to 10,000 men during the fifth century and tending to decline,[30] it was the qualitative or moral superiority of this trained and disciplined infantry army that allowed Sparta to claim the hegemony of the Peloponnese and much of the rest of continental Greece.

At some point in the sixth century, the Spartans seem to have taken a conscious and prudent decision not to use their military power for further territorial expansion. Perhaps it was felt that further conquest, with the political problems involved, might threaten Sparta's internal stability; certainly, there was a desire to keep the Spartan army close to home and to avoid unnecessary military commitments outside the Peloponnese. Later on, Sparta refused to assist the Ionian Greek cities in the islands of the eastern Aegean and along the coast of Asia Minor, threatened by the expansion of the Persian empire. The refusal meant that the Peloponnesian League would be seriously limited by its lack of naval power and overseas allies; for this, Sparta was attacked for preparing the way for Athenian maritime imperialism. Instead of conquering and taking on far-flung commitments, Sparta chose to use its military reputation to gain peace in the Peloponnese via a system of alliances made initially with neighbouring city-states; Greek particularism and regional security were balanced as these allies retained much of their autonomy but were linked to Sparta through reciprocal defence pacts. As one historian has put it, instead of trying to conquer the Peloponnese through war, Sparta became its *hegemon*.[31] Sparta's hegemony, the Peloponnesian League, was built up through a series of unequal bilateral treaties with cities of, and beyond, the Peloponnese. The first of these, with the warlike city of Tegea, committed the Tegeans 'to expel the Messenians' from their territory. Later treaties presumably bound Sparta's allies, as a fifth-century treaty bound Athens, to help put down the *helots* in the event of an uprising in Sparta: 'Should the slave population rise, the Athenians shall help the Lacedaemonians with all their might, according to their power.'[32]

The Peloponnesian League, or 'the Lacedaemonians and their allies', as Sparta's *hegemonia* was called, became the most formidable power bloc in the Greek world, persisting for two centuries until it was finally wound up in the 360s. Sparta's primacy was recognized by all members of the alliance: the treaties were not concluded as between parties of equal standing, and Sparta was acknowledged as *hegemon* with the automatic right to command the allies in war.[33] The allies swore to have the 'same friends and enemies' as Sparta, there was no right of secession from the alliance, and the hegemony was intended to be a permanent fixture. However, the League functioned as a loosely knit grouping without a permanent bureaucracy or a large standing army, and its activities, before the Peloponnesian War, seem to have been infrequent and spasmodic.[34] The allies of Sparta paid no tribute, a point which Thucydides stressed in his initial sketch of the two great alliances. Sparta could appeal to its allies for 'contributions' but it lacked any direct control over their financial resources. The degree to which Sparta was able to act on behalf of its allies was determined less by absolute principles than by the circumstances of the particular case. Until the late fifth century when the exigencies of war led the Spartans to emulate Athenian practices and to assume the role of imperial overlord, each of the allies enjoyed, at least in principle, the right to make its own laws, choose its own leaders, and try its own citizens in its courts.

Sparta's power as *hegemon* was greater during wars or moments of crisis, yet even in these cases it was unlikely to be absolute, for Sparta's alliance was bicameral. There were, in effect, two chambers – the Spartan state, and a League congress of all the allies (Sparta included). The vote of Sparta was equal to the sum of the allies' votes; each had the power of veto. A congress of the Peloponnesian League prevented Sparta from intervening in Athens in about 503 to overthrow the commons[35]. Thereafter it was a potential check on Sparta's power unilaterally to involve the allies in a war or to make peace at the end of a League action.

The procedure adopted by the Spartan alliance is shown in Thucydides's account of the outbreak of the Peloponnesian War in 431: first there was a debate in the Spartan assembly to decide the policy of Sparta, and then there was a second debate in a congress of the allies – also held at Sparta – where each ally (including the Spartans) had a single vote (1.66–88 and 1.118–25). One cannot read the debates at Sparta without gaining the impression that, on the eve of the war, the member-states in the Spartan alliance were independent, unafraid to admonish their *hegemon* about 'the duties of supremacy', and able to use the machinery of the League to press their interests. If anything, the allies of Sparta, particularly Corinth, felt that the leader of their confederacy was insufficiently aware of the dangers of Athenian expansionism, and that its inaction was risking the safety of its friends; they did not complain of losing their autonomy to the Spartans. Sparta did consult and listen to its allies, and the allies did not regard their membership in the League as something that detracted from their freedom. This was in sharp contrast to the way power was organized in the rival Athenian coalition, and it may partly explain why opinion in Greece was so overwhelmingly pro-Spartan when the war began in 431.

## The Dual Hegemony

The Athenian-led alliance which historians call the Delian Confederacy differed from the Peloponnesian League in some important ways. Athens won its hegemony in the war with Persia, but its power was measured in ships and financial reserves rather than *hoplite* soldiers. It was a maritime league whose origins lay in the crisis of the great Persian invasion of 481/479, the decisive experience of the Greeks, and in the collective actions taken by the Greek states resisting Persia. Sparta rather than Athens was *prostates tes Hellados*, the natural leader of the alliance of Hellenes fighting the Persians. But the Athenians emerged from the war at the head of a far-flung protectorate based on seapower that covered much of the Aegean, including the offshore islands and coastal cities of Ionia, the Hellespont, Delos (headquarters of the alliance), and other islands of the Cyclades. The 31 city-states that resisted King Xerxes did not stay united after the defeat of Persia's naval and military forces in 480/79. The panhellenic alliance gave way to the more familiar spectacle of rivalry and jealousy (*phthonos*) within the Greek system.[36] Such is the nature of international politics that the dissolution of a common fear typically heralds the breakup of a wartime coalition, as old antagonisms reassert themselves and the victors begin to squabble over the spoils. After the defeat of Persia, Athens in effect succeeded to the hegemony of Greece at sea while Sparta retained its traditional peninsular supremacy, much of the rest of Greece lining up behind one pole or the other. The states-system that emerged from the Persian crisis was thus bipolar, an unstable dyarchy in which the *hegemonia* was divided between a restless, aggressive, imperialist Athens and a quiescent, isolationist, *status quo*-orientated Sparta.

Thucydides examines the origins of Athens' hegemony and its

transformation into the Athenian empire in his Pentecontaetia, or fifty-year period, a digression in Book One (89–117) on the growth of Athenian power from the end of the Persian War in 479 to the outbreak of the Peloponnesian War in 431. He prepared this skeletal fifty-year history because 'the history of these events contains an explanation of the growth of the Athenian empire' (1.97). Like the Archaeology, the Pentecontaetia is not a narrative history but a synopsis of the growth of *dynamis* and *hegemonia* at sea: land power, in the form of Sparta, is shown to be in constant retreat in the face of the rising naval power of the Athenian confederacy. His analysis of how Athens came to acquire its supremacy in the wake of Persia's defeat focuses on those sources of hegemony analysed in the Archaeology to account for past collective actions such as the Greek expedition to Troy: fear, the love of gain, the development of superior naval power, and far-sighted leadership were the primary elements in the creation of the Athenian hegemony.

The Hellenic alliance that had been formed in 481 under Sparta's leadership moved to the offensive in the spring of 478, following the retreat of the Persian forces across the Aegean. Now the war was to be carried by sea to the Persian king's territory, his land ravaged in revenge for the sacking of Greek cities, and those Greeks liberated that were still under Persian rule. This ambition had the potential to vault Athens, the dominant naval power of Greece, to the head of a large maritime protectorate of Greek islands and cities on the coast of Asia Minor and the trading routes they commanded. Sparta had neither the seapower nor the political will to prevent it. Indeed, Sparta was viewed in the region as an unacceptable choice for the hegemony. The Spartan regent Pausanias led a fleet of Greek ships up to Byzantium to evict the Persians, and, having compelled the town's surrender, then frightened his own allies with his violent behaviour. Pausanias had 'gone native' in Asia, wearing Persian dress, going about Byzantium with Medes and Egyptians as bodyguards, and acting toward the Ionian Greeks like an overbearing despot. It was at this point, according to Thucydides, that the Ionians turned to the Athenians and their 200-ship navy and sought protection. The Athenians, full of self-confidence and ambition after the flight of the Persians, seized their opportunity.

... the violence of Pausanias had already begun to be disagreeable to the Hellenes, particularly to the Ionians and the newly liberated populations. These resorted to the Athenians and requested them as their kinsmen to become their leaders, and to stop any attempt at violence on the part of

Pausanias. The Athenians accepted their overtures, and determined to put down any attempt of the kind and to settle everything else as their interests might seem to demand (1.95).

Recalled from Byzantium to Sparta to face charges of misconduct and Medism, Pausanias was forced to give up his command. (Pausanias was also suspected of the far worse crime of intriguing with the *helots* in Sparta to bring about an insurrection: 'and such indeed was the fact', adds Thucydides [1.132]). When the Spartans sent out a replacement with a small force, they:

found the allies no longer inclined to concede to them the supremacy. Perceiving this they departed, and the Lacedaemonians did not send out any to succeed them. They feared for those who went out a deterioration similar to that observable in Pausanias; besides, they desired to be rid of the Median war, and were satisfied at the competency of the Athenians for the position, and of their friendship at the time towards themselves (1.95).

Sparta was conceding the Athenian claim to the *hegemonia* at sea, probably with considerable relief: 'they desired to be rid of the Median war'. To have desired otherwise would have been contrary to Sparta's very nature. Sparta's interest was the security of Sparta and the Peloponnese, not the liberation of the overseas Greek city-states from Persia. In its social and political makeup, Sparta was a conservative land power, not a democratic seapower; Spartan men were trained to fight as *hoplite* infantry soldiers, not (as in Athens) as naval officers, rowers and seafaring rabble. Moreover, the Spartan state lacked the financial resources to build and harbour a fleet large enough to contest the hegemony at sea. For these reasons, and also because it was less likely than most states to be carried away in the first flush of victory, Sparta resisted the temptations of *pleonexia*, refused to grasp for more, and settled for a division of the hegemony with Athens.

The Athenians, on the other hand, were ambitious for power; it was this ambition, not some altruistic urge to help their Ionian 'kinsmen', that moved them to organize and lead a maritime confederacy of some 140 widely scattered city-states, a new force to be reckoned with in the Greek states-system. Thucydides provides a highly condensed description of the Athenian-led Delian Confederacy. It suggests the complexity of motives and interests in the alliance and gives some insights into the role of *phoros*, tribute; in the Athenian league.

The Athenians, having succeeded to the supremacy by the voluntary acts of the allies through their hatred of Pausanias, fixed which cities were to contribute money against the barbarian, and which ships, their professed object being to retaliate for their sufferings by ravaging the king's country. Now was the time that the office of 'Treasurers for Hellas' was first instituted by the Athenians. These officers received the tribute, as the money contributed was called. The tribute was first fixed at four hundred and sixty talents. The common treasury was at Delos, and the congresses were held in the temple. Their supremacy commenced with independent allies who acted on the resolutions of a common congress (1.96–7).

This important passage contains an ambiguity which merits discussion because of the light it casts on Thucydides's methods. He is concerned throughout the *History* to make sharp distinctions between the 'professed objects' or pretexts of politicians and states and the real (though often concealed) motives and interests that underlie their actions. He develops an approach to political causation that emphasizes the opposition of stated, superficial pretexts (believed by the vulgar and credulous) and the deeper, true causes (discernible only by 'exact observers' such as himself). The pretexts might be expressed in religious, ideological or ethnic terms, whereas the true causes are usually formulated in terms of a motive inspired by relationships of power, as in Thucydides' judgement that the real reason for the Peloponnesian War (though the reason least often given) was the fear aroused in Sparta by the growth of Athenian power (1.23). He writes in Book Six that the Athenian pretext for invading Sicily in 415 was to assist a 'kindred' (Ionian Greek) city there and perhaps to acquire some of its reputed wealth. Many Athenians believed this, but the true reason for the invasion, according to Thucydides, was that Athens was 'ambitious in real truth of conquering the whole' of Sicily, and much else besides (6.6).

In the passage quoted above, Thucydides states that the 'professed object' or pretext of the Athenians in assessing tribute was to enable the new alliance to obtain revenge by plundering Persia; that is, the Athenians said that tribute would be assessed and then used to mount allied expeditions into Persia, taking booty as compensation for losses suffered by the Greeks in the war.[37] Another, deeper and concealed motive is implied, but Thucydides leaves his readers to speculate as to what it may have been. On first reading, he seems to imply that the Athenians intended from the start to convert their confederacy of autonomous allies into a tribute-paying empire of subject-cities, but that they veiled their true purpose by leading their allies on looting expeditions in Persia and elsewhere. However, had the Athenians been that cynically farsighted or the allies that credulous, Thucydides would not have gone on to say that 'their supremacy commenced with independent allies who acted on the resolutions of a common congress'. A second interpretation of the passage yields a more plausible meaning: namely, that Athens as *hegemon* used the common strategy of making expeditions against Persia as a pretext in order to gain control over which allies paid tribute in money, and which in ships. The Athenians used the allies' *fear* of Persian reprisals and their *greed* for booty to centralize control over the financial 'burden-sharing' arrangements of the league. Fear and the love of gain ensured the acquiescence of the allies in the new hegemonial system: the strong control the weak for their mutual advantage. The mechanism of financial control, Thucydides goes on to say, was the office of 'Treasurers of Hellas', instituted by the Athenians to collect the tribute. Aristeides, an Athenian, is said to have made the first assessment. The allies and Athens swore to have the 'same friends and same enemies', and the lumps of iron that were thrown into the sea by the ambassadors at the oath-taking signified that the oaths would be kept until the iron floated; the league was to be permanent.

While the formation of the naval confederacy was proceeding in the Aegean, Themistocles led the Athenians in the rebuilding of their city and its walls. Thucydides begins to develop his conception of leadership through his analysis of this remarkable but low-born Athenian statesman, who led his city through the crisis with Persia, and transformed Athens into a great naval state: 'he first ventured to tell them to stick to the sea and forthwith began to lay the foundations of the empire' (1.93). Themistocles had in the 480s persuaded the Athenians to use a larger share of their private and public resources, including the proceeds from newly discovered beds of silver, for defence rather than consumption. It was Themistocles who grasped that Persia was the real threat to be met, and that seapower rather than the *hoplite* infantry held the key to Athens' future. Because he linked the navy to the growing patriotism of the *demos* and their enmity toward Persia, the building of a fleet of 200 trireme warships and the development of Piraeus as a major harbour were already under way before the Persian invasion. Again, it was Themistocles who led the Athenians through the harrowing invasion of Persia's land and naval forces, persuading them to fight at sea in spite of the defeatist utterances of the Delphic oracle[38] and the spectacle of so many Greek cities submitting to Persia or staying neutral. When the Athenians were compelled to evacuate their city and to transport their families to the nearby island of Salamis, the Spartans wanted to withdraw the allied forces to the Isthmus. But Themistocles threatened to move his ships and the Athenians to Siris in Italy, and this forced the Greeks to wage everything on a naval battle in the narrow straits of Salamis in September of 480. The Greek victory at Salamis did not end the war, but because of these dramatic events the Athenians 'became a naval people' (1.18).

Thucydides illuminates Themistocles's natural qualities of leadership: his judgement in crises, his intuitive feel for the right action, and particularly his farsighted intelligence. It is Themistocles's *natural* judgement and powers, his native genius for grasping the decisive elements in emergencies, that Thucydides emphasizes. 'By his own native capacity, alike unformed and unsupplemented by study, he was at once the best judge in those sudden crises which admit of little or no deliberation, and the best prophet of the future, even to its most distant possibilities'; he could 'excellently divine the good and evil which lay hid in the unseen future' (1.138). These attributes of leadership, so vital in a war leader, came from Themistocles's untrained ability to divine human nature: he knew the future because he knew the nature of man and understood war. To use power effectively in a great international crisis or in war, leadership demands the qualities of 'military genius' that Carl von Clausewitz set out in his famous nineteenth-century study, *On War*.[39] These include: a capacity to cope with the uncertainty and unpredictability of war, courage in the face of personal danger, the willingness to assume the burden of making very difficult decisions, the gift to mobilize the moral or human forces in war, and a fierce ambition for honour and fame. Themistocles possessed all of these in full measure, and Thucydides, a difficult critic to please, is unstinting in his admiration. His encomium tells us, in effect, that Themistocles knew that Sparta would one day fight Athens for the hegemony of Greece, and that he had begun to prepare the Athenians for it.

*Hegemonia* was won and lost in war. Themistocles proclaimed Athens' right, earned in the war with Persia, to speak and act as Sparta's equal in the post-war system of states. Athens had been gutted by the Persians and the desire to fortify it with new walls seems unremarkable. But walls represented more than physical security. Sparta sent ambassadors to Themistocles to request that work on the walls be stopped; instead of walling up their city the Athenians should join with the Spartans and throw down the walls in all cities outside the Peloponnese. Thucydides notes that Sparta was acting at the prompting of its allies, who were alarmed at the power of Athens' fleet 'and the valour which she had displayed in the war with the Medes'. The diplomats did not voice these suspicions, but urged 'that the barbarian, in the event of a third invasion, would not then have any strong place, such as he now had in Thebes, for his base of operations, and that Peloponnese would suffice for all as a base both for retreat and offence' (1.90). Sparta and its allies plainly wanted to keep Athens, now paramount at sea, vulnerable to military pressure on land from the armies of the Peloponnesian League. However, unilateral disarmament cannot be imposed upon a power that has emerged victorious from a great war; such a fate is reserved for states that have lost a war or are very weak, and Athens was neither of these. The Athenians dismissed the envoys and Themistocles himself hurried to Sparta, where he used deception and all his diplomatic skills to postpone any action by the Spartans, while the whole population of Athens laboured to raise the walls to the height from which defence was possible.

The episode of the walls, as written by Thucydides several decades after the events, bristles with the incipient tensions and fears between the two leading Greek power. His account stresses the reciprocal apprehensions, the lack of trust, the unspoken suspicions of the two powers in the immediate aftermath of the common victory over Persia. Athens was fearful of a pre-emptive attack; Sparta's fear of the growing power of Athens was already palpable. Diplomacy's role here was not to conciliate or reduce uncertainties but to temporize and deceive the adversary while rearmament proceeded.

Informed that the walls of Athens were high enough for defence, Themistocles openly told the Spartans that:

Athens was now fortified sufficiently to protect its inhabitants; that any embassy which the Lacedaemonians or their allies might wish to send to them should in future proceed on the assumption that the people to whom they were going was able to distinguish both its own and the general interests; . . . that they now thought it fit that their city should have a wall, and that this would be more for the advantage of both the citizens of Athens and the Hellenic confederacy; for without equal military strength it was impossible to contribute equal or fair counsel to the common interest (1.91).

The Spartans were still friendly to Athens for the part it had taken in the war, and so they accepted this *fait accompli*, albeit with secret annoyance. It was a capitulation, amounting to *de facto* recognition of Athens' claim to an equal status as a hegemonic power. The walls were intended to assert this claim and to provide the Athenians with the independence they would need to develop their great supremacy at sea. The walls of Piraeus, the main harbour, were built to massive thickness. Themistocles, who thought Piraeus more valuable than the upper city, believed they could be defended 'by a small garrison of invalids', the rest being freed for service in the fleet. 'For the fleet claimed most of his attention . . . indeed, he was always advising the Athenians, if a day should come when they were hard pressed by land, to go down into Piraeus, and defy the world with their fleet' (1.93).

**Conclusion**

From his analysis of seapower and hegemony in an earlier Greece Thucydides developed his ideas about Athenian imperialism and its part in the origins of the Peloponnesian War. The *arche* (empire) was yet another stage in the consolidation of Athens' rising power and the development of Greece. Only a dozen years after the creation of the Delian naval confederacy and Themistocles's challenge to Sparta, the allies of Athens began to chafe under the harsh and exacting leadership of the Athenians. Some states attempted to leave the alliance and were forced to return; others which had been neutral were forced to sign up. And the Athenians, who had the power to determine which allies would pay tribute in cash and which would contribute ships, used their position to build up their own fleet while disarming their allies. If the Athenians 'had more than their fair share of service, it was correspondingly easy for them to reduce any that tried to leave the confederacy'. For this, Thucydides wrote, 'the allies had themselves to blame, the wish to get off service making most of them arrange to pay their expense in money instead of in ships, and so to avoid having to leave their homes' (1.99). It is human nature both to want to rule and to resist being ruled. If the allies of Athens preferred the quiet life, they had no-one to blame but themselves if the Athenians subjugated them. Indeed, the Athenians themselves later asserted that they had been 'compelled' to advance their empire by fear, the desire for honour or glory, and the need for profit; they denied having done anything unusual in having increased their power, for it had always been the law that the weaker should be subject to the stronger (1.75–6).

Success and prosperity had encouraged the Athenians imprudently to believe they could always have more, and this immoderation led them to forget that power used without self-restraint provokes fear and hatred in others. Whereas hegemony had encouraged the weak to consent to the leadership of the strong for reasons of mutual advantage, the empire acknowledged no limits to the rule of force and was bound to provoke hatred and fear. As formulated by Thucydides, the growth of Athenian power was one side of the real cause of the war; the other side was Sparta's *fear* that Athens was likely to become even stronger. Weakened by *helot* revolts and regional tensions, 'slow to go to war except under the pressure of necessity', the Spartans finally decided 'that they could endure it no longer, but that the time had come for them to throw themselves heart and soul upon the hostile power, and break it, if they could, by commencing the present war' (1.118). Sparta's decision finally to resist Athens's ambition, daring and *pleonexia*, its grasping for more, marked the end of the unopposed growth of the empire and the beginning of a struggle for primacy that would exhaust the whole of Hellas.

International historians will find in Thucydides's history of the Peloponnesian War no dogmatic precepts or laws of international relations. Yet it is to this one great inquiry into war that historians and political scientists owe many of their fundamental and enduring ideas about the struggle for power and justice among sovereign states. These include: the primacy of war and peace; the causes of war as the focus of inquiry; power defined as military and political power; the nature of the international anarchy; the motives and interests that lie behind great power expansionism; and the tensions between justice and advantage in international politics. There is no conception of a balance of power in Thucydides, but there is a well developed theory of leadership, hegemony, that seems to have relevance in today's post-Cold War environment. And beyond these points, there are themes in Thucydides that will have special resonance for those who studied international history with Donald Cameron Watt: in particular, a strong interest in seapower and naval strategy, an equally strong interest in the assumptions, perceptions, and psychology of leadership, an emphasis on the immediate as well as the deeper origins of crises and wars, and, perhaps above all, an abiding scepticism of all conventional wisdoms and all conclusions drawn from inadequate historical evidence.

### NOTES

1. Thucydides, *The Peloponnesian War*, trans. Thomas Hobbes, with Notes and Introduction by David Grene (Chicago, 1989) (1st pub. 1629).
2. Among others, see Werner Jaeger, *Paideia: the Ideas of Greek Culture*, Vol. 1 (New York, 1945), p. 383; J.B. Bury, *The Ancient Greek Historians* (London, 1909), p. 78.

3.  Thucydides, *The Peloponnesian War*, trans. R. Crawley (New York, 1982). All citations are from this translation.
4.  A.W. Gomme, *A Historical Commentary on Thucydides*, Vol. I (Oxford, 1945), p. 113.
5.  Simon Hornblower, *Thucydides* (London, 1987), pp. 30–1.
6.  Werner Jaeger, *Paideia: the Ideas of Greek Culture*, p. 386.
7.  A good analysis on these lines is in Cynthia Farrar, *The Origins of Democratic Thinking* (Cambridge, 1988), pp. 140ff.
8.  John H. Finley, Jr., *Three Essays on Thucydides* (Cambridge, MA, 1967), p. 9.
9.  Thucydides here anticipates the argument made by Karl Marx in the mid-nineteenth century on the unanticipated effects of British imperialism in India. Marx (who knew Thucydides and other classical historians) said that British capitalists would lay the foundations for India's unity by introducing railways and capitalist industry into the country. As Minos was said to have opened the seas to navigation and made it possible for the Greeks to overcome their isolation and to accumulate wealth, so the English bourgeoisie was expected to unify India through a material revolution in communications and transport. Imperialism, rooted in self-interest, has the potential to create material progress even for those whom it exploits.
10. Martin Wight, *Power Politics*, 2nd ed. (Harmondsworth, 1986), p. 139.
11. Machiavelli argues in *The Discourses*, Book 2, Ch. X, that it is not gold but good soldiers that are the sinews of war, and he cites Sparta's defeat of Athens in the Peloponnesian War as evidence. 'Wealth will not only not defend you, it will cause you to be plundered all the sooner.' But Sparta had to rely on Persian gold to finish off Athens. Thucydides was well aware of the danger that wealth, especially when very unevenly distributed, could pose to a stable political community by promoting class hatred and private gain at the expense of the public interest. 'Indeed, after the Lacedaemonians, the Chians are the only people that I have known who knew how to be wise in prosperity. . . .' (8.24).
12. Thucydides notes that the Spartan general Brasidas learned while marching against Amphipolis that 'Thucydides possessed the right of working the gold mines in that part of Thrace, and had thus great influence with the inhabitants of the continent . . . .' (4.105).
13. See John H. Finley, Jr., *Thucydides* (Cambridge, MA, 1942), pp. 87–9.
14. An exception may be the orator Demosthenes in speeches delivered about 350. Especially see, 'For Megalopolis' and 'On the Liberty of Rhodes', in A.N.W. Saunders (ed.), *Greek Political Oratory* (Harmondsworth, 1970).
15. Martin Wight, 'The states-system of Hellas', in Hedley Bull (ed.), *Systems of States* (Leicester, 1977), p. 65.
16. Thucydides was by no means the only fifth-century Greek thinker to set out an unromantic, pessimistic theory of human progress. A useful discussion is in W.K.C. Guthrie, *The Sophists* (Cambridge, 1971), pp. 60ff.
17. M.I. Finley, *Ancient History. Evidence and Models* (New York, 1986), Ch. 5.
18. See the speech of Hermocrates of Syracuse at 4.61, and the comments of W. Robert Connor, *Thucydides* (Princeton, 1984), pp. 122–3.
19. Xenophon, *Cyropaedia* [The Education of Cyrus], trans. Walter Miller (London, 1914), especially Bks. 1 and 8; also, James Tatum, *Xenophon's Imperial Fiction* (Princeton, 1989).
20. Xenophon, *Hellenica*, I, trans. C.L. Brownson (London, 1918), Book IV, 6.2.
21. Hedley Bull, *The Anarchical Society* (London, 1977), pp. 215–16.
22. Xenophon, *Hellenica*, III.3, describing a conspiracy of *helots* in the 390s, says that by casual count in the market, they outnumbered the Spartiates by 40,000 to 40!
23. Wight, *Systems of States*, p. 57.
24. Hornblower, *Thucydides*, p. 177.
25. F.E. Adcock, *The Greek and Macedonian Art of War* (Berkeley, CA, 1957), p. 10.
26. Leo Strauss, *The City and Man* (Chicago, 1968), p. 151.
27. Hornblower, *Thucydides*, pp. 162ff.
28. See Victor Davis Hanson, *The Western Way of War: Infantry Battle in Classical Greece* (New York, 1989), Ch. 4.
29. Herodotus, *The History*, trans. David Grene (Chicago, 1987), 7.104.
30. J.F. Lazenby, *The Spartan Army* (Warminster, 1985), pp. 57–9.
31. Victor Ehrenberg, *From Solon to Socrates* (London, 1968), p. 45.
32. From the Spartan-Athenian treaty of 421, as cited by Thucydides in 5.23 of the *History*.

33. Sir Frank Adcock and D.J. Mosley, *Diplomacy in Ancient Greece* (London, 1975), p. 231ff.
34. Ibid, p. 232.
35. Herodotus, 5.91–92.
36. Simon Hornblower, *The Greek World 479–323 BC* (London, 1983), pp. 15–31.
37. Hobbes' translation here is: 'When the Athenians had thus gotten the command by the confederates' own accord for the hatred they bare to Pausanias, they then set down an order which cities should contribute money for this war against the barbarians, and which galleys. For they pretended to repair the injuries they had suffered by laying waste the territories of the king.' Thucydides, *The Peloponnesian War*, trans. by Thomas Hobbes, 1.96.
38. Herodotus (7.140-3) says that the Athenians played the decisive part in the resistance to Persia, and did so in spite of the 'dreadful oracles' from Delphi. A first oracle, which simply counselled the Athenians to flee from their certain destruction to the remotest ends of the earth, was followed by a second, which held out the hope that the Athenians might be saved by 'a wall of wood'. Themistocles 'counseled them to prepare for a fight at sea, since the ships were their wooden wall'. The Delphic oracle somehow survived this débâcle. Its defeatism can be likened to the pro-appeasement establishment newspapers of Britain, France and the United States in the 1930s.
39. Carl von Clausewitz, *On War*, trans. Michael Howard and Peter Paret (Princeton, 1976), Book 1, Ch. 3.

# The Great Illusion: Concerning the Future of War in Our Age

## MARTIN VAN CREVELD

A great illusion is spreading among public opinion in the most 'advanced' democratic countries – the illusion that, now that the West has 'won' the Cold War, armed conflict and perhaps even history itself are coming to an end. Such a view is incorrect. Large-scale *conventional* war – meaning war waged by governments at the hands of their regular armed forces – may indeed be at its last gasp; however, war itself is not only alive and well but is about to enter a new epoch. As the old forms of war disappear and are replaced by new ones, the same may happen to the type of political organization by which it is waged, namely the state.

By far the most important reason why large-scale *conventional* warfare is on its way out is, of course, nuclear weapons. From the moment the first bomb was dropped on Japan its power stood revealed for all to see. From that moment, too, the nuclear arms race got under way. It has lasted to the present day. Though the first two atomic bombs were comparatively primitive, each was a thousand times more powerful than anything previously employed in war. Scarcely ten years after Hiroshima it became possible to build weapons more powerful than all the devices ever used by man in all wars since the beginning of history. After another five years, research into the development of still more destructive weapons had virtually come to a halt, not because they could not be made but because they would only make the rubble bounce.

The USA ws the first country to acquire the bomb. In September 1949 its monopoly was broken by Stalin's USSR. The testing of hydrogen bombs by the superpowers in 1952–53 represented an important development, although its significance was nowhere as great as that of the first atomic bomb. Later Britain, France, China and India joined the club. A number of other countries, such as Israel and

Pakistan, have not tested nuclear weapons openly but are widely believed to possess them clandestinely. A still larger number of countries could easily produce the bomb but do not intend to do so. This situation is perhaps the first time in history when any number of governments have deliberately forgone weapons which, from the technical and economic point of view, they could acquire easily enough.

The reluctance of many states to develop nuclear weapons is readily understandable when set against the political benefits which ensue, or do not ensue, from their possession. Developing a nuclear arms programme has put a tremendous strain on the resources of poor countries such as China, India and probably Pakistan. All three either already have a nuclear arsenal or are on the edge of acquiring it, yet none could translate ownership into significant political advantage. China has not been able to recover the lost province of Formosa, or even 'punish' neighbouring Vietnam, an incomparably smaller military power. India has not been able to reunite the subcontinent – if that is indeed its aim – nor has the bomb been helpful in solving the problem of Tamil separatism in Sri Lanka or of Muslim irredentism in Kashmir. Finally, Pakistanis sometimes justify their nuclear programme by their fear of Indian conquest, pointing out that no nuclear country has been wiped off the map. This is true enough, but ignores the fact that the number of non-nuclear states that have been wiped off the map since 1945 is also very small.

The political benefits that possession of nuclear weapons has conferred on medium powers such as Britain and France are, if anything, smaller still. Obviously the bomb has not helped either country to regain or retain its former great-power status. The bomb came too late to prevent the loss of their colonial empires; had it come earlier it could have done little to slow down, let alone stop, the disintegration of those empires. Today the nuclear arsenals at their disposal almost certainly cannot prevent their remaining overseas possessions from being occupied by a determined aggressor, even one who does not himself have nuclear weapons. For decades on end, the rationale adduced by both countries to justify the expenditure was the need to deter a Soviet attack if the American guarantee failed. This line of reasoning was plausible, except that it could only be put into effect at the cost of national suicide which would be certain, swift, and final.

The superpowers themselves undoubtedly derived a large part of their status from their uniquely powerful nuclear arsenals. Still, even in their case it has proved almost impossible to translate this status into tangible political benefits. In June 1945 Stalin declined to be properly impressed by President Truman's announcement of the bomb during the Potsdam Conference. During the next four years the American nuclear monopoly failed to stop the Soviets from consolidating their East European Empire; George Kennan at his Moscow post noted how the Soviet Foreign Minister, Vlacheslav Molotov, contrived to act as if the US did not have the bomb or, alternatively, as if he had it too. The bomb did not save Czechoslovakia from Communist rule in 1948. Nor could it prevent China from falling to Mao Tze Dong, an event which for decades was considered the single greatest defeat ever suffered by the West in its struggle with world communism.

Since by the early 1950s the Soviet Union was also in possession of nuclear arms, year by year the likelihood of their being used declined. General Douglas MacArthur in Korea wanted to use the bomb against China, only to be dismissed when he made his demands public. The US between 1954 and 1958 repeatedly waved nuclear weapons at China, to what effect remains unknown. Khruschev rattled intercontinental missiles (which, it later turned out, he did not possess) in connection with the Suez Crisis of 1956 and the Berlin Crisis of 1961. Perhaps the last time when anybody seriously threatened to use nuclear weapons was during the Cuban Missile Crisis of October 1962. Even then, the entire way President Kennedy handled the crisis was designed specifically to ensure, as far as possible, that nuclear weapons would *not* have to be used. The chances of the President actually ordering the button pressed were, according to National Security adviser MacGeorge Bundy, one in a hundred. Still, one in a hundred sufficed to give the world a fright which has lasted to the present day.

Having effectively neutralized each other, the superpowers discovered that the utility of nuclear weapons was limited even in their dealings with countries that did not possess them. Since 1945 both the USA and the USSR have seen their influence subject to many fluctuations, especially in the Third World. The US first 'lost', then 'won', a whole series of countries from Egypt to Indonesia and from Somalia to Iraq. For the USSR over the decade and a half since 1973 the process has often worked in reverse: it 'lost' Chile and 'gained' Ethiopia (subsequently 'lost' once again). To list the dozens of ·cases when, often following a domestic coup, a third-world republic switched allegiance from West to East or *vice versa* would be both tedious and irrelevant. As far as anyone can determine, *none* of these changes was influenced to any significant extent by the question of which power, the US or the

USSR, possessed the more powerful nuclear arsenal.

The reason why the political impact of nuclear weapons has been so small is, of course, that nobody can show how a nuclear war could be fought without destroying the world. This has not been for want of trying. Attempts to devise a 'warfighting doctrine' got under way during the 1950s. This was a period when schoolchildren all over the Western world were put through nuclear alarm drills adapted from the Second World War. They were made to file out of class into basements, or else to dive under their desks, cover their heads with their hands, and close their eyes. Meanwhile houseowners were told to dig shelters in their gardens. The shelters had to be stocked with provisions that would last for a few days or weeks until the worst of the radiation was over. People in danger of being caught in the open were advised to take advance notice of the nearest available shelter. To be on the safe side they were told to wear light-coloured clothes, wide-brimmed hats and sunglasses.

Nor were 'preparations' confined to the time of the actual attack. Serious strategists have engaged in calculations designed to show that, if the superpowers' populations could be evacuated in time and evenly dispersed across their respective continents, most of them would survive the blast of nuclear weapons. If they also had shallow dugouts they might even live through the initial period of radiation. How to survive a nuclear winter – assuming that there is such a thing – was a different issue altogether. There was talk of stockpiling food, medical supplies, fuel and earthmoving equipment for the post-nuclear scene. Few countries other than Switzerland did much to put these ideas into effect, and even many Swiss find it hard to take them seriously.

While thinkers strategized and teachers drilled, the politico-military leadership were busy devising ways to fight a nuclear war. Naturally, their first priority was to ensure their own safety. Billions were invested in early-warning installations, blast- and radiation-proof bunkers, airborne command centres, etc. The exact state of these preparations has been kept secret; still, judging from the relatively well-publicized American programme, present-day equipment should give about twenty minutes' warning. Theoretically, fifteen minutes should suffice to whisk America's President away from Washington D.C. Forty-six other key officials are being tracked around the clock and preparations for their evacuation are said to have been made. Some two hundred more have the *right* to be transported out of the capital during business hours. In fact, not even the President's own survival can be guaranteed against a carefully planned nuclear first strike using sea-launched missiles on a depressed trajectory. Whether the President, assuming he has survived, will be able to contact whatever retaliatory forces have ridden out the attack is moot.

Given these problems, many attempts were made to render the world safe for nuclear war by imposing limits on it. One early suggestion was that the nuclear powers agree not to use bombs with a yield greater than 150, or 500, or whatever, kilotons. Another bright idea was that they agree to use them only against selected targets, such as military forces, bases or installations. The attempt to ban the most powerful weapons and avoid cities – the most important targets by far – was commendable in itself. However, it begged the question as to why belligerents who could reach such an agreement should go to war at all, especially one that threatened to end the existence of both.

How to conduct a war *with* nuclear weapons was not, however, the only problem confronted by military planners. It was equally important to consider ways and means by which conventional forces could operate *in* such a war and still survive, let alone retain their combat power. The Americans, for their part, beginning in the mid 1950s, divided traditional divisions into smaller and more mobile units. Linked by the small, transistorized communications systems that were coming into service at that time, these new units were supposed to operate in a decentralized, dispersed mode unlike any previous one in history. They were to leap from place to place, dodging nuclear explosions by opening and closing like huge accordions. To this end they would require novel types of equipment, beginning with giant cross-country landwalking machines and ending with flying jeeps.

Serious attempts to design a 'nuclear warfighting strategy' again proliferated during the 1970s. Rivers of ink were spent devising ways to use new weapons such as Multiple Independent Reentry Vehicles and cruise missiles. Small, accurate warheads would provide the President with 'flexible options'. They might be used for 'warning nuclear shots across the bow'. Instead of going to full-scale war, the US would be able to destroy a military base here, perhaps even a small city there, acting with deliberation and constantly monitoring the other side's reaction. The goal was achieving 'escalation dominance', that is frightening the enemy into submission. The US might even 'decapitate' the Soviet Union by striking at selected government, party, and KGB command and communication centres. The arcane phraseology resembled medieval theological debates. Still, each of these terms was simply a euphemism for using nuclear weapons in ways which would not, it was hoped, bring about the destruction of the world, at any rate not automatically.

During the Carter administration, this line of reasoning was reversed. American officials now worried about what would happen if the USSR used *its* MIRVed missiles to 'take out' America's land-based deterrent. For several years various schemes were floated to prevent this from happening. One was to station the missiles under the sea or else on moving platforms that would crawl over the bottom of lakes. Another was to load them on giant trucks and shuffle them from one firing position to the next along an underground 'racetrack' half as large as the American midwest. A third scheme proposed digging holes thousands of feet deep. The holes would be sealed, and the missiles inside them provided with special equipment that would enable them to screw their way up to the surface in the aftermath of an attack.

Fortunately for the national debt, none of these proposals was adopted. 'The best available estimates' – in truth, mere 'guesstimates' – indicated that, even in a 'clean' Soviet strike directed against America's missile fields, as many as twenty million people would be killed. This would happen even if *none* of the two to three thousand warheads involved missed its way and landed, say, on Los Angeles or Chicago. In the face of such vast 'collateral damage' the question of retaliation – especially limited retaliation – turned out to be academic. Towards the mid 1980s, this particular wave of nuclear warfighting doctrines followed its predecessor and died. The cause of death was the same in both cases, namely choking on its own absurdities.

To sum up, over the last 45 years it would be difficult to point out even a single case when a state of possession of nuclear arms was able to change the *status quo* by threatening their use, let alone using them. In other words, their political effect – if any – has been to enforce caution and freeze existing borders. The most important reason behind this state of affairs is that nobody has yet figured out how to wage a nuclear war without at least risking global suicide. Nuclear weapons are instruments of mass murder. Since there is no defence, the only thing they are suitable for is an act of butchery without precedent in history. They cannot be employed, however, for waging war in any meaningful sense of that term. The chasm separating the apocalyptic implications of nuclear weapons from the puny attempts to 'use' them for sensible ends is tremendous, even inconceivable.

When the first nuclear weapons were built, they were considered unprecedentedly powerful tools for making and winning war. In fact, ten years had not passed before they threatened to put an end to war itself. Nor was the problem confined to nuclear conflict only. By the mid 1950s both superpowers had assembled fission bombs numbering perhaps in the low hundreds and were busily building fusion devices. In such circumstances the possibility of a conventional attack being launched against either of them also appeared increasingly unlikely. With each superpower now in control of the larger part of a hemisphere, an attack against either could only be successful if it was very large. A very large attack would surely be answered with nuclear weapons, particularly if it threatened to become successful.

With the superpowers thus virtually immune to attack, conventional as well as nuclear, attention turned to their allies. However, it soon transpired that the dog that can take care of the cat can also take care of the kittens. In neither West nor East (as far as we know) was there anybody who could devise a way to attack a superpower's close allies without risking Armageddon. From the 1948 Berlin blockade to the last West Berlin crisis in 1961, the superpowers manoeuvred like two dogs testing each other's resolve. Though there were some tense moments, ultimately the testing did not work and both sides ended up conceding defeat. This situation was literally built into concrete when one side erected the Berlin Wall and the other tacitly accepted it.

The division of Europe into two zones of influence closed the doors of the most important theatre where conventional warfare might still be waged, a fact which the recent demolition of the wall and the reunification of Germany have merely confirmed. In 1953 the end of the Korean War created a similar situation on the other side of the globe, and it too was soon cemented by permanent fortified lines. Basically this left only two places where large scale conventional fighting could still take place, along the Indo-Pakistani border and in the Middle East. If only because they could not manufacture all their own arms, the states of those regions were also tied to the superpowers. India, Pakistan, Israel, Egypt, Syria and all the rest fought the superpowers' wars by proxy. Incidentally, they also acted as laboratories where new weapons and doctrines were tested.

As the little powers fought each other the superpowers watched, though taking care to bring the fighting to an end as soon as their own welfare appeared to be even remotely threatened. Many members of their military establishments probably felt jealous of the combatants, in particular of the Israelis who, thanks to their very diminutiveness, were still able to play the game of war. Those military establishments themselves made immense efforts to find ways whereby a superpower could engage in large-scale conventional warfare in a nuclear world. They were, however, frustrated by a simple dilemma. If conventional forces were to stand the slightest chance of surviving a nuclear war they would have to disperse and hide. If hide and disperse they did – discarding much of their heavy equipment in the process – they would no longer be capable of waging conventional war. Thus nuclear weapons threatened the continued existence of conventional forces. Yet if fighting was to take place at all, the only forces which could engage in it without threatening to blow up the world were conventional ones.

The task of trying to square the circle fell to the Kennedy administration. Its solution consisted of going all out for conventional war, ignoring nuclear weapons. A new strategic doctrine, known as 'flexible response', was articulated and officially adopted by NATO in 1967. Its essence consisted of a confidence trick: henceforward preparations for conventional war in Europe and elsewhere were to proceed *as if* the threat of nuclear escalation did not exist. While flexible response doctrine caused conventional forces to flourish, most Western analysts believed that a determined Soviet attack could only be stopped by using 'tactical' nuclear weapons. As early as 1955, a series of wargames played on behalf of the Supreme Allied Commander, Europe (SACEUR) had shown that employing such weapons would cause so much devastation in West Germany that there would be little left to defend. Thus it came to pass that, during the last quarter century, much of the Western effort aimed at preparing a defence against the USSR has amounted to a gigantic exercise in make-believe.

The dampening effect of nuclear weapons made itself felt even in wars where nobody threatened their use. As a result, the USA for one has only been able to employ its conventional armed forces in cases where its vital interests were *not* at stake. The war fought in Korea, a small appendix of Asia several thousand miles away, provides a case in point. The American chiefs of staff recognized this fact even at the time, emphasizing that the really significant areas were Japan and the Philippines. The same applied to Lebanon (1958), Vietnam (1964–72), the Dominican Republic (1965), Cambodia (1972–75), Lebanon (1983) and the Persian Gulf (1987–88). Looking back, so microscopic were the stakes for which United States troops were supposed to shed their blood that most of these cases could hardly even be explained to the American people. On occasions such as the Mayaguez Affair (1975) and Grenada (1983), so puny were the opponents against which American forces pitted themselves that hostilities took on a comic-opera character.

Nor was the United States the only one to suffer from the dampening effect of nuclear weapons. The USSR deployed naval forces to cover the Cuban landing in Angola in 1976, helped the Ethiopians defeat the Somalis in 1979, and sent some advisers to Central America during the 1980s; all of these were marginal issues, however, far removed from the centre of Soviet power. Though Mao at one time denied the relevance of nuclear weapons in a war against an undeveloped country such as China, his own frantic efforts to acquire the bomb prove otherwise. Be that as it may, after China developed a nuclear arsenal and a second-strike missile force to deliver it the clashes along the Chinese–Soviet border – which at one time threatened to escalate into a major war – came to an end. Since then China's single largest military effort has consisted of its 15-mile drive into Vietnamese territory in 1978. Attempting to teach Vietnam a lesson, the Chinese ended up by learning one themselves.

Among the former colonial powers, France, since its defeat in Algeria, has been fairly active in Africa. However, it did not have the occasion to employ forces larger than a regiment, nor in all probability would French public opinion have condoned such an involvement if it had been attempted. After the unhappy experience of the Suez Crisis in 1956 Britain's career as a conventional power appeared to be over. When, much to the government's surprise, Britain did go to war over the Falklands in 1982 this was only made possible by the fact that the Falklands were totally unimportant from any political, strategic or economic point of view.

The (presumed) introduction of nuclear weapons seems to have made a difference even in the Middle East. According to internationally published sources, the first Israeli nuclear device became operational in 1969. The possibility that Israel *might* have the bomb did not escape Arab notice at the time. This may well have been one reason why the October 1973 War was as limited as it was. Though the Arabs did have the necessary delivery systems, Israeli home territory was scarcely attacked at all. Neither the Egyptians nor the Syrians tried to advance very far beyond their respective armistice lines in the Sinai and on the Golan Heights. Even so rumour, taken up by *Time* magazine, has it that, on the fourth day of the war, the Israeli government came within a whisker of losing its head and ordering the bomb to be used.

Whether or not this incident actually took place, this and subsequent reports must have attracted the Arabs' attention. Possibly as a result, there have been no more large-scale conventional wars in the Middle East since 1973. Israel, to be sure, did invade Lebanon in 1982. Prime Minister Menahem Begin, a man whose military knowledge was amateurish at best, was told by his advisers that 'Operation Peace for Galilee' would be a small one. It was supposed to penetrate no more than 25 miles into Lebanon, avoid entanglement with the Syrians, last perhaps three days, and keep casualties to a few dozen. Had he known it would turn into a war, he would never have ordered it; once he realized it *had* turned into a war he underwent a nervous collapse and resigned.

A final interesting case in point is the Iran–Iraq War, which represents by far the largest conventional conflict fought anywhere in the world during the decades since 1953. When the war broke out in the autumn of 1980 it at first seemed as if the Iraqi military could score a rapid victory over the Iranians whose army was disintegrating and whose society was in turmoil. The Iranians under Khomeini made a surprising recovery, however. For almsot eight years they not only held off the Iraqi regular forces but assumed the offensive. They drove into their opponent's territory and, in the spring of 1986, it appeared as if their next offensive would take them to the vital oil-producing region of Basra. Assisted by tens of billions dollars' worth of equipment sold to them by the principal military powers, the two sides became embroiled in protracted warfare.

A million or so casualties later, the belligerents found themselves back at their starting points. The Iranians were taught that, in the face of massive firepower assisted by gas, their fanatic young troops would not be able to achieve a breakthrough except on the road to heaven. The Iraqis learnt that conventional military superiority alone was incapable of inflicting a meaningful defeat on a large country with almost three times their own population. Both sides were constantly hampered by the fear that a serious interruption in the flow of oil would lead to superpower intervention (in fact oil prices started falling not long after the war broke out, helping the war to stay localized). Both wanted a ceasefire, and both were relieved when one was finally concluded.

As the twentieth century is drawing to an end, it may be too early to celebrate – or lament – the demise of conventional war among regular, state-controlled, armed forces. Some facts, however, do stand out. Since 1945 no superpower has engaged another in conventional hostilities and, indeed, in almost all cases even the threat of launching such hostilities against a superpower has bordered on the ludicrous. The superpowers' non-nuclear allies have also been virtually immune to conventional war, except when launched by the power which claimed to offer them 'protection' (for example the Soviets in Eastern Europe). Korea was the last example of a superpower engaging in large-scale conventional warfare against a non-nuclear country. The number of cases when nuclear countries other than the superpowers fought conventional wars may also be counted on the fingers of one hand. Though Britain had acquired nuclear weapons in 1952, their existence proved irrelevant to the Suez campaign. Perhaps the only others are the 1973 Arab–Israeli War, the 1982 Falkland Islands War and the 1991 Gulf War.

Admittedly, countries not in possession of nuclear arsenals have engaged each other in conventional war more frequently. The largest clashes took place in the Middle East, between China and Taiwan, India and China, and along the Indo–Pakistani border. However, in the 1970s nuclear weapons seem to have been introduced into these regions. Whether or not this is the reason, since then the incidence of conventional war has undergone a marked decline. Egypt and Israel have signed a peace treaty. In the face of endless provocations Israel and Jordan are unofficially at peace, and even Syria's president Assad has been dropping occasional peaceful hints. China has declared its intention of using only peaceful means to regain Taiwan. Though the Indians still dispute their border with China another war between the two countries does not appear likely so long as both retain their nuclear arsenals and, as important, their national cohesion. Meanwhile India and Pakistan remain at loggerheads. They are unlikely to fight another war, however, and in 1989 they agreed to refrain from bombing each other's nuclear installations in case of war.

If one looks, not at how many conventional wars there have been and by whom they were fought but at the way that they ended similar conclusions emerge. Out of several dozen such conflicts, very few have led to internationally recognized territorial changes. One exception was the 1948–49 war in the Middle East which led to the establishment of Israel. Another was the Indo–Pakistani War of 1971 which, though it established Bangladesh, did not result in the drawing of new frontiers. There may have been a few other cases, but on the whole the trend is clear. 'Employing armed force for acquiring territory' has, after all, been declared unacceptable by international law. The signs are that, faced by actual nuclear weapons or by the ability to build them quickly, states have grown wary not merely of territorial expansion but of conventional war itself. There is, of course, no way to predict the future, but everything considered the

Iran–Iraq War may well have been among the last the world will see.

Though conventional war may be on its way out, the same is not true of war as such. Since 1945 there have been perhaps 160 armed conflicts around the world, more if struggles like the French against Corsican separatists and the Spanish against the Basques are included. Of those, perhaps three quarters have been of the so-called 'low intensity' variety. The principal characteristics of Low Intensity Conflict (LIC) are as follows. First, they tend to unfold in 'less developed' parts of the world; the numerous small-scale armed conflicts which do take place in 'developed' countries are usually given a variety of other names such as 'terrorism' or, in the case of Northern Ireland, 'troubles'. Second, very rarely do they involve regular armies on *both* sides. Third, most LICs do not rely primarily on modern, high technology, crew-operated, weapons. Excluded are high-performance aircraft, tanks, missiles, heavy artillery, and many other devices so complicated as to be known only by their acronyms.

Besides being numerically predominant, LICs have also been far bloodier than any other kind of war fought since 1945. The clashes between Hindus and Muslims from 1947 to 1949 probably claimed over a million lives. Up to three million people perished during the Nigerian Civil War between 1966 and 1969. Well over a million died in the 30-year Vietnamese conflict, perhaps another million in the rest of Indochina. A million probably died in Algeria, another million in Afghanistan where there have also been some five million refugees. The conflicts which took place in Central and South America were much smaller, yet certainly they involved hundreds of thousands of deaths. In addition, armed conflict occurred in the Philippines, Tibet, Thailand, Sri Lanka, Kurdistan, Sudan, Ethiopia, Uganda, Western Sahara, Angola, and half a dozen other places. The total number of dead has been put at twenty million or more.

Uncertain as they are, these figures are *much* larger than those generated by any post-1945 'conventional' conflict. To this rule there have been only two exceptions: the Korean War, where most casualties were civilians, and the eight-year Iran–Iraq War. For the rest, the following example may give an idea of the orders of magnitude involved. Fifteen years of civil war in Lebanon, a country with a population of approximately 2.5 million, are said to have claimed over 100,000 dead (this figure has remained constant for several years, indicating that nobody bothers to count any longer). By contrast Israel – a country justly famous for the number and scale of the wars it has fought – had lost a total of some 14,000 killed in the four decades of its existence. Of those 14,000 fully 6,000 or 43 per cent, fell during the 'War of Liberation' in 1948–49. That war, when considered from the point of view of the forces engaged and the weapons used, was itself in many ways a 'low intensity conflict'.

If politics is what wars are all about, then LICs have been politically by far the most significant form of war waged since 1945. Only one or two of the several dozen 'conventional' conflicts waged since 1945 resulted in the establishment of new frontiers. During the same period the consequences of LICs, numerically about three times as strong, have been momentous. All over the 'Third World', Low Intensity Conflict has been perhaps the dominant instrument for bringing about political change. Under the name of 'wars of national liberation', LICs have helped bring about the disappearance of colonial empires which between them controlled approximately one half of the globe, *without a single conventional war*. In the process, some of the strongest military powers on earth have suffered humiliation, to the point of helping put an end to the entire notion of the white man's inherent superiority.

Perhaps the best indication of the importance of LIC is that its results, unlike those of conventional wars, have usually been recognized by the international community. Often, indeed, recognition preceded victory rather than followed it, shedding interesting light on the interaction of right with might in the modern world. Considered from this point of view – 'by their fruits thou shalt know them' – the term LIC itself is grossly misconceived. The same applies to related ones such as 'terrorism', 'insurgency', 'brushfire war', or 'guerrilla war'. The truth is that what we are dealing with here is neither of low intensity nor some bastard offspring of war. Rather, it is WARRE in the elemental, Hobbesian sense of the word, by far the most important form of armed conflict in our time; so much so that *all* of the 15 to 20 wars now being fought in various places around the world are of this type.

The fact that present-day armed violence is overwhelmingly of the 'low intensity' type will scarcely surprise the inhabitants of the developing countries in which these wars are taking place. Nor is it necessary to remind the reader that those countries, the *locus classicus* of LIC, have as their populations approximately four-fifths of all people living on this planet. If anyone should be startled at all, it is the citizens of the 'developed' world and, even more, the members of their 'defence' establishments who for decades on end have prepared for the wrong kind of war.

The reasons why, until recently, large numbers of intelligent people in both East and West have either ignored or missed the truth are easy to find. In 1945, having just gone through the horrors of total war, most developed countries heaved a sigh of relief. They were only too happy to return to the good old days when wars were directed by governments and fought by armies, preferably on the territory of some far-away third country. During the 1950s there arose a whole 'limited warfare' school of thought which sought to codify those ideas. Meanwhile most people were content to watch war on TV. They had not the slightest intention of risking their lives, however, and when President Lyndon Johnson hinted that general mobilization might be necessary to win the war in Vietnam he was forced from office.

A curious vicious circle was created. Regarding each other as their most important enemies, the superpowers in particular thought in terms of nuclear and conventional war. Estimating armed force in terms of what it takes to wage nuclear and conventional war, they looked at each other as their most dangerous enemies. Thus the military establishments of developed countries clung to nuclear and conventional war because these were games with which they had long been familiar and which they liked to play. They were also games in which those forces held virtually all the cards, be they military, technological, or economic.

As far as many developed countries were concerned, the exercise in make-believe probably could have gone on for ever. Though preparing for nuclear and conventional war was expensive, its very cost kept a vast military–industrial complex content and prosperous. Unfortunately, there were those who regarded this kind of war as part of a vast plot designed to perpetuate the rule of developed countries over undeveloped ones. All over the so-called 'Third World' numerous movements of national liberation sprang into being. Most did not have an army, let alone a government, though without exception they claimed to represent the people. Usually they called themselves by some local variant of 'freedom fighters'. Others called them guerrillas and terrorists, or else resorted to a large repertoire of still less complimentary epithets. If – or so they claimed – their aims were not criminal, their methods often were, and so was the treatment they received. Semantics apart, very often they were both able and willing to employ warlike violence to achieve their ends.

Judged by ordinary standards, none of these movements stood the slightest chance of success. Often the economic resources at their disposal were minimal. Consequently they had to resort to bank-robbing or drug-dealing, blurring the distinction between war and crime. Militarily they were very weak, especially at the outset. They had neither regular organization and experience, nor heavy weapons. They were too weak to carry arms openly; they could not afford to wear uniform and thus turn themselves into easy targets. Unable to abide by the established rules of war, they refused to fight as if it were a tournament, one army against another. Using a combination of violence and persuasion, they drew the populations to their side and intimidated the enemy. Their methods, admittedly, were not pleasant. However, there was nothing particularly pleasant about the methods of conventional war which, to select but two recent examples, included gassing opponents to death and destroying entire cities by fire.

Pleasant or not, LIC was very effective – so much so that, from Algeria to Vietnam, Lebanon, Afghanistan, Sri Lanka, Cambodia and Namibia, *every* regular army which fought them was defeated. Usually the insurgents did not even have to close to the kill before the regular forces broke. Withdrawal frequently was accompanied by the feeling that counter-insurgency was not 'their' kind of war, and that it would end up destroying them even if, as happened once or twice, something like military 'victory' seemed within reach. Either way, over much of the world the new form of war has already taken over. Though decolonization is now all but complete, LIC has not been interrupted in its march of conquest. Even today it is ravaging many developing countries from Colombia to the Philippines. Much of this is the work of ragtag bands of ruffians out for advantage, hardly distinguishable from the *écorcheurs* ('skinners') who devastated the French country-side during the Hundred Years War. Now as then, they have turned entire societies into bloody chaos.

Nor is there any reason to think that the comparatively small number of developed countries will continue to enjoy immunity for ever. On numerous occasions in the past their embassies have been attacked, their ships hijacked, their aircraft bombed out of the sky with heavy loss of life. Some of their citizens have been taken hostage and held out for ransom. Others were murdered, others still threatened with execution unless they bowed to the dictates of some mad mullah in a faraway capital. To make things worse, many now contain sizeable minorities – whether Muslims, as in Western Europe, or Blacks and Hispanics, as in the US – who sympathize with the struggles going on in their countries of origin, and who may themselves resort to violence to protest social and economic discrimination. Today, to believe one is safe from LIC is to be either very foolish or blind.

Long-established, stable countries like Britain, France, West Germany, Italy and Spain, to mention but a few, all have their own indigenous terrorists. Some terrorists claim to be on the left, others on the right. Many are inspired by nationalist considerations. All have this in common – they are dissatisfied with the existing order and are determined to use violence to alter it. Excluding those active in the developing world, the organizations with which they are affiliated number in the dozens and may soon exceed a hundred. Many of their members are strongly motivated, highly educated, and fully capable of taking advantage of modern technology from computers to plastic explosives. In the past such organizations have proved themselves willing and able to co-operate with each other, forming a kind of terrorist international. Nor have they refrained from establishing contacts with other organizations whose motive for resorting to violence is not primarily political, such as drug traffickers, Mafiosi, and the like.

The attitudes of individual states to terrorism have changed over time. Still, usually these movements were able to obtain finance, weapons, training, and asylum from one source or another. Like self-transplanting weeds, they could not be eradicated simply by being uprooted at one particular place. The prevalence of terrorism has often been blamed on the unwillingness of liberal-democratic countries to take the tough measures necessary for its suppression. Advocates of this view pointed to the fact that, through much of the post-war period, Eastern Bloc totalitarian states with the Soviet Union at their head had been able to contain terrorism within very narrow bounds. However, Russia itself has a history of terrorism as long and honourable as that of any other state. As the 1980s gave way to the 1990s there were abundant indications that people living within the borders of the USSR, Muslims in particular, were about to follow the example of their brethren outside. As Soviet dominance weakened East European national rivalries began to return and, as has already begun in Yugoslavia and Romania, will presumably resort to violence when it suits their purposes. Finally, the US, as the most violent 'first world' society by far, has always had something resembling LIC within its borders, except that, in the US, even organized violence is seldom politically motivated and is usually known as crime.

Like a man who has been shot in the head but still manages to stagger forward a few paces, conventional war is all but finished. Brought face to face with the threat of LIC inside their borders, some of the largest and mightiest empires that the world has ever known have suddenly begun falling into each other's arms. Should present trends continue, then the kind of war between states with which we have been familiar since the Peace of Westphalia seems to be on its way out. The rise of LIC may, unless it can be quickly contained, end up destroying the state. In the long run, the latter's place as the chief political entity in which humanity is organized will be taken by warmaking organizations of a different type.

The compelling factor behind the inability of states to fight each other is the spread of nuclear weapons. From Central Europe to Kashmir, and from the Middle East to Korea, they threaten to turn large-scale war into attempted suicide. This point is not new. The first to suggest that 'close intermingling with the enemy' represented conventional forces' best hope of avoiding nuclear destruction were the 'tactical nuclear warfighting' theorists of the late 1950s. Their analysis was correct but, seen in retrospect, did not go far enough. The unlimited range of modern delivery vehicles, their ability to reach any point in enemy territory, the sheer power of the nuclear warheads that they carry, and the absence of an effective defence -- all of these are well on the way to rendering national frontiers meaningless. If fighting is to take place at all, then not only the armed forces but the political communities on whose behalf they operate will have to become intermingled with each other. If and when such intermingling takes place, it is very likely that the forces fielded by these communities will no longer be of the conventional kind.

If territorial states are decreasingly able to fight each other, then the concept of intermingling already points to the rise of LIC as an alternative. The essence of LIC is that it does not require a large, distinct, territorial base. It circumvents and undermines the modern state; which is why that state in many ways is singularly ill-suited for dealing with this kind of war. On the whole, the best that developed countries from Britain and Northern Ireland to Italy (and, most recently, the Eastern Bloc from Yugoslavia to Armenia and Uzbekistan) have been able to do is to contain terrorism. An amount of violent activity which even as late as the 1960s would have been considered outrageous is now accepted as an inevitable hazard of modern life, so much so that the casualty rate is often compared with that caused by traffic accidents. Moreover, LIC is fast becoming an export commodity of developing countries with little else to sell. Throughout the Third World numerous new states were never able to establish themselves *vis à vis* other kinds of social entities, including in particular ethnic groups and tribes. In the face of their quarrels, those states began to fall apart before they had become properly established.

What makes this scenario all the more credible is that war represents perhaps the most imitative activity known to man. Strategy is by definition interactive; any attempt to defeat the enemy must be preceded by an endeavour to understand him. By fighting, belligerents who were originally very dissimilar will come to resemble each other, first in the methods that they use and then, gradually, in other respects. Resembling each other, provided only the struggle lasts long enough, the point will come where the reasons for which they originally went to war are forgotten. One need not share Hegel's view concerning the primacy of war in human affairs to agree that one important way by which human societies of any kind develop their internal structure has always been through fighting other societies. After all, no community illustrates this fact better than the modern state itself; an organization which acquired its characteristic institutions partly through the need to fight its opposite numbers.

Doubtless the process by which LIC spreads and the state loses its monopoly over armed violence in favour of other organizations will be gradual, uneven and intermittent. Things happen at a different pace in different parts of the world. To hazard a guess, among the first to be affected will be states in Asia, Africa, the Caribbean, and Latin America; and indeed some would say that in many of them the process has already begun. Similarly, in large, heterogeneous empires such as the Soviet Union (including some of the other Warsaw Pact members), the process is already well under way. China and India are also likely candidates. Both countries are afflicted by expanding populations, making it almost impossible to solve their pressing economic problems. Both contain entire peoples whose memories of former political independence, even greatness, have by no means been erased. Given a suitable opportunity, they are increasingly likely to have a go at it.

The USA is another large, multiracial society where weapons are widely available and where the tradition of internal violence is second to none. During most of their history abundant natural resources, an open frontier, and – later – global expansion enabled Americans to raise their standards of living. As they did so, from time to time they fought a war in which their aggressions found an outlet. However, all three factors no longer exist. The frontier was closed long ago. America's economic viability has been on the decline since about 1970. Partly as a result, so has its ability to dominate the rest of the world, a process which the recent eclipse of the USSR is unlikely to halt. As

Americans were forced to run faster and faster just to stay in place, social tensions mounted and so did escapism – the use of drugs – until it was described by President Reagan as 'our number one war'. America's current economic decline must be halted. If not, one day the crime that is rampant in the streets of New York and Washington D.C. may develop into LIC by coalescing along racial, religious, social and political lines, and run completely out of control.

If only because they have strong traditions to fall back on, some of the oldest states, particularly Japan and those of Western Europe, may be able to hold out the longest. Japan is particularly fortunate because it is isolated, exceptionally homogeneous and, at present, rich. Yet even today Japanese politicians shudder at the possibility that 'huddled, teeming, masses' from poor countries in the region may start arriving on their shores. West European states are likely to see their sovereignty undermined as much from above, at the hands of international organizations, as from below. Should Europe be united, then whatever form its organization assumes almost certainly will not resemble a 'state' as the term is understood today. Integration may cause regional pressures for independence on the part of Basques, Corsicans, Scots and a host of other peoples to grow; the first to succeed will act as a trojan horse for the rest. Most likely not all these movements will employ violence to gain their ends. Still, and also in view of the growing numbers of resident, non-European, non-Christian people, in the long run the possibility exists that LIC will break out and sweep at least part of the European continent.

Assuming all this takes place, what will the community which may one day take the place of the state as the principal warmaking entity be like? In the past, war has been made by numerous entities – tribal societies existing from prehistoric times until recently; city states of the kind that were common in the ancient world and also in late-medieval and early modern Europe; royal despotisms such as the ancient Assyrian, Persian, Hellenistic and Roman Empires; feudal social structures such as those at one time dominant in both Europe and Japan; religious associations seeking to establish the glory of this god or that; private mercenary bands commanded by warlords; and even commercial organizations such as the British East India Company and its opposite numbers in other countries. Many of these entities were neither 'political' (politics being inextricably mixed up with a host of other factors) nor in possession of 'sovereignty' (a sixteenth-century term). Nevertheless they *did* engage in purposeful, organized, large-scale violence: that is, war.

No more than Froissart in the fourteenth century could foresee the replacement of the feudal political system by the modern one which is based on states, can we today foresee what new order will arise after the latter's collapse. However, the fact that already at present *none* of perhaps two dozen armed conflicts being fought throughout the world has states as both belligerents may permit an educated guess. In most of Africa the entities by which the wars in question are waged resemble tribes – indeed they *are* tribes, or whatever is left of them under the corrosive influence of modern civilization. In parts of Asia and Latin America the best analogy may be the robber barons who infested Europe during the early modern period or else the vast feudal organizations which warred against each other in sixteenth-century Japan. In North America and Western Europe future warmaking entities will probably resemble the Assassins, the group which, motivated by religion and allegedly supporting itself on drugs, terrorized the medieval Middle East for two centuries.

In the future, war will be waged not by armies but by groups whom we today call terrorists, guerrillas, bandits and robbers, but who will undoubtedly find more formal titles to describe themselves. Their organizations are likely to be constructed on charismatic rather than institutional lines and to be motivated less by 'professionalism' than by fanatical, ideologically-based loyalties. While rooted in a 'population base' of some sort, that population probably will not be clearly separable either from its immediate neighbours or from those, always the minority, by whom most of the active fighting is done. A warmaking entity of any size will have to be 'in control' of a territorial base of some sort. However, that base is unlikely to be either continuous, impenetrable, or very large. Probably its frontiers – itself a modern term – will not be marked by a clear line on a map. Instead, there will be the occasional roadblock cropping up at unexpected places, manned by ruffians out to line their own pockets as well as those of their bosses.

The most important single demand that any political community must meet is the demand for protection. A community which cannot safeguard the lives of its members, subjects, citizens, comrades, brothers, or whatever they are called is unlikely either to command their loyalty or to survive for very long. The opposite is also correct: any community able and, which is even more important, willing to exert itself to protect its members will be capable to call on their members' loyalty even to the point where they are prepared to die for it. The rise of the modern state is explicable largely in terms of its military effectiveness *vis à vis* other warmaking organizations. If, as seems to be the case, that state cannot defend itself effectively against internal or external LIC, then clearly it does not have a future. If the state *does* take on LIC in earnest then it will have to win quickly and decisively. Alternatively, the process of fighting itself will undermine the state's foundations. Indeed, the fear of initiating this process has been a major factor behind the reluctance of many Western countries in particular to come to grips with terrorism. This scenario is certainly not imaginary; even today, in many places around the world, the dice are on the table and the game already well under way.

## NOTE

1. The Gulf War, which broke out after these words were written, at first sight seems to belie the thesis advanced on these pages. It should be remembered, however, that this war was only made possible by the fact that, at the time, Iraq was the one country in the world which, while it did have large, powerful, and advanced conventional forces, did not yet possess nuclear weapons.

# Why Wars Do Not End: Some Observations on the First World War

## MICHAEL GRAHAM FRY

There is a vast literature on the origins and conduct of war generally, and specifically on the causes and unfolding of the First World War. The literature on war termination is substantial; that specifically addressing the prolongation of war is, in contrast, very modest. Indeed, the central puzzle of why wars are not brought to a negotiated settlement is almost invariably a residual theme in studies of the conduct of wars and how they end. The literature dealing with ethics and war is concerned almost exclusively with origins and conduct, and ignores the moral issues involved in the prolongation of war.[1]

The First World War, in all its concatenations and dimensions, was the major event of the twentieth century. Militarily it was essentially a European and Near Eastern war with global appendages. At sea the war was fought primarily for control of the Atlantic and the Mediterranean. It ultimately involved all the major powers. The war was fought from August 1914 to November 1918 to a military conclusion that still left victory something of an abstraction. It had its interlocked military and diplomatic rhythms, and a surreal fascination for participants. It took on mechanistic, system-like properties, and developed a momentum generated by emotions and moral precepts that went far deeper than the governing assumption that war was a legitimate instrument of policy. The war became commendable and satisfying to elites and attentive publics; it remained politically and psychologically easier to wage war than to terminate it through negotiation. But the costs, particularly the level of human suffering, were tragically high. They prompt speculation still about the political benefits of a shorter, less devastating and destructive conflict –

evolutionary solutions to Russia's ills, less fertile breeding grounds for extremism in Germany, a less paranoid France, more creative and economically viable arrangements in Eastern Europe, a revitalization of the mentalities of the European concert and a sounder peace settlement. But the war ran its course, and one is left contemplating the Europe that would have resulted had the Central Powers largely crafted a settlement in 1918 or even dictated peace and gathered in the immense harvest of the Treaty of Brest–Litovsk. In other words, was not it worthwhile to fight on to prevent a 'German peace'? The answer at the time for *Entente* statesmen, whatever wavering occurred, was in the affirmative; it has retained much of its justification since then.

These considerations reflect what one might call countervailing, ethical-emotional burdens that were borne by participants in the various policy communities. Hardly any of Europe's statesmen found their involvement in the decision to go to war in August 1914 an intolerable, debilitating memory, except perhaps Sir Edward Grey, the British Foreign Secretary. But decisions to prolong the war were very hard to live with and heartrending. Living with the carnage, the sacrifice, the cost, and the unanticipated and uncontrollable consequences became a spiritual and psychological burden, and a moral dilemma, which added immensely to the physical stress and strain of office, and the uncertainty of it all. Witnessing what was judged to be the incompetence and apparent indifference of the generals was hard enough for politicians to take; being unable to effect change added frustration to sorrow. On 28 December 1917, for example, David Lloyd George, Britain's Prime Minister from December 1916, told C.P. Scott, editor of the *Manchester Guardian*

... I am in a very pacifist temper. If people really knew the war could be stopped tomorrow ... But, of course, they don't know and can't know ... The thing is horrible and beyond human nature to bear and I feel I can't go on with the bloody business; I would rather resign.[2]

Two days later he agreed with Sir Maurice Hankey, secretary to the War Cabinet, and Philip Kerr, a prominent member of his secretariat, that peace was desirable for there was little chance of securing better terms in 1918.[3] Richard von Kuhlmann, the German Foreign Secretary, claimed to have felt the same way in the spring of 1918. Such sentiments provided a great incentive to negotiate, especially for men who believed that individuals shaped history, and that history was a terrible and formidable judge with an interminable memory. What would history say of them if they prolonged the war unnecessarily, if they threw away any legitimate opportunity to negotiate peace? This incentive to negotiate rested also on the presence of shared values between the belligerents. The First World War, at least until 1917, until the *Entente* confronted Bolshevism in power in Russia and what they concluded was unrepentant militarism in Germany, was less ideological than the Second World War. The Kaiser was not Hitler, not anti-Christ. But these were fading assumptions. The enemy 'became' responsible for war not out of blunder but out of choice. Germany, for example, had enjoyed several options in 1914 and had decided, consciously and deliberately, on war. Its war aims were gargantuan. Germany was fighting the war unjustly, and the atrocities grew in their frequency and severity. Lloyd George talked of assassinating Enver Pasha, the Turkish War Minister, in November 1917; Winston Churchill, seeking political rehabilitation as Minister of Munitions, was prepared to consider the use of gas attacks on the Western Front in the desperate days of the late spring of 1918. But such schemes were seen as fleeting aberrations, out of character. From the *Entente* perspective it became essential to punish the aggressor, exorcise Prussian militarism, democratize Germany, indict war criminals and make Germany pay the cost of the war, but not to benefit the Bolsheviks.[4] The war became a matter of justice and righteousness. Elites, military and civilian, found robust political and psychological defences to enable them to cope with the dilemmas and the resulting stress. Personal, party, governmental, national and international causes were being served by fighting on that were just and justifiable. Patriotism fed a sense of duty, even destiny. War made the nation fitter and one could construct from its sacrifices societies fit for heroes. Gains were to be made, territorial and non-territorial, that were legitimate, necessary and reasonable, even modest and indispensable rather than excessive and indefensible. The war became an opportunity to reform the international system, alter the nature of diplomacy, initiate new rules of the global game, serve the cause of collective security, and build barriers against alien ideologies. Victory came to be viewed, in fact, as the only guarantee against a resumption of war. Sacrifice now would prevent even more terrible sacrifice in the future; death would save lives.

When a balance was struck between these contending considerations it pointed to prolonging the war. Several factors determined that judgement. First, was the nature of wartime diplomacy. The war had its diplomatic system, autonomous, discrete and integrated. Belligerents were involved simultaneously in its five parts – a negotiated peace, separate peace arrangements to undermine the opposing alliance, the defence of the integrity of one's own alliance, the courting of neutrals and the search for new allies, and the definition of war aims, which were called peace desiderata. The diplomatic initiatives, the bargaining and negotiating to pursue these ends could not be disaggregated, and that itself constituted a formidable obstacle to peace. The purposes of a negotiated as opposed to a separate peace were fundamentally at odds with one other. When contacts were made and discussions initiated, statesmen found it extremely difficult to judge exactly what was transpiring, to determine precisely why, with what motive and for what purpose talks were underway. And the stakes were too high to permit error.

When Austria-Hungary or Germany offered to negotiate on Alsace-Lorraine or Belgium, was this an attempt to bring about a general peace, or France's defection from the *Entente*? When Habsburg agents made contact in Denmark or Switzerland was the purpose to extricate the Habsburg Empire from the German alliance and the war, to draw the *Entente* into peace negotiations on terms favouring the Central Powers, or to bring about Italy's defection? When Britain and France responded to Austria's initiatives were they seeking peace or Austria's defection, hoping to be able to persuade Italy and the south Slavs to lower their aspirations? Italy's appetite for territory, even though codified in the Treaty of London of April 1915, came to be regarded, in most quarters, as outrageously excessive and utterly unjustified. And what motivated the agents of the Ottoman government, Enver Pasha included – playing Germany's game, preserving the Ottoman Empire territorially, or, if Arab lands were to be lost, finding compensation in the east and south east and serving Pan-Turanian dreams, and/or filling their pockets with *Entente* gold (and there was plenty of that from secret service funds), and boat tickets to the Americas? Who could say with any certainty? Far better in the circumstances to fight on.

And that was sound judgement all round, beyond the problem of discerning motive and intent. 'Peace kites', Hankey's phrase, traced circles of improbability across the sky. If allies, Italy for example, would not relinquish part of their war aims, there could be no separate peace arrangements with a member of the opposing alliance; without disrupting the enemy alliance there could be no victory, no realization of war aims. If Britain, for example, consulted its allies beforehand, they could veto negotiations; if Britain went ahead unilaterally, its allies would repudiate any unacceptable arrangement, and re-examine their loyalties. For Britain, there was the added complication of the Dominions. Arthur Balfour, the Foreign Secretary, when handling the German initiative that came by way of Madrid, in September–October 1917, found a compromise. How to handle Russian sensitivities emerged as the major problem. Britain would receive any German communication on peace; to do otherwise, to give a point-blank refusal, would discourage the German 'peace party' and encourage pacifism at home. Balfour would *inform* the Allied ambassadors of that decision, a step that fell short of *consulting* the Allies, but one that was an advance on secrecy. That was as far as Lloyd George, disillusioned with the Russian situation, would go.[5]

The fact of the matter was that when the German government took the initiative, as it did prominently three times between December 1916 and September 1917, and more opaquely in April and September 1917, involving Belgian officials and Aristide Briand, the French radical leader but out of office, it was seeking to sow dissension within the *Entente*, particularly between Britain and France, as a war measure, as a preface to seeking peace on its own terms after victory.[6] Its contacts with Russia from March to June 1917 and after October 1917 were to serve the same purposes. That was why Austrian initiatives, carefully monitored and leading, it was hoped, to the detaching of either France or Italy from the *Entente*, and without involving any significant threat that Austria would desert the Central Powers, were not necessarily to be discouraged. But Count Czernin, the Emperor Karl's Foreign Minister, and the Prince Sixte affair in 1917, brought complications that were decidedly unacceptable. Czernin was not willing to sign a separate peace with the *Entente* and march the Habsburg Empire out of the war, but his views on what were acceptable general peace terms were not what German politicians in office could accept, let alone the generals. But nothing came of Czernin's flirtations with Britain or the United States in the first two months of 1917. Prince Sixte, a plausible French royal, along with his mother and sister, the Empress Zita, became a conduit between the Emperor Karl and the French government of Alexander Ribot between February and June 1917. Lloyd George was brought into it in April. But it was impossible to come to any conclusion other than Karl, and Czernin, to the extent that he was involved, were seeking either to detach France from the *Entente* by an offer of Alsace-Lorraine or draw the *Entente* into a general peace on Austrian terms.[7]

Attitudes in London and Paris complemented those in Berlin and Vienna. Germany had to be fended off, Austria, Bulgaria and Turkey pursued. Lloyd George reasoned that because he saw immeasurable value in and distinct opportunities for disrupting the enemy's alliance, his counterparts in Berlin must have reached precisely the same conclusions. He saw the Sixte affair entirely as a way to bring about a separate peace with Austria. He worked with sanguine energy, and absolutely no success, at St-Jean-de-Maurienne in April 1917 and elsewhere, even to the detriment of Near Eastern policy, to convince Sydney Sonnino, the Italian Prime Minister, to lower Italy's territorial expectations. In all this, Lloyd George clearly was in error, as Foreign Office officials pointed out with a mixture of dismay and satisfaction. But Lloyd George persisted with the strategy until it was irrelevant, seeking also with 'a bribe and a blow' to detach Turkey from the Central Powers. For if Austria or Turkey were genuinely free to negotiate then, he reasoned, there was no danger of being drawn into discussions with Germany. The trap could not be sprung. It never was, but not because Lloyd George's reasoning was sound.

*Entente* statesmen and officials, moreover, judged German initiatives through Madrid in September 1917, for example, to be insincere moves to divide the Allies. Kuhlmann was up to the old trick of seeking to separate France from Britain, and Russia from the Allies. He was an 'Easterner' who would make modest sacrifices in the West so as to bid for hegemony from a power base newly created in the East. That is what an inconclusive, 'patched up' peace would invite. Balfour concluded that Germany would back off when it learned that Britain would not proceed unilaterally. Georges Clemenceau, to be the French Prime Minister from November 1917, would have the traitor Joseph Caillaux shot, rein in Briand, and refuse to negotiate with Germany even if France was promised Alsace-Lorraine, the left bank of the Rhine and Holland! He would stand resolute with England.[8]

'Peace kites', then, were flown frequently in the months from December 1916 to October 1917. But to see those months as a promising high season for peace would be to confuse initiatives to bring about various separate peace agreements with genuine attempts to negotiate a general settlement to the war. Before December 1916, few officials or politicians took the soundings that occurred sufficiently seriously to warrant detailed historical analysis, except when third-party mediation was involved. The fact was that the military balance before December 1916 gave neither side a clear edge, tipping towards the *Entente* in the summer of 1916 and back to the Central Powers by November. Both sets of belligerents, caught up in the prosecution of the war, saw victory as attainable and the costs of achieving it as acceptable.

After October 1917, Germany and its allies, still united in intent and purpose, had grounds to risk reaching for victory, and sufficiently large territorial appetites to savour the anticipated rewards – the confirmation of Germany's expansion in the east, codified in the Brest-Litovsk and related treaties, Turkey's Pan-Turanian visions, the consolidation of the Habsburg Empire, and acquisitions at the expense of Greece and Serbia for Bulgaria. Russia's disintegration and then its defection, United States sloth, allied food and manpower shortages, both real and perceived, the continued effectiveness of submarine warfare, and the shattering of the Franco-Russian *entente*, which meant that Germany had the solution to the problem of war on two fronts that had eluded it since 1914, seemed ample reason to make the sacrifices necessary to achieve victory. The Central Powers could look forward to dictating peace terms at the peace conference. Czernin remained the advocate of a general peace, but Kuhlmann's differences with the generals were largely about how Germany could control Eastern Europe and why, and not about the necessity for that control. A series of military offensives launched on the Western Front from 21 March 1918 accompanied attempts to consolidate Germany's hold on Eastern Europe, Romania and Western Russia and secure unfettered access to their resources, and thrusts into the Caucasus, Trans Caspia, northern Persia and Turkestan. 'Peace kites' flown by Germany, as it prepared for the March 1918 offensive, and even after March, were designed, as they had been in 1917, to carry away individual members of the *Entente*. Austrian contacts with French, United States and British representatives in February and March 1918, the Kerr–Skrzynski (the latter of the Austrian mission in Berne) meeting, for example, in mid-March, were futile and predictably so. Czernin wanted to engineer a general peace; the Allies wanted to detach Austria from Germany. Allied leaders concluded, with some wavering, that, despite the Russian débâcle, it was not time to parlay.

Jan Smuts, the South African member of the British War Cabinet, wobbled most, George Curzon not at all. Lord Milner, at the War Office from April 1918, spoke often in private of the desirability of ending the war by negotiation. He detested Bolshevism, but he was driven essentially by one central purpose – to ensure that the British Empire left the war in an invincible position, and with the United States as a co-operative ally.[9] Russia, from the final months of 1917 was uppermost in Lloyd George's calculations. He said things in the War Cabinet and privately that are not difficult to misinterpret.[10] He would not endorse the position of his predecessor, Herbert Asquith, that Germany must surrender territory occupied in the West *and* in Russia and Poland as a pre-condition of peace. He was willing to discuss the consequences of making peace at Russia's expense, especially as France, the United States and British opinion, in his view, would not balk at such a strategy. In his memoirs, Lloyd George wrote: 'We would not have kept up the War in order to undo the Treaty of Brest–Litovsk'.[11] But his principal concern, in fact, was to retain Russia as a weapon against Germany, to see Russia fight on to liberate its territory from German control. And Balfour never let him forget the negative consequences of Germany leaking to Russia, before or after the Bolshevik seizure of power on 7–8 November 1917, that Britain was willing to sell out its ally.

Some historians depict Lloyd George's Trade Union speech of 5 January 1918 as an offer of peace to the Central Powers, to be arranged largely at Russia's expense. This interpretation is unsound. The speech was a war not a peace move, a stratagem to bring about victory ultimately, motivated by domestic and international considerations, beyond the categorical advice of Sir William Robertson, the CIGS, that the military situation, whatever its dangers, demanded that the Allies, if they would make the necessary sacrifices, should not enter a peace conference at that time.[12] At home, Lloyd George wanted to ensure radical and socialist support by the appearance of moderation, assuring a socialist delegation on 28 December 1917 that British aims contained nothing that was perpetuating the war.[13] Incidentally, his speech would rebuff once again the irritatingly persistent Lord Lansdowne. Lloyd George was, in fact, seizing the moral high ground from the socialists, as well as from Germany, the Bolsheviks and President Woodrow Wilson. The preening response of Ramsay Macdonald, the socialist leader, to the speech indicated that, at least as far as the socialists were concerned, he had had some success. The danger in this gambit lay in alienating Lloyd George's conservative, nationalist and imperialist supporters. But it was an acceptable risk. The payoff would be that his government and the sacrifices it had asked, and would ask, of the nation would be legitimated. The nation would unite behind a prime minister who demonstrated both moderation and a sense of purpose and direction.

Abroad, Lloyd George wanted to undermine Germany's negotiations with the Bolsheviks, and evade a peace conference convened at Germany's timing, to ratify Germany's war aims. That meant also finessing the peace terms published by Czernin, which were sufficiently appealing that they had to be discredited by citing their vagueness and the lack of sincerity that lay behind them. Lloyd George wanted control of the terms and timing of any peace discussions. The propaganda value of the Trade Union speech was expected to be substantial. The propaganda apparatus would demonstrate that Germany could have peace at any time that it decided to be reasonable, and that the allies were not seeking to destroy Germany. The speech was, in effect, to set out the maximum contrast with Germany's treatment of Russia and the essential harmony existing between Britain and the United States. These benefits would produce two further advantages. The speech would unite the Allies and harness the United States more closely to the *Entente*, providing for a more vigorous and less detached American war effort. But, while assuring President Wilson of their common purpose, Lloyd George was confirming British leadership of the *Entente*, signalling that pre-eminence had not been surrendered to the United States.

Second Lloyd George intended the speech to encourage prospects for separate peace agreements with Austria and Turkey, despite the mounting evidence that such arrangements were far less likely to be made, and that the payoffs from them were by then quite modest. Smuts and Philip Kerr had been sent to Switzerland in the third week of December 1917 to meet with Austrian and Turkish representatives. Their instructions were specific – not to get drawn into discussions of a general peace with Germany. They held to their brief and, in so doing, confirmed that neither Austria nor Turkey would desert the German-dominated alliance. Lloyd George, by mid-January 1918, had lowered his expectations; separate peace talks would not cause Austria to leave the war but might undermine its war effort and discourage military assistance to Germany on the Western Front.

Finally, the Trade Union speech of 5 January 1918 was intended to find some advantage in the Russian situation, if a degree of certainty could be detected. Lloyd George and his colleagues were not sure who ruled, where and for how long, what Bolshevik as opposed to German aims were, and whether the Allies should pray for order or anarchy in Russia. There were diplomatic and propaganda, military and territorial benefits to be secured. It seemed essential to demonstrate to all factions in Russia that Britain would stand by Russia if it continued to prosecute the war against the Central Powers, just as Britain was remaining loyal to France and Italy. The Trade Union speech condemned Germany's treatment of Russia in its negotiations with the Bolsheviks, so as to undermine those negotiations, cultivate differences between the negotiators over, for example, Trotsky's peace terms, and give heart to all anti-German elements in Russia. Perhaps the various factions would value the assurance of continued support more than the threat that accompanied it. The threat was that Britain would not fight on to secure Russia's war aims if Russia itself did not continue to prosecute the war. Clearly, the threat would impress the opponents of the Bolsheviks – nationalist, pro-Allied and anti-Germany elements – far more than the Bolsheviks, but who could predict how any of them, including the Bolsheviks, would respond?

Militarily, the War Cabinet was seeking to limit Germany's benefits from Russia leaving the war – keeping Russian resources out of German hands; preventing the complete disintegration of the Eastern Front; and making it hazardous for Germany to transfer divisions to the Western Front. The most pessimistic forecast saw Russia actually joining Germany and Turkey in an offensive in Asia. It seemed vital at least to embroil Germany in Russia and to delay the opportunity for Germany to exploit the Ukraine. And Lloyd George was most reluctant to activate the scheme for intervention in Siberia, using the Japanese. Territorially, Lloyd George wanted to save Romania but not necessarily to create Poland.

But Lloyd George and his colleagues were not sure whether British policy would appear to be, or should be, anti- or pro-Bolshevik, or, for that matter, which stratagem, in support of or hostile towards the Bolsheviks, could be construed as a threat to or an opportunity for Russia. It could be argued that recognizing the Bolshevik government would encourage it either to fight the Germans or at least to turn away from its negotiations with Berlin, drag them out and even reject Germany's terms as unacceptably harsh. In both circumstances, the Bolsheviks would seek to infect Germany with the red virus. Lenin could be told that Russia was free both to choose its future and of its obligations to the allies, so that he could rally moderate elements to his government. There was nothing certain about all this, but at least Lloyd George did not want to push Lenin into Germany's arms until he was already, definitely and irrevocably, there. Alternatively, Britain and its allies could opt for an avowedly anti-Bolshevik strategy, looking for assistance from Whites, moderates, subject nationalities or a military junta, while giving the strategy credibility by launching military intervention in Russia. That was, some argued, the surest way to recreate the Eastern Front. Perhaps either strategy could be defended as being in Russia's best interests. But neither strategy should be seen as evidence that the Lloyd George government was willing to acquiesce in German control of Euro-Asia, whether or not Austria or

Turkey could be detached from Germany. Such a result would be, despite its neatness, a contradiction, making war in the future more likely and only temporarily ensuring the security of the Empire.

Ultimately, one must ask what assumption governed Lloyd George's reasoning. It was that Germany was negotiating with the Bolsheviks so as to remove Russia from the war, on Germany's terms, as the final preparatory step to seeking victory on the Western Front in the spring of 1918. A general peace would follow, securing Germany's war aims. The fact that the Central Powers had, on Christmas Day 1917, appeared to accept the Bolshevik call for a peace without annexations and indemnities could not be taken at face value, any more than Czernin's preferences could be embraced. Lenin was less the problem in the sense that, ideologically, he called a plague on all capitalist states; Germany and Britain were equally condemnable. But his preference to retain power and the force of circumstances were driving him irresistibly into a separate peace with Germany. It followed, in Lloyd George's opinion, that Germany would not accept peace on the terms laid down in his Trade Union speech, for those terms reflected Germany's perception neither of its current military situation nor its prospects for 1918. The German military and the Kaiser believed that more could be extracted from the war, and that, as they were dictating the tempo and the direction of the war, that they should attempt to secure every possible advantage from it. Lloyd George's response was to accept the risk involved. His task, his supreme challenge, was to hold his nerve and hold on, conserve manpower, reduce the enemy's armies by a defensive strategy in France, and find hope in the long haul, the United States and technology. He must look for a breakthrough in the contacts with Austrian and Turkish agents, or in revolutionary elements in Germany, and discover grounds for optimism in defeating the submarine, blockading the Central Powers, and watching strain and war-weariness sap enemy morale. Thus, one must conclude that, in the first week of January 1918, the War Cabinet was not signalling peace. Nor was President Wilson in his Fourteen Points speech.[14]

Subsequently, Lloyd George told the Imperial War Cabinet, in his opening speech on 11 June 1918, that there was no question of a negotiated peace at that time. The military balance still favoured the enemy. Negotiations would produce a German demand for control of Eastern Europe and Russia, in return for making concessions to the Allies in the West. And a settlement based on such terms would merely create the conditions for a future war, launched, predictably, by

Germany.[15] This statement, as always with Lloyd George, served other purposes. But it was genuine enough on the issue of peace. Lloyd George was not averse to Lord Newton, head of the delegation to prisoners-of-war talks in The Hague, and Sir George Cave, the Home Secretary, listening to German overtures, carried by Prince Hatzfeldt and others. But 'peace kites' were by then the Foreign Office's preserve, an unmistakable indication of their unimportance. Foreign Office officials concluded that Newton 'had been had'.[16] In any case it was no time for the Prime Minister to risk falling foul of the imperialist, nationalist press.[17] And Lloyd George's responses to Austrian, Turkish and Bulgarian initiatives, and any proactive steps he took himself in 1918, through Smuts, Kerr or Sir Basil Zaharoff, the Greek financier, were, as they had been in 1917, attempts to disrupt the enemy alliance.

The *Entente* weathered the military crisis of the spring and summer of 1918. From early August victory rushed toward them, to the surprise of every Allied government. None of them had expected victory until the second half of 1919; some felt it would not come until 1920 if at all, and that was a measure of perceptions of German power. The final Austrian peace move came in September 1918, only to be overtaken by the Bulgarian armistice. From that point on, Allied leaders wrestled with the merits of various armistice schemes and Turkey's attempt to escape unscathed territorially from the war, issues kindling disputes over leadership of the *Entente*. By then a negotiated settlement had become irrelevant.

Finally, the diplomacy of the war was conducted through regular and unorthodox channels, and both bilaterally and multilaterally. It was, on peace matters, handled almost invariably, and certainly in its early stages, by agents and officials of individual governments, but always in the context of working alliances. A rough loyalty tended to prevail, but sorting out the details of burden-sharing, of compromising on publicly stated war aims, was difficult. Peace diplomacy brought strain to intra-alliance loyalty, threats to unity, even when a significant degree of shared values existed. While Germany dominated the Central Powers, Austria and Turkey, and even Bulgaria, had both sovereign rights and bargaining power. The *Entente* was more a coalition of equals, making unilateral initiatives even more difficult. Thus, intra-alliance bargaining over what war aims were indispensable was difficult. Should the British Empire, for example, return Germany's colonies in order to liberate Belgium and restore Alsace-Lorraine to France? Not if the Dominions and the imperialists had their way. When each alliance was in contact with the enemy, it also kept an eye on significant neutrals, initially the Ottoman Empire and especially the United States before April 1917. Their preferences could be discounted but not dismissed. In a sense, the 'old diplomacy' had come apart. It could no longer meet the challenges it confronted; the 'new diplomacy', with its amended rules of the game, was not yet filling the vacuum.

It is the essence of war that its diplomacy and military operations are conducted simultaneously. That provides the second consideration. Diplomatic and military trends unfold side by side but often at a different pace. Judgements about the military balance, the state of the war and its prospects, are made regularly. These assessments, as was suggested in a preliminary way above, are made at the same time by both sets of belligerents. In the First World War these interlocked assessments combined unavoidably in ways that determined that the military situation never appeared to favour a negotiated peace. A negotiated peace, by definition, as opposed to a dictated peace, imposed and acquiesced in, requires the consent of all parties. It became an axiom in the First World War, perhaps in every war, that military success and diplomatic prospects were mutually reinforcing. That is, the greater the degree of military success achieved, the better the bargaining position one enjoyed, and the more likely the enemy would be to negotiate. That axiom was false and it undermined prospects for a negotiated peace. The military successes of each set of belligerents, even Germany's assault on Russia in 1917, were never decisive. They merely encouraged the opposing coalition to fight on, in expectation that the tide would turn, that attrition would wear the enemy down and that over the long haul it would prevail.

The archives reveal time and again how enormously formidable the Central Powers, anchored by German resources and resolve, looked to the leaders of the *Entente*. Yet at two dramatically pivotal points in the war, in December 1916 and in the weeks following the Bolshevik revolution, the attraction of the long haul prevailed. *Entente* politicians put a good face on the possibility of the United States turning against their cause in December 1916; they did not lose their nerve when Russia in effect left the war in December 1917. The *Entente* would fight on without the United States; Russia's disintegration and the collapse of the Eastern Front was not an occasion to despair but one requiring creative strategic responses. And it was not paradoxical that military reverses actually produced reinforcing reactions. Russia and France soaked up defeats and did not call for peace, until the Bolsheviks seized power and looked for a way out of the war. Each ally judged it vital to keep the other in the war; each fought on and supported the other diplomatically, therefore, rather than walk down the path of extrication. Germany and Austria, enjoying military success or suffering reverses, were bound together, inextricably.

Furthermore, a negotiated peace requires that all parties view the military situation as being at a stage which provides a basis for bargaining. In fact, there never was a time when both sets of belligerents took that view, and that is scarcely surprising. When Germany took the initiative, as it did between December 1916 and September 1917, it did so, as Professor Farrar has shown, for tactical reasons. The *Entente*, once augmented by the United States, viewed the current military situation as temporary and Germany's peace initiatives as ill-motivated and insincere. The Central Powers were offering peace because they had the upper hand; they wanted to negotiate because they enjoyed a superior bargaining position. Or, and seemingly equally persuasive to some despite being quite contradictory, the confident nation, it was argued, never initiates negotiations, never seeks to compromise. The military mind found such reasoning attractive. The initiation of a peace move was a sign of weakness, of a loss of will, nerve and national unity. It was evidence that the initiator's resources were becoming over-strained, an indication even of a certain desperation, brought on perhaps by mounting disunity at home or within the initiator's alliance. Either way, the *Entente* must fight on. Britain, especially, would not negotiate under the threat of submarine warfare, would never concede that naval power had turned on the island race.

Such reasoning rested in part on the fact that just as power is an elusive concept, so calculations about a state's or an alliance's strength, and that of the enemy, not always enlightened by intelligence reports, are difficult to make precisely and with assurance. That is the case whether or not the assessments are comparative. Exactly where a state or an alliance stands is hard to know, and from calculation statesmen and officials move logically to perception and even intuition. The parameters of the calculations were predictable – manpower, industrial production, munitions and weapons supplies, food production, shipping, financial resources, and alternative sources of supply – but judgements had to be made also about unity, morale, will, momentum and technological change. When statesmen needed reasons to rally the nation behind the war effort, they claimed that the enemy's suffering and war-weariness were, or would surely become, intolerable. Even if the enemy appeared to be winning at any particular point in the war, he would ultimately lose. It was a matter of stamina; at best there would be stalemate. After all, from the British perspective at least, historical precedent favoured the *Entente*; the maritime powers, on this occasion joined by the United States, would defeat the Continental land based coalition.

Finally, the diplomacy of the First World War demonstrated that a state negotiates not only when it has the upperhand militarily over the enemy, but also when it dominates the military effort of its own alliance. That was always the case with Germany, despite consultations that could degenerate into heated, intra-alliance wrangling. Within the *Entente* such calculations were difficult, even risky to make. But the British government, for example, found decidedly appealing the prospect of negotiating after France had peaked and before the United States became dominant. As Russia foundered, as Italy's case even for equality was wrapped ever more in pretension than credibility, and as Japan remained peripheral, the challenge proved irresistible for the *Entente*'s elder statesman, Lloyd George. The threat to British pre-eminence came, unavoidably, incrementally, from the United States. But, after all, Britain could not leave the war without providing for the security of the Empire.

There are references above to neutral states. The fact that the peace initiatives of December 1916 and 1917 involved third parties provides the next consideration. In December 1916 the United States was both initiator and intermediary; so was the Holy Father, Benedict XV, in August 1917. In September 1917 the government of Spain was the messenger for Germany, just as Prince Sixte had been for Austria.[18] These third parties were not, to put it mildly, a homogeneous group, but they shared certain debilitating features. They were all known to be or regarded in *Entente* policy circles, to varying degrees, as not impartial, tainted because of being used by the initiator, Germany. The Pope, unavoidably, and Spanish officials were, in addition, suspect because of their ties to Roman Catholic, pro-Austrian cliques. All three inter-mediaries complicated rather than lubricated the peace process, bringing with them complexity and inserting uncertainty of various forms. Viewed from Washington and the Vatican, the prize was as glittering as the tactical choices were tough; the risk of failure was predictably high. To initiate a peace move unilaterally was to invite rebuff. Consulting only one side beforehand was obviously dangerous; consulting both did little to improve the prospects of success. To act as an intermediary in response to one side was to invite condemnation. And keeping the roles of initiator and intermeidary separate was well nigh impossible.

In the midst of meetings between French and Austrian agents in Switzerland, orchestrated by Paul Painlevé, the French War Minister, and approved by Alexandre Ribot, the French Foreign Minister, and Lloyd George, the Pope, on 16 August 1917, published his peace note. His motives were credible but he had, and was known to have, consulted only the Central Powers beforehand. Neither the *Entente* nor the Central Powers appreciated the terms of peace he proposed. The Germans most certainly did not want the Franco-Austrian contacts to prosper, seeing them, quite rightly, as a device to divide its alliance and likely to lead to unwelcome peace discussions. Kuhlmann's response, therefore, was to initiate a move by way of Spain, a move intended to divide Britain and France and ensure that any peace discussions served German war aims. The contacts at the same time between Briand and van Lancken, an official in the German administration in Belgium, and involving Belgian officials, were to serve the same purposes for Germany. The tangled personal relationships between Painlevé, Prime Minister from 13 September, Ribot, still Foreign Minister, and Briand, put an end to these feelers. The Kuhlmann initiative via Spain prompted in London, as was noted above, a debate between Lloyd George, Balfour and Walter Long, the Colonial Secretary, over the merits of consulting the Allies, particularly Russia, and the Dominions before responding. In one sense, the significance of the Papal initiative and the Spanish messenger service lay there. The Pope's initiative was finessed; the Central Powers, the Allies insisted, must state their terms before progress could be made. The approach through Spain could not be ignored. But the news that Britain was informing its Allies was enough for Kuhlmann to break off the exchange. Neither the Pope nor the Spanish foreign office could salvage anything from the incident. They had no relevant resources with which to assert pressure on the belligerents. They could exact no price, threaten no sanctions. They were suspect conduits and ineffective.

The United States, however, was a powerhouse of resources, but were they sufficiently mobilizable to make Woodrow Wilson an irresistible mediator? The mission of Colonel Edward House, Wilson's wandering envoy, in 1916, produced an unequivocal rejection from the German chancellor, Theobald von Bethmann Hollweg, coupled with mild contempt for the President and the conviction that he was sympathetic to the *Entente*. It left British leaders, with Edward Grey most reluctant, convinced that in the hierarchy of desirable outcomes, a general peace orchestrated by the United States, at its timing and without allied prior consent, stood a very poor fourth in a list of four. The ranking was clear – victory without United States military intervention but with its economic assistance; victory after United States military intervention; and United States mediation requested by the *Entente* in order to escape the consequences of defeat, if not a military stalemate.[19] Lloyd George, then Secretary of State for War, egged on by Lord Northcliffe, the press magnate, delivered the *coup de grâce* to the House initiative, by releasing the text of his interview with Roy Howard, head of United Press of America, in *The Times* on 28 September 1916. *The Times* praised the interview as 'apposite in form, excellent in substance, and most opportune in season'.[20] Lloyd George defended his action to an outraged C.P. Scott:

. . . he had positive and documentary evidence that Gerard, the United States ambassador at Berlin, had gone to America with a proposal to Wilson that he should propose mediation and Wilson would be under very strong temptation to do this in order to conciliate German–American opposition to his re-election which would probably turn the scale. Once mediation was proposed, it would have been difficult to refuse and once the war was stopped it would have been impossible to resume it. But the time for a settlement was for us extremely unfavourable and for the Germans favourable.[21]

On 12 December 1916, six days after the capture of Bucharest, the German government issued its peace note. It was an artifact of the complex policy process in Berlin, and within the Central Powers alliance. The peace note was an attempt by Bethmann Hollweg, Count Burian, the Habsburg Foreign Minister, and the German military to make political capital at home and abroad, to secure extensive war aims by taking advantage of the military situation, and to help ensure that unrestricted submarine warfare did not result in precipitate American belligerency. The Allies rejected the German peace note outright on 31 December. Wilson, however, on 19 December, had made an attempt at mediation, and the issue in essence became whether American resources were indispensable to the *Entente* war effort? The fact was that *Entente* leaders, fully aware of the increasing dependence on American financial and economic aid, came to the conclusion, in January 1917, that alternative sources of finance and *matériel* were available. They agreed that the United States would not intervene decisively against the *Entente* if they rejected mediation from across the Atlantic. Their reply, on 10 January 1917, made the point as tactfully as possible. Clearly, both wishful thinking and risk-taking had come to the fore. Lloyd George put the argument that the United States

would not threaten the *Entente* cause either by withholding resources
from it or by making them available to the Central Powers. No lofty
motives were involved in Wilson's initiative, no Atlanticist ideology
flourished in Washington. Put simply, Lloyd George insisted, the
United States had so much invested in the *Entente* war effort that it
could not sit by and tolerate a German victory. Self-interest would, in
the last resort, bring the United States to the side of the *Entente*. They
must ensure, in the meantime, that German slanders, suggesting that
Britain was compelling very reluctant allies to fight on so that it could
seize Germany's colonies, did not take root in the United States.

The assessment of United States behaviour rested in part on a certain
contempt for and disgust with President Wilson, 'the quintessence of
a prig', recently on the hustings, in the clutches of Jews with their
money and control of the press, the irresponsible and dangerous Irish,
and an assortment of Bryanites, Anglophobes, Francophobes and
Germanophiles. Sir Cecil Spring-Rice, the British ambassador in
Washington, reported that while Wilson was not entirely in their
hands, German agents had engineered his peace note. The President, a
peculiar character, seeking the Nobel peace prize, must be handled
with care.[22] Few matched F.S. Oliver, the influential imperialist, in his
invective. Wilson was 'detestable', 'immoral', a 'cold-blooded, hot-air
materialist', an 'ass', and an astute calculator of United States interests.
Such views brought no dissent from the generals, relieved as they were
that their own politicians were solid, firm in their determination in
December 1916 to evade the German–American trap.[23] *Entente*
leaders had little sympathy for Wilson's genuine and heartrending
dilemmas as he campaigned for re-election, faced the consequences of
his oratory after being re-elected, tried to keep the United States out of
the war, and attempted to mediate a settlement. They could, and they
had sound intelligence on the point, gamble on German impatience.
Germany would most assuredly launch unrestricted submarine
warfare that winter.

One can, in retrospect, see this as a failure of Wilsonian diplomacy.
The President did not know how to use the economic, financial and
moral weapons he held. A negotiated peace under his auspices was the
answer to the most fundamental of predicaments – either being drawn
into the war because of submarine attacks on American shipping or
appeasing Germany and becoming the object of transatlantic liberal
contempt. A negotiated peace would be the greatest of political and
diplomatic triumphs. What a way to begin a second term! But
Germany ensured that no such outcome resulted in the winter of

1916–17. Wilson's mediatory contacts with Vienna in February 1917 were inconsequential, and by early April the United States was at war. Third-party mediation, then, even when the mediator was the formidable United States, did not enhance prospects for a negotiated settlement to the First World War.

The question of war aims was at the core of discussions in both alliance groups about peace. It provides the fourth consideration. War aims were both territorial and non-territorial, embracing trade and financial matters, political change, and the rules that should govern the functioning of the international system. The appetites of individual governments and alliances for territorial gain and economic advantage from the war grew sufficiently in the first two years of the war, that respective, minimum levels of what came to be regarded as indispensable war aims undermined prospects for the successful negotiation of peace. No party to the conflict would sign a renunciatory peace. There are grounds for arguing, as some have, that Germany was, consciously, by intent, more expansionary and imperialistic than any other belligerent, but that the differences were merely ones of degree. Against that, it is true that the Lloyd George government, for example, spent far more time seeking to curtail rather than feed territorial appetites. Only Japan and the Dominions, after December 1916, were allowed to consolidate and even enhance their territorial war aims.

But overall, except for moments of gloomy despair, escalating devotion to the spoils of war expanded the boundaries of what was deemed non-negotiable, of what could not be the subject of bargaining. Leaders set out positions on war aims publicly, and moderated them only for political and propaganda purposes. There occurred an escalation of expectations. The reasoning was essentially circular. War aims served vital national and imperial needs. They justified the growing expenditures and sacrifices. They protected alliance unity. They served higher goals and purposes. And thus the nation must fight on, make even greater sacrifices, expend more assets, lead the allies to victory, and secure what its leaders had concluded it could not survive without. This escalation of expectations occurred to the extent that neither set of belligerents would settle for the *status quo ante* of 1914. The Central Powers were not at war to preserve the British and French Empires, let alone see them expand. German conservatives and the Germany military expected the war to 'deliver' preferred aims, and nothing less. The *Entente* was not at war to see German power, managed by a risk-taking, aggressive, militarist, Prussian autocracy, remain intact, let alone be augmented. The *status quo ante* would mean simply that the war would be resumed within ten years. It might come sooner than that, and be a more formidable challenge, if Germany left the current war in control of greater resources than before 1914. Far better, therefore, to fight on, even into 1919 and 1920. That became a bedrock assumption of both civilian and military elites in the *Entente*.

Two dilemmas lay beneath the debate within the *Entente* from April 1917. Lord Esher, residing in Paris and a prominent, quasi-official contact with French opinion and political leaders, saw the tactical one – France and the United States expected Britain to relinquish claims to the German colonies in the peace bargaining. If Britain refused, the unity of the *Entente* was threatened; if it agreed, the security of the Empire was placed in jeopardy. Albert Thomas, French socialist and confidant of Lloyd George, captured the broader dilemma in August 1917. *Entente* war aims, in a response to the Pope or the socialists convening in Stockholm, would have to be moderate, democratic and defensible. But a peace settlement that was a compromise would not be lasting.[24]

And in all this, politicians and their advisers had little difficulty in discovering higher purposes for the war, great principles that were at stake. At home they ranged from the preservation of the old and revered order to being the necessary condition of reform. Abroad, the war might confirm the value of established, well-tried methods, or demand a new order where law not force would govern, where public right not militarism would reign, where conference diplomacy would supplant pre-emptive behaviour, and where freedom from coercion would flourish. These latter views sent those who held them in several directions in their response to the challenges of managing dissent, imperialism, Atlanticism and prospects for a League of Nations. In Philip Kerr's case they found a platform in Lloyd George's oratory.[25]

As Rankeians are today a rare academic species, it seems safe and even wise to look to domestic political considerations for the fifth factor that undermined prospects for a negotiated peace. The composition of governments in several belligerent states changed substantially at various times during the war, with 1917 being something of a watershed. Monarchs survived, except the Tsar, but no head of government who had helped decide on war in 1914 remained in office beyond that winter, except in Constantinople. All wartime policy communities were coalitions of a kind, and some of them were quite artificial and temporary. They were responsible to several constituencies – monarchs, legislatures, political parties, segments of society, interest groups, influential and sceptical attentive audiences at home and abroad. Transaction costs were high and decision-making structures complicated. Motives were as many as there were constituents to be satisfied. Those who came to power in 1916–17 concluded that their predecessors had lost office, neither because of the decision for war in 1914 nor the failure to negotiate peace, but because of their inability to prosecute the war effectively. Leadership meant the pursuit of victory. Peace without victory would be a miserable prize, pointing to political rejection. Such reasoning made politicians victims of their own oratory, captives of their public diplomacy, their declaratory policies. Logically, it seemed, reputation and political prospects were wrapped up in victory, in securing the nation's war aims, in providing commitment, and in honouring the sacrifices already made, not betraying them.

This reasoning, the political attraction of victory, became more powerful, more alluring, as governments made increasing demands on society, as they sought to extract more resources for the purposes of war. What else could governments promise but victory when they were drafting sixteen-year-old boys? In that way the pursuit of national unity, social cohesion, governmental stability and an effective war effort became a process of reinforcement, a conscription of commitment, a form of psychological entrapment. It had its less elevated but equally understandable side – staying clear of peace initiatives in deference to nationalist and imperialist opinion, and avoiding the return to power of the 'old gang'. In sum, politicians easily equated the pursuit of victory with personal, party and governmental imperatives, and concluded that there was little future politically in a negotiated peace. There were, in a word, insufficient political incentives to open peace talks in a serious, sincere way. That was where judgements about political legitimacy and about risk came into play. Risk, as always, had two faces – of policy failure and political vulnerability.

The sixth consideration also had two faces, one turned inward toward society, the other outward to the world of transnational links. The potential for revolution in the First World War was a matter of perception and judgement, fed by intelligence reports and missions of inquiry. Revolution was expected, and came twice, in Russia. It seemed more likely to occur in France and Italy than in Britain, probable in Bulgaria, and more possible in Turkey and Austria-Hungary than in Germany. The forces providing social stability and bolstering domestic morale – patriotism, political opportunity, social advancement, economic gain – competed with war weariness, economic hardship, personal and group sacrifice, financial strain, food shortages and general disillusionment. The latter forces took on greater significance the longer the war dragged on.

There was a certain amount of wishful thinking in both groups of belligerents about the conditions in enemy states and the potential for revolution. The stronger socialists were in enemy countries the more likely that dissent would escalate into revolution seemed a credible hypothesis. But anticipation was tempered by the sense that revolutionary conditions did not respect national boundaries. Given the Russian example, perhaps it was better for all parties, ally and opponent, to get out of the war without dramatic social upheaval, whatever the military advantages to be gained from revolution weakening the enemy.

Dissent in wartime, calling for peace without victory, is a fragile plant. In the First World War, radicals, pacifists, socialists, and communists tended to be overwhelmed by the passions of war, wrapped skilfully, deliberately, in the flag, the cause, and the closing of ranks, the party truce, the *union sacrée*. Dissent, in fact, could be and was branded as treason by governments bent on countering defeatism and pacifism. Indeed, on occasions, more leniency was promised to the enemy than to dissenters at home. Dissenters were beguiled by their political opponents, co-opted, shouted down by propaganda, undermined by censorship, evaded through secrecy, threatened with punishment and punished severely.

Lloyd George's courting of labour, for example, began on the first day of his premiership. Radicals like Arthur Ponsonby, in the summer of 1918, wanted to believe that Lloyd George had not lost all sense of the larger moral issues. The prime minister, the hope for post-war reform, was merely, and temporarily, captive of the war machine. The radical in him was numbed not dead. Few could read a colleague better than Lloyd George; he could finesse the likes of Ponsonby. He respected, he said, those radicals who demanded peace; that was not treachery. But timing was the essence of peace negotiations; it would be fatal to seize the wrong opportunity at the wrong time. Indeed, one needed prior assurances on terms before entering into negotiations. No prime minister could be expected to risk both policy and personal failure. When the time was ripe, he would, without fear of the jingoists, seek peace. Until then, Lloyd George would fight on to defeat a resolute and confident enemy, and thereby ensure that the peace would be permanent. Lloyd George warned Ponsonby that the people were with him. During the Boer War he, as a dissenter, had addressed great and enthusiastic meetings, only to see radicalism swamped at the next election. That, he predicted, would happen at the end of the war; dissenters would do well to think again.[26]

Governments, their internal unity and political prospects not seriously threatened by their decisions in 1917 to avoid peace negotiations, did not hesitate to deal sternly with those who disagreed. Milner, within the British war cabinet, was most firm on that score – Ramsay Macdonald, the Labour leader, using Quaker money and stirring up discharged veterans and 'shirkers', wanted to stop the war by calling a general strike; E.D. Morrell was the mastermind of the pacifists and was perhaps a German agent. The government must counter these revolutionaries, who were also pro-German and pacifist, if it was to stop the rot and prevent Britain following Russia 'into impotence and dissolution'.[27] The nationalist press, appearing every day, usurping political discourse and undermining the influence of legislatures, chose not to challenge governments on what it regarded as the necessary pursuit of order and stability.

Ineffectual at home, certain radical leaders tried to function as intermediaries. Some of Europe's socialists looked to transnational diplomacy, to clarion calls from socialist gatherings to bring a halt to the war. The conference to convene in Stockholm in September 1917 seemed to some to hold significant promise. Perhaps Europe's socialist leaders, Arthur Henderson for example, Labour's representative in the British War Cabinet, could, through oratory, manifesto and influence, bring the belligerents to the peace table. They never could. In part this was because of old dilemmas, sometimes reappearing in new forms – socialism's relationship to nationalism and patriotism; peace moves aiding the enemy; sympathy for post-Tsarist Russia translating into support for Germany. But essentially governments were not especially vulnerable to socialist pressure on the issue of peace, and had adequate weapons to combat it. Henderson's dismissal, for example, in August 1917 was not, in the short run, a particularly debilitating error. That is not to argue that radical and socialist opinion did not influence policy in other ways. It did; the content, timing and elaborate preparations for Lloyd George's Trade Union speech demonstrated that. But dissenters could never get governments to the peace table.

Civil–military relations, far more problematic and divisive for policy communities, provided the seventh obstacle to peace negotiations. This is a complex issue, involving heterogeneous groups, resting on unresolved definitional problems, and clouded by the military's complicated role in the 1914 crisis. Historians would do well to question the 'cult of the offensive' which has entranced political scientists in their efforts to use 'the 1914' case' to construct theory. But once the war was under way, the charisma of the military leaders rose, unless they were exposed in their incompetence and disgraced by defeat. Many of them were vindicated, even Douglas Haig, the commander of British forces in France. In policy debate their expertise was difficult to discount, their advice not easy to ignore, let alone dismiss. Military figures became identified with loyalty, patriotism, service and the national will; the press made heroes of them if they were not goats. Politicians who opposed them played a dangerous game. The field commanders, as opposed to staff officers, were particularly invulnerable. Prominent military and naval figures showed themselves as adept at manipulating the press as any politician. Both 'frock' and 'brass-hat' had reason to censor bad news from the front.

The fact was that, as they joined in the debate on grand strategy, the military, with warnings and caveats, and using every occasion to press for their preferred strategies and the resources to implement them, spoke out against peace negotiations, which they judged invariably to be premature. The assessments of the CIGS for the British War Cabinet in the last days of December 1917 and on into early January 1918, provide ample evidence for the point. Any discussion in Berlin of a general peace, in December 1916 for example, or of war aims, meant a complex debate involving the Chancellor, the Foreign Minister, the Kaiser and the generals, with Erich von Ludendorff most prominent, all with an eye to the socialists at home and Germany's allies, especially Austria-Hungary. These debates resulted in the harsh and eminently rejectable peace note of 12 December 1916, and then the severe treatment of Russia and Romania in March 1918. The German generals largely had their way with politicians who acquiesced all too easily in annexationist policies and who, in truth, preferred expansion by subtler means, such as use of East European and Baltic nationalism.

The war was the military's test and its opportunity; there was no substitute for victory. Generals and admirals agreed, therefore, that what was necessary strategically was possible, and what was probable was certain to occur. The nation could shorten the war by escalating it. New technologies – the submarine, the tank, poison gas, massive long-range guns, airpower – would be decisive. Diplomacy must serve military policy not the reverse; and if the outcome seemed in doubt it was because of diplomatic not military failure. This line of argument tended to unite politicians and generals against diplomats, depicted as inept, in their joint determination to find a military solution to the war. That is why it is misleading, for example, to see Lloyd George simply as the scourge of the Foreign Office or the enemy of the generals. He used the Foreign Office to combat the generals, the War Office to evade the diplomats, and both to render the Colonial Office impotent. But generals demand to be allowed to prosecute the war vigorously without political interference or restriction. Frequently, however, because of the success of their advocacy, they have to be rescued from their determination, their stamina, and their folly. Then military pusillanimity emerges, with generals pleading with politicians to extract the nation from the unwinnable war. Subsequently, some concoct a 'stab in the back' thesis to explain the defeat.

But generals never see it that way. Politicians, they insist, demand sacrifices and commit resources to the war, but never adequately so, never to the point of providing enough men and materiel to permit the military to secure victory. And the amateur strategist in any politician bedevils the enterprise from its inception. Yet, even then, generals and politicians, weighing very much the same evidence, perforce found more common ground at the time than they did later in the battle of memoirs and the writing of history. Robertson was usually reasonably frank with Haig. In late September 1917, on the heels of Germany's recent peace move, Robertson saw Germany as '. . . much more anxious at the present time for peace than she has ever been before'. He would consider peace on the terms rumoured to have been offered, but he did not think that Germany would offer such terms until its armies had been further defeated. The politicians, assessing the dual impact of Russia's pending collapse and United States involvement, preferred to concentrate less on the Western Front, hammer at Germany's allies and detach them by way of separate peace agreements. Robertson saw his task as confirming the wisdom of a continued Western Front strategy, but confessed to Haig that '. . . I stick to it because I see nothing better, and because my instinct prompts me to stick to it, than to any convincing argument by which I can support it'. Stagnation militarily may well destroy the nation's determination to fight on, but Robertson could see no easy solution. Finally, Robertson reported, he and Lloyd George were at odds over air power – whether to use it on the Western Front or for home defence. Lloyd George, in the War Cabinet, had given a '. . . harrowing description of the destruction of the house and the sight of blood on the walls!! They have really lost all sense of proportion'.[28]

Elite debates actually over whether or not to negotiate peace provide evidence of the eighth factor. The debates were conducted in a boundedly rational fashion for the most part. Statesmen do not set out to be irrational; officials do not advise so as to be ignored. Both, of course, succeed some of the time. And, when decision-makers make their cost-benefit calculations, they divide costs into two parts, albeit in a rough and ready fashion, that is between costs already incurred, what might be called sunk costs, and costs to be anticipated, to be borne in the future. Anticipated costs were deducted from the benefits to be gained from fighting on. They were, therefore, an incentive to negotiate peace. But costs already incurred, the investment in the war, representing both resources committed and the commitment to war aims, were added to benefits. Incurred costs provided, therefore, a strong incentive to fight on. The archives are very clear about that. This preference had further consequences. It reinforced the tendency to accept risk, to indulge in wishful thinking and the psychological comfort that brings, and to remain faithful to current policy rather than to adapt. It fed the predilection to see established policy as sound, attractive and efficacious; it avoided the need and the political risk to admit that errors were being made. The preference to regard sunk costs as an investment in the war also justified the escalation of war aims, and undermined the case for cutting losses. It made another increment of effort worth while, a further sacrifice acceptable, the expenditure of more lives and bullion defensible. This process constituted a form of psychological entrapment, feeding incremental thinking, and pointing away from negotiation.[29] It held Clemenceau, for example, in its grasp. Debate in decision sessions brought reasoning of dubious quality, when goals, for example, were evaluated simultaneously with the probabilities of their being reached. If the nation demands something, it becomes attainable; if an object can be achieved, it is desirable.

Finally, an examination of the exchanges on peace in 1917 provides evidence that bargaining theorists, it would seem, have missed. In the First World War, the advantages from initiating negotiations were quite temporary and transitory. The 'other side' easily countered and offset those advantages. If a government or alliance grouping took the first step, they gained the moral high ground, unless their insincerity, their tactical ploy, was immediately exposed. They controlled the timing of the negotiations, to their own advantage. The initiating party secured a certain propaganda advantage, which also made it easier to evade responsibility publicly for any failure. Finally, to initiate contacts was to cause uncertainty in the other camp about the initiator's intent and purpose, and about appropriate and necessary responses. Was the initiator sincere, were negotiations a threat to alliance unity, was the initiative a sign of weakness, even despair, justifying an optimistic view of the military balance, and should the offer be summarily rejected?

These exchanges sometimes involved agents with chequered histories and dubious credentials. The sequence of initiation and response was complex, and remains difficult to track down. In the course of the preliminary soundings and as the issue of peace took some shape, it became clear, quite early, that the initiator's control of the timing could appear to be, and could be made publicly to seem to be, a crude attempt to use a temporary advantage. The initiator reached for the moral high ground only to find that it could not use its military advantage to force negotiations, and that the reacting party could evade the call to the bargaining table with ease. If the initiating government failed to state its terms it seemed evasive and disingenuous, and the other side countered. If the initiator stated peace terms, it had showed its hand and given away a bargaining asset. Peace terms that were set out and were modest would be judged inept or worse, that is as an attempt to produce defection in the enemy coalition, to mollify dissent at home or undermine domestic unity in enemy states. Terms that were stiff could easily be made out to be vindictive, even rapacious, damaging the initiator's standing. Either way, ample justification could be found for their rejection. *Entente* statesmen concluded on every occasion between December 1916 and October 1917 that Germany, the initiator, was insincere, and that judgement was sound. This reaction, to the extent that it was predictable, deterred the initiation of peace moves, made them rare events, and a marginal calculation in German grand strategy. Germany's reactions both to Lloyd George's Trade Union speech and Wilson's Fourteen Points, in January 1918, were consistent with this argument and quite predictable.

Negotiating peace is always a formidable challenge, and frequently a protracted affair. In the First World War the final peace process began on 28 September 1918 with Bulgaria's surrender. The process entails reaching agreement on a cease-fire and its maintenance, on an armistice and its revisions, and on a comprehensive settlement and its implementation. The process has its own sequence and logic. But there can be advantages to breaking the sequence, and opportunities for the defeated to exploit. The Ottoman government, for example, proposed, on 4 October 1918, a peace not an armistice. The initiative was dismissed, quite rightly, as a final attempt to divide the *Entente*, as a belated move to escape from the war relatively unscathed.

Negotiations, once entered into, are likely to be prolonged, intense and complex. The outcome is, by definition, uncertain. Actually to begin to negotiate is to give new strength, a fresh set of weapons, to the militarily weaker party. It is difficult for the stronger party to assert discrete and precisely applied amounts of military pressure once negotiations have started, to calibrate a renewed offensive, for example, with rounds of bargaining.[30] Gross threats are hard to deliver effectively. The correct mix of coercion and diplomacy is difficult to implement.

The very act of negotiation is understood to be, predictably, a threat to alliance unity. It increases incentives to pursue individual war aims rather than the common cause, to repeat demands that allies make the concessions necessary to lubricate the bargaining. In the First World War negotiations required the revelation of secret treaties, private bargains and war aims that were difficult to justify. Negotiations once started are difficult to suspend. Better then to have secured one's war aims before entering into peace talks.[31] A war put temporarily on hold, statesmen felt in the First World War, would be almost impossible to restart. And should that predicament arise, then surely the democracies would find it more difficult to resume hostilities than the autocracies. Parliamentary governments, it was assumed, probably incorrectly, would find it more of a challenge to overcome public war-weariness and reverse the feelings of great relief that the fighting had been suspended. And knowledge of this predicament, shared by both sets of belligerents, would damage the bargaining power of the democracies during the peace negotiations. The enemy – the Prussian militarists, for example – would exploit the situation. Perhaps that had motivated the initiator, Germany, all along? Better not to get into negotiations in the first place. The perilous state of the morale of the French Army in 1917 seemed ample justification for such reasoning within the *Entente*. And the failure of negotiations once started would invite an outburst of propaganda, and fuel recrimination and blame. Charges would be levelled at more than the enemy. The likelihood of defection from within each alliance would escalate. Governments would come under spirited attack at home. In sum, negotiating peace, bargaining to end a war, was a dangerous affair. Victory, it was assumed, would sweep away most problems.

This *tour d'horizon*, part theory, part history, stops short of ten commandments, let alone fourteen points. One could go on. There were no extensive cultural distances and incompatible negotiating styles involved in the peace process in the First World War. Japan was not a significant factor. There were no common enemies, external to the conflict, ideological or military, to unite the belligerents. Bolshevism secured a tenuous grasp on Russia in November 1917. But it was, to the Central Powers, an asset to be used rather than a cause for fundamental strategic realignment. For the *Entente*, the Bolsheviks in power were a further complication in the Russian débâcle. Responding creatively and judiciously would test Allied ingenuity and nerve. It seemed wise, however tragic the drama, however risky the enterprise, however costly the effort, to fight on. Peace without victory was, after all, summer without sun, jugged hare without wine. It was, in fact, an insipid thing.

## NOTES

1. Of the historical literature one might consult H. Weinroth, 'Peace by Negotiation and the British Anti-War Movement, 1914–1918' (unpublished paper); W.B. Fest, 'British War Aims and German Peace Feelers during the First World War (December 1916 to November 1918)', *The Historical Journal*, xv, 2 (1972), pp. 285–308; L.L. Farrar, Jr., *Divide and Conquer: German Efforts to Conclude a Separate Peace, 1914–1918* (New York, 1978); A.J.P. Taylor, *How Wars End* (London, 1985); Charles S. Maier, 'Wargames: 1914–1919', in Robert L. Rotberg and Theodore K. Rabb, *The Origin and Prevention of Major Wars* (Cambridge, 1989), pp. 264–71; and David Stevenson, *The First World War and International Politics* (Oxford, 1988), pp. 103–5, 135–6, 140-44, 162–9 and 183–205. Gordon S. Craig and Alexander L. George, *Force and Statecraft* (Oxford, 1990), pp. 229–46, bridges historical and theoretical approaches. The purposes of the theoretical literature are to be found in the special issue of *The Annals*, William T.R. Fox (ed.), 'How Wars End', 392 (Nov. 1970); S. Rosen, 'War, Power and the Willingness to Suffer', in Bruce K. Russett (ed.), *Peace, War and Numbers* (Beverly Hills, 1972), pp. 167–83; D. Wittman, 'How Wars End: a Rational Model Approach', *Journal of Conflict Resolution* 23, 4 (1979), pp. 743–63; Bruce Buena de Mesquita, *The War Trap* (Yale, 1981); P.R. Pillar, *Negotiating Peace. War Termination as a Bargaining Process* (Princeton, 1983); Francis A. Beer and Thomas F. Mayer, 'Why Wars End: Some Hypotheses', *Review of International Studies*, 12 (1986), pp. 95–106; and J.F. Dunnigan and H. Martel, *How to Stop a War: The Lessons of Two Hundred Years of War and Peace* (New York, 1987). See also Michael Walzer, *Just and Unjust Wars* (New York, 1977).
2. Scott diary, 28 Dec. 1917, C.P. Scott papers.
3. Hankey diary, 30 Dec. 1917, Lord Hankey papers.
4. Lord Curzon was the first to raise the issue in the British war cabinet of indicting German leaders.
5. Balfour to Lloyd George, 24 Sept., Lloyd George papers, F/3/2/30; Hankey to Walter Long (Colonial Secretary), 6, 8 and 11 Oct., Long to Balfour, 7, 9 and 11 Oct., Balfour to Long, 8 and 10 Oct. 1917 and Batterbee to Long, 10 and 11 Oct. 1917, Walter Long papers, 947/515; and Balfour to Buchanan (ambassador to Russia), 4 Oct. 1917, FO/800/205. These exchanges reflected both Dominion, Tory and Colonial Office determination to strip Germany of its colonies and Long's difficulties in championing consultation with the Dominions, in the face of evasion from Lloyd George, Balfour and Andrew Bonar Law, the Chancellor of the Exchequer.
6. Professor Farrar is convincing on this point in his *Divide and Conquer.*
7. Francis Bertie (Ambassador to France) to Balfour, 14 April 1918, FO/800/161.
8. Briand to Ribot, 20 Sept., Lloyd George papers, F/160/1/8; Bertie to Balfour, 23 Sept. and 11 Oct., ibid., F/51/4/39 and 44; Bertie to Lloyd George, 24 Sept., ibid., F/51/4/40; and Murray to Lloyd George, 24 Oct. 1917, ibid., F/41/5/2.
9. Fisher diary, 15 Aug. 1918, H.A.L. Fisher papers. Milner was blamed unfairly at the time as a defeatist, and then as a conspiratorial, early appeaser.
10. Scott diary, 28 Sept. and 20 Oct. 1917, C.P. Scott papers; Balfour to Lloyd George, 24 Sept., Lloyd George papers F/3/2/30, and War Cabinet, 27 Sept. 1917, ibid., F/160/1/12 and Cab. 23/3; Buchanan to Balfour, 2 Oct. and Balfour to Buchanan, 4 Oct. 1917, Lloyd George papers, F/3/2/32; Buchanan to Balfour, 8 Oct., ibid., F/3/2/33; and Balfour memorandum,

11 Oct. 1917, ibid., F/160/1/5.
11. David Lloyd George, *War Memoirs*, II (London, 1936), p. 1930.
12. War Cabinet, 3 and 4 Jan. 1918, Cab. 23/5.
13. Meeting between Lloyd George and a Labour delegation, 28 Dec. 1917, Lloyd George papers, F/217/4 and Ramsay Macdonald diary, 28 Dec. 1917, Ramsay Macdonald papers, PRO 30/69/8/1.
14. Cecil to Spring-Rice, 5 Jan. 1918, FO/371/3436. This interpretation summarizes the argument in chapter four of my second volume on Lloyd George and foreign policy 1916–1922, tentatively titled *And Fortune Fled*. Thomas Jones, a member of Hankey's secretariat, captured some of this: 'The line now is to publish a declaration on war aims as a counter offensive to the offer of the Central Powers to the Bolsheviks . . . The idea is to make it ultra-democratic, to go to the further point of concessions, so as to produce the maximum effect in Turkey and Austria, and not less to support the war spirit at home which is seriously weakened . . . and through the distrust of the Cabinet's War Aims' (Jones diary, 1 Jan. 1918, Thomas Jones, *Whitehall Diary*, Vol. I, 1916–1925, ed. Keith Middlemas (London, 1968), p. 42).
15. Lloyd George statement, Imperial War Cabinet, 11 June 1918, Cab. 23/41.
16. Lloyd George-Kuhlmann conversation, May 1933, Lloyd George papers, G/262 and War Cabinet, 6 June 1918, Cab. 23/6. Kuhlmann depicted himself as sincerely pursuing a settlement, only to be dismissed on the advice of his Conservative and military opponents. Newton seemed to accept the argument that Germany's terms were moderate – concessions in Western Europe and over colonies in return for a free hand in the East – and that the German generals were neither expansionist nor dominating policy in Berlin (Headlam-Morley to Tyrell, 8 Aug. 1918, FO/800/206 and Villiers (Hague) to Hardinge, 12 June 1918, Hardinge papers, Vol. 38).
17. F.S. Oliver to Carson, 13 July 1918, Lloyd George papers, F/6/2/39.
18. Various Scandinavian would be intermediaries, if not certain Belgian politicians, can be left in historical obscurity.
19. Michael Fry, *Lloyd George and Foreign Policy, Volume I, 1890–1916. The Education of a Statesman* (Montreal, 1977), pp. 218–35.
20. Ibid., p. 235.
21. Ibid., pp. 235–6.
22. Hardinge to Lloyd George, 14 and 15 Dec., enclosing copies of telegrams exchanged between Grew and the German government, Lloyd George papers, F/3/2/1 and 2; Foreign Office to Hankey, 16 Dec., and Spring-Rice to Foreign Office, 24 Dec. 1916, ibid., F/60/2/2 and F/160/1/4.
23. Oliver to Carson, 26 Jan. and Carson to Lloyd George, 29 Jan. 1917, Lloyd George papers, F/6/2/11; Robertson to Haig, 16 Dec. and Robertson to Esher, 18 Dec. 1916, Robertson papers, 1/22 and 1/34.
24. Esher to Robertson, 9 April 1917, ibid., 1/34; and Thomas to Lloyd George, 17 Aug. 1917, Lloyd George papers, F/58/1/16.
25. Kerr to Balfour, and Kerr to Sir Horace Plunkett, 5 Dec. 1916, FO/800/201.
26. Lloyd George-Ponsonby conversation, 27 June 1918, Arthur Ponsonby papers, file 1918–1919.
27. Milner to Lloyd George, 26 May and 11 June 1917, Lloyd George papers, F/38/2/5 and 8.
28. Robertson to Haig, 27 Sept. and 3 Oct. 1917, Robertson papers, 1/22.
29. Frank Edmead, *Analysis and Prediction in International Mediation* (United Nations Institute for Training and Research, 1971); C.R. Mitchell, M. Nicholson, K. Webb, H. Blumberg and P. M'Pherson, *Conflict Termination Project*, Working Papers 1 (Analyzing the Process of Conflict Termination) and 2 (Conflict Termination and Decision-Making); C.R. Mitchell and M. Nicholson, 'Rational Models and the Ending of Wars', *Journal of Conflict Resolution* 27, 3 (1983), pp. 498–520; C.R. Mitchell, 'Conflict Termination, Utility and Rational Decision-Making', (unpublished paper, 1983); and K.K. Pieragostini, 'A Decision-Making Analysis of the Reversal of Government Policy', (PhD dissertation, University of Kent at Canterbury, 1981).
30. Professor Douglas Stuart made this point in response to an initial version of this essay.
31. Balfour to Bertie, 8 Oct. 1917, Long papers, 947/515. Yet just weeks before Balfour had not dismissed Kuhlmann's expectation that the *Entente*, to secure peace, would have to reduce its war aims (Balfour to Bertie, 17 Sept. 1917, Lord Derby papers, 920 DER (17), WO).

# The Making of a
# Foreign Minister:
# Louis Barthou (1862–1934)

## ROBERT J. YOUNG

On 17 April 1934 the French government sliced through the tangled
knot of European disarmament. At least, so it first appeared. By means
of a formal Note addressed to London, the government of Gaston
Doumergue declared its unwillingness to wait a moment longer for
the Geneva-based Disarmament Conference to devise formulae
acceptable to all parties. The security of France, the Note pronounced,
could no longer be mortgaged to the elusive prospect of some
international agreement, particularly since Hitler's Germany had
withdrawn from that conference the previous year and now seemed
bent on hastening the pace of its own rearmament. Accordingly, while
France in no way intended to repudiate the ideal of disarmament or to
withdraw from the two-year-old international discussions, it was
resolved to satisfy its security needs by whatever means were available. This neither committed France to accelerated rearmament,
nor ruled it out. It did raise, expressly, the possibility of consolidating
its existing ties with Allied and other friendly powers, perhaps even of
extending them.[1]

There was no mistaking the new and decisive ring which the Note
struck against the rim of recent convention, at least so it seemed. After
all the political turbulence resulting from the passage of seven
governments in two years, at last there seemed to be in place a
government with guts. More than that, the cabinet formed by
Doumergue in February 1934 was a coalition government which had
ignored only the distant extremes of the political spectrum, and a
government deep in political experience and leadership. Doumergue
was a former premier and a President of the Republic. Edouard

Herriot and André Tardieu, currently ministers of State, were ex-premiers, as was Pierre Laval, now at the Colonial Ministry. Indeed, almost all members of the cabinet had previous ministerial experience, including the 72-year-old Minister for Foreign Affairs, Louis Barthou.

The Note of 17 April carried his signature, a cachet which seemed appropriate for two reasons. Not only was he the minister responsible, but he seemed to epitomize this government of personally energetic, politically conservative senior citizens. Doumergue was 73, his War Minister, Marshal Pétain, was 78, Herriot was in his sixties, as was Louis Marin, at Public Health, Albert Sarraut, at Interior, and Louis Germain-Martin, at Finance. Some of the key youngsters in the cabinet, people like Tardieu and Laval, were already over 50. These were men whose memories extended back, without effort, to the carnage of 1914–18. Pétain had withstood the *Boches* on the battlefield of Verdun; Barthou had confronted them by securing parliamentary passage of the three-year military service law in 1913; Germain-Martin, a veteran member of the Chamber's Finance commission, knew how much the Germans had cost the French Treasury over the past several decades; Tardieu, and his chief, Premier Georges Clemenceau, remembered them from the anguished days of the Paris Peace Conference; and Herriot had tired of their reparations stonewalling and their armaments violations in the 1920s. These were men who had seen it all before, heard it all before, men who would not be gulled by German blandishments or seduced by the soft and empty assurances which came from friendly foreign capitals. That, at least, was how it seemed.

What more fitting, one might even say predictable, that a political veteran like Barthou, a man who had wrapped himself in the flag for most of his political life, should come up with the Note of 17 April. An elderly member of an elderly Senate, a politician who for 40 years had drawn intense fire from the socialist-communist left, Barthou looked very much like a man resolved to establish a new order based on the old. The Note was his way of reminding the Germans who had won the war, telling them and the world that the Third Republic had regained its composure and its resolution. And this was no subterfuge, no hollow utterance, for everyone knew that the Germans had killed his son in December 1914. Some knew that he had declined the offer to become ambassador to Germany after the war, on the grounds that his wife could not bear to be among Germans.[2] From all this, eventually, came the April Note, signed by him, publicly acclaimed by him, and widely represented by the contemporary press and historical commentators as the work of his hand. As Charles Micaud once observed, Barthou personified the 'traditional foreign policy of the Right'.[3]

In fact, one might be tempted to quarrel with this conclusion, even while accepting the accuracy of the evidence on which it is based. Barthou's record did evince moments of Germanophobia, before the war and the death of his son, as well as afterwards. The problem is that there is evidence of another order, evidence which speaks to his temperamental centrism, his native dislike of extremes and extremism, his inherent distrust of dogmatism. It is then that one must turn to the question of character, and what the French call *formation*. One does so out of an uneasiness with what often happens in our studies of ministerial performance. Too often cabinet ministers are assessed as if they had no past. They are portrayed as more or less skilled respondents to the forces of the present, mindful of the current pressure-points, but too often as if they had no memory. It is a notion, one supposes, that is consistent with the stereotyped, waffling politician, that creature of the moment who floats at will only because he has jettisoned his principles on take-off. It is, in short, a simple-minded view.

Barthou in 1934 cannot be understood solely in terms of 1934. Indeed, this attempt to address him as a foreign minister takes as its point of departure a remark he once made about Ernest Renan: 'The nest may not always determine the distance of the flight to come, but the child does explain the man.'[4] It is to this 'nest' that one must first turn, and to the early years of the fledgling, for it is there and then that one detects Barthou's early, formative impressions of foreigners and foreign cultures. Without some sense of those impressions, one cannot address the controversy which slowly has arisen about his part in the Note of 17 April 1934. The fact is that Barthou's *formation* renders up evidence of the childhood revulsion he felt for Germany, to take but one example, *and* a sometimes unrestrained celebration of Germanic culture.

He was born in August 1862 in the small south-western town of Oloron-Sainte-Marie, foothill country between the departmental capital of Pau to the north and the snow-capped Pyrenees to the south. His father was a hardware merchant whose shop was situated on the Rue Sablière, a narrow lane which followed the eastern contours of the Oloron river. Nine years later his address changed, although not the location of his home above the shop, when the street was renamed the Rue du Général Chanzy, in 1871, in memory of a French general who had distinguished himself in the Franco-Prussian war of the previous year.[5] At an early age, therefore, Louis Barthou caught a local glimpse of a drama played out on a continental stage, one which – in his youthful eyes – pitted French heroes against foreign villains.

No doubt he was familiar with the name of General Chanzy, well before the municipal authorities decided to rename the Rue Sablière. Some 60 years later he could still recall that afternoon in September 1870. For a few days he had been his father's eyes on the world. Confined to the shop, Isidore Barthou had despatched his eight-year-old son to make pencilled notes of the official military bulletins posted on the walls of the local prefecture. That day, the one a septuagenarian would never forget, the young Louis had returned with the news of France's defeat at Sedan. But the word had outpaced him. Isidore, a republican, and no friend of the chastened emperor Napoleon III, was in tears. More stunning still for the breathless child was the fact that he had found his father commiserating with their neighbour Touan, the draper, Touan, the bonapartist![6] That day, at the age of eight, Louis Barthou learned the difference between what was superficial and transient, and what was profound and constant. Thereafter, 'France' meant for him something that towered above ephemeral political differences.

Formal schooling complemented these formative influences. In 1875, at 13 years of age, Louis Barthou secured entry to the prestigious *lycée* at Pau, which he attended for the ensuing four years and where his quickness of mind and restless energy earned for him the nickname of quicksilver, *vif-argent*. How well he remembered, so many years later, that moment when the new boys had been taken into the assembly hall and shown the prominently featured device: 'Children, never forget 1870–1871.'[7] From then, until graduation, no effort was spared to ensure that every lad remembered the French defeat of 1870, that every lad kept alive the memory of Alsace and Lorraine, the two French provinces incorporated into Germany by the victor's treaty of Frankfurt. The curriculum might well have been traditional – with emphasis upon Latin, Greek and French literature – but more than one teacher recalled with tears the recent humiliation of 1870. Two decades later, Barthou still remembered Georges Edet. It was this remarkable French professor who had addressed the graduating class in August 1879, spoken of France's expectations of them, and stirred their patriotism with passionate references to the Republic's great victory at Valmy in 1792.[8] Little wonder that Barthou, upon returning to the school twelve years later as newly elected deputy for the Basses-

Pyrénées, should have taken national revival as a natural theme for this audience. 'You will be part of this reawakening', he promised this next generation. 'We'll make soldiers out of you.'[9]

As he saw it, his education to that point had been distinguished by one great strength, and one great weakness. They had been taught to be patriots, reared partly on the texts of great French writers like Jules Michelet and Victor Hugo, partly on press accounts from Paris of the speeches delivered in the Chamber by that great republican hero, Léon Gambetta.[10] But they had been poorly tutored in modern languages. Partly this was because of the weight of tradition, which gave more emphasis to the languages of the ancients. Partly it was because of a cultural and regional bias. Those who were pressed to study a modern language, like Barthou, generally chose Spanish. English commanded no priority, a condition which prevailed despite – or perhaps because of – the visible influence of a prominent English community in the resort area of Pau. German was even more warmly despised. Indeed, those boys who had been compelled to study the language of the enemy were held by the others to have been 'martyrisés'.[11]

There is no sign that this deficiency was remedied, at least by any formal requirement, during the next half-dozen years of Barthou's academic career. He enrolled in the law faculty at Bordeaux in 1879, completed his master's degree there, and by 1886 had secured his doctorate in law from the University of Paris. By the following summer he was practising law back in Pau. By then too his ambivalence about Germany was very much in evidence. He was drawn, for example, to the artistry of German musicians – Bach and Mozart, Schumann and Schubert, but especially to the old romanticism of Beethoven and the new wave released by Richard Wagner.[12] Partly for that reason, he was depressed and frustrated by his rudimentary knowledge of German, a shortcoming made more manifest by his brief visit to western Germany in the autumn of 1887. It was then, so it appears, that the 25-year-old Barthou resolved to improve his capacity in the language of the enemy.[13]

That he continued to so regard Germans is beyond doubt. Indeed, the abbreviated nature of his trip to Germany that September of 1887 stemmed entirely from this fact. He had found himself in Cologne on 2 September, the anniversary of France's defeat at Sedan. Incapable of being in the company of Germans celebrating this national occasion, the young lawyer had advanced his departure date and fled to Amsterdam where, incidentally, he was not much taken by the Dutch either.[14] The fact is that, however much he could appreciate the beauty of Cologne's great cathedral, however much he was moved by the canvases of the great Dutch masters, no pleasure equalled the return journey to France. Indeed, he expressed relief that the German authorities had declined to let him stay in Alsace-Lorraine for more than 24 hours. A longer visit would have been too painful, witnessing on the one hand the callous behaviour of the German regime, on the other the 'stoical courage' of a people still true to France, of a people's unrelenting 'hatred for the conqueror'.[15]

Much of what Louis Barthou learned in the autumn of 1887 only confirmed what he already knew. Earlier that year, and as a supplement to his career in the Pau Appeals Court, he had become a regular contributor to *L'Indépendant des Basses-Pyrénées*, the pro-republican daily newspaper. Under the tutelage of Emile Garet, press director and celebrity among moderate republican circles of Béarn, Barthou concentrated mainly on issues of domestic political importance. However, from time to time he ventured opinions on the world of international politics. In these signed articles, written mainly between 1887 and 1888, are glimpses of how Barthou, in his mid-twenties, perceived the European arena.

Everything hinged on the German problem, and the theft of Alsace and Lorraine in 1870. France would never accept the loss; neither would the loyal citizens of the captive provinces. Accordingly, Germany would continue its attempts to reduce France to silence, first by isolating the Third Republic diplomatically, second by intimidating it with occasional threats of war. From that, certain conclusions flowed. The German chancellor, Otto von Bismarck, was the single greatest threat to European peace. It was his 'fatal genius' that had so confounded his royal masters, confounded them to such a point that the stability of Europe now depended on 'the arbitrary will . . . of a single man'.[16] And who would ally with France to contain the hazards so casually thrown up by the German chancellor? Italy, under the direction of Prime Minister Francesco Crispi, seemed secure in Germany's wake. His peaceful assurances notwithstanding, Crispi was a Francophobe who was intent on maintaining the alliance with Germany and Austria–Hungary.[17]

Barthou was no more optimistic when it came to England. Although he never commented on what it had been like to spend a good part of his youth in 'la ville anglaise' of Pau, it is clear that he never evinced any particular affinity for England or things English. Part of this distance derived from his fiercely republican loyalties, sentiments which caused him to regard the Irish as 'an oppressed people', and to compare, unfavourably, what he saw as the English monarchy's halting political and social reforms with the republican liberties and social progress already in evidence in France.[18] Part of it also derived from the fact that England was France's greatest imperial rival, and never more so than in the 1880s and 1890s when colonial expansion was seen by many Frenchmen as the key to the national revival that had to precede any redressing of French grievances against Germany. Certainly Louis Barthou was an enthusiastic supporter of the Republic's colonial policies in North Africa and the Far East, and a particularly vocal defender of the controversial Jules Ferry. For that reason at least, Barthou was sharply critical of England's steadily tightening grip on Egypt. The convention recently signed between England and Turkey, he wrote in May 1887, was an absolute 'masterpiece of diplomatic duplicity'. England, it is said, will withdraw from Egypt in three years, *if* circumstances allow for it. In short, Barthou forecast, 'she will never get out!'[19] The English, he said, were masters at mouthing high principles while getting their own way.

Tsarist Russia, he ventured, was quite different. In 1875 Tsar Alexander II, the 'glorious liberator of the serfs' had managed to defuse one of Bismarck's war scares. By so doing, he had 'saved our country from irreparable disaster'. More recently, German provocations were continuing the process of nudging France and Russia together. Bismarck's latest threat of confrontation had again been proved idle, thanks – so Barthou implied – to the restraining offices of the Russian Tsar. The trick for France was to be patient, patient enough to let German bungling slowly propel Russia towards the Third Republic.[20] And as for the shameless taunt of French monarchists that Russia would never ally with republicans, Barthou simply dismissed it as fraudulent. The forms of government were of no account when it came to alliances. What mattered, solely, was a perception of mutual interests.[21] By the late 1880s, it was clear that the journalist Barthou was convinced of the interests which were slowly bringing France and Russia together.

For the next 25 years, essentially until 1914, Barthou's attentions turned to international politics only rarely. After a brief period as a city councillor in Pau, he embarked on a national political career with his election to Parliament in 1889. Shortly thereafter, a succession of cabinet posts came his way, including those of Public Works, Interior, and Justice. The duties associated with those offices, together with the drama of domestic crises such as the Panama scandal, the Dreyfus affair, and the Separation issue, kept his gaze on domestic problems. To be sure, he continued to vote approval and funds for the Republic's colonial programmes and for the alliance with Russia which had been slowly fashioned in the early 1890s. He continued to be a strong voice for national revival, and a firm critic of anything which detracted from that recovery – whether alcohol abuse, indifferent physical education programmes, or the declining birth rate. But very rarely did he make foreign policy central either to his parliamentary speeches or to his ongoing journalistic endeavours. On the surface, therefore, there was not a great deal to suggest that some day Louis Barthou might distinguish himself in the portfolio for foreign affairs. Apart from a brief period of service on the Chamber's foreign affairs commission in 1911–12, there was indeed little in his own background that would explain the historical conclusion he reached in 1913 about that colourful eighteenth-century figure, the Comte de Mirabeau. Mirabeau, Barthou wrote, would not have been a complete statesman had he not been equally alive to foreign as well as domestic issues.[22]

Below the surface, therefore, one can detect a process of maturation which not only carried Louis Barthou briefly to the premiership of France in 1913 but also was part of his growth towards the Foreign Ministry two decades later. This maturation may be said to have had three components: domestic political experience, international travel, and personal culture.

Barthou's pre-war political career can be summed up by the trilogy republicanism, patriotism, centrism. Brought up in a republican home, and schooled as part of a generation of patriots, he was a centrist both by temperament and intellectual persuasion. He spoke with equal passion against monarchism and anarchism, against the rival blindness of conservatism and of revolutionary socialism, against the debilitating effects of clerical influence in French society and the tiring divisions induced by radical anti-clericalism. Characteristically, he would enter each post-election parliament – never once having been defeated at the polls – and try to swing his weight *against* the triumphant coalition in the Chamber. In other words, if the left had gathered steam in the most recent electoral contest, he was inclined to shift slightly to the right. In the reverse situation, he was more likely to vote with the left.[23] It was his way of combating excess and, if the truth were told, of limiting the liabilities of mercurial mass politics.[24] Expressed differently, it was his way of articulating the link between moderation and pragmatism. One did one's best to adjust to circumstances as they were, not merely how one wished them to be – even if it meant being called a shallow opportunist by self-seen men of principle. One accepted the need for orderly change, even if it meant criticism from those who wanted no change, and from those who wanted no order. In a sense, the political credo of the politician who turned 52 in August 1914 had been inscribed in the dissertation of the 24-year-old doctoral candidate: 'Revise without rupturing and repair without renouncing, that should be the motto of the lawmaker bent on reform.'[25]

Travel, too, had helped shaped Barthou's horizons. Indeed, one of the most interesting comments offered in October 1934, on the occasion of Barthou's assassination, came from Gabriel Hanotaux. Barthou, his old political comrade in arms observed, was a truly modern man : because he travelled.[26] In 1934, following Barthou's celebrated ministerial trips to countries in eastern Europe, the remark seemed as obvious as it was true. What was less well known was the extent of his pre-war travel. Even before his trip in 1887 to Germany, Holland and Belgium, Barthou had been several times across the border into Spain. In 1894, as Public Works Minister, he had made an official visit to Liverpool and London. Thereafter, primarily as a private tourist, he had paid occasional visits to Austria–Hungary, Italy, Egypt, Spain, the Sudan, Morocco, Canada and the United States. More significantly, because more frequent and enduring in influence, were his annual trips to the Lucerne area of Switzerland and to the Bayreuth festival where each year he was captivated by the music of Richard Wagner.

Two features of these pre-war travels merit comment. First, despite his lingering reservations about the German regime of Kaiser Wilhelm II, Barthou had none about the Teutonic cultural achievement. He was ecstatic, for example, about the art collections of Dresden, and totally enchanted by performances of Beethoven and Wagner in the Vienna Opera. In fact, he was much impressed by the fact that German audiences were more easily won over to the music of Wagner than their French counterparts. He even found it comforting to think that the Kaiser, whom he despised, did not share his own people's admiration of Wagner. Germans and Austrians, Barthou ventured, had a deep appreciation of fine music, an art form which they made available at much more reasonable prices than was the case in Paris.[27] Moreover, the Germans were impressive in another way. They had a talent for teaching and learning foreign languages, including French, which he found the German middle class learned with some degree of fluency. By contrast, the French school system was decidedly inferior, that is to say that it was too traditional in its methods. A French *lycéen* might well be able to translate a page of Goethe, but would collapse from the effort of buying a train ticket in Berlin.[28] This was why he had made some effort to develop his own spoken German, and why he had employed a German nanny to facilitate his own son's progress in the language.[29]

Second, impressed as Barthou was by certain features of Germanic society, as a Frenchman he was in no danger of being overwhelmed by anything foreign. Often he compared what was French with what was foreign, rarely conceding the advantage to the latter. The International Art Exhibition in Dresden in 1901 was altogether outstanding, largely because of the presence of French artists and sculptors. The museums of Vienna were outstanding, the more so as they nearly approached the quality of the Louvre.[30] In short, there was in Barthou not only an impulse to compare things foreign with things French, but very much to associate the meaning of 'France' with the genius of French artists and composers. In this sense, he was never entirely away from his country, for he was forever finding France wherever he went – in the galleries of Dresden, the bookshops of Vienna, the architecture of Quebec City, the contours of Rodin's 'France' unveiled in 1912 on the shores of Lake Champlain.[31]

Predictably, the seam is fine between Barthou's travels and what can be called his personal culture. What is already implicit is that this was a man of very considerable finesse, all the more impressive for being self-acquired. He was of course steeped in the literature of France, from the eighteenth-century masters like Voltaire and Denis Diderot to his own contemporaries – Edmond Rostand, Pierre Loti and Anatole France – to name only those with whom he enjoyed particularly close personal relations. More striking, however, and more instructive here, was his quite exceptional adulation of the two German composers, Ludwig von Beethoven and Richard Wagner. It was over the former that Barthou actually chose to contradict one of the greatest of his French heroes, Victor Hugo. Hugo could not see beyond Beethoven's Germanic soul, and accordingly had attributed but mortal status to the composer. Barthou was indignant. Beethoven, he said, was for all men and for all time as close as men ever get to immortality.[32] Wagner was no less so, childlike in many ways and yet truly a man of genius, one whose music often reduced Barthou to tears, one whose life inspired Barthou to write a full-length biography as well as a succession of articles for literary journals.[33]

Although he tried to elevate them beyond the boundaries of mere nation, these were in fact Germans whom he was applauding. And in that fact lay more ambivalence, for Louis Barthou was far from having made his peace with Germany. During his visits to Germany in 1901 and 1902 he claimed that he was haunted by unpleasant recollections from his first visit in 1887.[34] In 1902 he again found himself in Cologne in the month of September, and again had to witness some of the anniversary celebrations of 1870. It was no easier for him at 40 years of age than it had been when he was 25. 'I curse', he wrote, those Frenchmen 'who are crazy enough to propose reconciliation now, despite the humiliation we continue to suffer from the defeat and our acceptance of it.'[35] Twelve years later, in 1914, when he was 52, and the war was on, and his son was dead from a German artillery shell, the anger spilled beyond bounds. Louis Barthou was enlisted as a state propagandist, and during the course of the war churned out speech after speech excoriating the *boches*, both leaders and followers. The day of judgement was at hand, he thundered in the press and at the podium, even in those dark days when a French victory seemed utterly remote. Germany would pay for its perfidy. Revenge would be sweet because it would be just. Alsace and Lorraine would be returned to the fold, the Kaiser and his murderous generals would be put on trial, and the German people would pay for the damages they had caused. Never again, he swore, would he shake hands with a German.[36]

There is no doubt that during the 1920s Louis Barthou enhanced his reputation as a conservative nationalist and an unrepentant Germanophobe. For instance, in 1919 he switched his role from that of passionate wartime propagandist to that of Parliament's official *rapporteur* on the Versailles peace treaty with Germany. Predictably, some would have said, he criticized many of that treaty's provisions – notably the imprecision of the Anglo-American guarantee of French security – and came perilously close to suggesting that Clemenceau had been hoodwinked by President Wilson and Prime Minister Lloyd George. He also expressed regret that France had not insisted on a permanent occupation of the left bank of the Rhine and on the immediate trial of the Kaiser as a war criminal.[37] Such public pronouncements proved but the vanguard of action. In 1921, in his capacity as War Minister, Barthou ordered French troops to engage in a temporary occupation of several German cities, as part of a campaign to make the Germans fulfil their reparations obligations to France. In 1922, as the principal French delegate to the Genoa Conference, he was blamed for scotching hopes of a broad European reconciliation involving Britain and Russia as well as Germany. In early 1923, as chairman of the International Reparations Commission, he was held up as Premier Raymond Poincaré's supple henchman, the 'fixer' who had set things up for France's dramatic military occupation of the Ruhr.

However much one is tempted to qualify and contextualize these characterizations, there is no denying them some basis in fact. At the same time, there are other bodies of evidence which can be brought in to reinforce the image of this traditional hardliner. For one, his much publicized intransigence about enforcing all the terms of the Versailles treaty brought him into frequent conflict with the British government. Personally, he did not much care for British leaders – least of all Lloyd George whom he considered to have been a pernicious influence at and after the Paris peace conference.[38] What bothered him most, as it had in 1887 over Egypt, was British hypocrisy, the way their government always wrapped self-interest with the ribbons of lofty principle. And got away with it! Indeed, in March 1920 Barthou caused a considerable stir in Parliament and press by remarking on the way the British government had rallied to the cause of European reconstruction – *after* it had ensured the destruction of the German Navy and Air Force.[39] Moments such as these, together with subsequent Anglo-French duelling at the Genoa conference and in the Reparations Commission, were in themselves enough to harden the image of Louis Barthou as an obstacle to European reconciliation.

And of course there was more to it than that. By the time he was 60, in 1922, he was seen by many as a familiar fixture on the political right. A man who had fought a duel with Jean Jaurès in 1895, who as minister had broken postal strikes in 1906 and 1909, who in 1914 had discredited that left-wing darling, Joseph Caillaux, Louis Barthou had become a favourite *bête noire* of the French left.[40] When he served briefly as Foreign Minister in October–November 1917, the parliamentary left had given him a frosty reception; and only the extreme exigencies of the war situation had saved him from further criticism from the radical left when he called the victorious Russian Bolsheviks thugs and terrorists. When one adds to this his characterization of Bolshevik propaganda in France as 'criminal behaviour', his negative portrayals of the Soviet delegates at Genoa, and his positive – if cautiously expressed – appreciation of the progress made by the new fascist regime in Italy, there can be no mistaking one vivid impression of Louis Barthou – a social conservative, a lifelong opponent of socialism and communism, a man of traditional, bourgeois calculation and countenance.[41]

That may be so, but what is true should not be confused with the truth. Just as there was an ambivalence in Barthou before the First World War, so too is that ambivalence readily detectable in the interwar period. Nor should this come as a surprise, as long as one keeps in mind that governing, centrist impulse in his character. When one does, the mix of inherent moderation and pragmatism makes highly improbable a decisive shift to any political extreme. In fact, the problem at this moment is that the current impression of Barthou is now too stark, too clear. For improved obscurity, one might draw upon the two familiar examples of Barthou and England, Barthou and Germany, both of which need to be filled out with new references to what has been called earlier his personal culture.

Louis Barthou, as has been suggested, had no pronounced affinity for England. While it is true that he was familiar with some of the English Romantics, like Byron and Shelley, and that he had included a few works by Kipling and Swinburne on the shelves of his library, there are few traces of English contributions to his cultural lexicon. On the contrary, there are frequent signs of resentment over what he took to be Britain's customary blend of hypocritical and successful self-aggrandizement. But what is missing from the version so far recalled is his recognition that *entente* with England was essential to France's security. In March 1920, when he had criticized the English government before the French Parliament, he had also underlined the critical importance of that government's contribution to the recently successful war against Germany. Indeed, he had no misgivings about judging the Anglo-French alliance as 'essential to world peace'.[42] In subsequent speeches and articles in the early 1920s Barthou renewed this emphasis, even while insisting that France maintain an equality within this partnership. To that end he several times invoked the judgement of his personal heroes. Mirabeau had stressed the importance of friendship with England. So too had Gambetta, almost a century later. So too had Alphonse Lamartine, that astute poet-statesman who had referred to 'the happy necessity of the alliance with England', but who had added – with Barthou's chosen emphasis – that this alliance '*must not be without constraints, nor without prudence, nor without qualifications*'.[43] Seen in this light, it is no wonder that in February 1934 Anthony Eden first judged Barthou 'a nasty old man at heart', but subsequently as the man responsible for having made Anglo-French relations 'better . . . than I had ever known them'.[44]

A similar if considerably sharper ambivalence was apparent when it came to Barthou's appraisal of Germany. As witnessed earlier, until the mid-1920s he was emphatic about the need for a strict enforcement of the Versailles treaty clauses. His was not a voice which condemned the treaty as too harsh, not one which recommended liberal and lenient interpretation of its provisions on arms and reparations. He made it clear that even if Germany was greater than its Prussian component, that component still remained part of Germany and part of the German character. In 1919, for his assessment of the Versailles treaty, he had borrowed the phrase that war was Prussia's national industry. In 1932 he recalled Danton's rebuke to the Convention – 'Will any of our arguments kill a single Prussian?' – and judged it an eloquent appeal, 'simple and sublime'. This was not a man who forgot quickly or forgave readily.[45]

At the same time, he was a man who always had shrunk from fanaticism. Having spent three years during the war writing pieces that seethed with hatred, it was not long before Louis Barthou was advising French readers that: 'Hatred is a poor counsellor; . . . it perceives badly, and it judges badly'.[46] It was in pragmatic recognition of this that Barthou behaved at Genoa with much more diplomatic grace and agility than pleased the stiff Poincaré. Unlike his premier, who did not much care how the Conference foundered as long as it did so, Barthou was determined to ensure that France alone could not be blamed for the anticipated failure. Accordingly, he was more genial and accommodating than Poincaré wanted or his British, Italian, German and Russian counterparts at Genoa had frankly expected.[47] The same proved true of his years at the Reparations Commission (1922–26), at least once the Ruhr occupation had been engineered in January 1923.

In fact, as early as November 1922 the British ambassador in Berlin reported an interesting exchange between the German Chancellor, Joseph Wirth, and Barthou, who, in his capacity as chairman of the Reparations Commission, was making the first formal visit by a high-level French statesman to post-war Germany. On this occasion he urged Wirth to avoid provoking more discussion about who had been responsible for the last war. 'Your speech the other day,' Barthou remarked, 'brought out Poincaré in a bitter attack; further, it has induced Viviani to write his infernal *mémoires*. What is the good of that? These recollections merely stir up animosity and prolong hate.'[48] Subsequently, particularly in the course of 1924, Barthou slowly adopted more conciliatory language toward Germany; and by 1926 the British delegate to the Commission concluded that Barthou had been able 'to secure the confidence of our former enemies and to ensure the respect of the whole world'.[49]

By then as well this alleged Germanophobe already had returned to his pre-war regimen. Not only was he spending the better part of every August in the German–Swiss resort area of Burgenstöck, near Lucerne, but he was also taking a week almost every summer in

Bayreuth, among Germans, indulging in the delights of *Tannhäuser, Lohengrin, Die Walküre, Siegfried* or *Götterdämmerung*. Indeed, even when it came to musical events in Paris, Barthou kept a particular watch for visiting German performers such as Bruno Walter or Wilhelm Furtwängler.[50] And as of January 1930 he began what were to be the last four years of his life broadcasting and writing about the troubled genius of Richard Wagner. In all probability he knew more about German society than most French public figures of his day, and a good deal more about German culture. Indeed, it is a measure of his respect for the language, as well as a mark of his progress in it, that Barthou affirmed that Wagner, whom he had discovered so many years earlier, was really only fully satisfying in the original German.[51]

It was in Burgenstöck in August 1932 that Barthou reflected on what the future held in store. He was not worried about himself. At 70 years of age, his wife and son both dead, he anticipated no future, certainly not one that would involve new ministerial responsibilities. But he worried about Europe, eyeing the storm clouds on the horizon, trying to assure himself that peace was safe in humanity's acquired disgust of war. He thought of his old friend Aristide Briand, so recently deceased, and praised this peacemaker for his vision of a reconciled Europe. He had done so while Briand was alive – describing his policies as the only ones that made any sense – and he had done so again, in March 1932, when he had called the deceased Briand 'the apostle of a universal faith', that of peace.[52] Accordingly, when as minister he himself first met the Chamber's foreign affairs commission, in March 1934, it was entirely consistent that he should represent himself as a successor of Briand. 'He was my friend', the minister avowed. 'I renounce neither that friendship, nor that policy.'[53]

But only six weeks later, this same minister was to squelch prospects for a European disarmament convention. The Note of 17 April, so critics alleged and supporters boasted, had ended the promise, or the charade, of disarmament talks. It meant the return of the intransigent hardliners, men of strong words who were prepared to risk confrontation with Germany. Or it meant the revival of political realism, men of strong words whose very presence diminished the likelihood of confrontation. As if uncertainty of such magnitude was not enough, the Foreign Minister only added to the confusion. Having first privately denied authorship of the Note, Barthou then laid official claim to this allegedly dramatic initiative, and then went out of his way to deny that the Note was either dramatic or novel. It is this latter argument which brings together the accumulating impressions of Barthou's

character, with the case *against* his authorship of the April Note.
Certainly some sort of synthesis is needed to explain the following
conundrum. While critics jeered and proponents applauded the April
Note for its newfound spirit of resolution, Barthou himself emphasized
to Parliament that the Note was in no sense a departure from previous
French policy. Rather, he stressed the continuity between his approach
and that of his predecessors, framed them both in the language of conciliation and pacification, and affirmed that France was still prepared to
consider any new initiatives on the matter of disarmament. In short,
nothing had changed. The Note of 17 April was no bold new initiative,
and its author no vigorous innovator. As Barthou said in May to the
Chamber's foreign affairs commission: 'We are in favour of a convention. . . . We support the broad policy of the Disarmament
Commission.'[54]

At the same time, he emphatically denied any desire or intent to
address the German problem by means of a diplomatic encirclement of
Germany. Some observers, knowing that he had been personally close
to the pre-war Foreign Minister, Théophile Delcassé, saw in Barthou
the imminent revival of the old pre-war combinations, in particular the
alliance with Russia. Aware of that friendship, built in part on the
generational, regional and ideological affinities which linked the two
men, aware too of Barthou's early advocacy of alliance with Russia in
the late 1880s, one cannot be unmoved by the suggestion that in 1934
he held up Delcassé as a model.[55] Indeed, Barthou said as much
himself. What is critical, however, is to know how he assessed Delcassé
– critical and instructive. Far from having been the man behind some
master plot to encircle Germany, Delcassé, Barthou observed, had
strengthened the foundation for European peace through his efforts at
Anglo-French and Franco-Italian reconciliation. In fact, Barthou
remarked in early October 1934, there had been nothing either
aggressive or provocative in the diplomacy of Delcassé, just as there
was no encirclement design in his own policy.[56]

Whether or not one accepts such assurances depends in part on how
one sees Barthou's role in April 1934 and in part on how one reads his
character. As for the first, the evidence is simply overwhelming against
his authorship of the Note, his own protestations notwithstanding.
Briefly put, on the very eve of the cabinet meeting which endorsed the
thrust of the 17 April Note, Louis Barthou had made known his own
preference for a more conciliatory line. Anticipating Premier
Doumergue's resistance to anything 'soft', Barthou ensured that
several key members of the diplomatic corps, of the parliamentary

commissions, and of the press contingent, were aware of his own position.[57] Just as he had argued at the time of the Genoa Conference in 1922, so too he argued in 1934. France had to refrain from any action which might be held responsible for the failure of the Disarmament Conference. Such an attribution would tarnish the reputation of the Third Republic, further frustrate France's relations with a British government ostensibly bent on a disarmament convention, and, conversely, generate more international sympathy for a disconsolate Nazi Germany. Instead, France had to retain the moral leadership acquired by Briand – to whose grave Barthou made a special pilgrimage in early April 1934 and before whose tomb he pondered what his old friend would have done in his place. The answer, he knew, was to remain flexible, not to concede to Hitler's demands on the arms issue, but to hold out hope for French concessions *if* some of France's own requirements could be satisfied through evidence of German conciliation.[58]

But the cabinet had said 'no' – no more concessions, no more accommodation. They hoped, it seemed, to make the Germans tremble with the sound of a loud voice, a tactic which the Foreign Minister regarded as empty posturing and over which he contemplated resignation. But he judged the stakes to be too high. Resignation now was likely to revive the acute ministerial instability of which he had been a chief and public critic for the past two years. Now that the country had a broad-based national coalition under Doumergue, it would be reckless to test its fragility within the first few months of its existence.[59] So Barthou stayed, and said that the Note was his, that the cabinet had been unanimous, that the disarmament discussions could continue – that nothing had changed.

Such a construction is as consistent with Barthou's character as it is with the historical evidence. What one detects in the controversy surrounding the April Note, as in that of the ensuing six months of his ministry, are the marks of moderation and pragmatism. As for the disarmament issue, he did not wish to be – nor was he – a spokesman for a recalcitrant traditionalism which saw military deterrence as the only assurance of peace. At the same time, he was no star-struck idealist when it came to the League of Nations as principal guarantor of French security. He had hopes for the League, but no illusions, which is to say that no international organization could in itself solve a German problem which was older than he was. Accordingly, it was fitting to resort to the familiar as well as the new, bilateral conventions as well as the League, ideally bringing the two together, but minimally having entente or alliance ready as backup. It is in recognition of this latter, pragmatic, calculation that so many scholars are convinced that Barthou's real if unspoken objectives in 1934 were an alliance with Russia and an alliance with Italy.[60]

Judging strictly from his character, it is likely that he would have pursued both, had it been necessary to do so. No admirer of Bolshevism, and recently disturbed by the excesses of Italian fascism, Barthou would not have baulked at tying France to either power. As he had written 50 years before, it was mutual interests, not common forms of government, that determined alliances. However, neither evidence nor character suggest that he was prepared to pursue those objectives *à outrance*. Instead, he laid the foundations for the Soviet Union's membership in the League of Nations, a step which would mark Russia's return to the fold of international respectability without expressly alarming Germany by the prospect of a new Franco-Russian alliance. Similarly, he minimized German anxiety about a Franco-Italian accommodation, in this case by delaying negotiations until the Italians had smoothed out some of the irritants in their relations with France's quasi-ally, Yugoslavia. There is in all this a pragmatism and a prudence which accord poorly with any characterization of Barthou as a blinkered, right-wing idéologue, but remarkably well with the temperament of a political centrist and man of inherent moderation. As Maurice Vaïsse has written, Barthou was not a man 'to rupture' but 'rather a man to repair'.[61]

The same qualities are even more evident, if in different measure, when it comes to Barthou's approach to relations with Great Britain and Germany. As for the first, one might contrast the judgement of one senior British diplomat with that of a distinguished French historian. Sir Robert Vansittart, in 1934 the senior permanent official in the British Foreign Office, concluded that Barthou 'had more value than any French Foreign Minister since Delcassé'. Four decades later, Professor Duroselle observed that Barthou's mark of distinction lay in the fact that he alone of French ministers in the 1930s was prepared to act independently of Britain.[62] Barthou himself would have detected no contradiction, for he had never forgotten Lamartine. France needed England, but the best way to fulfil that need was to ensure that England never took France for granted. Accordingly, one spoke one's mind to the English, even lectured them, if one recalls Eden's early indignation at the new French Foreign Minister. Indeed, Barthou had long held candour to be one of the greatest virtues, even in international politics. 'I detest obsequiousness,' he once wrote, 'as debasing for those who express it as for those at whom it is directed.'[63] That is why, for example, he had said in 1926 that the only way to solve international problems was to get them out on the table, look one's counterpart 'straight in the eyes' and speak one's mind. That is why, in June 1934, he delivered a searing indictment of the way in which the League of Nations too often tried to paper over unresolved differences with cosmetic assurances of mutual accord. The 'unanimity' which was so often proclaimed, he said, was in reality nothing but 'misunderstandings' and 'contradictory propositions'; worse, they would never be addressed until someone had the courage to admit they were still there. Of course, not everyone wished to be upbraided by the truth; and not everyone appreciated, as Eden put it, how 'appallingly witty' Barthou could be 'at the expense of his allies'. Nevertheless, it was that same Eden who soon came to recognize that Barthou was often correct in his judgement, 'even if he seasoned all he had to say with bitter aloes', and that the combination of his perception and his candour had strengthened rather than weakened the Anglo-French *entente*.[64]

It is in the light of such an appraisal that scholars continue to mourn the death of Barthou in October 1934. They do so out of a belief that a breakdown in the Anglo-French dialogue was central to the approaching tragedy of the Second World War, and from a sense that he was perhaps the one French statesman who had proved capable of both clearing the air and taking some initiative. Oddly, the same argument might be advanced when it comes to Franco-German relations. Oddly and remarkably, for here was one who had been schooled in a hatred for Prussia, whose only child had been killed by Germans, and who went to the grave still loathing the fallen and discredited Kaiser Wilhelm II. Nevertheless, it was this great admirer of German culture who, by 1922, was dissuading others from stirring up controversy about war guilt and, by 1926, was warning readers that hatred was poor counsel. Aristide Briand was already becoming Barthou's paragon of sensible, peace-sensitive diplomacy, and Théophile Delcassé he now praised as a man inspired less by a willingness to confront than a desire to conciliate.

Certainly this was how Barthou repeatedly tried to represent his own policies before the French Parliament and its commissions. The language, consistently, was that of conciliation and collaboration. The sentiment, we may surmise, was still in the spirit of Briand, and of Lamartine before him: 'there may be more action in . . . fighting, but there is a hundred times more true patriotism in peace!'[65] So it was that a man who had good reason to detest Germans, and good reason to admire them, cautiously continued to make his peace with them. In May 1934, for instance, he acknowledged to one German diplomat how men had to change with the times. He first recalled his ealier, wartime vow never to shake hands with a German, then the fact that he had been the first French political leader to negotiate in post-war Berlin, and then, the point of the exercise: 'I desire an understanding with Germany, this I tell you eye to eye, as a man of honour.'[66] The following month, when he received Joachim von Ribbentrop in Paris, Barthou 'suddenly . . . took hold of both my arms and said, apparently quite spontaneously: "Please . . . look me straight in the face and believe when I say that . . . I have the most ardent desire to achieve agreement with Germany."'[67] Indeed, even after the massacre of Hitler's domestic political enemies in late June, and the Nazi-inspired assassination of the Austrian Chancellor Dollfuss in early July – outrages which literally sickened Barthou – the French Foreign Minister continued to maintain his commitment to a 'policy of cooperation'.[68] Appalled as he was by the evidence of Nazi barbarism and duplicity, he maintained to the end his interest in accommodating post-war Germany. By so doing, he retained his own flexibility. By so doing, he kept alive both the alternative of a Germany reassured by the provisions of League-based collective agreements, and that of possible French alliances with Russia and Italy in the event that Germany proved intractable before the League. Therein, of course, lies the controversy which has surrounded the diplomacy of Louis Barthou.

This essay has sought to expose Barthou by slowly peeling away the crust of competing legends. In a sense, it is more of a technical achievement, an old portrait restored, than a new canvas. What has been lifted is the patina of doubt which had accumulated slowly during the exchanges between Barthou's defenders and detractors, between those whose own predilections cause them to fasten upon either his testimonials to the League or to those of alliance, but not both. Accordingly, some have seen him as a 72-year-old traditionalist, uncomfortable with the rhetorical idealism of the League, intent on surrounding Germany with hostile diplomatic combinations. Others, more familiar with his pronouncements in the contemporary press and before attentive parliamentary commissions, are struck by his passionate commitment to European reconciliation through negotiation and accommodation. For some, therefore, the inspiration was Delcassé; for others, Briand.

Barthou would have insisted on both. A friend of Delcassé, he knew that there had been no intention of risking a war by threatening

Germany's security. A friend of Briand, he knew that there had been no intention of risking a war by doing anything to exacerbate the insecurity of France. Briand had played upon, expoited, his media-induced image as prophet of peace, a cause for which his genuine passion was so ably enlisted. But no one knew better than Barthou that Briand was as cunning a politician as the Third Republic had seen, that his reputation as wrecker of French cabinets was well founded, that underneath his stainless cloak of peacemaker there had remained a shrewd and seasoned statesman. Accordingly, what one sees in Barthou is both a man genuinely anxious to draw Germany into multilateral conventions designed to strengthen Europe's hold on peace, and a man prepared to back up conciliatory language with the tougher instruments of alliance diplomacy. He favoured the former but, if necessary, would accept the latter – rival options of which his realism and pragmatism could allow him to speak with equal sincerity. To the end, he remained the centrist, ready to shift his weight from one foot to the other, not in the absence of principle, but rather because of it.

Barthou spent a lifetime upholding moderation against fanaticism, and adaptability against rigidity. In 1933 he described all fanaticism as 'odious', but only because he had learned so well the catechism of his early mentor and tenacious moderate, Emile Garet. In 1933 he used Hugo's metaphor to treat the question of consistency in politics, but only because his schoolboy reading had lasted a lifetime. To be too rigid, too wedded to the same principles, so Hugo had written, was like preferring dead trees to those still growing.[69] Just as romanticism welcomes movement, so must statesmen respond to change, partly as a matter of principle, and partly as a matter of character. Not surprisingly, some mocked him, calling him 'Passe-Barthou', the all-purpose politician who personified the passkey approach to politics. What they missed, however, was the commitment to adaptability, as a matter of principle. For them, movement implied a lack of character, for him it was the essence of character – whether it was expressed in a schoolboy nickname like *vif-argent*, in a penchant for travel, in an adoration of romantic literature like that of Hugo and Loti, or the music of Chopin, Beethoven and Wagner, or in that desire of April 1934 to retain for France a continuing role in the international dialogue over disarmament.

NOTES

1. 'Communication', 17 April 1934, *Documents Diplomatiques Français*, vi, no. 104, pp. 270–72.

2. Bernard Auffray, *Pierre de Margerie (1861–1942) et la vie diplomatique de son temps* (Paris, 1976), p. 399.
3. Charles A. Micaud, *The French Right and Nazi Germany, 1933–1939* (Durham, NC, 1943), pp. 33–34. See also John Rison Jones, Jr. 'The Foreign policy of Louis Barthou, 1933–1934' (unpublished doctoral dissertation: University of North Carolina at Chapel Hill, 1958), pp. 164–9.
4. Barthou, 'Fêtes du centenaire d'Ernest Renan', *Académie Française*, 2 Sept. 1923, p. 22.
5. Barthou, 'Souvenirs de la Rue Sablière', in *Plaisir du Béarn* (Paris, 1931), pp 25–37. The street was renamed the Rue Louis Barthou in 1934.
6. Barthou, 'Pour ceux qui avaient huit ans en 1870', in his *Lettres à un jeune français* (Paris, 1916), pp. 135–40.
7. Ibid., p. 139.
8. See article by Barthou in *L'Indépendant des Basses Pyrénées*, 8 April 1904.
9. See the report of his speech in *L'Indépendant*, 1 Aug. 1891.
10. See Octave Aubert, *Louis Barthou* (Paris, 1935), pp. 22–3; Jules Bertaut, *Louis Barthou* (Paris, Sansot, 1919), 4–6; Barthou, *Emile Garet, 1829–1912* (Pau, 1912); 'Souvenirs de la Rue Sablière', *Plaisir du Béarn*, p. 35.
11. Aubert, *Louis Barthou*, p. 23.
12. Ibid., p. 140.
13. Barthou, *Notes de Voyage. En Belgique et en Hollande. Trois jours en Allemagne* (Pau, 1888), pp. 14-15.
14. Ibid., p. 24.
15. Ibid., pp. 15-16; and his article 'Choses d'Allemagne', in *L'Indépendant*, 27–28 Feb. 1887.
16. See Barthou, 'Les excitations allemandes' and 'Le règne de M. de Bismarck', in *L'Indépendant*, 1 June and 17–18 June 1888.
17. See Barthou, 'L'Italie et l'Allemagne', 'Le discours de M. Crispi' and 'France et Italie', in *L'Indépendant*, 7 and 28 Oct. 1887 and 22 Feb. 1888.
18. See Barthou, 'En Angleterre', *L'Indépendant*, 22 Oct. 1887.
19. Barthou, 'La Convention Anglo-Turque', *L'Indépendant*, 28 May 1887.
20. Barthou, 'La France et la Russie en 1875', and 'La France et la Russie', in *L'Indépendant*, 24 and 27 May 1887.
21. Barthou, 'Situation extérieure', and 'Les Alliances européennes', in *L'Indépendant*, 22 Feb. 1887 and 2 March 1888.
22. Barthou, *Mirabeau* (Paris, 1913), p. 207.
23. For example, see Jean Bousquet-Mélou, *Louis Barthou et la circonscription d'Oloron (1889–1914)* (Paris, 1972), p. 94.
24. In his first electoral campaign of 1889 Barthou had been shaken by the caprice of some voters. One constituent, having mistaken Barthou for a rival candidate, started cheering for that rival. Once corrected, he had turned with equal enthusiasm to cheers for Barthou. It was a lesson about the 'fragilité du suffrage universel' that stayed with him to the end of his life. See his *Promenades autour de ma vie* (Paris, 1933), p. 187.
25. Barthou, *Droit Romain de la distinction des biens en meubles et immeubles. Droit Français de l'Origine de l'Adage 'vilis mobilium possessio' et de son influence sur le code civil* (Paris, 1886), p. 223.
26. Gabriel Hanotaux, 'Un homme de gouvernement', unidentified, undated press clipping from October 1934, in 'Dossier Barthou', *Bibliothèque Historique de la Ville de Paris*. Claude Farrère made the same point in his eulogy to Barthou, of 23 April 1936, *Académie Française*, p. 30.
27. See his sixth letter, from Vienna, of August 1902, and the seventh letter, from Dresden, of Sept. 1902, in *Impressions et Essais* (Paris, 1914), pp. 35–48.
28. Ibid., letter three, Vienna, August 1902.
29. See Aubert, *Louis Barthou*, p. 23. Interview with Marcel Gilbert, 4 May 1982. Maître Gilbert's mother was a cousin of Barthou.
30. Barthou, *Impressions et Essais*, pp. 10–11, 38–9.
31. His accounts of Dresden and Vienna are found in *Impressions et Essais*. The best account of his trip to Canada and the United States, in 1912, is to be found in the articles by Gaston Deschamps in *Le Temps*, 10, 18, 19, 21 May and 4 June 1912.
32. Barthou, 'Autour de *William Shakespeare* de Victor Hugo', *Revue de Paris* (1 Aug. 1920), p. 458.

33. The book, dedicated to his wife Alice, was entitled *La vie amoureuse de Richard Wagner* (Paris, 1925).

34. *Impressions et Essais*, p. 4.

35. Ibid., p. 50.

36. The principal speeches are contained in three volumes: *L'Heure du Droit: France. Belgique. Serbie* (Paris, 1916); *Lettres à un jeune français* (1916); and *Sur les Routes du Droit* (Paris, 1917).

37. Barthou, *Le Traité de Paix* (Paris, 1919); *Journal Officiel, Chambre des Députés, Débats*, 2, 3, 18, 24 Sept. 1919, pp. 4099–114, 4124–9, 4422–3, 4543, 4550–3.

38. Barthou, 'Paix du dehors et paix du dedans', *Annales* (20 June 1920), n.p.; for a fuller appraisal of Lloyd George, see 'Les raisons de la France', *Annales* (14 April 1933), pp. 413–14.

39. *JO, Députés, Débats*, 25 March 1920, pp. 717–23. See also *The Times*, 30 March 1920 and 14 April 1920.

40. Barthou's role in the Caillaux–Calmette affair of 1914 is discussed more fully in my biography, *Power and Pleasure: Louis Barthou and the Third French Republic, 1862–1934* (McGill-Queen's University Press, 1991).

41. See his remarks as Foreign Minister to the Senate's Foreign Affairs Commission, 12 Nov. 1917, *Archives du Sénat*, p. 1052–4; 'L'année décisive de la paix', *Annales* (9 Jan. 1921), n.p.; 'De Bossuet à Briand en passant par Moscou', *Annales* (15 Jan. 1930), n.p.

42. *JO, Députés, Débats*, 25 March 1920, p. 723.

43. Barthou, 'Les vraies bases de l'Entente Cordiale', *Annales* (29 Aug. 1920), pp. 164–5; 'Les espérances françaises', *Annales* (1924), pp. 131–58, the translated text of which can be found in Crewe to FO, 27 Jan. 1924, Public Record Office, FO 371, 9730, C1516/32/18.

44. Eden to Simon, 18 Feb. 1934, *PRO* (Simon Papers), F0 800, p. 289. By 17 May Eden's appraisal had softened considerably, now describing Barthou as 'a foxy old gentleman who has certain affinities with D(avid) L-G(Lloyd George), ibid.; and then Earl of Avon, *The Eden Memoirs. Facing the Dictators* (London, 1962), pp. 108–9.

45. Barthou, *Le Traité de Paix*, p. 94; and his *Danton* (Paris, 1932), p. 336.

46. Barthou, 'Sur Anatole France', *Revue de France*, iii (May–June 1926), p. 606.

47. My own appraisal of Barthou's role at Genoa is very much in line with that initiated by Jean de Pierrefeu in *La Saison Diplomatique. Gênes (Avril–Mai 1922)* (Paris, 1928) and developed by Renata Bournazel, *Rapallo. Naissance d'un mythe* (Paris, 1974), pp. 151–74 and Stephen A. Schuker, *The End of French Predominance in Europe. The Financial Crisis of 1924 and the Adoption of the Dawes Plan* (Chapel Hill, 1976), pp. 205–7.

48. D'Abernon (Berlin) to Curzon, 9 Nov. 1922, PRO, FO 371, 7487, C 15606/99/18.

49. Lord Blanesburgh's testimonial to the retiring Barthou can be found in the minutes of 24 Aug. 1926, Series AJ5, Vol. 536, p. 9, *Archives Nationales*. This Series is the archive of the Délégation française à la Commission des Réparations.

50. Gustave Samazeuilh, 'Un hommage à Louis Barthou', *La République des Pyrénées*, 26 Nov. 1964, in the Collection Georges Coustel, *Bibliothèque municipale de Pau*.

51. Barthou 'Richard Wagner et Judith Gauthier (Documents inédits)', *Revue de Paris* (15 Aug. 1932), p. 740. See also 'Au retour de Bayreuth', *Cahiers de Radio Paris* (1930), pp. 577–83; 'Impressions de Bayreuth', *Les Annales* (1 Sept. 1930), pp. 193–5; 'Richard Wagner et Judith Gauthier', *Revue de Paris* (1, 15 Aug. 1932), pp. 481–98, 721–52; 'Richard Wagner cinquante ans après sa mort', *Les Annales* (10 Feb. 1933), pp. 153–5.

52. Barthou, *Promenades autour de ma vie*, pp. 27–8; 'Au Seuil du Nouveau Septennat', *Annales* (1 June 1931), pp. 509–10; 'Aristide Briand', *Annales* (15 March 1932), n.p.

53. Commission des Affaires étrangères, 2 March 1934, p. 16, *Assemblée Nationale*; *Le Temps*, 7 March 1934, p. 3.

54. Commission des Affaires étrangères, 9 May 1934, pp. 33–49, *Assemblée Nationale*. See also *JO, Chambre, Débats*, 25 May 1934, pp. 1261–2.

55. See, for instance, General Maurice Gamelin, *Servir* (Paris, 1946–1947), ii, p. 131. Barthou and Delcassé were both from the French south-west – Delcassé having been born in Pamiers in 1852, only ten years before Barthou. Both entered Parliament for the first time in 1889, and served together in the cabinets of Charles Dupuy in 1894–95.

56. Barthou, *A la mémoire de Delcassé. Discours à l'inauguration d'une plaque commémorative, le 3 octobre 1934*. (Paris, 1935); and Wladimir d'Ormesson, 'L'Intérêt Général', Oct. 1934,

unidentified press clipping, in 'Dossier Barthou', *BHVP*; Paul Bastid, 'La paix est blessée, *Vu* (numéro spécial, 12 Oct. 1934), n.p.

57.  See André François-Poncet, *Souvenirs d'une ambassade à Berlin* (Paris, 1946), pp. 175–6; Jules Laroche, *La Pologne de Pilsudski. Souvenirs d'une ambassade, 1926–1935* (Paris, 1953), p. 154; Jean Fabry, *De la Place de la Concorde au cours de l'Intendance* (Paris, 1942), p. 55; Geneviève Tabouis, *Vingt ans de 'suspense' diplomatique* (Paris, 1958), p. 171; François Piétri, 'Souvenir de Barthou', *Revue des Deux Mondes* (1 March 1961), p. 67; Pierre Etienne Flandin, *Politique Française, 1919–1940* (Paris, 1947), p. 72. Authorship of the Note is more fully discussed in my *Power and Pleasure: Louis Barthou and the Third Republic, 1862–1934.*

58.  Tabouis, *Vingt ans*, p. 171.

59.  See Tabouis, *Vingt ans*, p. 170; Maurice Vaïsse, 'Louis Barthou et la note du 17 avril 1934', in *Barthou, un homme, une époque*, edited by Michel Papy (Pau, 1986), pp. 167–72.

60.  For instance, see F. Kupferman, *Pierre Laval* (Paris, 1976), pp. 34, 38; J.B. Duroselle, 'Les milieux gouvernementaux français en face du problème allemand en 1936', in *La France et L'Allemagne, 1932–1936* (Paris, 1980), p. 377.

61.  Maurice Vaïsse, *Sécurité d'abord. La politique française en matière de désarmement, 9 décembre 1930–17 avril 1934* (Paris, 1981), p. 531.

62.  See Lord Robert Vansittart, *The Mist Procession* (London, 1958), p. 492; J.B. Duroselle, 'Les milieux gouvernementaux . . .', *La France et l'Allemagne*, p. 377; also *La Décadence, 1932–1939* (Paris, 1979), pp. 92–9.

63.  Barthou, 'Lettre-préface', *Catalogue des Livres de F.L. Schmied* (Paris, 1927), n.p.

64.  See the text of Barthou's interview with an Italian newspaper, as reproduced in *Le Temps*, 2 May 1926; also the text of Barthou's speech to the League, 5 June 1934, *Ministère des Affaires Etrangères*. Series S.D.N., Sous-Série II(Désarmement), Vol. 891, pp. 46–9 and Earl of Avon, *Facing the Dictators*, pp. 93–5.

65.  Barthou, *Lamartine. Orateur*, p. 147.

66.  Von Lersner (Geneva) to Berlin, 31 May 1934, *Documents on German Foreign Policy*, Series C, ii, no. 475, p. 859.

67.  Frohwein to General Schönheinz, 23 June 1934, ibid., iii, no. 31, p. 79.

68.  Commission des Affaires étrangères, 6 July 1934, p. 32, *Assemblée Nationale*.

69.  Barthou, 'Anatole France – *Les Dieux ont Soif'*, *Conférencia* (1 May 1933), p. 491; 'L'esprit de la politique', *Conférencia* (1 March 1933), p. 279.

# 'A Greater and a Higher Ideal': Esme Howard, Imperial Unity, and Canadian Autonomy in Foreign Policy, 1924–27

## B.J.C. McKERCHER

For my part I feel that Mr. King's ideal of a league of free and equal people is a greater and a higher ideal than that of a centralised Empire.

*Esme Howard, September 1924*[1]

During his tenure as British ambassador at Washington from 1924 to 1930, Sir Esme Howard played an important role in helping the Canadian government of William Lyon Mackenzie King achieve autonomy in conducting foreign policy.[2] Interestingly, Canadian historians who have written about this aspect of their country's development give the credit for this significant change in the intra-imperial relationship almost entirely to Canadian leaders. Largely ignored is any consideration of not only Britain's international position in the process that led to autonomy, but also the endeavours of British diplomatists like Howard. Yet the historical record shows that Howard and other British statesmen were fundamental to the process whereby Canada gained control over its own foreign policy. Howard was especially prominent, since the first Canadian permanent diplomatic mission in a foreign country was established at Washington in 1927.

Howard had had a lengthy connection with imperial affairs since his entry into the British diplomatic service in 1885. His work as a diplomat, plus labours for Britain in other ways, made him sympathetic to Canadian demands for autonomy in foreign policy after 1924 and

led him to assist Mackenzie King. Then, following the 1926 Imperial
Conference and the establishment of the Canadian Legation at
Washington early in 1927, Howard did what he could to aid Vincent
Massey, the newly appointed Canadian minister, in carrying out
Ottawa's directives in the American capital. Admittedly, there were
imperial diehards in Britain who arrogantly assumed that all parts of
the Empire should fall in line with foreign policy as dictated by
London, but they had been largely discredited by the Chanak crisis in
1922. Moderate men, at once more realistic and flexible in their
approach to imperial affairs, came to dominate the making and
execution of British imperial policy. Howard exemplified such
moderate thinking. He reckoned that loosening the ties binding the
dominions to Britain was the only means by which the Empire could
continue to exist in an increasingly difficult world. Thus Britain's
position as the only truly global power, the *sine qua non* for which was
the Empire, could be sustained. To ensure Britain's status as *the* world
power meant responding wisely to the new international order that had
been created at the Paris Peace Conference; an integral part of this
challenge involved responding to the determination of the dominions,
led by Canada and the Irish Free State, to make and implement their
own foreign policy. Put more crudely, it meant reacting wisely to
dominion desires not to be bound by a common imperial foreign policy
which might serve British interests more than those of the dominions.
Of course, Howard was not of primary importance in the success
enjoyed by the Canadians in getting control over foreign policy. This
reflected the endeavours of Canadian nationalists led by Mackenzie
King. But Howard played an important role in the process; hence it is
useful to revise the prevailing view that Canadian leaders were solely
responsible for achieving complete independence in the making of
Canada's foreign policy in the latter half of the 1920s.

   Canadian historians who have considered the autonomy question
have tended to look at the issue excessively from the perspective
of Canada. Reflecting the introspective nature of Canadian historiography, this tendency can most charitably be called the 'professional Canadian' view. It highlights the role of Canadian leaders and
their diplomatic initiatives in international history to such an extent
that the historical reality is distorted. In terms of the specific issue of
Canadian foreign policy autonomy, Canadian historiography is
marked by two constant threads: first, a narrow focus on the legal bases
of autonomy granted over several years; and, second, a conscious effort
to interpret past events so as to have them play into an on-going debate

about the nature and direction of Canadian foreign policy. Almost completely absent are considerations of inter-state power politics and the impact of personality and policy on the British side.

The focal point of this Canadian historiography is the towering political figure of Mackenzie King and the key role he played in the drive for Canadian foreign policy autonomy. The story is well-known.[3] He rose to power in December 1921 and for the next decade, except for a brief three months in opposition in 1926, controlled Canadian foreign policy as both Prime Minister and Minister of External Affairs. During his first ministry, he struggled with moderate success to distance his country from Britain – a key element of which is seen in Canada's concluding the 1923 Canadian–American Halibut Treaty without the counter-signature of a British diplomatic agent. But the 1926 interregnum between his two governments heightened his antipathy towards legal ties with Britain. In June of that year he asked the British governor-general, Lord Byng, for a dissolution of Parliament. Byng refused on constitutional grounds and instead asked the Conservative Party leader, Arthur Meighan, to form a ministry. Meighen failed, and Mackenzie King won the ensuing election in September. The dispute with Byng galvanized Mackenzie King into securing Canadian sovereignty in all political matters. Coupled with this, Mackenzie King's party, the Liberals, had its power base in Quebec. Here lay the essential political reality. In 1917 Canadian unity had been shaken when the Conservative government of Sir Robert Borden had introduced conscription, and anti-conscription riots had broken out in Quebec with a corresponding anti-Quebec backlash in English Canada; French-Canadians did not want to fight and die for Great Britain. This led Mackenzie King thereafter to oppose any notion of a common imperial foreign policy.

To involve Canada in international crises where Canadian interests were threatened was one thing, but to do so to defend those of Britain was quite another. Hence, Mackenzie King took every opportunity after 1921 to distance Canada from British foreign policy. The Canadian response to Chanak and the signature of the Halibut Treaty showed this. But it was his effort after the King-Byng dispute that caused the pace to quicken. Working primarily with the Irish Free State – which he had been doing since 1923 – Mackenzie King saw his dreams with regard to foreign policy realized at the 1926 Imperial Conference. At that time, bowing to dominion pressures, the British government through Lord Balfour, a former Prime Minister and respected imperial statesman, declared that Britain and each dominion were united by a common allegiance to the Crown but, collectively, they constituted a Commonwealth of autonomous nations. This meant that Britain and the dominions could pursue independent foreign policies. From this basis, Canada and the United States exchanged permanent diplomatic missions in 1927, followed soon after by similar Canadian exchanges with Japan and France. Moreover, Britain established a High Commission at Ottawa in 1928 to handle government to government relations, thereby reducing the governor-general to a powerless head of state. The next year, when an imperial gathering declared that the domestic legislation of British and Dominion Parliaments be considered equal in all ways, the final bonds restricting Canadian autonomy were sundered. Although Mackenzie King's second government fell from power in 1930, the promulgation of the so-called Statute of Westminster in 1931, giving legal status to all the gains made since 1926, was the end of a long and difficult road for the autonomists within the British Empire.

The debate among Canadian historians centres on Mackenzie King, and it breaks down into two schools of thought. The 'Liberal' school has elevated Mackenzie King and his efforts to distance Canada from the clutches of an imperial foreign policy to the point where he embodies all that is noble about the country's quest for diplomatic autonomy.[4]. Proponents of this school deride the Prime Minister's opponents of the time, chiefly the Conservative Party and pro-British members of his own government, for their desire to ensure that Canadian ties with the mother country were not damaged in any way. A corollary of this is the assertion that because of the key position of Quebec within the Canadian confederation (and not simply because it was the satrap of the Liberal Party), Mackenzie King and his supporters had at heart the true interests of a bicultural Canada. This school has reached new levels of character assassination in a recent study of twentieth-century Canada where three leading 'Liberal' historians have used the term 'moss-backs' to castigate those Canadians who wanted a strong imperial connection with Britain in the 1920s.[5]

Best labelled 'anti-Liberal', the other school encompasses both Conservative and left-wing historians who take issue with key elements of the 'Liberal' interpretation. Epitomized by the work of Donald Creighton, the Conservative view argues that Canadian independence from Britain conformed to the established pattern of the British Empire's constitutional development: a long, slow, and steady separation of the British and Canadian polities, of which the events of the 1920s were merely the culmination of more than a century of effort by a succession of leaders.[6] Although these historians do not necessarily see intimate Anglo-Canadian relations as being beneficial to Canada, they regard Mackenzie King's policies as simply the culmination of an inexorable movement of the northern dominion away from the economic, diplomatic, military, and political orbit of Britain. More telling, the Conservative school argues that the result of the way in which Mackenzie King broke the bonds with Britain led to increasing dominance of Canada by the United States. Thus, an element of anti-Americanism permeates 'Conservative' historiography, in which the legacy of British subjects who fled the new American Republic after the Revolutionary War and then played an integral part in Canada's subsequent economic, political, and social development is important. Left-wing critics of the 'Liberal' school have shorter historical vision than either of the other two strains of thought. While they seem always to have entertained anti-British views,[7] they have been concerned more with the increasing American dominance of Canada that has been a cultural, economic and political fact for Canadians throughout much of this century. The nub of this left-wing argument is that the Liberal Party of Canada has consistently pursued policies which, even if inadvertently, have pushed Canada firmly into the camp of the United States. This contention had particular importance during the Cold War and Vietnam war periods,[8] and it has not abated since the collapse of the Soviet Empire in Europe. For left-wing Canadians, Liberal foreign policy since Mackenzie King has supposedly denied Canada the ability to pursue an independent foreign policy – that is, a foreign policy that should be the antithesis of that pursued by the United States.[9]

At the present time, significant changes are occurring in Canadian foreign policy. A Conservative government in the 1980s moved to strengthen Canada's position in the western hemisphere by turning its back on Britain and Europe, concluding a free trade agreement with the United States, joining the Organization of American States, and reducing troop commitments to NATO. Arguments by the left-wing now attack economic alignment with the United States, and historical precedents are being exhumed to aid in this endeavour. For the same reasons, the 'Liberal' school now argues that the Liberal Party is and always has been suspicious of the United States. Indeed, in a recent study, the anglophobe doyen of Canadian 'Liberal' historians argues that historically, it was British weakness tied to Conservative not Liberal foreign policies that pushed Canada away from Britain and led to the forging of the firmer ties with the United States which have restricted Canadian sovereignty.[10] The past is being used to serve the present.

It follows that the 1920s are a watershed in terms of Britain, the Canadian drive for autonomy in foreign policy, and the intra-imperial relationship. However, thus far, little serious consideration has been given to the British side of the equation, especially to the role of the British ambassador at Washington in the success enjoyed by Canadian nationalists after 1924. That the shift in control over Canadian foreign policy-making was as benign and bloodless as it was derived not just from the skill of Mackenzie King and his advisers. In an important way, it also came from Howard. He not only shared Mackenzie King's convictions about 'a league of free and equal people', he also recognized that the Empire was changing and that Britain had to respond to this with reason and flexibility. That the Canadian question did not damage further already strained Anglo-American relations in the latter half of the 1920s – a more important foreign policy consideration for London – was as much a testament to Howard's skills and vision as it was to those of the men at Ottawa.

Howard came to Washington as British ambassador in February 1924 well-equipped to deal with the Canadian element in Anglo-American relations. Much of this derived from his character, which had been shaped during his youth. Born in 1863, he came from the landed gentry of northern England.[11] His father's family was a line of Howards descended from the dukes of Norfolk, who had been prominent in English politics and society since before the Tudors came to the throne. The Longs, his mother's family, had been founders of the English colony in Jamaica in the seventeenth century, while his maternal grandmother was a descendant of the important eighteenth-century Whig Prime Minister, Sir Robert Walpole. Although enamoured of country pursuits, horses and the hunt, his father was a hard-nosed businessman who had become wealthy in part by investing in railroads, the greatest development in nineteenth century industrial Britain. Through his father, Howard came to appreciate not only the traditions of his class, but also recognize that progress and change were inevitable and had to be faced squarely. In sharp contrast to his father, his mother had been raised in a literary family; in her early life she had travelled widely with her parents, living on the Continent and being exposed there to a range of different cultures. While she held firmly to her own beliefs, she was by all accounts an unpretentious, clear-thinking and considerate woman, tolerant of those whose opinions and ways of life differed from her own. Thus, Howard was the recipient of a rich family heritage and tradition, an appreciation for things modern, and the refined tastes of European, and not just English, culture. By the time he completed his education in the upper echelon of English public schools – Farnborough and Harrow – he possessed the background for diplomacy.[12] With three years studying languages in France, Germany and Italy – and languages proved to be his forte as he eventually spoke ten of them – plus a year in a London 'crammer', he passed stiff examinations and entered the diplomatic service in April 1885.

By the mid-1920s, Howard had emerged as one of Britain's leading ambassadors. His cultured background, lack of insularity and social grace were the basis of this achievement.[13] To these was added his expertise in the craft of diplomacy. His service had provided valuable lessons about the hard edge of foreign policy and how to use them effectively to protect Britain's position as a power of the first rank. The most important involved the absolute necessity of handling and assessing situations both cold-bloodedly and dispassionately. Only this could bring success. He also learnt how to represent British interests by handling difficult leaders with tact and sympathy, leaders whose backgrounds occasionally differed from his and whose countries' interests did not always parallel those of Britain. This does not imply that Howard toadied to his host governments. When the situation demanded that Britain's case be put forcefully, he never shirked his duty. During the Great War, for example, he assailed the pro-German Premier of neutral Sweden, Hjalmar Hammarskjöld, for the hypocrisy of the official Swedish criticism of British blockade policy. Hammarskjöld's arguments conveniently ignored Germany's violation of Belgian neutrality in 1914.[14]

Howard also came to understand completely the importance of national strength – economic, military, and political – in under-pinning foreign policy. The conviction that armed strength must support foreign policy strategies remained constant throughout his career. Britain could only remain a great power if it was willing to back its foreign policy with force; and, in the ultimate expres-sion of this attitude, this led him to endorse unreservedly the war against the central powers between 1914 and 1918, although he knew its terrible cost in lives and money. Finally, Howard's eminence as a diplomat came from a lesson he first took to heart in Bismarckian Germany: that, at times, it was essential to work with powers whose

internal policies were anathema to everthing in which liberal English-
men believed. This derived from the cold reality that Britain's foreign
policy interests sometimes coincided with those of such powers. Hence,
sentiment had no place in the pursuit of British foreign policy. By the
same token, Howard understood the corollary of this: British interests
did not necessarily parallel those of powers which shared the liberal
democratic outlook of Britain. In this way, Howard was an advocate of
Palmerston's famous adage that Britain had no eternal friends or
enemies, just eternal interests.

Howard's character, plus his success at mastering what he called
'the grammar of diplomacy', made him an admirable choice as
ambassador to the United States. In the post-1918 period, the United
States existed as the one great power that seemed able to threaten
seriously Britain's status as the only world power. The rise of the pro-
business Republican Party to national power in the 1920 elections –
taking the White House and both houses of Congress – heralded the
advent of a political leadership in the United States which endeavoured
consciously to ensure that the economic gains made during the war
were protected and expanded at British expense.[15] Subsequent
American efforts to collect war debts from Britain can be seen in this
light, as can the rising prominence of the aggressive economic and
financial nationalist, Herbert Hoover, the American secretary of
commerce after 1920.[16]

But more than this, both American trade and United States *amour-
propre* as a great power had suffered as a consequence of the successful
British blockade of the Central Powers from 1914 to 1917.
Conditioned by the teachings of Admiral Mahan, American navalists
began to demand 'a navy second to none' in the latter part of the war
and in the Peace Conference period.[17] At the Washington conference
of 1921–22, the Republican administration of Warren Harding
enjoyed a partial victory in this respect by achieving formal Anglo-
American parity in capital ships, those over 10,000 tons like
battleships, and aircraft carriers.[18] By early 1924, it seemed only a
matter of time before Washington moved to extend parity to vessels
below 10,000 tons. However, at the Washington conference, the
British had refused to limit such warships, especially cruisers, the main
maritime weapon for attacking and enforcing seaborne blockade.
When Howard arrived at the American capital in February 1924,
although the naval issue was eclipsed temporarily by other matters
centring on European security and American participation in the
reconstruction of the German economy via the Dawes Plan, the

question of Anglo-American naval limitation had yet to be resolved. These economic, financial, and naval issues all had an impact on whether Britain could remain the only truly global power. In all this, the American question impinged on the matter of the preservation of the Empire, especially the crucial problem of Canada. With increasing warmth developing in Canadian–American relations, seen graphically in the levels of American investment in the northern dominion, and with Mackenzie King working to torpedo any notion of a common imperial foreign policy in the aftermath of the Chanak crisis, the preservation of the imperial edifice assumed some urgency for British leaders.

This was particularly so for Howard for two reasons. The first concerned the formal position of the British ambassador in the Canadian–American diplomatic relationship. Although an autonomous dominion which possessed a foreign ministry – the Department of External Affairs – since 1909, Canada lacked diplomats serving abroad. There was a high commissioner at London and a commissioner general at Paris, but beyond this the British diplomatic service represented Canadian interests. This derived from a certain timidity among Canadian leaders about Canadian diplomats being involved in relations with other countries, as well as from the important matter of economy – the British did not charge Ottawa for handling Canada's diplomatic business.[19] Hence the British embassy at Washington handled Canadian affairs with the United States. This occurred in a byzantine fashion. The embassy would discuss issues with American officials and report on them to the Foreign Office. The Foreign Office would relay the information to the Colonial Office, then responsible for Dominion affairs. After deliberating, which might mean seeking additional information from the Washington embassy, the Colonial Office would contact the Canadian government through the governor-general at Ottawa. The reverse procedure also applied.

The second reason was more important, and it derived from Howard's view of the Empire and how best to ensure its unity in a changing world. Like the lessons he had learned in diplomacy, Howard's beliefs about the Empire were formed principally by experience. His initial exposure to imperial affairs came in his first posting after entering the diplomatic service. In this period, thanks to the efforts of his elder sister, the wife of the Earl of Carnarvon, he was seconded to the staff of the Viceregal Lodge at Dublin following his brother-in-law's appointment as viceroy of Ireland in June 1885. Although Howard's time in the Irish government proved to be brief, he imbibed heavily of the brand of imperialism championed by the viceroy.

Carnarvon had twice been Colonial Secretary, in 1866–67 and from 1874 to 1880; in his first tenure he had presided over granting Canada dominion status in 1867. He assumed responsibility for Irish affairs at a difficult moment. Supported by the majority of the Irish population, nationalists were demanding home rule from Britain; they were opposed by the Anglo-Irish gentry who, powerful within the Conservative Party at Westminster, were obstructing reform.[20] Carnarvon had to deal with this, and in so doing he helped expose Howard to the problems of imperial administration. Like other Victorians who believed strongly in the Empire as the *sine qua non* of British global power, Carnarvon reckoned that the Empire had to be preserved at all costs. But where most British leaders tended to see the Empire as a static entity, Carnarvon did not. It was a living organism that changed with time and new circumstances; hence, the purpose of British policy should be to recognise change and shape policy accordingly.[21] Consequently, Howard came to share his brother-in-law's belief in reform when resistance to legitimate grievances only spawned trouble.[22]

Moreover, Howard's ideas about maintaining the Empire involved more than just meeting the legitimate grievances of subject peoples. At the end of 1890, he had resigned from the diplomatic service because he felt that a career in diplomacy stifled his ambitions. He believed then that there were 'two great ideas at present in embryo in England. 1. the so-called "Federation of the Empire"[.] 2. State Socialism'.[23] What he wanted to do was 'to help in anyway – in the smallest way – to assist in the development of either or both of these'. Although he returned to diplomacy in 1903 – he had married by then and wanted to give his wife and family some security – he spent almost thirteen years pursuing the 'great ideas'. His focus came to rest on the Empire. In 1897, he helped form a syndicate to cultivate rubber in the West Indies. When it later became evident that rubber cultivation would be unprofitable, Howard bought out his partners and put the bulk of his fortune into a new effort to grow cocoa.[24] Even though he returned to the diplomatic service in 1903, he continued to work his plantation, through an on-site manager, until his death in 1939. The Empire had to be viable economically to survive. Consequently, Howard did not pontificate about the Empire: he did everything possible to strengthen it from within, putting all of his resources into the scales to do so.

More than this, when the Boer War broke out in 1899, Howard saw it as his duty to fight for the Empire. He had had previous experience in South Africa when, in 1891, he led a gold-prospecting expedition into Rhodesia.[25] His travels were edifying, allowing him to witness the greed of Cecil Rhodes' British South Africa Company which, in a classic expression of the desire for power without responsibility, wanted the protection of the British government but not its directions. This was balanced by several discussions with Rhodes and others in South African politics, which confirmed for Howard that sensible demands for change in imperial administration had to be met, but not to the extent that the Empire was weakened and the international equilibrium upset. Eight years later, following the Boer attack on the British colonies, Howard saw a vital economic and strategic region of the Empire threatened. Laying his life on the line, he willingly joined the fight and served with distinction in a 'yeoman' company.[26]

All of this shows that Esme Howard had wide experience with a variety of imperial questions before he took up his post at Washington in 1924. Conditioning his views about the Empire, these experiences were an important counterpoint to his skill in the craft of diplomacy. He did more than talk about imperial problems; he also did what he could to foster imperial unity, growth and development. Indeed, his imperialism reflected a belief that the British Empire, as much as possible, had to function as a single entity in international affairs if Britain's position as a global power was to be maintained.

Howard did not come to Washington unschooled in the Canadian question. As counsellor of the British embassy between 1906 and 1908, he had been charged with responsibility for handling the Canadian-American relationship;[27] the ambassador at the time, Sir James Bryce, had more pressing issues to tackle, all of which involved working to improve Anglo-American relations strained by a series of questions beginning with the Venezuela boundary dispute in 1895–96.[28] Trusting Howard completely, Bryce had given his subordinate a free hand in controlling policy relating to Canada. This was no easy task. Canadian relations with the United States had become embittered in the late 1890s over a boundary dispute along the Alaska panhandle. When London sided with Washington over this matter in 1903 to help ameliorate Anglo-American differences, Ottawa felt aggrieved.[29] Thus, Howard spent two years doing all possible to repair Anglo-Canadian relations while attempting to remove the bitterness between Canada and the United States caused by the Alaska boundary dispute and other outstanding problems like those over disputed fishing rights. By the time he left Washington in late 1908, Canadian relations with the two great English-speaking powers were on the mend. He had travelled several times to Canada, meeting with the political and financial elite in Toronto, Ottawa, and Montreal.[30] He had supported

Sir Wilfrid Laurier, the Liberal Prime Minister of Canada, on a range of issues involving the United States, chiefly North Atlantic fishing rights and tariff reciprocity. Crucially, Howard formed a friendship with a rising young Canadian civil servant, Mackenzie King, then a member of the Department of Labour, who had gone to Washington to settle problems involving Japanese immigration.[31] All of this meant that Howard had had experience with that byzantine bureaucracy that dominated Canadian relations with the United States and, just as important, had some idea about how the political life of Canada functioned. That he became friendly with Mackenzie King was an added benefit.

Upon arriving in Washington in 1924, Howard discovered that a range of Canadian–American issues needed resolution. These included the diversion of Lake Michigan waters southward to help the city of Chicago solve its water and sewage problems, the American desire to construct a seaway along the St Lawrence River to augment waterborne trade between the Atlantic to the Great Lakes, and the importing of bootleg Canadian liquor into the United States in defiance of prohibition.[32] Along with the need to ensure good Anglo-American relations, which had been undermined by the conduct of his predecessor, Sir Auckland Geddes, Howard found that the success of Bryce, who had left Washington in 1913, had been tarnished by more than a decade of inadequate British representation at the American capital. As a firm believer in Anglo-American amity, Howard had much to do. He immediately set about improving the British image in the United States. Building on the goodwill that had been recently engendered by the settlement of the British war debt to the United States and the afterglow of the Washington conference, Howard embarked on a series of public appearances and speeches.[33] This strategy of public engagements included visits to Canada. Within months of taking up his new post, he was preparing to visit Toronto, Ottawa, Montreal and Quebec City to meet with Canadian political, business and financial leaders, so as to learn first-hand of their concerns, and to assess the state of Anglo-Canadian relations for the Foreign Office.

Howard's Canadian trip, which lasted from 30 June to 9 July 1924, dealt with two issues. The first concerned improving Britain's image, which had been damaged by Geddes. George Wrong, a senior member of the History Department at the University of Toronto, was one of Howard's Canadian friends since his days in Bryce's embassy. In private correspondence before Howard's trip, Wrong told Howard candidly that Geddes had been a disaster because he 'did not really know Canada'.[34] Wrong elaborated:

[Canada] is in a state of mind like that of a young man just freed from parental control. He has a sensitive dignity and is suspicious that his full manhood may in some way be ignored. Geddes was not quick enough in sympathy to understand this. He kept saying publicly and privately that he could look after Canada's business at Washington and that a Canadian representative would be a fifth wheel in [*sic*] a coach.

According to Wrong, Geddes 'knew only Montreal and chiefly its English-speaking circle. This is very influential but it is a small minority in a French *milieu*'. Geddes had angered Canadian nationalists, mainly in Toronto, a city which Wrong admitted 'in some ways has a rather unpleasant and hyper-critical temper'. None the less, Geddes had blundered in such a way that a strong imperial connection, favoured by Wrong, had been shaken. Furthermore the tremors of discord started by Geddes had penetrated into Mackenzie King's office at Ottawa.[35]

The second issue involved Canadian representation at Washington. In 1921 a Canadian, Merchant Mahoney, had been appointed Canada's representative at the American capital. But while Mahoney had an office at the British embassy, he was an unofficial envoy with no formal standing with the State Department. Consequently, the advocacy of Canadian interests suffered. On top of this, the Canadian government had appropriated funds in 1921 to give official status to a Canadian representative, but successive ministries – the Conservatives under Meighen and the Liberals under Mackenzie King – had been reluctant to go ahead with the project because of the implications this had for separate representation in a foreign country.[36] Still, pressures were mounting in Canada to force Mackenzie King to raise the status of Canadian representation in Washington and, on 4 June 1924, Howard received a memorandum from Mahoney setting out the need for him to be recognized by the State Department as the official Canadian agent.[37] Seeing merit in this proposal, Howard warmly recommended it to Sir Eyre Crowe, the permanent under-secretary at the Foreign Office.[38] In the ambassador's view, Mahoney's elevation would reduce the embassy's workload while giving Canada increased status in official Washington. This would also help safeguard Canadian sensitivities which, with the massive amount of diplomatic work engendered from the purely Anglo-American relationship, were sometimes hurt. Howard referred to the fact that occasionally important Canadians came to the United States and, because the embassy knew nothing of their presence in Washington, they did not have easy access to the appropriate departments of the American government. To emphasize Mahoney's importance, thereby demonstrating British respect for Canadian opinion, Howard recommended that Mahoney be ranked immediately under the counsellor, the second-ranking British diplomat (an earlier effort to have a Canadian diplomat placed in the embassy above the counsellor had failed because of Canadian nationalist opposition to this diplomat speaking for the Empire whenever the ambassador was away).[39] But the important point here is that Howard recognized that the existing situation concerning Canadian representation could not continue. Crowe supported Howard but, unwilling to be seen dictating to Canada, wanted the initiative for such a change to come from Mackenzie King's government.[40]

This was the background to Howard's visit to Canada, which proved to be a ringing success in terms of cementing a firm Anglo-Canadian relationship within the confines of the Empire. In reporting on his mission, Howard acknowledged that the desire for improved representation in Washington consumed prominent Canadians.[41] This concern reached a peak when journalists in Ottawa queried Howard about his views on the matter: would separate Canadian representation lead to a separation of Canada from Britain and the Empire? Howard gave a frank response. As he told Ramsay MacDonald, the British Prime Minister and Foreign Secretary:

I stated that I did not see in the appointment of a Canadian Minister any tendency towards separatism. I said the advisability of such an appointment was one of which the Canadian Government was the best judge. So long as the Canadian Government desired me to look after Canadian interests at Washington it would be my duty, honour and pleasure to do so to the best of my ability. If later they considered the appointment of an envoy necessary, it would be my duty, honour and pleasure to assist him in any way that I could.

Howard had not spoken these words without consulting MacKenzie King and Lord Byng – he did not want to repeat Geddes's indiscretions. Both Prime Minister and governor-general supported Howard. This was critical because just at that moment the Canadian Parliament was debating whether to accede to the Lausanne Treaty, the treaty settling matters finally with Turkey. In addition, the Irish Free State had chosen to appoint its own representative to Washington.[42] The two issues were connected: an unfavourable British reaction to the dilatory attitudes of Canadian parliamentarians might push Mackenzie King into conforming precipitously to the Irish model. But Howard's realism helped defuse a difficult political issue in Canada. As Mackenzie King told him, 'in spite of the appointment of an Irish envoy, the question was for the moment in abeyance [in Canada], and indeed there does not seem at the present moment to be any great demand for it throughout the Dominion'.

In assessing privately his handling of this thorny question, Howard confided in Crowe.[43] Beyond what official Ottawa thought of his statement, which Howard characterized as 'quite frankly the way I feel about the question', he observed that the general Canadian reaction was quite positive. He even quoted from a letter he had received from Wrong which reported that Canadian press and parliamentary opinion, especially among extreme nationalist MPs, had been decidedly supportive.[44] It seemed that as long as Howard held such views, Canadian interests might best be represented by the British ambassador in Washington. Howard had pushed the memories of Geddes's unfortunate showing sufficiently into the shadows, so that Britain's image in Canada had improved. Imperial unity had been protected and, even if Mackenzie King later reversed himself and pressed for separate Canadian representation at Washington, legitimate Canadian desires for foreign policy autonomy would be received favourably by the British ambassador.[45]

Howard unexpectedly encountered two other issues on his Canadian tour which indicated that leaders in both English and French Canada worried about external problems affecting the economic and social fabric of the country.[46] The first centred on the high levels of American investment in the dominion. Even in Quebec, Louis Alexander Taschereau, the nationalist Premier, decried American investment as designed less to help Canada and more to increase exports, including hydroelectric power, southwards. As Howard remarked to MacDonald, 'the general feeling was that they would be far more satisfied to see this development carried out by English capital and with the object of increasing the industrial production of Canada herself'. Such concerns fitted in with Howard's established views that the Empire would underpin British foreign policy effectively only if it was strong economically. This required a commitment from British and other imperial investors to put their money into Canadian industrial development. The second issue involved the need to get 'more immigrants of the right class from the British Isles'. In this, as in the matter of investment, Howard reported that Canadian leaders wanted 'so far as possible, cooperation between the Dominion and the

Home Government in order to secure the best results for both'. Although Howard subsequently found it difficult to meet Canadian desires on both these issues,[47] he did what he could to support Canadian endeavours.

However, Howard's Canadian trip in 1924 led him to state his beliefs publicly in the United States about the Empire. Canadian opinion had to be reassured about his role in the diplomacy of the North Atlantic triangle. Just as crucial, as many Americans were wary of the Empire's power in international affairs, he must give consideration to wider international questions in which Britain and the United States were fundamentally concerned. For these reasons, and because the American presidential-congressional elections, scheduled for November 1924, meant that foreign policy issues touching Britain were certain to be ventilated, Howard took the opportunity of an invitation to speak in mid-September 1924 to the British Empire Club at Providence, Rhode Island, to put his views about the Empire on the public record.

In this speech, he sought to show that he was at one with Canadian nationalists while, at the same time, indicating to his American audience that although the Empire remained as strong as ever, it posed no threat to the United States. A month earlier, the Canadian Prime Minister had spoken at Toronto about the evolving Empire, and Howard used verbatim Mackenzie King's thesis as the basis of his remarks:

The essential feature of the Imperial situation today is the transformation of what was formerly an Empire in the all [that is, universal] sense with a central Government in complete and unquestioned control over the subordinate colonies and plantations overseas, into a league of free and equal nations. The transformation is now practically complete in domestic affairs. It has gone far, though not so far, in foreign affairs.[48]

Howard thus indicated his unabashed support of Mackenzie King's 'ideal of a league of free and equal people' as 'a greater and higher ideal than that of a centralized Empire'. Importantly, however, such a league was not a distant goal: it was increasingly a hard fact of international life. Those who did not see this were 'foolish and mistaken', especially those in Britain who 'love to look at a map of the world and see the areas that are coloured red forming parts of the Empire, who like to think of the sun never setting and so on'. A new era in diplomacy had begun with both the Allied victory in the Great War and the Paris Peace settlement, and the latter, Howard emphasized, had seen separate dominion representation in the British Empire Delegation. While not hiding the fact that difficulties had arisen in the intra-imperial relationship since the war, Howard argued that these were being eliminated by London's desire to meet the legitimate demands of nationalists within the Empire. On this basis, he reckoned that the Empire would survive in the altered form advocated by Mackenzie King. In a veiled attack on anglophobe elements in the United States, he also deprecated those who saw the changes under way within the Empire as portending its break-up. The only result of a break-up would be a destabilization of the global balance of power, something that would assuredly be inimical to American interests. Accordingly, Howard advocated increased co-operation between the changing British Empire and the United States. To underscore this he pointed out that the Dawes Committee discussions, then reaching fruition at London, showed how the British Empire and the United States could work together successfully to resolve a fundamentally important international crisis, in this case the economic reconstruction of Germany.[49]

Judging from the publicly expressed favour with which well-placed Canadians like Wrong greeted Howard's speech, the ambassador had done much to reassure nationalists in Canada that he would not block *à la* Geddes their efforts to get a fair hearing in either London or Washington.[50] The specific impact of his words in the United States, on the other hand, is more difficult to gauge. The Providence speech was one of 16 that Howard made in his first year as ambassador in order to improve Britain's image in the United States. That a lack of critical comment about his views on the Empire appeared in the American press can be taken as suggesting that Americans were also reassured. On one occasion in his first year, when he explained the policies of the British Labour government about normalizing relations with Bolshevik Russia, he was attacked by an American anti-communist group which mistakenly believed that he also advocated United States recognition of the Russian regime.[51] But along with his other speeches, which were favourably received by general American opinion,[52] the absence of press criticism concerning his ideas about the Empire and its relationship with the United States suggests that the Providence speech found acceptance in powerful quarters in the United States. That American politicians, embroiled in the 1924 election campaign, did not seek to score easy points on this matter with voters by exploiting the latent anglophobia present in their country,[53] says even more.

Although issues concerning the evolving Empire failed to excite

American politicians at that moment, those touching naval questions did not. To improve his party's sagging fortunes, the Democratic presidential candidate, John Davis, made scathing comments about how British naval power vastly exceeded that of the United States because the Republicans, in office during the Washington conference, had sold out American naval interests.[54] This came to naught, as the Republican Party, under Calvin Coolidge, retained control of the White House and both houses of Congress. But following his inauguration in March 1925, Coolidge indicated a desire to call a second Washington conference to extend limitation to warships under 10,000 tons. This immediately affected Canada and the other dominions. The Americans seemed prepared to send only a single invitation to Britain and the other imperial governments, a function of the American argument that the naval forces of the entire British Empire had to be counted as a single unit in any extension of the Washington treaty. If accepted by British and dominion statesmen, this American argument would erode the gains made by Mackenzie King and others about there being no common Imperial foreign policy.

From April to October 1925, the possibility of a second Washington conference and its implications for Canada impinged on Howard's diplomacy. Ultimately the chance for such a conference evaporated when, in the summer of 1925, the League of Nations called for a general disarmament conference to deal with land, air and sea weapons. To produce a draft treaty as the basis for negotiation, a Preparatory Commission was established. Upstaged by these events, the Coolidge administration abandoned separate naval talks and joined the League endeavour. But, despite, the stillborn American initiative, Howard's handling of the issue of dominion representation showed his continuing support for the Canadian quest for foreign policy autonomy.

When American diplomatic feelers were put out just before Coolidge's inauguration about the possibility of holding naval talks, Mackenzie King's government informed London that Canada would attend only if it received a separate invitation.[55] For a variety of reasons, a quick decision by authorities at Whitehall was delayed on both the matter of separate invitations and the more pressing question of whether Britain would attend. A Conservative ministry under Stanley Baldwin had taken office in November 1924; it was then in the midst of reforming the Colonial Office by splitting off those departments responsible for dominion affairs and creating a Dominions Office. Thus, legal opinions on the matter of separate invitations were slow in coming.[56] Second, and perhaps more important, the new Foreign Secretary, Austen Chamberlain, had become enmeshed in delicate manoeuvres to create a regime for European security by reconciling Franco-German differences in western Europe – the Locarno negotiations.[57] As a central feature of Chamberlain's strategy involved using the League as a mechanism to bring the French and Germans together, the Foreign Secretary wanted to give the international organization as much influence as possible in the European settlement. Supporting naval talks in Washington might endanger this aim because the League would be bypassed in arms limitation. Not surprisingly, when a League-sponsored general disarmament conference seemed likely, Chamberlain saw that as a better method of protecting British security.[58]

Howard knew of these developments,[59] but this did not restrain him from doing what he could to assist the autonomist bent of the Mackenzie King government and promote good Anglo-American-Canadian relations. On 28 April 1925, Howard spoke with quiet force before the Canadian Society of Washington on the improvement of American relations with the dominions, particularly Canada.[60] At this moment, the American Pacific fleet was sailing on a goodwill mission to Australia and New Zealand. Actions like this, Howard stated, could only improve relations between the United States and the 'great democracies of the Southern Seas'. But because Canada and the United States were contiguous, 'special and continual demonstrations of friendship' like the Fleet visit did not have to be undertaken. As he had done at Providence, he laid out the need for increased co-operation between Britain and its dominions, on one hand, and the United States, on the other. 'The bond between us is all the stronger because it is a voluntary bond, a simple straightforward bond as between friends,' Howard remarked. 'The greater the friendship, therefore, not only between the Britishers of Great Britain and the United States of America, but also between the more distant parts of the Great British Commonwealth and the United States, the better we are pleased.' Howard chose his words wisely. He spoke of the 'Commonwealth' not the 'Empire', the latter term having been exorcised from Mackenzie King's lexicon. Just as crucial in the wider diplomatic sense, he reaffirmed the need for pan-Anglo-Saxon collaboration, and he left no doubt that, as far as British statesmen like him were concerned, American closeness to the dominions was not perceived as a threat to imperial unity. Hence, the United States could work as closely with the dominions as it did with Britain on matters like naval limitation. It is not surprising that a copy of Howard's speech reached Mackenzie King.[61]

But public speaking needs to be supported by action. Behind the scenes, Howard did what he could to influence the dilatory debate in London. Knowing the general thrust of Foreign Office–Colonial Office thinking that separate representation had to occur – the difficulty hinged on the legal method of doing so – Howard suggested that, as the ambassador at Washington, he could accept any American invitation in the name of Britain and its Empire. This could then be sent to London for separate despatch to the dominion capitals.[62] Nothing revolutionary would come from such a procedure, nor would any new legal precedent be established, since, as Howard pointed out, this was precisely how he handled issues in Canadian–American relations all of the time. While the Foreign Office found nothing to quarrel with in this suggestion, the new Dominions Office dithered; it wanted direct consultations with Howard, scheduled to be on leave in Britain in late September.[63]

On 8 October 1925 Howard and Robert Craigie, a senior member of the Foreign Office American Department, met with the assistant secretary of the Dominions Office, Harry Batterbee.[64] The three men agreed that Howard's earlier proposal of a general invitation channelled through his embassy would be followed should the Americans not agree to issue separate ones. However, should the Coolidge administration accept the notion of separate invitations, the Dominions Office wanted these to come from the American ambassador in London, thus conforming to a precedent established at the time of the Genoa conference in 1922. In this meeting the sensitivities of the ministry responsible for dominion affairs – the new Dominions Office – were balanced by the diplomatic requirements of the man on the spot – Howard. Howard had done much to protect Canadian interests in Washington and London, giving the Mackenzie King government no cause to complain. The principle of separate invitations to the dominions had been protected, and a strategy to enforce it, especially if the Americans later refused to follow the Genoa precedent, had been determined.

For most of the next twelve months, Howard's handling of the Canadian question reverted to more mundane aspects of day-to-day diplomacy. This involved asserting Canadian claims to sovereignty in areas where an American expedition to the North Pole contemplated crossing the Canadian Arctic, observing the progress of Canadian–American fisheries negotiations held in Washington, and monitoring problems between Canada and the United States over territorial waters in the Great Lakes and along the St Lawrence River.[65] Howard had nothing to do with the only major Anglo-Canadian diplomatic problem that arose at this time: Canadian unwillingness to sign the Locarno treaty.[66] Mackenzie King's government saw no Canadian interests involved and only future danger in joining with Britain to guarantee the Franco-Belgian-German border.[67] As the diplomacy of this question centred on Ottawa and London, the Washington embassy was bypassed. More important, Howard had much to handle in terms of the Anglo-American relationship, chiefly an American presentation of claims against Britain arising out of its blockade of the Central Powers during the Great War.[68] Howard and the Foreign Office set out to resolve the problem in Britain's favour. Success came only in May 1927.

None of this means that Howard ignored the need to keep Mackenzie King reassured about the goodwill of the British embassy and its resolve to aid Canada in its foreign policy endeavours. He demonstrated this commitment in two ways. On a personal level, Howard reinforced his friendship with the Canadian Prime Minister by sending him a copy of Carnarvon's biography when it appeared in late 1925. Howard hoped that 'the facts about Canada may perhaps interest you'.[69] At the official level, Howard made another visit to Canada in late April and early May 1926. Mackenzie King's diary leaves no doubt that he worried about the negative effect created by the assertion of Canada's independence in foreign policy.[70] Drawing on all his skill as a diplomat, Howard allayed Mackenzie King's unease in two private conversations. As Mackenzie King observed:

The conversation, which lasted an hour or more[,] left one with the feeling that relations between Canada & U.S. (excepting the diversion problem) were all that could be desired, and that so far as Grt. Britain was concerned[,] Sir Esme was quite satisfied as to our attitude on all questions.

Even on the matter of Canada rejecting a role in the Locarno agreements, Howard soothed Mackenzie King's anxieties. 'I also spoke of our attitude towards Lacarno [sic] agreement. Sir Esme said he thought we were right not to become a party, when U.S. was not, he saw the position quite clearly'.

Sensing that Mackenzie King needed additional reassurance that the embassy at Washington would continue to do all in its power to aid Canada in resolving its differences with the United States, Howard

took the initiative and asked the Canadian Prime Minister to send him
Ottawa's views privately about the chief problems in Canadian-
American relations.[71] After reading them, Howard confided in
Mackenzie King that 'I feel sure that they will be extremely helpful to
us'.[72] Howard subsequently used them in his diplomacy with the
Coolidge administration.[73] Thus, in terms of both his personal and
official relationships with Mackenzie King, he showed that he was
doing everything possible to promote Canada's interests in the United
States. Such consideration was part and parcel of the *realpolitik* of
keeping British interests protected in the North Atlantic triangle.

Howard sought to explain this to Chamberlain in reporting on his
trip to Canada.[74] Canadian leaders, including those in Quebec who saw
Britain as a bulwark protecting its liberties, still worried about eventual
annexation by the United States. Admittedly, some Canadians, mainly
those in the Prairie Provinces who saw the United States as essential to
their economic prosperity and whose population contained a 'number
of American farmers and foreign immigrants who naturally have no
sentiment for the Empire', supported closer ties with the Americans.
Howard reported that Mackenzie King and other leaders believed 'the
best and only way to discourage a tendency to desire annexation is to
foster and promote a feeling of pride in Canadian nationality'. But
narrow British policies, which Canadians might perceive as keeping
their country in a position of political inferiority to Britain, would only
increase pro-Americanism in Canada. Although he did not say so, the
delay and obstruction that marked Dominion Office handling of
separate invitations to a new Washington conference could be
construed in that way. Realism about the Canadian question had to be
the order of the day in London:

If [the Canadians] want to give up the appeal to the Privy Council why not let
them? If they think it matters to them to make a change in their national flag so
as to make it more national, why worry? If they think it important to be
diplomatically represented outside the Empire, why pull a wry face? The
important thing is really to build up a national local feeling in the Dominions
and to let them know that we approve.

If political leaders in Britain, Howard went on, wanted to preserve
the imperial connection, conceding equal status to Canada and the
other dominions which shared the same views would be helpful. The
nub of Howard's letter was to inform his superiors at London that this
was how he intended to handle the Canadian question as long as he
remained ambassador at Washington.

His admonition to Chamberlain proved to be timely, because the summer and autumn of 1926 became a watershed for Canada and the intra-imperial relationship.[75] Just as Howard wrote, the King–Byng dispute erupted, precipitating the political crisis that rocked Canada until the general election in September returned the Liberals with a majority. This result, claimed Mackenzie King, embodied a mandate to force a major constitutional change in Canada's status within the Empire. Coming just before the 1926 Imperial Conference, which began in London on 19 October, it set the stage for the Canadian Prime Minister and his allies, chiefly the Irish Justice Minister, Kevin O'Higgins, to press the British to concede formally that each independent government within the 'Commonwealth' had a right to pursue its own foreign policy. Success came during the conference when Balfour made his famous statement to that end, the critical passage stating that the dominions were 'autonomous communities within the British Empire, equal in status, in no way subordinate to one another in any aspect of their domestic or external affairs, though united by a common allegiance to the Crown, and freely associated as members of the British Commonwealth of Nations'.[76] In addition, by the time of the Imperial Conference, a significant change had occurred within the Canadian foreign-policy-making elite. A year earlier, Oscar Skelton, a leading Canadian academic, the biographer of Mackenzie King's hero, Laurier, and a staunch nationalist, had been appointed under-secretary of state in the Department of External Affairs. A protégé of the Prime Minister, Skelton appears to have been instrumental in stiffening Mackenzie King's resolve to push for increased autonomy in Canadian foreign policy, a crucial influence when one considers Mackenzie King's fear of offending the British. No doubt existed after the Imperial Conference that Skelton would continue pressing for as much foreign policy independence as Ottawa could grasp following the Balfour Declaration. The net result of all of this was that, as 1926 drew to a close, the devolutionists within the Empire, with Mackenzie King somewhere near their head, had accomplished a great deal. Howard's handling of the Canadian question entered a new phase.

Earlier in 1926, rumours surfaced that the Mackenzie King government intended to go through with the long-anticipated move of establishing a separate Canadian diplomatic establishment at Washington.[77] During his Ottawa visit in April and May, Howard had told Mackenzie King that he knew of these rumours; presaging what he later told Chamberlain, Howard indicated to Mackenzie King that

neither the embassy in Washington nor the government in London
had difficulty with this Canadian move – that had been made clear
to Howard during the discussions about a possible second Washington
naval conference in 1925. All Howard desired as Britain's
representative was that Canada did not act precipitately. As
Mackenzie King noted in his diary: '[Howard] seemed interested in
knowing what was probable in way of Canadian representation at
Washington, he welcomed it cordially . . . the only request he made
was to see that the Br. Govt. were informed of the step in advance, and
our representative accredited in the same manner as the Irish Rep. had
been'.[78]
    Mackenzie King's quarrel with Byng and the constitutional issue it
spawned – which the Liberals exploited to full advantage in the
election campaign to deflect charges of scandal made by their
opponents – led him finally to seek for the appointment of a Canadian
minister at Washington. The first breath of this came within days of the
election with unconfirmed press reports that Massey, a defeated
Liberal Cabinet minister, would be chosen.[79] There then ensured
intricate discussions in London over the next three months about the
precise ways to achieve this goal. Using his presence at the Imperial
Conference to show his determination in the matter, Mackenzie King
was ready to proceed once Balfour made his declaration. On the
British side, the Foreign Office, pulling the Dominions Office along,
wanted to ensure that the precedent established by the 1924
appointment of the Irish Free State minister was applied to the
Canadian case. A key element in the Foreign Office's concern involved
the necessity of the two dominion representatives having the same title:
the Irish had opted for a minister plenipotentiary; but the Canadians
wanted an envoy extraordinary and minister plenipotentiary. While
the United States government did not set much store by such titles,
those of the other powers did. A precedent established in Washington
where British and Canadian diplomats both served might later impair
British representation in other capitals. Should dominion ministers
later be appointed in those places with ranks higher than senior British
diplomats *en poste*, the power of these diplomats might be reduced.[80]
But this amounted to a procedural question, much as did the method
by which the monarch should grant approval of Massey's appointment
and the means of informing the Coolidge administration of Canadian
intentions and then securing American agreement to the Canadian
nomination.[81]
    The substance of the Canadian decision remained more important

and preoccupied Howard, since it touched on the relationship which he and his successors would have with the Canadian legation. The reality of the situation was that Mackenzie King had simply made operative a policy that had been pending for half a dozen years and which Whitehall had endorsed even before Howard took the Washington embassy. As Howard had spelled out to Chamberlain in May, no advantage would accrue to Britain by pulling 'a wry face' at the justified action of an autonomous dominion. He saw clearly that if British and imperial interests were to be maintained in North America and the wider world, which meant a strong Canada working with Britain within the Empire and resisting Americanization as much as possible, a sound working relationship between British and Canadian diplomats had to be created in Washington. Howard had learnt earlier in his career that the personal side of diplomacy set the tone for an effective ambassadorship.[82] On top of this, Geddes's blunders had shown the resentment that could be caused by British failure to countenance Canadian sensitivities. Howard consequently decided that he must show Mackenzie King and men like Skelton that the Washington embassy would promote Canadian interests whenever it could. This would not mean giving unsolicited advice or interfering in whatever diplomacy Mackenzie King, through Massey, decided to pursue. Rather, it would mean giving unreserved support when asked. And with other issues in Anglo-American relations surfacing – the blockade claims question and, with the Preparatory Commission dead-locked by Anglo-French differences, the Coolidge administration's preference for separate naval talks – Howard's energies would have to be directed elsewhere.

On leave in Britain during the Imperial Conference, Howard spoke with Mackenzie King privately to demonstrate that he would support whatever the Canadian government sought in its establishment of a legation in Washington.[83] At the same time, both in London and when he returned to the United States, Howard conferred with Chamberlain over how best he, as ambassador, should handle Massey's presentation of his credentials. This led to a difference of opinion between them which, though it proved to be relatively minor and was resolved in Howard's favour, exposed Howard's resolve to avoid Geddes's misadventures. The problem centred on Howard's role in the presentation. Chamberlain had been told by Mackenzie King that the Canadian government would like Howard to accompany Massey, which Chamberlain agreed would be 'a courtesy' but 'not as a right or privilege asserted by us'.[84] About this there was no disagreement.

However, the Foreign Secretary wanted the minimum of fuss, which translated into having Howard inform the State Department that he would accompany Massey to the White House to present his letters of appointment to Coolidge.[85] Howard saw danger in this which could damage Canadian self-esteem. He wanted to consult with the State Department on its desires and then co-ordinate with Massey, who had latitude in this matter from Mackenzie King. Obviously, Howard wanted to do something that would not only demonstrate in Washington the extent of imperial solidarity then and there, but also establish a binding precedent for the future.[86] He won the day over Chamberlain's objections and, more important, garnered the support of the Dominions Office and the Foreign Office American department for future accreditations.[87]

When Massey arrived in Washington in mid-February 1927, no impediments existed to block the smooth transition in the handling of affairs with the United States. Both Howard's reports and Massey's memoirs emphasize this; they also show that imperial unity had not been weakened in any way.[88] Massey's memoirs are particularly telling. He relates how Howard's management of his official arrival in Washington, with embassy members and the Irish minister present at the train station, showed 'the solidarity of the British Empire' as the transition process began. This was further underscored by the arrangements that the ambassador had worked out concerning the credentials ceremony. On 18 February, the American chief of protocol invited Massey to come on his own to the White House. There he met Howard, who had arrived earlier and separately, and together the three men were ushered into a meeting with Coolidge. The chief of protocol then introduced Massey as 'the Canadian Minister, accompanied by His Britannic Majesty's Ambassador'. While Howard had nothing to do either with summoning Massey to the White House or with the official ceremony, his being there showed Britain's silent support for the new minister. Massey appreciated the symbolism: Canada was achieving its rightful place as an independent state *within* the Empire. As he had explained in a letter to Howard in January when the latter was co-ordinating the presentation of credentials: 'I myself should be most grateful for your presence on this occasion which, as a matter of fact, will symbolise the invaluable support you are giving your junior colleague during his initiation, and for which he will always be most grateful.'

On 18 February 1927, a new era in the diplomacy of the North Atlantic triangle began. For Canadian nationalists like Mackenzie

King, it meant that their assertion of increased independence within the confines of the Empire was bearing fruit even while imperial unity, the best protection against Americanization of the country, remained as firm as ever.[89] For British leaders, the Empire had not been weakened externally – an essential political element in Britain's status as the only global power – while internal modifications had been made with care and caution.[90] The Americans understood that Britain intended to support Canada to the best of its ability, something expressed tangibly in the excellent personal relationship existing between the British ambassador and the Canadian minister.[91] In this, Howard's skill shone through. He had balanced between Ottawa and London since the September 1926 Canadian election, as he had done before, and he had made certain that imperial solidarity would not be weakened by Canada's assertion of its legitimate rights. Massey's retrospective assessment explains his key role:

As a professional diplomatist with a long and distinguished career, [Howard] conformed to the highest traditions of his Service but had an imagination that enabled him to understand and accept the changes that were taking place, one of which was, of course, the establishment of the Canadian legation in Washington. His view and mine about this innovation were identical. We both felt that the Canadian mission in Washington, far from impairing the diplomatic unity of the Empire, could strengthen it and produce an even greater solidarity.[92]

The establishment of the Canadian legation at Washington proved to be fortuitous for Howard. Eight days before Massey presented his credentials, Coolidge issued invitations for naval limitation talks, the idea being that any agreement by the great naval powers could be foisted on the seemingly moribund Preparatory Commission.[93] Britain and Japan joined with the United States to this end at Geneva from June to August 1927. But this conference failed, and the failure so embittered Anglo-American relations that, until the advent of the London naval conference in January 1930, they constantly threatened to rupture. During this time, Howard found himself increasingly directing his energies to keeping relations running smoothly between the two English-speaking powers. That Howard could devote his attention more fully to Anglo-American rather than Anglo-Canadian relations came in part from the establishment of the Canadian legation and his good personal and working relationship with Massey. Howard estimated that one-third of his and the embassy's time before February 1927 was consumed by handling Canada's relations with the United

States.[94] As both he and Massey later recorded, Howard was genuinely relieved at being able to hand this aspect of the embassy's responsibilities over to the Canadian minister and his staff.[95] But this was not merely a question of fobbing off work. As Howard had argued since February 1924, if the Canadians wanted to take on such tasks, they should be encouraged to do so. The arrangement conformed to the expectations of Canadian nationalism; and it was fashioned within an evolving imperial relationship that seemed to gather added strength as the decade progressed.

Despite his more pressing problems, Howard did not ignore Canadian concerns after February 1927. He saw it as his duty to support Massey in Washington and Mackenzie King in Ottawa whenever the need arose. He did this, however, only when asked. When Coolidge, for instance, issued invitations to the powers for separate naval talks, Canada and the other dominions were included with Britain in a general invitation to the British Empire. Howard stood aside while Mackenzie King and his advisers worked successfully with the Irish Free State to get what amounted to individual dominion invitations.[96] Along the same lines, the Washington embassy remained aloof from Canadian–American exchanges on territorial waters, the St Lawrence seaway, and those other unresolved questions.[97] The Canadians had to earn their diplomatic spurs, and it would profit Britain nothing for Howard and his staff to involve themselves unasked in these matters.

Indeed, one of Howard's arguments before February 1927 held that if Canadians were allowed to manage their country's relations with the United States, the imperial connection would become stronger. Evidence of this came by August 1927. In a letter to a colleague at the Foreign Office, John Balfour, the first secretary at the embassy, explained the situation:

As regards the general relations between the U.S.G. and the Legation in particular and Canada in general: it is not uninteresting to observe that the assumption by the Canadians of the task of carrying on their own diplomatic affairs with the great and glorious U.S.A. has the [?real] advantage of bringing home to them the fact that dealings between the two great North American countries are not all beer and skittles. Thus I never meet Beaudry [first secretary, Canadian legation] without his [?having] some minor grouse or other about the difficulty of getting the U.S. authorities to see eye to eye with Ottawa's wishes. . . .[98]

Such attitudes on the part of the Canadians boded well. 'These foolish little straws shew that the wind does not blow Canada consistently in the direction of the U.S.A.', Balfour added, 'and I personally am not particularly fearful that closer relations between Canada and the U.S.A. will necessarily involve a weaning of the former's allegiance to the imperial connection.'

Of course, when Canadian–American issues touched British interests, Howard acted. As the Coolidge conference ended in failure, Baldwin and the Prince of Wales were on an official visit to Canada. When it was discovered that the American vice-president, Charles Dawes, was to attend the opening ceremonies at the new Peace Bridge joining Canada and the United States at Buffalo, New York, Howard ensured that the British party and Mackenzie King attended.[99] Anglo-American relations could be further damaged if anglophobe elements in the United States were able to portray the absence of the British party and a Canadian delegation as an official snub of the Coolidge Administration. Also, later in 1927, both Mackenzie King and Lord Willingdon, the new governor-general, made separate visits to the United States on goodwill missions. Howard ensured that these went off without a hitch so that the British image in the United States did not suffer.[100] Mackenzie King appreciated Howard's efforts in this regard, and his positive attitude towards the Canadian legation. Mackenzie King sent him warm Christmas greetings and enclosed a copy of a new book he had just published.[101] The Willingdon visit did create some difficulty, because of King George V's discomfiture at Mackenzie King's desire for Willingdon to be treated in the United States as Canada's head of state rather than as the King's viceroy.[102] As Howard later explained to the disgruntled monarch:

Our policy if we want to hold the Empire together is, I think, to encourage the national feeling in the Dominions in every way we can. To do this we have ourselves to recast our old ideas about the Empire based on the fundamental conception of a Mother country, head of the house and still ruler in it, and a number of minors not yet completely of age. We must rather take as our pattern a firm in which the father has taken his sons into partnership and allows them an equal say in the household.[103]

Howard subsequently ensured that Canadian self-esteem was preserved during Willingdon's sojourn in the American capital, with very positive results for both Anglo-Canadian and Canadian-American relations.[104] When he retired in 1930, Howard left Anglo-American relations and the Anglo-American-Canadian triangle better than he found them.

It follows that the historiography of the autonomy question needs to be revised. While no one doubts that the lion's share of the credit for the change in the intra-imperial relationship in the 1920s, at least as far as Canada is concerned, should go to Mackenzie King, it is undeniable that British officials like Howard deserve their due.[105] The problem at the time for Howard and others who implemented British foreign and imperial policy was not whether Canada and the other dominions should have more autonomy over their external relations. If the British Empire had any chance of survival, and especially after Chanak, then those responsible for the myriad facets of imperial policy within the British government had to approach policy-making with reason and flexibility. Imperial policy could not be made in a vacuum. A new international order had been created at the Paris Peace Conference. Matters affecting the Empire, just like those influencing other concerns of British external policy, had to be pursued with a wider perspective. This was the case concerning the Canadian drive for autonomy in foreign policy. It concerned more than just the Anglo-Canadian relationship. It touched the rest of the Empire and, more telling, it affected Britain's relationship with other great powers like the United States. It might be true, as the doyen of Canadian 'Liberal' historians moans, 'that British historians, like British politicians, fail to understand Canada and Canadians'[106] – although Massey certainly did not think this of Howard. It is probably more true that Canadian historians fail to understand Britain and the British. Canadian politicians, at least Mackenzie King and Skelton, were more perceptive.

Consequently, 'professional Canadian' historiography needs to be less parochial; it needs to appreciate the position of Canada in the context of the past, and not the past as defined by the present. In the 1920s Britain was a global power; Canada, perhaps the most important British dominion, was a minor one. Britain had global interests to protect, interests tied to its Empire. British politicians and officials who dominated government and the diplomatic service after 1918 were more than willing to meet the legitimate desires of nationalists like Mackenzie King. Such willingness was purely pragmatic; it was necessary to preserve and reinforce the Empire. In this equation, matters of power politics were fundamentally important, as were issues in diplomacy, tied as they were to personality and policy. Esme Howard's first three years at Washington and his role in the achievement of Canadian autonomy in foreign policy by 1927 shows this clearly. He was a gifted diplomat, refined, cultured, and schooled in the hard world of great power politics. He understood from the time he served at Dublin that Britain's ability to remain a power of the first rank was linked to the preservation of the Empire. When he went to the United States in 1924, he knew that he faced difficulties on several fronts including Canada. His predecessor had damaged Britain's image among Canadian leaders by failing to appreciate their nationalist desires. Howard sought to reverse this. He travelled to Canada often; he met with Canadian leaders, treating them as equals in order to understand their concerns; and he weighed successfully the impact of his work on Canadian issues with more important ones concerning the United States. Moreover, he did this in a fashion that aided the Canadian drive for autonomy, removing difficulties blocking the path of Mackenzie King, Skelton, and others. He encouraged Canadians at every turn, whether from the public platform or by secret diplomacy. And in doing so, he willingly shouldered criticism that sometimes descended on him from his political masters in London, including King George V. That the Canadian question did not damage further already strained Anglo-American relations – a far more important foreign policy consideration for London – is as much a testament to Howard's skills and vision as to that of the men in Ottawa.

## NOTES

1. Howard 'Address to British Empire Club at Providence, 17 September [1924]', in Howard MSS [Cumbria County Record Office, Carlisle] DHW 5/20.
2. The approach adopted in this paper owes much to Donald Watt's seminal chapter 'The Nature of the Foreign-Policy-Making Elite in Britain', in his *Personalities and Policies. Studies in the formulation of British foreign policy in the twentieth century* (London,1965), pp. 1–15. It also has been influenced by his *What About The People? Abstraction and Reality in History and the Social Sciences* (London, 1983), which sets out clearly the precepts of 'the new international history'.
3. See J.M. Carland, 'Shadow and Substance: Mackenzie King's Perceptions of British Intentions at the 1923 Imperial Conference', in G. Martel (ed.), *Studies in Imperial History: Essays in Honour of A.P. Thornton* (London, 1986), pp. 178–200; R. Cook, 'A Canadian Account of the 1926 Imperial Conference', *Journal of Commonwealth Political Studies*, 3(1965), pp. 50–63; J. Hilliker, *Canada's Department of External Affairs*, Vol. I: *The Early Years, 1909–1946* (Montreal and Kingston, 1990), pp. 87–134; C.P. Stacey, *Canada in the Age of Conflict*, Vol. II: *1921–1948. The Mackenzie King Era* (Toronto, 1981), pp. 3–121; and P. Wigley, *Canada and the Transition to Commonwealth: British–Canadian Relations 1917–1926* (Cambridge, 1977).
4. R.M. Dawson, *William Lyon Mackenzie King: a political biography*, Vol. I: *1874–1923* (London, 1958); and H.B. Neatby, *William Lyon Mackenzie King*, Vol. II: *1924–1932* (London, 1963). For an example of 'Liberal' over-statement so typical of the 'professional Canadian' view, see the comment: 'The [foreign] policy for the most part was that of Mackenzie King, the extraordinary man who dominated Canada, Canadian politics, and the Commonwealth from 1921 to 1948.' (J.L. Granatstein, 'Foreign and Defence Policy', in J.L. Granatstein and P. Stevens (eds), *A Reader's Guide to Canadian History*, Vol. II:

*Confederation to the Present* (Toronto, 1982), p. 60.) Some British scholars have also been mesmerized by Mackenzie King; see N. Mansergh, *Survey of British Commonwealth Affairs: Problems of External Policy* (London, 1952), *passim*. Mackenzie King did respond to the crisis in Europe in the late 1930s by bringing Canada into the second World War on Britain's side; for 'Liberal' interpretations of this, see J.L. Granatstein and R. Bothwell, '"A Self-Evident National Duty": Canadian Foreign Policy 1935–9', *Journal of Imperial and Commonwealth History*, 3(1975), pp. 212–33; and B. Neatby, 'Mackenzie King and National Unity', in H.L. Dyck and H.P. Krosby (eds), *Empire and Nation: Essays in Honour of Frederic P. Soward* (Toronto, 1969), pp. 54–70.

5.  R. Bothwell, I. Drummond, and J. English, *Canada, 1900–1945* (Toronto, 1987), 238.
6.  See D.G. Creighton, *Dominion of the North: A History of Canada* (Boston, 1944), plus the revised edition (Toronto, 1958); idem. with P. Fox, *The Long View of Canadian History* (Toronto, 1959); and idem, *Canada's First Century* (Toronto, 1970). Also of interest is D.G. Creighton 'Conservatism and National Unity', in R. Flenley (ed.), *Essays in Canadian History* (Toronto, 1939), pp. 154–77; idem, 'Canada in the English-Speaking World', *Canadian Historical Review*, 26(1945), pp. 119–27; and idem, 'The United States and Canadian Confederation', *Canadian Historical Review*, 39(1958), pp. 209–22. The hard line of Creighton, though not his intellectual rigour, has been softened to a degree by younger Canadian historians of this school. For an example of this which looks at the development of increasingly bureaucratic government in Canada, admittedly with an emphasis on domestic policy, see D. Owram, *The Government Generation. Canadian Intellectuals and the State, 1900–1945* (Toronto and London, 1986).
7.  For instance, see F. Scott, *Canada Today* (Toronto, 1938); and F.H. Underhill, *In Search of Canadian Liberalism* (Toronto, 1960). The monthly multi-disciplinary journal, *Canadian Forum*, was a vehicle for left-wing writing in Canada in the inter-war period, and British foreign and domestic policy was particularly singled out for criticism. For example, cf. M. Ayearst, 'The Colonial Complex', *Canadian Forum*, Vol. 14 (Oct 1933), 14-15; M. Gelber, 'The Liberal Facade', ibid., Vol. 16 (May 1936), pp. 17–19; and F.M.A. Gerube, 'The Chamberlain Way to War', ibid., Vol. 18 (1938), pp. 439–40.
8.  Representative are M. Baldwin, 'The Myths of the Special Relationship', in S. Clarkson (ed.), *An Independent Foreign Policy for Canada?* (Toronto, Montreal, 1968), pp. 5–16; A. Lamorie [pseud.], *How They Sold Our Canada to the USA* (Toronto, 1976); all of the articles in R. Swift and R. Clarke (eds), *Ties That Bind: Canada and the Third World* (Toronto, 1982); and G. Stevenson, 'Continental Integration and Canadian Unity', in W.A. Axline *et al.* (eds), *Continental Community? Independence and Integration in North America* (Toronto, 1974), pp. 194–217. For a balanced left-wing critique, see D. Smith, *Diplomacy of Fear. Canada and the Cold War, 1941–1948* (Toronto, 1988); and idem, 'Canada and NATO', in R.G. Haycock and K.E. Neilson (eds), *The Cold War and National Defence* (New York, 1990), pp. 171–84.
9.  This is the thrust of Clarkson, *Independent Foreign Policy*.
10. J.L. Granatstein, *How Britain's Weakness Forced Canada Into the Arms of the United States* (Toronto, 1989).
11. On Howard's family background and early life, see Lord Howard of Penrith, *Theatre of Life*, Vol. I: *Life Seen From the Pit, 1863–1905* (London, 1935), pp. 13–48; and B.J.C. McKercher, *Esme Howard: A Diplomatic Biography* (Cambridge, 1989), pp. 2–8.
12. On the nature of the Victorian diplomatic service, and the requirements for diplomats, cf. R.A. Jones, *The British Diplomatic Service, 1815–1914* (Waterloo, Ont., 1983); and Z.S. Steiner, *The Foreign Office and Foreign Policy, 1898–1914* (Cambridge, 1969). Also see Z.S. Steiner, 'Elitism and Foreign Policy: The Foreign Office before the Great War', in B.J.C. McKercher and D.J. Moss (eds), *Shadow and Substance in British Foreign Policy, 1895–1939. Essays Honouring C.J. Lowe* (Edmonton, 1984), 19–56.
13. See Howard, *Theatre of Life*, I, 64–102; idem, Vol. II: *Life Seen From the Stalls* (London, 1936), pp. 13–484; and McKercher, *Howard*, pp. 10–268.
14. Howard, *Theatre of Life*, II, pp. 239–41. Cf. Howard telegram (unnumbered) to Grey [foreign secretary], 2 Oct. 1916, Howard MSS DHW 4/Official/8; and Howard telegram (unnumbered) to Grey, 11 Oct. 1916, Howard MSS DHW 5/6.
15. See K.M. Burk, 'The House of Morgan in Financial Diplomacy, 1920–1930', in B.J.C. McKercher (ed), *Anglo-American Relations in the 1920s: The Struggle for Supremacy*

(London and Edmonton, 1991), pp. 125–57; F.C. Costigliola, 'Anglo-American Financial Rivalry in the 1920s', *Journal of Economic History*, 37(1972), pp. 911–34; R.A. Dayer, *Finance and Empire. Sir Charles Addis, 1861–1945* (New York, 1988), pp. 109–306; M.J. Hogan, *Informal Entente: The Private Structure of Cooperation in Anglo-American Economic Diplomacy, 1918–1928* (Columbia, MO, 1977); and C.P. Parrini, *Heir to Empire: United States Economic Diplomacy, 1916–1923* (Pittsburgh, 1969).

16. J. Brandes, *Herbert Hoover and Economic Diplomacy: Department of Commerce Policy, 1921-1928* (Pittsburgh, 1962); M.D. Goldberg, 'Anglo-American Economic Competition 1920–1930', *Economy and History*, 16(1973), pp. 15–36; and J.H. Wilson, *American Business and Foreign Policy, 1920–1933* (Lexington, KY, 1971).

17. D.F. Trask, *The United States in the Supreme War Council: American War Aims and Inter-Allied Strategy, 1917–1918* (Middlestown, CT, 1961); and idem, *Captains and Cabinets: Anglo-American Naval Relations, 1917–1918* (Columbia, MO, 1973). Also see S.W. Roskill, *Naval Policy Between the Wars*, Vol. I: *The Period of Anglo-American Antagonism, 1919–1929* (London, 1968), 71–130.

18. T.H. Buckley, *The United States and the Washington Conference, 1921–1922* (Knoxville, TN, 1970); J.R. Ferris, *Men, Money, and Diplomacy. The Evolution of British Strategic Policy, 1919–1926* (London, 1989), pp. 98–102, 114–15; M.G. Fry, *Illusions of Security. North Atlantic Diplomacy 1918–22* (Toronto, 1972); Roskill, *Naval Policy*, I, pp. 204–33, 300–30; and H. and M. Sprout, *Toward a New Order of Sea Power: American Naval Policy and the World Scene, 1918–1922* (Princeton, 1940).

19. Hilliker, *External Affairs*, pp. 43–53, 57–70, 71–3, 84–6, 90–6.

20. See A.B. Cooke and J.R. Vincent, *The Governing Passion: Cabinet Government and Party Politics in Britain 1885–1886* (London, 1974) *passim*; A. Hardinge, *The Life of Henry Howard Molyneux Herbert, Fourth Earl of Carnarvon, 1831–1890*, Vol. III: *1878–1890* (London, 1925), pp. 160–216; and R. Rhodes James, *The British Revolution. British Politics 1880–1939* (London, 1977), pp. 81–103.

21. Cf. the Earl of Carnarvon, 'Imperial Administration', in the Earl of Carnarvon, *Essays, Addresses and Translations*, Vol. III, ed. R. Herbert (London, 1896), pp. 3–29; and B.A. Knox, 'Conservative Imperialism 1858–1874: Bulwer Lytton, Lord Carnarvon, and Canadian Confederation', *International History Review*, 6 (1984), pp. 333–57.

22. Howard, *Theatre of Life*, I, 61.

23. Howard to his mother, 1 and 20 June 1890, Howard MSS DHW 3/9.

24. On his rubber plantation, see Howard, *Theatre of Life*, I, pp. 214–59; and McKercher, *Howard*, pp. 25–8, 32.

25. Howard, *Theatre of Life*, I, pp. 103–41; and McKercher, *Howard*, pp. 14–17. Also see the diary Howard kept on this journey in Howard MSS DHW 1/15.

26. Howard, *Theatre of Life*, I, pp. 274–316; and McKercher, *Howard*, pp. 30–2. Also see his untitled mss recording his capture and escape from the Boers in the summer of 1900 in Howard MSS DHW 1/15.

27. Howard, *Theatre of Life*, II, pp. 101–42; and McKercher, *Howard*, pp. 75–95.

28. See A.E. Campbell, *Britain and the United States, 1895–1903* (Glasgow, 1960); C.S. Campbell, *Anglo-American Understanding, 1893-1903* (Baltimore, MD, 1957); and B. Perkins, *The Great Rapprochement. England and the United States, 1895–1914* (New York, 1968).

29. N. Penlington, *The Alaska Boundary Dispute: A Critical Reappraisal* (Toronto, 1972).

30. See Howard to Stafford Howard, 12 Sept. and 8 Dec. 1907, and 9 March 1908, Howard MSS DHW 5/86.

31. For instance, see Mackenzie King to Howard, 3 Dec. 1908, Howard MSS DHW 4/Official/ 15.

32. On the Chicago water diversion, see Pope [under-secretary of state, Department of External Affairs] to Chargé d'Affaires, British Embassy, Washington, in Department of External Affairs, *Documents on Canadian External Relations* [hereafter *DCER*], Vol. III: *1919–1925* (Ottawa, 1970), pp. 856–8; on the seaway, see Howard to Hughes [US Secretary of State], 12 March 1924, ibid, pp. 929–30; and on liquor smuggling, see Hughes to Howard, 2 April 1924, ibid, pp. 978–9. Cf. Stacey, *Age of Conflict*, II, pp. 44–9.

33. McKercher, *Howard*, pp. 280–4.

34. Except where noted, the following paragraph is based on Wrong to Howard, 14 June 1924,

Howard MSS DHW 9/42. Also of interest is Wrong to Howard, 10 March 1924, Howard MSS DHW 5/25.

35. For example, Mackenzie King diary, 30 Oct. 1922, Mackenzie King MSS [National Archives, Ottawa] MG 26 J13 1922.

36. Hilliker, *External Affairs*, pp. 81, 105–06; and Stacey, *Age of Conflict*, II, pp. 31–4.

37. Howard to Crowe [permanent under-secretary, Foreign Office], 4 June 1924, enclosing Mahoney memorandum for Howard, 4 June 1924, Howard MSS DHW 5/15.

38. Ibid.

39. See paraphrases of Administrator telegrams to Colonial Secretary, 1 April and 6 May 1920, *DCER*, III, pp. 17–18, 21.

40. Crowe to Howard, 26 June 1924, Howard MSS DHW 5/15.

41. Except where noted, this paragraph is based on Howard despatch to MacDonald [British Prime Minister and Foreign Secretary], 14 July 1924, FO 371/9633/4531/3673.

42. On Lausanne, see the correspondence between the Colonial Secretary and the Governor-General from 22 Feb. to 19 May 1924, *DCER*, III, pp. 93–111; cf. Wigley, *Transition to Commonwealth*, pp. 206–16. On the Irish question, see Colonial Secretary to Governor-General, 22 April 1924, and Governor-General to Colonial Secretary, *DCER*, III, pp. 40, 43; cf. D. Harkness, *The Restless Dominion. The Irish Free State and the British Commonwealth of Nations, 1921–31* (London, Dublin, 1969), pp. 63–7.

43. Howard to Crowe, 31 July 1924, Howard MSS DHW 9/42.

44. See Wrong to Howard, 25 July 1924, ibid.

45. After his Canadian trip, Howard informed Mackenzie King that Mahoney's official recognition would meet with no opposition from Britain, but the Canadian government had to put forward a request 'in this sense'; see Howard to Mackenzie King, 13 July 1924, Howard MSS DHW 5/15.

46. Howard despatch to MacDonald, 14 July 1924, FO 371/9633/4531/3673.

47. See Broderick [commercial counsellor, British Embassy, Washington] to Howard, 23 Dec. 1924, Howard MSS DHW 5/15; and Armstrong [British consul-general, New York] to Howard, 22 Jan. 1925, and Howard to Armstrong, 26 Jan 1925, Howard MSS DHW 5/13.

48. Howard 'Address to British Empire Club at Providence, 17th September [1924]', Howard MSS DHW 5/20.

49. See G.P. Auld, *The Dawes Plan and the New Economics* (Garden City, NY, 1927); and R.W. Boyden, 'The Dawes Report', *Foreign Affairs*, 2(1924), pp. 583–97. Cf. S.A. Schuker, *The End of French Predominance in Europe. The Financial Crisis of 1924 and the Adoption of the Dawes Plan* (Chapel Hill, NC, 1976), especially 171–393.

50. See G.M. Wrong, 'Relations with the United States', in *The Canadian Annual Review of Public Affairs*, Vol. 24: *1924–1925* (Toronto, 1925), pp. 78–89.

51. McKercher, *Howard*, pp. 282–3.

52. Ibid, pp. 280–3.

53. On Foreign Office perceptions of American anglophobia, see B.J.C. McKercher, 'The British Diplomatic Service in the United States and the Chamberlain Foreign Office's Perceptions of Domestic America, 1924–1927: Images, Reality, and Diplomacy', in McKercher and Moss, *Shadow and Substance*, pp. 221–48.

54. Howard despatch to MacDonald, 30 Oct. 1924, with enclosures, FO 371/9619/6701/435.

55. Amery [Colonial Secretary] to Chamberlain [Foreign Secretary], 16 March 1925, FO 371/9619/6701/435.

56. Harding [Dominions Office] to Craigie [Foreign Office], 10 Aug. 1925, with Craigie to Howard, 27 Aug. 1925, FO 371/10637/4065/49.

57. See J. Jacobson, *Locarno Diplomacy. Germany and the West, 1925–1929* (Princeton, 1972).

58. Chamberlain to Howard, 4 Nov. 1925, Chamberlain MSS FO 800/258.

59. For instance, Amery to governors-general of Canada and South Africa, 4 April 1925, FO 371/10636/1411/49; Chamberlain to Howard, 18 March 1925, Chamberlain MSS FO 800/257; and Chamberlain to Howard, 4 June 1925, ibid, FO 800/258.

60. 'Address of Sir Esme Howard at the Banquet of the Canadian Society of Washington, Wardman Park Hotel, April 28, 1925', in Howard MSS DHW 5/20.

61. See the copy in Mackenzie King MSS MG 26 J2 Vol.12.

62. Howard despatch (734) to Chamberlain, 14 May 1925, FO 371/10637/2681/49.

63. Mounsey [Foreign Office treaty department] minute, 29 May 1925; Wellesley [deputy under-secretary, Foreign Office] minute, 29 May 1925; Chamberlain minute, 30 May 1925; and Craigie to under-secretary, Colonial Office, 11 June 1925, ibid; and Harding to Craigie, 10 Aug. 1925, FO 371/10637/4065/49.
64. 'Memorandum respecting the Issue of Invitations for the Dominions to attend a Disarmament Conference', 10 Oct. 1925, Batterbee, FO 371/10637/5274/49.
65. On the American polar expedition, see the files in FO 371/10650/3157, as well as Howard despatch to Chamberlain, 25 Feb. 1926, enclosing Howard to Byng, 25 Feb. 1926, FO 371/11171/1293/39. On fisheries, see the files in FO 371/10650/2786, as well as Howard despatch to Chamberlain, 25 Feb. 1926, FO 371/11195/1295/1295. On territorial waters, see the files in FO 371/11194/997, as well as the documents in *DCER*, III, pp. 862–73, 897–8, 935–42.
66. See Stacey, *Age of Conflict*, II, pp. 77–83; and Wigley, *Transition to Commonwealth*, pp. 206–47.
67. Governor-General to Dominions Secretary, 8 Jan. 1926, *DCER*, IV, pp. 679–81.
68. B.J.C. McKercher, 'A British View of American Foreign Policy: The Settlement of Blockade Claims, 1924–1929', *International History Review*, 3(1981), pp. 358–84.
69. Howard to Mackenzie King, 17 Oct. 1925, Mackenzie King MSS MG 26 J1 Vol. 116.
70. Except where noted, this and the next paragraph are based on Mackenzie King diary, 30 April and 1 May 1926, Mackenzie King MSS MG 26 J13 1926.
71. Mackenzie King to Howard, 26 May 1926, enclosing External Affairs memoranda on 'The Chicago Diversion', 'Revised Rush-Bagot Agreement', and 'Pelagic Sealing Convention', with enclosure, all 25 May 1926; and 'The *Eastwood*', no date, Mackenzie King MSS MG 26 J1 Vol. 132.
72. Howard to Mackenzie King, 22 June 1926, ibid.
73. See the files in FO 371/11194/997.
74. Howard to Chamberlain, 11 May 1926, Chamberlain MSS FO 800/259.
75. Except where noted, the following paragraph is based on Neatby, *Mackenzie King*, II, pp. 177–91; Stacey, *Age of Conflict*, II, pp. 83–9; and Wigley, *Transition to Commonwealth*, pp. 248–77.
76. Cmd.2768: *Summary of the Proceedings of the Imperial Conference, 1926*, p. 9.
77. For instance, British Library of Information, New York despatch to Foreign Office, 27 Feb. 1926, FO 371/11193/1332/977.
78. Mackenzie King diary, 1 May 1926, Mackenzie King MSS MG 26 J13 1926.
79. Amery telegram to governor-general of Canada, 24 Sept. 1926, FO 371/11193/5138/977. Cf. V. Massey, *What's Past is Prologue. The Memoirs of the Right Honourable Vincent Massey, C.H.* (Toronto, 1963), pp. 109–11.
80. See Mackenzie King to Chamberlain, 5 Nov. 1926, with Chamberlain minute, 6 Nov. 1926, Craigie minutes, 8 and 15 Nov. 1926, Selby [Chamberlain's private secretary] minute, 15 Nov. 1926, and Selby to Stamfordham [King George V's private secretary], 15 Nov. 1926, FO 371/11193/5800/977; and Stamfordham to Selby, 17 Nov. 1926, FO 371/11193/6008/977.
81. On the monarch's approval, see R.I. Campbell [Foreign Office American Department] to Wellesley, 26 Oct. 1926, FO 371/11193/5756/977; and Chamberlain to King George V, 26 Oct. 1926, with the King's initials, FO 371/11193/5800/977. On American agreement, see Foreign Office telegram (223) to Chilton [British Embassy, Washington], 30 Oct. 1926, FO 371/11193/5756/977; Chilton telegram (258) to Foreign Office, 1 Nov. 1926, FO 371/11193/5757/977; Selby to Chamberlain, 17 Nov. 1926, FO 371/11193/6008/977; and Balfour [British Embassy, Washington] despatch to Chamberlain, 22 Nov. 1926, with enclosures, FO 371/11193/6444/977.
82. McKercher, *Howard*, pp. 11-14, 115-18, 272.
83. See Chamberlain minute, 9 Nov. 1926, FO 371/11193/5800/977 which reports a Mackenzie King meeting with Howard and two senior Foreign Office officials.
84. Chamberlain minute, 20 Nov. 1926, FO 371/11193/6099/977.
85. Howard to Chamberlain, 18 Nov. 1926, with minutes, and Craigie to Chilton, 26 Nov. 1926, both ibid; Chamberlain minute, 21 Jan. 1927, FO 371/12020/396/14; and Chamberlain minute, 16 Feb. 1926, FO 371/12020/560/14.

86. Howard telegram (45) to Foreign Office, 19 Jan. 1927, FO 371/12020/396/14; and Howard telegram (56) to Foreign Office, 25 Jan. 1927, FO 371/12020/560/14.
87. On Howard's views being accepted by the American government, see Kellogg [US Secretary of State] to Howard, 29 Jan. 1927, FO 371/12020/560/14. On their approval, see R.I. Campbell minute, 15 Feb. 1927, with Wellesley and Vansittart initials, both 16 Feb. 1927, and Vansittart to under-secretary, Dominions Office, 26 Feb. 1927, Ibid.; plus Dixon [Dominions Office] to under-secretary, Foreign Office, 23 March 1927, and Vansittart to Howard, 6 April 1927, FO 371/12020/1787/14.
88. The rest of this paragraph is based on Howard despatch to Chamberlain, 18 Feb. 1927, FO 371/12020/1305/14; and Massey, Prologue, pp. 121–4 for the quotations. Massey's papers are restricted, and the portion of his official biography dealing with his American appointment (C. Bissell, The Young Vincent Massey (Toronto, 1981), pp. 112–23) shows its 'professional Canadian' bias by ignoring Howard's efforts for the new minister. On Howard's efforts in Washington, see the correspondence of January–February 1927 in the Mackenzie King MSS MG 26 J1 Vol. 141, especially Howard telegram (2) to Willingdon [governor-general of Canada], 19 Jan. 1927; Howard telegram (4) to Willingdon, 25 Jan. 1927; Howard telegram (7) to Willingdon, 7 Feb. 1927; and Willingdon telegram (unnumbered) to Howard, 9 Feb. 1927.
89. For an indication, see Mackenzie King's comments at this time when he discussed expanding the Canadian diplomatic service: 'I laid it down that London was the highest & first of the appointments, on account of Eng. being part of Br. Empire. That Washington might rank second on account of importance of post, volume of business etc. & Paris third . . .', in Mackenzie King diary, 11 Jan. 1927, Mackenzie King MSS MG 26 J13 1927.
90. See Chamberlain to Amery, 29 March 1927, and Amery to Chamberlain, 1 April 1927, Chamberlain MSS FO 800/260 which show the important position of Canada in British thinking.
91. See the views of Kellogg, the American secretary of state, that Britain persuaded Canada to support a British hardline over naval limitation at the abortive Coolidge naval conference in the summer of 1927; Kellogg to Phillips [US minister in Canada], 9 Aug. 1927, Kellogg MSS [Minnesota Historical Society, St Paul, MN, microfilm edition] Reel 27.
92. Massey, Prologue, p. 124.
93. The rest of this paragraph is based on D. Carlton, 'Great Britain and the Coolidge Naval Conference of 1927', Political Science Quarterly, 83(1968), pp. 573–98; McKercher, Howard, pp. 300–51; idem, The Second Baldwin Government and the United States, 1924–1929; attitudes and diplomacy (Cambridge, 1984), pp. 55–199; and Roskill, Naval Policy, I, pp. 498–566.
94. Howard, Theatre of Life, II, pp. 516.
95. Ibid., pp. 517–18; and Massey, Prologue, pp. 128–9.
96. B.J.C. McKercher, 'Between Two Giants: Canada, the Coolidge conference, and Anglo-American Relations in 1927', in idem, Struggle for Supremacy, pp. 81–124.
97. DCER, IV, pp. 395–594.
98. Balfour to Thompson, 29 Aug. 1927, FO 371/12020/5415/14.
99. Howard telegram (unnumbered) to Mackenzie King, 19 July 1927, Mackenzie King MSS MG 26 J1; Willingdon to Howard, 25 July 1927, and Howard to Willingdon, 30 July 1927, both Howard MSS DHW 9/57; and Chamberlain to Howard, 22 Aug. 1927, ibid., DHW 9/51.
100. See Mackenzie King diary, 21–24 Nov. and 11 Dec. 1927, all Mackenzie King MSS MG 26 J13 1927.
101. See Howard to Mackenzie King, 20 Dec. 1927, Mackenzie King MSS MG 26 J1.
102. Howard telegram (435) to Foreign Office, 4 Oct. 1927, FO 371/12020/5837/14; Chamberlain telegram (unnumbered) to Howard, 13 Oct. 1927, and Howard telegram (unnumbered) to Chamberlain, 14 Oct. 1927, both FO 371/12021/6056/14; Howard telegram (unnumbered) to Chamberlain, 26 Oct. 1927, FO 371/12021/6293/14; and Howard despatch to Chamberlain, 8 Dec. 1927, with minutes, FO 371/12021/7332/14.
103. The correspondence between Howard and Stamfordham continued intermittently for months after the Willingdon visit. Finally, Howard wrote a long letter on the Canadian question summarising the views he had expressed in the correspondence; this quotation is

from Howard to Stamfordham, 11 July 1928, Howard MSS DHW 9/60.

104. British Library of Information, New York despatch to Foreign Office, 9 Dec. 1927, FO 371/12021/7298/14; Howard despatch to Chamberlain, 12 Dec. 1927, FO 371/12021/7482/14; Mackenzie King to Kellogg, 10 Dec. 1927, and Kellogg to Mackenzie King, 22 Dec. 1927, both Mackenzie King MSS MG 26 J1 Vol. 144; and Mackenzie King diary, 13, 16, and 31 Dec. 1927, all Mackenzie King MSS MG 26 J13 1927.

105. Significantly, Granatstein, *How Britain's Weakness*, provides almost no analysis to the 1920s.

106. Granatstein, 'Foreign and Defence Policy', 63.

# 'Salter's Soviet': Another View of All Souls and Appeasement

## SIDNEY ASTER

All Souls College and appeasement, like Geoffrey Dawson and *The Times* or the Astors and Cliveden, appear synonymously in any discussion of British foreign policy in the 1930s. They have been firmly wedded since 1961 when A.L. Rowse published his brief book *All Souls and Appeasement*. Therein appeasement was derided as the foreign policy of 'a class in decadence' which reduced Britain 'to a second-rate place in the world'.[1] Rowse contended that All Souls was an important venue for politicians, academics and other establishment figures who systematically plotted the intensification of appeasement as part of a campaign to reach a permanent agreement with Nazi Germany.

That is the picture which has generally entered subsequent examinations of appeasement and the origins of the Second World War. So ingrained has this association between All Souls and appeasement become that no attention is ever paid to an important reservation offered by Rowse. It was indeed true, he wrote, that several Fellows of All Souls played a leading role in the affairs of state and were prime figures in appeasement diplomacy. 'But it is equally true that a majority of the Fellows, particularly of the younger generation, as we were then,' he continued, 'were strongly opposed to the whole policy and course of conduct with which our foremost and best-known members were identified.'[2] Unfortunately, Rowse then devoted his acerbic pen to a passionate attack against the elder, patrician Fellows of the College. These included Lord Halifax, who succeeded Anthony Eden in February 1938 as Secretary of State for Foreign Affairs, the Chancellor of the Exchequer from 1937 to 1940, Sir John Simon, the long-serving editor of *The Times*, Geoffrey Dawson, and others in the alleged pro-appeasement lobby. The intensity of Rowse's feelings on the subject, however, led him to ignore largely the 'younger generation' who were anti-appeasement.

Between the extremes of Rowse's elder grandees involved in appeasement diplomacy and the younger, fiercely anti-appeasement generation, stood yet another Oxford manifestation, 'Salter's Soviet',[3] formally called the All Souls Foreign Affairs Group. Its existence as an unofficial discussion group, concerned with foreign policy towards Germany, Spain and Italy, as well as the threat offered to the British Empire from Japanese expansion, was neither a well-kept secret nor common knowledge. During the brief period from December 1937 to July 1938, the group met usually at weekends at All Souls, and occasionally in London at the Temple chambers of Harold Nicolson and Sir Norman Angell at 4 King's Bench Walk. Its documents on foreign policy were occasionally circulated for private study to the Foreign Office and to the editors of leading newspapers and weeklies for information. In later years its activities were first acknowledged by Sir Arthur Salter in his *Memoirs of a Public Servant*.[4] This was confirmed subsequently in the memoirs and biographies of several other participants.[5]

The records of the All Souls Foreign Affairs Group are incomplete. None of the participants preserved an entire set of documents. This was not for lack of organization. By January 1938 the group had the services of a secretary, Christina Hole.[6] Minutes were kept of the meetings, and these and occasional discussion papers were circulated among the group. However, an exact record of all the participants, or of those who attended a particular meeting, is impossible to collate. Few sets of minutes included the discussants, and Nicolson's unpublished diaries, a valuable source, did not always name all those who were present. In addition, later recollections tended to disagree on either leading or occasional members. After wide consultation in 1961, Sir Basil H. Liddell Hart[7] compiled a list suggesting that the following individuals, besides himself, participated at some point in the group's discussions: W.G.S. Adams,[8] Lord Allen of Hurtwood,[9] Sir Norman Angell,[10] William Arnold-Forster,[11] Alfred Barratt Brown,[12] Lionel Curtis,[13] H.A.L. Fisher,[14] H.V. Hodson,[15] Geoffrey Hudson,[16] Sir Walter Layton,[17] Harold Macmillan,[18] Gilbert Murray,[19] Harold Nicolson,[20] Alfred Reginald Radcliffe-Brown,[21] A.L. Rowse,[22] Sir Arthur Salter,[23] Arnold Toynbee,[24] and E.L. Woodward.[25] Salter later observed that Guy Wint,[26] his talented young secretary at the time, should also be included in the list of participants.[27] From the surviving minutes of the meetings, Lord Arnold,[28] who advocated an isolationist foreign policy,[29]must also be mentioned.

Some 21 individuals, therefore, participated in the All Souls Foreign Affairs Group, only eight of whom were at some point in their careers Fellows of the College. The convenors were Salter and Nicolson, although the chair was usually reserved to Allen. The inner core of members, those attending most regularly and acting as the Brains Trust, included the two convenors, as well as Allen, Angell, Hudson, Liddell Hart, Murray, Arnold-Forster, Rowse, Toynbee and Wint. The others attended irregularly or soon abandoned the group.

The driving force behind the formation of the discussion group, without a doubt, was Salter. In October 1934 he had been appointed Gladstone Professor of Political Theory and Institutions at All Souls. In addition, he had won a seat as an Independent MP for Oxford University at the 27 February 1937 by-election. In these roles, Salter strove hard to maintain one of the unique qualities of All Souls, what he called the 'bridge between the academic and the public life'.[30] Out of that concern and under his unique combination of patience, prodding and patronage, there emerged various seminars, off the record meetings and unofficial lobbying groups. The All Souls Foreign Affairs Group can be placed in the last of these categories. Shortly after its formation in December 1937, Salter explained the circumstances which had motivated him:

The reason why I proposed the meetings was that I found myself in grave doubt ... as to the course of policy to support and advocate, a doubt extending to some of the gravest issues presenting themselves; and in consulting others who started with a similar general outlook I found they were all experiencing equal, though not identical, anxieties. I hoped that we might help each other in clearing our minds and in solving the individual problem presenting itself to each of us as to his own line of conduct.[31]

Salter might also have had another objective. On 26 July 1935, *The Next Five Years: An Essay in Political Agreement* had been published to widespread approval. Its Foreword was followed by a list of more than 150 signatories, who endorsed the book but who had 'different political associations, and divergent views as to ultimate doctrine and policy'. However, they were agreed on an 'attainable programme of action' to be implemented over the next five years. The extensive section on international relations, for example, argued the case for 'Anglo–American co-operation and the strengthening of the collective peace system'. It could hardly have been mere accident, therefore, that five of the six original members who drafted the book in 1935 (besides

Salter, Allen, Arnold-Forster, Barratt Brown and Macmillan) were again brought together in late 1937.[32] At that stage, however, it was not yet clear whether the meetings would serve only discussion purposes or lead to a published statement about foreign policy.

Many years later, Salter reflected on the reputation of the group and its relation to Oxford life:

Outside Oxford itself the present image, both in the rest of England, in America and elsewhere, is distorted by a disproportionate emphasis on the association for two or three years of less than a half-dozen of Fellows with the policy of appeasement of Hitler in a College in which many Fellows, like Amery for example, were strongly opposed to that policy. Any such emphasis is fantastically unjust to the College as a mirror of its true character and influence.[33]

The objective of this essay, therefore, is to establish a record of one particular aspect of College life and thereby to contribute to an understanding of what Salter referred to as the 'true character and influence' of All Souls. It will also be suggested that 'Salter's Soviet' vividly demonstrates that the traditional dichotomy between appeasers and resisters is a simplification.[34] In addition, the analysis will enable the portrait offered by Rowse in *All Souls and Appeasement* to be assessed and placed in context. Such aims further relate to the wider questions of appeasement, public opinion and the origins of the Second World War. An examination of 'Salter's Soviet' might thus confirm that appeasement was never the one-dimensional phenomenon derided so often by its critics. Rather, it wore many masks, meant different things to different people and at different times. Indeed, it might not be a case of *All Souls and Appeasement*, but of appeasement at All Souls.

In early December 1937 Salter began to organize the first of the All Souls meetings. By the eleventh he had acceptances from Toynbee, Barratt Brown, Curtis, Macmillan, Layton, Allen and Liddell Hart. Other affirmative replies followed from Arnold, Arnold-Forster, Hudson, Hodson, and Radcliffe-Brown.[35] Nicolson also joined the group at its inaugural meeting on Saturday and Sunday, 18 and 19 December. His diary recorded:

Met by Nigel [Nicolson], who drives with me to All Souls where I go straight into dinner. After dinner we open our discussion on foreign policy. . . . Sleep at All Souls. Bitterly cold at night. . . . We meet again at 10.30 and continue with an interval at luncheon until 6 p.m.[36]

According to the minutes circulated afterwards by Salter, three questions were addressed: 'What is our power?' 'Where is the first challenge likely to occur?' and 'What steps should be taken to meet the challenge?' The discussants divided the world between League and anti-League powers. At the core of the anti-League combination were Germany, Italy and Japan, a group which could probably attract the support of Austria, Hungary and Bulgaria. Yugoslavia and Poland were deemed 'uncertain quantities', as were Turkey and Greece. No British policy, it was further assumed, 'could be based upon expectation of American assistance although that assistance (if ever available) would be [a] determinant'. There followed a discussion of the military balance of power. This led to the view that, in the event of war, Britain must concentrate in the first weeks on home defence against air attack.

The Sunday morning session agreed that, while provocation would most likely come from Japan and Italy, 'Germany was the centre of the whole problem'. But what precisely were its aims? One view was that the slogan *'Weltmacht oder Niedergang'* reflected Germany's ambitions; in the long term the target was the British Empire. The alternative view saw Germany as being satisfied with a greater *Reich*, incorporating all scattered Germans and seeking *'Grund und Boden'* in eastern Europe. Both sides, however, contended that 'the German state of mind was one that might lead to a general war'.

The question 'What should be done?' was finally raised and two alternatives were spelled out:

(a) the policy of Danegeld – or sops to Germany in expectation of her gratitude; (b) the Fabian policy of playing for time, avoiding head-on collisions, and waiting for the Fascist and Nazi spirit to 'burn itself out'.

It was generally agreed that (a) was futile and (b) too negative. Something more constructive was required.

What that might be led to an emerging view that 'British policy towards Germany should be one of firmness followed by conciliation'. The outline of 'A General Settlement' was then sketched as follows:

I. *We offer Germany:*–
(1) The *Anschluss*.
(2) An arrangement by which the Sudeten Germans would be granted 'cantonal status' by the Czech Government, on condition the latter retained adequate powers for military defence of the Czech State.
(3) Recognition of Germany's right to possess colonies. We should be

prepared to extend the Congo Basin system plus the Mandate system to all our tropical colonies, Germany to be given a pooled territory in the Cameroons. (4) A readiness to admit Germany's prior *economic* interests in Eastern Europe.

II. *We demand from Germany:–*

(1) An assurance that the extension of her influence in Eastern Europe will not entail any attack upon the autonomy or democratic institutions of other countries.

(2) An assurance that she would agree to a scheme for the limitation of armaments under which (a) Germany would be the strongest Power in Central Europe but (b) no single Power should be strong enough to dominate the collective force of the other Powers. In other words, preponderance but not supremacy.

(3) Germany not to support Italian ambitions in the Mediterranean and in Africa.[37]

A final meeting of some members of the group on Sunday evening concluded 'that, even if Germany declined the terms offered, the approach would have been worth making, as putting us right with our own public opinion'.[38]

The following day, 20 December 1937, Curtis revealed in a private letter the crucial role which Nicolson had played in emphasizing Germany's aggressive ambitions. Nicolson had argued that Germany was a nation whose youth were inspired by 'the heroic motive' which prepared them to die in pursuit of power. It was his further view that Foreign Office policy was to keep Germany and Russia apart and to deny them economic prosperity. To Curtis's riposte that the Germans were 'entitled to special economic privileges' in eastern Europe, Nicolson objected 'that this arrangement would so strengthen Germany that she would first dominate Europe and then us and the world'. None of this impressed Curtis much.[39]

In the interim the record of the meetings was shown to Anthony Eden, the Secretary of State for Foreign Affairs, who generally concurred with the analysis. Discussion of Japanese expansion in the Far East particularly interested Eden, who affirmed 'that American opinion was not as yet prepared to support the administration in any active policy which might lead to war with Japan'.[40] What the Foreign Secretary had picked up on was the group's agreement on 'the desirability of a firm stand at some stage against aggression; to be followed by the offer of generous terms for a general settlement'. As well, the group had concluded that this stand should be made on Far Eastern issues because 'further retreat before aggression might have

very dangerous consequences on the world situation as a whole. . . .'
Participants, however, were given little hope that the government,
Parliament or public opinion would condone such 'vigorous action' in
the Far East.[41]

The group that met to discuss this impasse at 3.30 p.m. on Saturday,
15 January 1938 included, for the first time, Murray,[42] Layton, Adams,
Rowse[43] and Woodward.[44] The discussion opened with a question.
With the knowledge that the 'affirmation of strength' in the Far East
was impossible without firm American support, what policy should be
pursued in that region? It was recognized that any boycott of Japanese
goods or League of Nations intervention raised the spectre of war. In
that case the only feasible policy was to facilitate the shipment of
supplies to China, institute a 'Trades Union boycott', particularly oil,
and in effect abandon Hong Kong if it were attacked. 'Therefore Far
East not an affirmation of strength but a demonstration of weakness',
was Nicolson's pithy summary of this portion of the discussion.

The meeting then returned to the question of relations with
Germany. One participant explained the Foreign Office view that 'the
greatest caution must be exercised to avoid any "head-on" collision'
with the Axis, 'that we should play for time, even at the cost of certain
immediate sacrifices', and 'do nothing which might create in Germany
a feeling of encirclement'. This description of official policy met with
considerable resistance. It was argued that the Foreign Office must
improve relations with Russia, especially as it was the only power which
could help resist a German drive to the east. In addition, trying to 'play
for time' was regarded as 'a purely negative policy and one which might
prove incorrect'. A position of pure rejectionism was not in the
character or purpose of the group. Instead, discussion then centred on
organizing 'a positive peace-group', based not on power politics but on
'a constructive economic policy'. The scheme included the settlement
of all outstanding debts with the United States, and the building of a
new economic order, associated with the League of Nations, which
might prove strong enough to attract both Germany and Italy. This
proposal, however, was opposed by those who argued that 'economics
depended on power'. And while the scheme might prove 'an adjunct' it
was not an alternative to a traditional balance of power policy.

It was clear by Sunday morning, 16 January, that discussions about
resistance must be balanced by those about conciliation. The question
was posed as to whether Germany could be trusted with the
organization of a British-style commonwealth in south eastern Europe.
When it was pointed out that such a scheme ran counter to Britain's

traditional balance of power policy in Europe, the question was raised as to whether Britain still had the power to enforce its will. In the subsequent discussion, policy options began to appear to be very limited.

The general feeling of the meeting was that any direct overtures to the present rulers of Germany would, at least until the armament programme was almost completed, be taken as a sign of panic and weakness. Yet if by evading all 'head-on collisions' we enabled Germany to obtain the resources of South-Eastern Europe and to purchase the neutrality of Russia, then her power would become almost invincible.

The problem was to discover what concessions could be made to Germany which would be neither dishonourable in intention nor disastrous in their effects on ourselves.[45]

On that inconclusive note the meetings drew to a close.

Liddell Hart wrote the following day to Salter approving 'the way so many individual viewpoints converged towards a common view of the main elements of the problem'. Salter's reply stressed what he called the 'real value' of the meetings.[46] On the other hand, Curtis complained to Dawson about Nicholson's attitude, which amounted to a plea to weaken Germany at all costs. 'The rest of them, with their minds concentrated on collective security, again talked as though they were prepared to plunge the world in war in order to assert it.' Curtis then pointed out that British approval of the Franco-Soviet pact would mean 'good-bye to any prospect of better understanding with Germany for us and indeed I should say to the last chance of avoiding a world conflagration'. He added that this would also destroy any plan advanced by him and generally approved at All Souls for the neutralization of Czechoslovakia. He urged Dawson to destroy his letter but also to do his best to counter such a possible development in British diplomacy.[47] Finally, Murray recorded a slightly different impression. 'I thought the advocates of conciliation at any price had their full fling,' he wrote to Liddell Hart, 'and on the whole did not get to any result, except perhaps about the neutralization of CzechoSlovakia.' To this the latter replied: 'the only security is collective'.[48]

The next meeting of the group was held on Sunday, 6 February 1938, at noon. It had been anticipated by Salter as 'the final meeting . . . on which the utility of these discussions will largely depend'.[49] There appears to be no record of these conversations and attendance was poor. According to Nicolson, besides himself, there were Murray, Salter, Arnold-Forster, Toynbee, 'plus the unimportant others' at All Souls. Nicolson's record continued:

We have a paper by Lord Allen which we take as an agenda. We discuss with great gloom the recent purge [of the high command and foreign ministry] in Germany and come to the conclusion that it means that Hitler has given Mussolini a free hand in Spain in return for a free hand in Austria. We are very disturbed.

We then go on with the agenda and come to several conclusions but we feel it is all very academic when one thinks of the raging activity of Berlin. We lunch there and we dine there. . . . Salter has flu and is very wretched. I expect he will pass it on to all of us. We thus adjourn at 11.00 p.m.[50]

Allen had emerged, not surprisingly, as the most persistent proponent of Anglo-German friendship. The material he had prepared for the meeting on 6 February 1938, known as 'Document C', detailed a foreign policy for Britain which combined 'a display of strength with an outline of proposals to meet legitimate grievances and claims. . . . The ultimate object is to rebuild a peacekeeping system between nations'. The document proposed to bring economic pressure to bear upon Japan, but only with the co-operation of the United States. Other measures included the continuation of the non-intervention policy in Spain, an increase in rearmament, the storage of food and other commodities, while at the same time leaving the door wide open to disarmament proposals. With regard to long-term policy, the central theme was 'Collective Action Against Aggression':

The League to be retained for its present members but this would not exclude the co-operation of other Powers on the basis of maintaining law and order.

All suggestions for emasculating the League Covenant by eliminating Article XVI should be avoided . . . . An intimation by Britain in some form to the effect that she was always prepared to join in making use of every opportunity, where conditions made it possible, to get a preponderance of force behind law, to implement the methods of the collective protection of law, either by economic or military joint action, such as was seen at Nyon.

Other measures included the disassociation of the League Covenant and the International Labour Organization Statutes, the elimination of the war guilt clause from the Treaty of Versailles, and the removal of any restriction on the union of Austria and Germany. The future of Czechoslovakia, as part of a wider European settlement, might include a cantonal system to deal with minority problems and the 'neutralization' of the country. Economic policy, a major preoccupation of 'Document C', emphasized the value of larger trading blocs, possibly linked with the League of Nations. Finally, the matter of procedure was examined.

> Direct overtures to Berlin, indicating our willingness to discuss above proposals, are at present undesirable, owing to the non-response to previous advances and the present state of mind of the German Government. It is important to avoid giving impression of weakness. The best course is that the Prime Minister and the Foreign Secretary . . . affirm their willingness to enter at any time upon negotiations for a comprehensive settlement.[51]

Participants were then invited to make revisions. The document subsequently went through several drafts co-ordinated by Wint.

There were adequate written materials when the Foreign Affairs Group next met at All Souls at noon, on Saturday, 26 February 1938. The wisdom of drafting a final document was debated at once by those present – Layton, Arnold-Forster, Allen, Salter, Curtis, Murray and Nicolson. Would it be for private or public circulation? Would it suggest amendments to present government policy or radical alternatives? One view held that this was the moment to show how 'a collective peace system could be recreated'. Another view was that criticism would only increase the government's difficulties. It was proposed, therefore, that one of the members prepare a draft document, which would be considered at the next meeting, along the following lines:

Chapter I. Contrast of the attitude to the League indicated in the Prime Minister's recent speeches and of the policy hitherto pursued. Possible implications of the new orientation.
Chapter II. Negotiations with Italy. Enumeration of possible Italian demands upon us, and of possible demands by us upon Italy.
Chapter III. Negotiations with Germany. Possible contents.
Chapter IV. Policy towards France.
Chapter V. Policy towards Russia.
Chapter VI. Conclusion. Long term aims of our policy and attitude towards the League.

Inevitably, the discussion turned to the significance of Eden's resignation as Foreign Secretary on 20 February 1938. The participants tried to separate the short-term issue, relations with Italy, and the long-term one, collective security and policy towards Germany. On the former, it was agreed that there might be little ground for a deal with Mussolini: 'he could offer words and we must give deeds'. On the latter issue, some argued for a clear understanding in advance between Britain, France and the USSR about those German actions which they would oppose and those in which Czechoslovakia should not expect assistance. Such a step would act as a 'possibly decisive deterrent' to German action, and ensure that Russia would not return to isolation. In contrast, others regarded Germany and Italy as unstable regimes. If war could be avoided, both would collapse in time. 'The policy therefore suggested was one of minimum commitment East of the Rhine', the minutes recorded, with the implication that it would be 'disproportionate' to endanger the empire on the issue of Czechoslovakia. A basis for a settlement, which gained some approval, rested on adopting a cantonal system in Czechoslovakia, an open door policy in the British Empire, and conceding German economic hegemony in eastern and central Europe. In conclusion, the group also recognized that further efforts must be made to improve air raid protection and home defence.[52]

The efforts to reach a consensus for publication was tending to emphasize differences rather than to speed unanimity. On this occasion Guy Wint first broke ranks. He feared that the document under discussion at All Souls would be 'extremely dangerous'. Its criticism of government policy would be seen as 'a challenge to the dictatorships' and 'make war infinitely more likely'. He wrote to Curtis, therefore, urging that Allen prevail upon Lord Lothian to advise the group on alternative policies before it proceeded any further.[53] Curtis needed no encouragement. Indeed, he used the opportunity to unburden himself of several concerns. He wrote to Allen on 28 February 1938 enclosing, with a request for the greatest secrecy, the letter from Wint. Curtis observed:

I have a certain respect for this young man's [i.e., Wint] judgement, more indeed than I have for that of Hudson or Rowse. . . . He is singularly free from the streak of fanaticism to which young intellectuals like Rowse and even Hudson are subject. We most of us were at their age. But I felt on Saturday that counsel was somewhat darkened by the atmosphere which Rowse and Hudson created, especially when they tended to represent the Cabinet as anxiously hoping for the victory of Franco. I dare say that is true of Duff Cooper [First Lord of the Admiralty] and possibly of Hailsham [Lord Chancellor]; but greatly doubt whether it goes further. Also in the mind of Rowse, who is one of my dearest friends, Lothian, who is another of my dearest friends, is public enemy number one.

Curtis went on to suggest that his own contribution had helped to clarify matters in the group, especially his arguments 'that sanctions and collective security are the cause of the present confusion rather than the cure for it'. He agreed that Lothian should be brought in to temper the views of 'people like Arnold-Forster and Rowse with a flame in their minds', and to discuss the proposed publication.

Allen's reply reinforced the compliment to Wint and continued:

Speaking in the strictest confidence I was sorry when Salter (without consulting me) brought Rowse into our discussions, but being a creature who attaches enormous importance to toleration I did not grumble. Groups, such as we have been working in, require . . . a combination of immense sincerity, founded upon opinions rigidly held, yet with a capacity for restrained expression and a passionate longing to enter into the hearts and minds of those with differing points of view. Men like Rowse are no doubt intellectually very alive, but they want to batter their opponents into submission . . . and take a certain pleasure in trying to prove other people to be either knaves or fools.

Allen then assured Curtis that he would consider extending an invitation to Lothian, but that he would never consent to sign any document which would hinder the government's peace efforts. Instead, he intended to pursue his 'Transitional Policy', that is, one which used the League with 'discretion'. What most worried him, however, was that at the next meeting both Curtis and Salter would be absent. This would leave him 'almost single-handed in resisting the ferocity, however sincere, of men like Rowse and Arnold-Forster'.[54]

It had been intended that the meeting of 16 March 1938 would discuss the question of publishing a statement, if agreement were reached. But given the pace of events in 1938, it was not surprising that individuals were often subject to changes in thinking. On 8 March several members of the All Souls group, including Curtis, Murray, Nicolson, Salter and Allen, met at Chatham House. They discussed a draft memorandum prepared by Toynbee for a speech he was to deliver there two days later. Toynbee's concern was with the consequences if Britain gave up the League. Would Britain sink to the position of a second-rate power like Holland or be destroyed in the process? Toynbee inclined to the latter view. Salter proposed an intermediate policy. He considered Russian help vital in any struggle with Germany. But with Russia 'out of the picture', he reasoned, 'we must play for time'. He argued therefore against any commitments to the Czechs, although he favoured 'defending Liberty on the Spanish front'. Murray pointed out that he was not biased against Nazism, only against 'the war ideology' of the dictator states. Curtis in turn digressed on the need for air raid protection. Nicolson as usual cut to the heart of the matter by stating that the real issue was 'between the traditions of our policy (namely to oppose the strong and to protect the weak) and an experiment in a new policy of trying to conciliate the strong'.[55]

Salter's remarks anticipated the conclusions of an eight-page memorandum, 'Notes on Foreign Policy', which he completed only hours before he sailed for New York. Salter advocated a case – which he described as 'a very painful one, but one personally I feel unable to escape' – for 'surrender east of the Holland–France line but not everywhere'. He endorsed such prior measures discussed by the group as an economic boycott of Japan, closer ties with the United States, further protection against air raids, and the rebuilding of a League system, based on principles of collective security and peaceful change. But he could not escape the following conclusion:

We have not, and cannot in the near future, secure such a combination of strength as will enable us to prevent without war (or probably even to defeat in war) the realization of the central core of Hitler's (and now Germany's) ambition – the association in some form of the Germans in Czechoslovakia and German Austria with the *Reich*.

Salter cautioned his colleagues to treat the document as confidential. But he must have later regretted not settling for the 'cooler reflection' he admitted the situation demanded.[56]

The document was indeed highly indicative of the sometimes volatile opinions in the group. For example, Wint plunged ahead and on 11 March 1938 produced an outline for a pamphlet intended to be 'very clear, simple, popular'. The first half advanced the view that 'the collective system can, in present circumstances, assure no *lasting* peace'. The second part detailed the objectives Britain might pursue: peace, and the defence of democracy in the British Empire. To achieve these goals, Wint argued, might involve giving Germany a free hand in eastern Europe, that is, 'a minimum of actual annexation of territory by Germany, and friendly agreements, economic and political, between Germany and the countries concerned'. Only such concessions, he stated, would lead to 'European appeasement', the ability to defend 'what is vitally important', and the ultimate re-establishment of the League system.[57]

The opening sentence of the minutes for the group on 16 March 1938, three days after the *Anschluss*, read: 'The meeting took place in the setting of the German coup in Austria, the apparent success of

General Franco's offensive in Aragon, and the agitation in London for the Government to take a more active line in Spain and Central Europe.' It was in fact the Spanish situation which first preoccupied the attention of the participants meeting in Norman Angell's chambers at 4 King's Bench Walk, in the Temple. The strategic consequences for France and Britain of an imminent collapse of the Spanish government were examined. This problem had been discussed at previous meetings. It had also formed a corollary to Salter's argument for 'surrender east of the Holland–France line'. Salter had argued that if 'we are strong enough to stand anywhere it is here [i.e., Spain]'. Liddell Hart then underscored the notion that a victory for Italy, Germany and the Nationalists in Spain would be a disaster for British interests. He left no doubt of his view that Chamberlain's policy was 'to put everything off until the Germans are in such a complete position of supremacy that we shall be unable to fight anyhow'. Pending the resolution of the Spanish situation and the Anglo-Italian negotiations, it was thought best to make no statement about Czechoslovakia.[58] What was finally approved by the end of the afternoon was an *aide-mémoire*, based on a draft by Liddell Hart, for distribution to newspaper editors. The covering letter stated that it was being sent '*for information and comment, but not for publication*'. The *aide-mémoire* argued that Franco would always remain subservient to his benefactors and bow to demands for strategic facilities. This would allow both Germany and Italy to threaten sea communications in the Mediterranean, France's third land frontier, and the Atlantic route to the Far East. But the eastern Mediterranean was described as an area where 'geography and sea-power still tell heavily in our favour'. Therefore, some form of effective action was required.[59] What precisely this might be was not spelled out.

The fluid European situation again spurred several members of the group to put pen to paper, canvass opinion across a broad political spectrum, or press the government for action. A written response to Salter's note of 8 March was circulated by Alfred Barratt Brown. He felt encouraged by Salter's 'restrained and restraining' approach, and thus wished to put forward some considerations without, as he put it, 'obtruding my Pacifism'. Barratt Brown criticized those who misinterpreted collective security as action designed to deter a general war. He continued: 'I appreciate the courage, however quixotic, of those who advocate that we should "put force behind law", even though the law is called in question and the force is inadequate to sustain it.' None the less, he wished the group to concentrate on 'the methods of political and economic appeasement on which we are all agreed'.[60] Something of the same sentiments was at the heart of the views which Allen continued to press. In an exchange of correspondence with Lord Robert Cecil, the 1937 Nobel peace prize winner and a pioneer of the League of Nations, he warned that a declaration in advance by Britain, France and Russia to defend Czechoslovakia would be regarded by Germany as an ultimatum, and hence should be avoided. Cecil replied that it was dangerous and useless to attempt to placate the dictators.[61] In public, too, Allen continued to campaign in favour of appeasement. Negotiations with the dictators must be free of any preconditions, he argued. Good faith was the result not the precondition of talks. 'Let us neither madden dictators with too rigid emphasis upon law', he stated, 'nor woo them with baits and concessions.'[62]

One of the younger members, Geoffrey Hudson, tried to evaluate some of the variables in the European situation in the note he circulated to the All Souls Group. He took it as a given that the British government had no intention of intervening in Spain or of committing itself to the defence of Czechoslovakia, and that the Soviet Union would fulfil the Czech–Soviet pact. To implement the last option might require passage by the Red Army across Poland against the wishes of that government. Was the All Souls Group, he asked, prepared to condone 'a Russian invasion of Poland in the name of collective security'? Hudson advocated a retreat by France and Britain behind the Maginot line, provided Spain could be rescued to form 'a London–Paris–Madrid axis'. This was a surrender, he admitted, yet it offered an opportunity to avoid a European war.[63]

Nicolson also had been using the time to clarify his own thinking on Czechoslovakia. He recorded in his diary on 22 March 1938:

. . . the only honest point of view is to say that it is a British interest but that we are not strong enough to defend it. . . . What we are trying to get the Prime Minister to do is to adopt our All Souls formula – namely pressure on the Czechs, to give greater concessions to the Sudeten Germans, coupled with some assurances that if they do that we will protect their future.[64]

This hardly represented an agreed 'All Souls formula'. However, Nicolson pressed ahead. He had already written to the permanent under-secretary of state, Sir Alexander Cadogan, revealing the existence of the Foreign Affairs Group. 'The meetings have been of considerable value to us in that they have done much to clear our minds.' Nicolson drew the attention of Cadogan to the *aide-mémoire* on Spain and warned that Italy and Germany 'were really occupying vital strategical points behind our backs'.[65] It was some time before Cadogan acknowledged receipt of Nicolson's letter. 'I . . . infer from it that you are in favour of immediate and open intervention by His Majesty's Government on the side of the Spanish Government', Cadogan wrote, and concluded that it would be contrary to official policy. Nicolson's response was forthright:

. . . if there exists the real danger of some agreement between Franco and the Dictator States . . . we should be prepared in conjunction with the French to take certain 'gages' such as occupying Minorca and Ceuta.
    The All Souls Group consist of such upright gentlemen that to suggest any such thing in writing would have been agony to their souls, but I quite see that any such action is not within the scope of present policy.[66]

In the interim, another member of the group drew up a 28-page memorandum, entitled 'Foreign Policy Now'. The mandate for the exercise derived from the meeting on 26 February 1938. The document was now expanded into nine chapters including such subjects as collective security, policy with regard to Spain, Italy, Germany, Czechoslovakia, China and Japan, and rearmament and economic matters. The Introduction pointed out that the paper was the outcome of six weekend discussions by a group 'from different political parties not including the extreme political Right or Left'. The group had had no prepared agenda and no intention to produce anything for publication. 'But certain conclusions emerged so clearly from our non-partisan discussions . . . that we finally decided to prepare and publish this paper.'
    'Foreign Policy Now' pointed out that 'survival for urban man' was the issue in a world war that had begun in September 1931 when Japan invaded Manchuria. 'Somewhere, somehow, some day, a stand will be made. Where? In what conditions? For what cause, and in what company, would British power be used, if it has to be used, in war?' asked the writer. On the long-term direction of British foreign policy, it was suggested that the reconstruction of a genuine 'Collective Peace System', dedicated to defending 'certain standards of peaceful behaviour', was still desirable. How this might be realized was then set out in a series of precise propositions.
    The second objective of the paper was to look at some of the short-term problems facing the country, particularly the question 'For what purpose shall this nation's power and influence be used?' The answer to that came through unequivocally. 'It is in Spain, rather than in

Czechoslovakia, that British power – which is still in the main naval power – can be brought to bear most effectively.' Non-intervention was decried as a 'disastrous experiment'. The prospect offered by forthcoming Anglo-Italian negotiations, and its possible contribution to European conciliation, led to this expression of caution:

> The blindest of all errors would be to attempt to buy a brief respite for ourselves by encouraging the allied dictators to direct their next explosion eastwards, southwards, anywhere rather than westwards, in return for such concessions on our part as would sustain their aggressive power.

The note of caution was also carried into the analysis of the ongoing Czech–German crisis. Expressions of sympathy towards legitimate German grievances were now regarded as 'academic'. 'The lesson of the Austrian *Putsch* is that we must hang together or we shall be hanged separately.' For the rest the comments on China, Japan and economic blocs of nations to fight the trend towards self-sufficiency reiterated previous areas of agreement. So too did the brief sections on rearmament and economic policy. Once again, the nation was urged to rearm for purposes of 'collective defence', to improve London's air defences, and to increase the storage of food and other essential commodities.[67]

What initially concerned the group when it next met on 23 March 1938 was the government statement on foreign policy expected the following day. Participants acknowledged that tensions created by the *Anschluss* had lessened, but that the European situation remained dangerous. It was noted that the government was showing greater awareness of the strategic importance of Spain. The discussion then turned to 'Foreign Policy Now'. The argument was advanced that if France were involved in war because of Czechoslovakia, Britain could not stay aloof. Therefore, 'the best course would be for us to join in a pledge to Czecho-Slovakia, in the hope that this would itself prevent the outbreak of war'. Another view attempted to limit Britain's commitment to France by an elaborate scheme of guaranteed and non-guaranteed frontiers. Finally, the continued *raison d'être* of the group itself was raised. Some wished the group to continue preparing a manifesto, while others held that its real function was discussion and the exchange of views.[68]

That inconclusive note resurfaced during the group's meeting on 31 March 1938 in Angell's chambers in the Temple. One of the participants described the government's foreign policy as one designed to avoid a crisis, and therefore open to taking 'grave political risks. . . . Its main fear was of a war breaking out as the result of drift'. Discussion then proceeded on the basis of this analysis. The opinion was offered that criticism would only force the government into repeated declarations of its determination to avoid war. This would allow the dictators to exploit the situation to their advantage. To this came the retort: 'If we advertised more clearly that we stand for law, individualism, etc., we should be able to mobilize behind us a great force of good will and thus increase our prestige.' Current European affairs were then subjected to detailed, but inconclusive, examination. Italian foreign policy, the question of recognition of Italy's conquest of Abyssinia, French domestic politics and a Franco victory in Spain were regarded as presenting 'alarming prospects'.

That left open the long-term implications of the situation in Europe. The most pessimistic view led to the scenario of a Nazi–Fascist domination of the continent, with an eventual 'Fascist revolution in England'. But could some lead, some rallying point, be given to the country? The strategic situation ruled out a League policy; while public opinion would not condone war 'in the defence of international law'. Some suggested a national appeal based on 'the defence of democracy'. Others toyed with the idea of dropping entirely the coercive functions of the League of Nations. The group 'agreed that it would welcome an initiative by the Government offering to make sacrifices in the cause of general appeasement, thus demonstrating that we did not merely stand for the status quo'. Finally, it was decided that a statement would again be attempted, as well as trying to make contact with groups in other countries. 'We are somewhat inconclusive,' Nicolson afterwards noted in his diary, 'but our main line is that a purely negative policy gets us nowhere and that there must be some more constructive drive.'[69]

The invitation to the next meeting stressed two factors requiring an early gathering. These were the conclusions of the Anglo-Italian agreement on 16 April 1938, which envisaged trading British recognition of Italy's conquest of Abyssinia for the withdrawal of Italian volunteers from Spain, and the forthcoming meeting of Parliament on 26 April. The group met at All Souls on 24 April, this time with Salter in attendance after his return from the United States, but with Liddell Hart and Nicolson abroad.[70] The minutes deal at length with the problems of 'appeasement and conciliation'.

Until recently we had stood for a policy of collective security and resistance to aggression. But now it was necessary to take into account other considerations – considerations of relative strength and vulnerability. . . .

We should recognize that the League as at present constituted was not able to fulfil the functions which we had expected of it . . . . there was in consequence no hope of appeasement through the League.

At present the capital task of diplomacy was not resistance to aggression whenever and wherever it might occur, but the preservation of peace – and of traditions of civilised Government, liberalism, mercy . . . . this meant that the primary effort of British policy should be directed not to resistance to aggression, but to appeasement and the finding of a *modus vivendi* with the aggressor states.

How this was to be translated into 'a middle policy between resistance and retreat' was difficult to articulate. It was accepted that the avoidance of war required 'the incorporation of all important irredentist communities within the *Reich*', the acquisition by Germany of colonies, the likely disappearance of Czechoslovakia, and a League without coercive functions. A wide range of other matters was also examined, but London's vulnerability to air attack was a particular matter of concern. 'It was fantastic that the fate of our civilization should depend on three or four thousand aeroplanes; and it was agreed that the whole scale of our programme should be transformed.' Finally, it was considered desirable to explore 'private and unofficial contact with Germany', a task for which some in the group 'were peculiarly fitted'. The line to be taken was to point out to the Germans 'that, if they were willing to co-operate with the other European powers they could probably fulfil peacefully most of their ambitions . . . but that their present methods threatened an explosion'. Before dispersing, the group decided to continue the work on a draft statement for publication.[71]

Despite the benefits of eight meetings and several extensive memoranda circulated for discussion, unanimity proved elusive. Allen now undertook the task of producing 'a clarifying statement of policy'. He privately wrote of the despair he felt at its hasty composition and the fact that it 'suffers from my attempt to meet points of view which are not entirely my own'.[72] The 29-page document which he produced by 10 May 1938 bore the title 'A Peace Policy for the Immediate Present'. In a covering note, he pointed out that his purpose was to frame 'a transitional policy'. The text attempted 'to outline a British foreign policy desirable in itself, immediately practicable in the broken circumstances of the present, and capable of rebuilding a system of international collaboration'.

Allen began by attributing many international problems to the 'mistakes' made at Versailles in 1919. That settlement, he argued, 'became synonymous with the selfish protection of the status quo . . . by those nations which at the time of the Peace Settlement were the most fortunate under the law'. He was prepared to accept that the situation now demanded 'an effort towards appeasement, even perhaps accepting certain breaches in morality such as that which occurred in Austria, as we make this new attempt to rebuild a system of international collaboration'. Such expediency, he conceded, would lead to 'casualties in morality'. But was it 'right to insist that British youth shall be killed and Europe involved in a ghastly catastrophe to sustain the existing integrity' of Czechoslovakia? He was prepared to believe that the 'neurosis of dictatorship' would pass, that arms were required in a rearming world, and that loyalty to the League no longer involved automatic obligations to collective defence. Most of all, he continued, Britain 'must hold out the hand of reconciliation even to the lawbreaker. To do this we shall have to accept as a *fait accompli* events which we regret and which have come about by illegitimate methods'.

The document then passed to practical proposals. Allen recommended support for the new Anglo-Italian agreement and recognition of Italian sovereignty in Abyssinia. Policy towards Germany required the eventual negotiation of 'a new Peace Settlement'. This might include separation of the League covenant from the peace treaties, the elimination of the war guilt clause, 'colonial reconstruction', and the recognition of Germany's 'special claims' in Czechoslovakia. He envisaged a four-power pact between Britain, France, Italy and Germany, the closing down of the Soviet Comintern, and Germany's return to a League of Nations without 'automatic obligations', and a Covenant that would be 'an instrument of social justice and economic welfare'. And he pleaded for a foreign policy based less on an appeal to law and more on upholding 'principles of human conduct, liberty and democratic forms of government'. Allen concluded with a scenario for his 'transitional policy' which, he wrote:

requires the exercise of prudence for a period of time during which we restore British armed strength, and promote military co-operation with democratic France and economic co-operation with democratic America. During that same period of time we shall also have made vigorous efforts towards appeasement. . . . If all these hopes should prove vain, we and other democratic nations will at least have gathered strength and restored a better moral foundation for a conflict if it should in the end be forced upon us.[73]

Allen had added what he called 'a special whip' to the notice of the next meeting set for All Souls on 15 May 1938. No record of those discussions survives. Nicolson afterwards wrote in his diary:

There is really a split between the realists and the moralists. Gilbert Murray and I do not approve of expedients. Allen says that peace should be bought at any price or almost any price. In fact he approves of the Government policy. We go on discussing till 7.0 and thereafter dine in Hall.[74]

Murray's own post-mortem supported Nicolson's impression. He wrote that the group once again showed

a tendency to split, Allen taking the line that the way to peace is to satisfy Germany; most of us thinking that resistance, and the maintenance of international law, more important. He would let Hitler have whatever he wants in Eastern Europe and more than Germany's original possessions in Africa.[75]

Toynbee had not been able to attend the meeting. However, in a letter to Allen on 11 May 1938, he refused to associate himself with the memorandum. He declared the 'transitional policy' to be a recipe for failure as well as 'morally wrong'. He regarded the Anglo-Italian agreement as an attempt to buy Italian neutrality 'at other people's expense and not out of our own pockets'. More generally, he returned to his belief that Britain could either abdicate its great power status or join the coming struggle against the European dictatorships, with the outcome being a 'World dominion' won by North America. Toynbee opted for the former policy. 'I am afraid my conclusion is gloomy', he wrote, 'but I have no belief at all in the possibility of "getting by" as the Americans say, in the next act of the tragedy.'[76] These observations were brought to the meeting and, according to Liddell Hart, 'created much commotion there'. The latter continued: 'Murray, Nicolson and myself were the only people who expressed agreement with it. Lionel Curtis, especially, remarked that twenty years of peace were worth any price.'[77]

Allen himself wrote to Toynbee on 17 May 1938, suggesting that the majority of participants agreed generally, while only a minority were opposed. He doubted that a sponsored document was on the cards.

In arguing about the present situation I am putting completely on one side my pacifist opinion, and am assuming that force must be put behind law in a world which remains armed. With that premise, my point is that to uphold under every conceivable circumstance the rule at a time when there is such a huge margin of doubt as to the capacity of aerial force to maintain the law is terribly serious. . . . It is for that reason that I am willing to take risks with morality during the transitional period in the hope – perhaps a vain one – that events will play into our hands.[78]

Shortly afterwards, following consultations with Salter, Allen reached outside the group. On 20 May 1938 he wrote to the Liberal journalist, J.A. Spender, describing the meetings over the previous five months of 'a very representative and distinguished group of international thinkers'. He emphasized that a statement was needed 'for the sake of public opinion, to help the rank and file of all the peace organizations, to restrain some expressions of the Opposition and to assist or bring pressure to bear upon the Government'. Allen confessed that the group had indeed considered his own most recent memorandum, one of several which he enclosed for Spender, and this had led to the suggestion that it might be rewritten by another hand. He continued:

Salter and I venture to beg you to consider whether you would, having read these documents, produce for joint signature and ultimate publication the right kind of document. You have the literary genius which I do not possess. You have the power of temperately expressing a new policy which would probably carry the support of many distinguished people.

He concluded with a proposal for a meeting, which would include Salter, to discuss the matter.[79]

Allen then undertook a letter-writing campaign to private correspondents,[80] the *Manchester Guardian* and, in particular, *The Times*. Dawson and some of his staff were very sympathetic to Allen's views and gave him access to the letter columns of the newspaper. In these, Allen threw his support behind a policy of 'collective action on two fronts simultaneously – conciliation and revision of the *status quo* on the one hand; the display of strength to protect lawful procedure on the other hand.'[81] At least one of his All Souls colleagues was less than complimentary about his flurry of activity. 'Allen's nerves are evidently upset', Murray observed.[82] Indeed, the latter now had little patience for Allen whom he regarded as 'taking the line that the way to peace is to satisfy Germany'.[83]

A meeting at All Souls, planned for 5–6 June 1938, never took place, possibly because of Allen's illness. Instead, two confidential papers were circulated on 29 June to members of the group. The first was a memorandum by Hudson on the Czechoslovak situation. The document emphasized the many weaknesses of the Czech state since its inception in 1919 and its precarious situation in 1938. The second, dated simply June 1938, was titled 'Memorandum by Mr J.A. Spender'. This took aim at the critics of Chamberlain who blamed him and his predecessors for policy failures in the Far East, Spain and central Europe. Spender argued that it was the duty of the government 'to mediate and pacify'. He continued:

But it cannot be expected to do single-handed what the Powers collectively have failed to do; and to reproach it as if it were guilty of a dereliction of moral duty when it declined this responsibility, seems to us unfair. . . .

Given Britain's worldwide responsibilities and the limits to its power, 'a distinction between what is desirable and what is possible' was required. Policy should be one of 'peace with all who are willing to make peace, irrespective of their internal forms of Government'. Finally, Spender advised bipartisanship in foreign policy which alone could prevent the misunderstandings which had set government and opposition at odds.[84]

Salter and Allen postponed the next meeting of the group, scheduled for 16 July 1938, because of the absence of several members. The Spender memorandum, therefore, never received a general airing. Curtis, for one, observed that he always doubted that the All Souls group would ever produce an agreed document. However, he praised Spender's effort as 'one of the wisest documents I have ever read'. He added that he would readily subscribe to it. Allen replied, more accurately, that the memorandum was 'not quite comprehensive' and informed Curtis that he would be meeting with Salter to discuss the future of the All Souls group.[85]

In any case, events and a desire for more tangible results overtook some of the group. As early as 4 May 1938, Wint had proposed that the crisis in central Europe demanded intervention by a British intermediary. He suggested that Salter go to Germany with a dual message: to warn that Europe was on the brink again as in 1914; and to advise that peaceful negotiations would lead to the satisfaction of many German demands.[86] Salter demurred, citing his long experience of international negotiations which had taught him the benefit of meticulous advance preparations. On the other hand, the proposal appealed to Allen, and he and his Quaker colleague, Corder Catchpool, went ahead with plans for a visit to Germany.

The July week-end meeting between Salter and Allen produced a draft letter to the editor of The Times. The note inviting signatures pointed out that the exercise was intended to unite 'many schools of thought', to avoid 'the usual ferocious demands' for unlimited British commitments, and at the same time make 'a practical proposal'.[87] The letter suggested that, if negotiations failed to resolve the crisis in Czechoslovakia, the principals involved 'declare their readiness to invite, through some suitable procedure, a third-party opinion as to the best solution, without necessarily binding themselves to accept the opinion so obtained'. On 26 July 1938, Allen sent the draft of the letter to Lord Halifax. The latter was asked whether such a publication 'would be helpful or at least not harmful'. Halifax's reply of 29 July, drafted in the Foreign Office, was far from encouraging:

. . . although the proposal made in the letter differs of course from the mission which Lord Runciman has undertaken, the fact that Runciman is about to leave for Prague with the apparent good will of both the disputants, puts rather a different light on it, and inevitably rather detracts from the value of the letter in its present form.[88]

Although the letter was withdrawn, Allen pressed forward in what had now become a personal mission. On 27 July he spoke in the House of Lords for the last time, pleading for a more humanitarian regime in Germany and repeating his wishes for an Anglo–German understanding. From 6 to 15 August he visited Germany and Czechoslovakia. The result, as he noted afterwards, was 'hours and hours of talk and NOTHING else whatever'.[89]

The All Souls Foreign Affairs Group, after the postponement notice sent out on 4 July 1938, was never reconvened. No formal decision was ever taken to wind up its affairs.[90] Its history remained preserved within the records accumulated during the nine meetings from 18 December 1937 to 15 May 1938. What then can be asserted with regard to the impact and historical significance of the All Souls Foreign Affairs Group? Indeed, what was its 'true character and influence'? During its brief life, the group served precisely the purposes designed by the participants. It acted as a Brains Trust on foreign policy. In this way, it helped leading individuals, drawn from various fields and with divergent political outlooks, to discuss, analyse and clarify. Thus informed, they were able to speak publicly on issues with the confidence that problems had been thrashed out by some of the most penetrating minds of the inter-war years.

In the initial meetings, the All Souls Foreign Affairs Group was agreed on a dual policy of firmness and conciliation. The proportions of these strategies, and the geographical area for their application, however, remained a matter for debate. Appeasers, either economic or political, with regard to Europe could be found to be resisters when contemplating the Mediterranean and the Far East, and vice versa. As the early months of 1938 passed with momentous changes unfolding in Europe, and particularly after the *Anschluss*, the group soon found itself deeply divided. The future of Czechoslovakia did not prove to be the stumbling block. Indeed, it was largely non-contentious; the neutralization in some form of that country had wide appeal within the group. What was never advocated was the defence of Czechoslovakia in all circumstances and under all conditions.

'Salter's Soviet', however, was never able to formulate an agreed public statement on foreign affairs. It could be argued that this was partly related to the unrelenting pressure of international events. Discussions in 1938 were often rendered obsolete by the headlines of the morning newspapers, or by radio news broadcasts. Another reason was that the group spanned the political spectrum, excluding the extremes of both right and left. Such diversity did not prevent agreement being reached on maintaining a tough line both in the Far East and the Mediterranean, hastening rearmament for defensive purposes, and avoiding the isolation of the USSR. Where the group found progress more difficult, if not impossible, was on two related questions. The first, as Toynbee put it at Chatham House on 10 March 1938, was 'Would firmness on our part . . . daunt the dictators, or would it madden them? Would an offer of unconditional negotiations win their hearts or swell their ambitions to outrageous dimensions?' The second was the great question of 'making a stand'. On this issue most of all, and justifiably so, 'the realists and the moralists' as Nicolson termed them, split. In essence, the group never came to a resolution of the dilemma, debated at its 24 April 1938 meeting, as to whether there was 'a middle policy between resistance and retreat'. What actually was worth the price of British lives? Between December 1937 and May 1938 the line of resistance floated worldwide, from the Far East to the Holland–France border. Failure to reach agreement on this fundamental question, for what purpose and with whom would British power be used, finally rendered it impossible to produce the desired declaration on foreign policy. In the end, the Allen prescription on 15 May 1938 of 'peace at any price' was never acceptable to the group.

In both the short and long term it cannot be contended that 'Salter's Soviet' – as a group – had any influence whatever on government policy or thinking with regard to international issues.[91] Rowse's contention

about the pivotal role of All Souls and its Fellows in the formulation
and implementation of appeasement therefore must be qualified. He
himself did so when he argues that the younger Fellows were opposed
to appeasement. 'Salter's Soviet' certainly provides yet further
evidence of that generation gap and the vigorous opposition within the
group. Even more, its records illustrate that few can lay claim to being
consistently either an appeaser or a resister. In a wider sense, however,
failure to agree on where to take a stand was the central issue at the
heart of appeasement. Prime Minister Neville Chamberlain himself
had the utmost difficulty with this question. Appeasement at All Souls
was no more successful.

## NOTES

For assistance at the editorial stage, the author is grateful to Michael Dafoe and Helen Hatton.

1. A.L. Rowse, *All Souls and Appeasement: A Contribution to Contemporary History* (London, 1961), p. 117.
2. Ibid., pp. v–vi, 113. Among the latter Rowse listed Richard Pares, Geoffrey F. Hudson, A.H.M. Jones, A.H. Campbell, Ian Bowen, Isaiah Berlin, Douglas Jay, Quintin Hogg, Dick Latham and Harry Davis. The American edition of the book was titled *Appeasement: A Study in Political Decline, 1933–1939* (New York, 1961). The two editions are the same, including pagination, except for some minor variations, as for example on p. 58, fn. 3, and pp. 109–10.
3. Sir Basil Liddell Hart, *The Memoirs of Captain Liddell Hart*, Vol. II (London, 1965), p. 150. The first contemporary use of this phrase appears in Curtis to Ivison Macadam, 2 March 1938, MSS. Curtis 12, fol. 39, Bodleian Library, Oxford.
4. Lord Salter, *Memoirs of a Public Servant* (London, 1961), pp. 259–60. There is also a fleeting reference in Rowse, *All Souls and Appeasement*, p. 59.
5. See, for example, Arthur Marwick, *Clifford Allen: The Open Conspirator* (London, 1964), pp. 176–8, Liddell Hart, *Memoirs*, Vol. II, pp. 149–50, Martin Gilbert, *Plough My Own Furrow: The Story of Lord Allen of Hurtwood as Told through His Writings and Correspondence* (London, 1965), pp. 399–405, Lord Salter, *Slave of the Lamp: A Public Servant's Notebook* (London, 1967), pp. 131–2, and Arnold J. Toynbee, *Acquaintances* (London, 1967), p.133.
6. Christina Hole (1896–1985). Subsequently, the noted authority on English folk customs and folklore, and prolific author of such books as *Traditions and Customs of Cheshire* (London, 1937), *English Folklore* (London, 1940), *Witchcraft in England* (London, 1945), and *British Folk Customs* (London, 1976).
7. Sir Basil Henry Liddell Hart (1895–1970). Military historian and strategist; military correspondent, the *Daily Telegraph*, 1925–35, and *The Times*, 1935–39; unofficial adviser to Minister of War, 1937–38; some 30 books include *Europe in Arms* (London, 1937), *The Defence of Britain* (London, 1939), and *Memoirs*, 2 vols. (London, 1965). For the list of participants, and the correspondence which led to its compilation, see Sir Basil H. Liddell Hart Papers, LH5/1, King's College, London.
8. William George Stewart Adams (1874–1966). Public servant; Fellow of All Souls, 1910–33; Gladstone Professor of Political Theory and Institutions, Oxford University, 1912–33; founded and edited the *Political Quarterly*, 1914–16; Warden of All Souls, 1933–1945) and then honorary Fellow, 1945.
9. Reginald Clifford Allen, Baron Allen of Hurtwood (1889–1939). Labour politician; three times imprisoned as a conscientious objector, 1916–17; treasurer and chairman, ILP, 1922–26; director, *Daily Herald*, 1925–30; supported 'national' labour group, 1931–36; publications include *Putting Socialism Into Practice* (London, 1924), *Britain's Political Future: A Plea for Liberty and Leadership* (London, 1934), and *Peace in Our Time* (London, 1936).

10. Sir Norman Angell (1872–1967). Publicist and author of *The Great Illusion* (London, 1910); *Peace With the Dictators?* (London, 1938), and some 35 other books; editor, *Foreign Affairs*, 1928–31; Labour MP, 1929–31; Nobel Peace Prize, 1933; memoirs in *After All* (London, 1951).

11. William Edward Arnold-Forster (1895–1951). With the Admiralty, 1914–18; joined the Labour Party, 1919; strong supporter of the League of Nations and frequent contributor to *Headway*; secretary to Lord Robert Cecil, 1929–31; artist specializing in pastel landscapes; author of *Why We Have Failed to Disarm* (London, 1927), *The Disarmament Conference* (London, 1931), *The Blockade, 1914–1919: Before the Armistice – and After* (London, 1939), and *The New Freedom of the Seas* (London, 1942).

12. Alfred Barratt Brown (1887–1947). Vice-Principal, 1921–26, and principal, 1926–44, Ruskin College, Oxford; member of the Quaker Executive Committee, 1914–18; twice imprisoned for his Christian pacifist views, first as a member of the No-Conscription Fellowship and then as a conscientious objector; books include *The Machine and the Worker* (London, 1934), and *Democratic Leadership* (London, 1938).

13. Lionel George Curtis (1872–1955). Public servant and exponent of federalist ideas; a founder of the *Round Table*, 1910; and of the Royal Institute of International Affairs, 1920–21; research Fellow, All Souls, 1921; author of *Dyarchy* (London, 1920); *The Prevention of War* (London, 1924), *The Capital Question of China* (London, 1932), *Civitas Dei*, 3 vols. (London, 1934–37), *Faith and Works, Or A World Safe for Small Nations* (London, 1943), and *With Milner in South Africa* (London, 1951).

14. Herbert Albert Laurens Fisher (1865–1940). Historian and statesman; introduced Education Act, 1918; Liberal MP, 1916–26; delegate to League of Nations Assembly, 1920–22; warden of New College, Oxford, 1925–40; publications include *James Bryce*, 2 vols. (London, 1927), *A History of Europe*, 3 vols. (London, 1935), and *An Unfinished Autobiography* (London, 1940).

15. Henry Vincent Hodson (1906–). Fellow of All Souls, 1928–35; editor, *Round Table*, 1934–39; and *Annual Register of World Events*, 1973–88; with Ministry of Information, 1939–41, and Ministry of Production, 1942–45; assistant editor, 1945–50, and editor, 1950–61, *The Sunday Times*; books include *Economics of a Changing World* (London, 1933), *Slump and Recovery, 1929–1937* (London, 1938), and *The British Commonwealth and the Future* (London, 1939).

16. Geoffrey Francis Hudson (1903–74). Fellow of All Souls, 1926–54; with the research department, Foreign Office, 1939–46; Fellow and director of Far Eastern Studies, St Antony's College, Oxford, 1954–74; author of *Europe and China* (London, 1931), *The Far East in World Politics* (London, 1936), with Marthe Rajchman of *An Atlas of Far Eastern Politics* (London, 1938), and *Fifty Years of Communism* (London, 1968).

17. Sir Walter Layton, 1st Baron Layton (1884–1966). Economist, and newspaper proprietor; with Ministry of Munitions, 1914–18; editor, *The Economist*, 1922–38; chairman, *News Chronicle*, 1930–50, and *Star*, 1936–50; with Ministry of Supply, 1940–42, and Ministry of Production, 1941–43; published *An Introduction to the Study of Prices* (London, 1920), *Allied War Aims* (London, 1939), and *How to Deal With Germany* (London, 1944).

18. Harold Macmillan (1894–1986). Publisher and politician; Conservative MP, 1924–29, 1931–64; Minister resident at Allied Headquarters in North-West Africa, 1942–45; prime minister, 1957–63; author of *Reconstruction: A Plea for a National Policy* (London, 1933), *The Middle Way* (London, 1938), and *Memoirs*, 6 vols. (London, 1966–73).

19. Gilbert Murray (1866–1957). Classical scholar and internationalist; Regius Professor of Greek, Oxford University, 1908–36; founder of the League of Nations Union and chairman of the executive council, 1923–38; besides numerous classical studies, works include *The Foreign Policy of Sir Edward Grey* (London, 1915), *The Problem of Foreign Policy* (London, 1921), and *Liberality and Civilisation* (London, 1938).

20. Sir Harold George Nicolson (1886–1968). Diplomat, author and critic; entered Foreign Office, 1909; married Victoria Sackville-West, 1913; with British delegation to Paris peace conference, 1919; served at Foreign Office and abroad, 1920–29; National Labour MP, 1935–45; governor of the BBC, 1941–46; his numerous books include *Curzon, The Last Phase* (London, 1934), *Diplomacy* (London, 1939), *King George V* (London, 1952), and *Diaries and Letters, 1930–1962*, 3 vols. (London, 1966–68).

21. Alfred Reginald Radcliffe-Brown (1881–1955). Professor of Anthropology, University of Sydney, 1925–31, University of Chicago, 1931–37; Fellow of All Souls and Professor of Social Anthropology, Oxford University, 1937–46; president of Royal Anthropological Institute, 1939–40.

22. A.L. Rowse (1903–). Stood as Labour candidate, 1929, 1935; Fellow, and later emeritus Fellow, of All Souls, 1925–74; author of many books of history, politics and reminiscences; the latter include *A Cornishman at Oxford* (London, 1965), *A Cornishman Abroad* (London, 1976), *A Man of the Thirties* (London, 1979), *Memories of Men and Women* (London, 1980), *Glimpses of the Great* (London, 1985), and *Friends and Contemporaries* (London, 1989).

23. Sir James Arthur Salter, 1st Baron Salter (1881–1975). General secretary, Reparation Commission, 1920–22; director, economic and finance section, League of Nations, 1919–20, 1922–31; Independent MP, 1937–50, then Conservative, 1951–53; Fellow of All Souls, 1934–75; Gladstone Professor of Political Theory and Institutions, Oxford University, 1934–44; head of British Shipping Mission, Washington, 1941–43; numerous publications include *Recovery* (London, 1932), *The United States of Europe* (London, 1933), and *Personality in Politics* (London, 1947).

24. Arnold Joseph Toynbee (1889–1975). Professor of Byzantine and Modern Greek Language, Literature and History, London University, 1919–24; director of studies, Royal Institute of International Affairs, 1925–55; director, research department, Foreign Office, 1943–46; editor, 1924–38, *A Survey of International Affairs*; numerous publications include *A Study of History*, 12 vols. (London, 1934–61); memoirs in *Acquaintances* (London, 1967), and the sequel *Experiences* (London, 1969).

25. Sir Ernest Llewellyn Woodward (1890–1971). Fellow of All Souls, 1919–44, 1962–71; Professor of International Relations, Oxford, 1944–47, and Modern History, 1947–51; editor, 1944–55 of *Documents on British Foreign Policy, 1919–1939*; and author of *The Age of Reform, 1815–70* (London, 1938); *Great Britain and the War of 1914–18* (London, 1967); and *British Foreign Policy During the Second World War*, 5 vols. (London, 1970–76); memoirs in *Short Journey* (London, 1942).

26. Guy Wint (1910–69). Author and orientalist; accompanied Sir Arthur Salter to China, 1933; wartime work in India for the Ministry of Information; on the staff of the *Manchester Guardian*, 1947–57; books include *The British in Asia* (London, 1947), *Spotlight on Asia* (London, 1955), *Commonsense About China* (London, 1960); and with Peter Calvocoressi, *Total War: Causes and Courses of the Second World War* (London, 1972).

27. Salter to Liddell Hart, 1 May 1961, Liddell Hart Papers, LH5/1. Salter also included the name of Leo Amery, but there is no evidence whatever that Amery ever attended the meetings. It was Wint who kept what Arnold Toynbee described as the 'admirable minutes' of the discussions. See Toynbee to Allen, 11 May 1938, Liddell Hart Papers, LH1/698.

28. Sydney Arnold, 1st Baron Arnold (1878–1945). Liberal MP, 1912–21; joined Labour Party, 1922; created a Labour peer and appointed under-secretary for the Colonies, 1924; paymaster-general, 1929–31; resigned from Labour Party for its alleged pro-war policies, 1938.

29. See, for example, *Parliamentary Debates, House of Lords*, Fifth Series, Vol. 104, 3 March 1937, cols. 505–9.

30. 'All Souls – College Affairs', n.d., Salter Papers.

31. Salter, 'Notes on Foreign Policy', 8 March 1938, Liddell Hart Papers, LH5/1. This is confirmed in Curtis to Brand, 20 Dec. 1937, MSS. Curtis 11, fols. 168–70.

32. *The Next Five Years: An Essay in Political Agreement* (London, 1935), pp. v–x, 1, 215–307. Geoffrey Crowther was the sixth member of the drafting committee. In addition, Angell, Curtis, Fisher, Layton and Murray were also among the signatories. The Next Five Years Group formally disbanded on 25 Nov. 1937. See Arthur Marwick, 'Middle Opinion in the Thirties: Planning, Progress and Political "Agreement"', *English Historical Review*, 79 (1964), pp. 293–5, and Thomas C. Kennedy, 'The Next Five Years Group and the Failure of the Politics of Agreement in Britain', *Canadian Journal of History*, 9(1974), pp. 45–68.

33. 'The Future of All Souls', 1962, Salter Papers.

34. William Norton Medlicott, *Britain and Germany: The Search for Agreement, 1930–1937* (London, 1969), p. 32, first suggested that, with proper analysis, 'the lines of distinction between the popular stereotypes, appeasers (or peacemakers) and warmongers (or resisters),

between the doves and the hawks of the nineteen-thirties, tend to disappear'.
35. Salter to Liddell Hart, 11 Dec. 1937, Liddell Hart Papers, LH5/1. In the event, Layton and Allen did not attend. As well, notes were not taken of discussions on the evening of 18 Dec. 1937. Meeting at All Souls College, Oxford, 18–19 Dec. 1937, Harold Nicolson Diaries, Balliol College, Oxford.
36. Entries of 18–19 Dec. 1937, Nicolson Diaries.
37. Conference on Foreign Affairs, 18–19 Dec. 1937 (Document A), Liddell Hart Papers, LH5/1. These were the minutes, circulated afterwards by Salter, with a letter A in the top left hand corner. Another document, Conference on Foreign Affairs, 18–19 Dec. 1937 (Document B) was also circulated. This contained a more free form summary of the discussions. The Harold Nicolson Diaries also include a set of minutes of the discussions. A comparison shows that they are a retyping of Documents A and B.
38. Conference on Foreign Affairs, 18–19 Dec. 1937 (Document B), Liddell Hart Papers, LH5/1.
39. Curtis to Brand, 20 Dec. 1937, MSS. Curtis 11, fols. 168–70. In Curtis to Allen, 20 Dec. 1937, MSS. Curtis 11, fol. 171, Curtis observed: 'Our real objective . . . should be to change the militaristic outlook in Germany we have created.' See also, Allen to Curtis, 22 Dec. 1937, MSS. Curtis 11, fol. 172. Nicolson's views can be followed in his 'Germany and the Colonies', *Fortnightly*, 142(1937), pp. 641–8.
40. Conference on Foreign Affairs, All Souls, 15–16 Jan. 1938, Nicolson Diaries.
41. Conference on Foreign Affairs, 18–19 Dec. 1937 (Document B), Liddell Hart Papers, LH5/1.
42. Murray was at the time trying to rewrite the League of Nations Union programme. He was convinced that 'The greatest issue now is Collective Security *plus* Peaceful Change.' Murray to Allen, 13 Dec. 1937, MSS. Murray 230, fol. 66, Bodleian Library, Oxford. See also, Murray to Salter, 29 Dec. 1937, and Enclosure, MSS. Murray 230, fols. 97–101.
43. Nicolson's pencil notes of the discussions record the presence as well of Toynbee. These notes occasionally serve to identify some speakers. However, they add little to the substance of the circulated record of the conversations. Notes, 6 pp., attached to entry of 15–16 Jan. 1938, Nicolson Diaries.
44. For an example of Woodward's views with regard to Germany, see his memorandum, 'Germany and Europe', 27 Jan. 1937, FO371/20734, C678/226/18, Public Record Office, London.
45. Conference on Foreign Affairs, All Souls, 15–16 Jan. 1938, Liddell Hart Papers, LH5/1; Notes, 6 pp., attached to entry of 15–16 Jan. 1938, Nicolson Diaries. Several days later, Arnold-Forster, described as 'Lord Cecil's right-hand man', was in Oslo as a representative of the International Peace Campaign. He was reported as being in favour of a boycott of Japan. See British Legation, Oslo, to Foreign Office, 25 Jan. 1938, FO371/22562, W1313/1067/98.
46. Liddell Hart to Salter, 17 Jan. 1938; Salter to Liddell Hart, 18 Jan. 1938, Liddell Hart Papers, LH5/1.
47. Curtis to Dawson, 17 Jan. 1938, MSS. Curtis 12, fols. 10–13. For an informative pen-portrait of Curtis, see Toynbee, *Acquaintances*, pp. 129–48.
48. Murray to Liddell Hart, 17 Jan. 1938; Liddell Hart to Murray, 19 Jan. 1938, Liddell Hart Papers, LH5/1. See also, Murray to Cecil, 19 Jan. 1938, MSS. Murray 231, fol. 95.
49. Salter to Liddell Hart, 18 Jan. 1938, Liddell Hart Papers, LH5/1.
50. Entry of 6 Feb. 1938, Nicolson Diaries. Liddell Hart was not present. See Liddell Hart to Salter, 3 Feb. 1938, Liddell Hart Papers, LH5/1. Allen's further views on foreign affairs can be followed in *Parliamentary Debates, House of Lords*, Fifth Series, Vol. 107, 17 Nov. 1937, cols. 115–31, 'A Constructive Peace Policy', *Contemporary Review*, 152(1937), pp. 11–20, *Peace in Our Time: An Appeal to the International Peace Conference of June 16, 1936* (London, 1936), and the chapter 'A Practical Peace Policy', in *Britain's Political Future: A Plea for Liberty and Leadership* (London, 1934), pp. 107–18.
51. 'Document C', Enclosure in Wint to Nicolson, 12 Feb. 1938, Liddell Hart Papers, LH5/1.
52. Entry of 26 Feb. 1938, Nicolson Diaries; Foreign Affairs Group, Meeting of 26 Feb. 1938, Liddell Hart Papers, LH5/1.
53. Wint to Curtis, 28 Feb. 1938, MSS. Curtis 12, fol. 32; original in Lord Allen of Hurtwood Papers, University of South Carolina, Columbia, SC.
54. Curtis to Allen, 28 Feb. 1938, MSS. Curtis 12, fols. 33–4; Allen to Curtis, 1 March 1938,

MSS. Curtis 12, fols. 36–8. Later, Rowse was to describe Allen as a 'distasteful figure . . . who had won an aureole for his sufferings as a pacifist. Enjoying invalidism, a fund was raised for his support, which he invested to such good purpose that he was henceforth not a member of the Independent Labour Party but, better, independent financially. This holier-than-thou type was created a Labour peer'. Rowse, *Man of the Thirties*, p. 202.

55. Christina Hole to Liddell Hart, 1 March 1938, Liddell Hart Papers, LH5/1; Curtis to Ivison Macadam, 2 March 1938, MSS. Curtis 12, fol. 39; Murray to Cecil, 4 March 1938, MSS. Murray 232, fols. 61–2; entry of 8 March 1938, Nicolson Diaries. For Toynbee's speech at Chatham House, which indirectly referred to the All Souls discussions, see 'The Issues in British Foreign Policy', 10 March 1938, Royal Institute of International Affairs Archives, 8/526, Chatham House, London. The revised version appeared in *International Affairs*, 27(1938), pp. 307–37.

56. Salter, 'Notes on Foreign Policy', 8 March 1938; and pencilled note by Salter attached and dated 8 March 1938, Liddell Hart Papers, LH5/1. See also, Salter to Curtis, 9 March 1938, Lionel Curtis Papers, Royal Institute of International Affairs Archives, Chatham House, London.

57. Wint to Curtis, 11 March 1938, and Enclosure, MSS. Curtis 12, fols. 58–62.

58. Foreign Affairs Group, 16 March 1938, Liddell Hart Papers, LH5/1; Salter, 'Notes on Foreign Policy', 8 March 1938, Liddell Hart Papers, LH5/1; Christina Hole to Liddell Hart, Liddell Hart Papers, LH5/1; entry of 16 March 1938, Nicolson Diaries.

59. Hodson to Liddell Hart, 16, 18 March 1938, and Liddell Hart to Hodson, 17 March 1938, Liddell Hart Papers, LH5/1. The signatories were Allen, Angell, Arnold-Forster, Hodson, Hudson, Layton, Liddell Hart, Macmillan, Murray, Nicolson, Radcliffe-Brown, Rowse and Toynbee. See Hole to Nicolson, 19 March 1938, Liddell Hart Papers, LH5/1. A copy of the *'Aide-Mémoire* on Spain' is attached to this last letter. The *News Chronicle* on 18 March used it as a basis for an article from a 'Military Observer'. For Liddell Hart's additional views at that time, see Angell to Liddell Hart, 18 March 1938, and Enclosures, Liddell Hart Papers, LH1/16/4–6, and Basil Liddell Hart, *The Defence of Britain* (London, 1939), pp. 63–70.

60. Note by Alfred Barratt Brown, n.d., Liddell Hart Papers, LH5/1.

61. Allen to Cecil, 19 March 1938; Cecil to Allen, 22 March 1938, in Gilbert, *Plough My Own Furrow*, p. 399.

62. Quoted in Gilbert, *Plough My Own Furrow*, p. 395.

63. Hudson, 'Notes on the European Situation', Enclosure in Christina Hole to Liddell Hart, 19 March 1938, Liddell Hart Papers, LH5/1. For a pen-portrait of Hudson see A.L. Rowse, *A Cornishman Abroad* (London, 1976), pp. 191–3.

64. Entry of 22 March 1938, Nicolson Diaries.

65. Nicolson to Cadogan, 21 March 1938, FO371/22641, W4440/83/41. The list of signatories which Nicolson gave to Cadogan left out Hudson and Radcliffe-Brown. To a fellow MP, Nicolson summed up his efforts thus: 'All I have tried to do is to wake people up to the Spanish danger.' Nicolson to Paul Emrys-Evans, 22 March 1938, Evans ADD.MSS. 58248, fol. 50, British Library, London.

66. Cadogan to Nicolson, 2 April 1938, FO371/22641, W4440/83/41; Nicolson to Cadogan, 4 April 1938, FO371/22642, W4471/83/41.

67. 'Foreign Policy Now', n.d. [19 March 1938], Liddell Hart Papers, LH5/1.

68. Foreign Affairs Group, Meeting of 23 March 1938, Liddell Hart Papers, LH5/1.

69. Foreign Affairs Group, Meeting of 31 March 1938, Liddell Hart Papers, LH5/1; entry of 31 March 1938, Nicolson Diaries.

70. For Nicolson's report to the Foreign Office on the conclusion of his tour of Bulgaria, Romania and Yugoslavia, see Nicolson to Vansittart, 2 May 1938, FO371/22342, R4737/94/67. On the same day he wrote to Angell: 'On the one hand I do not approve of Chamberlain's policy in all its aspects, yet on the other I cannot place any faith in the Opposition.' Nicolson to Angell, 2 May 1938, Sir Norman Angell Papers, Ball State University, Muncie, IN.

71. Christina Hole to Liddell Hart, 1 April 1938, 'Liddell Hart Papers, LH5/1; Foreign Affairs Group, 24 April 1938, Liddell Hart Papers, LH5/1. A meeting tentatively scheduled for 10 April appears to have been cancelled. See Christina Hole to Liddell Hart, 1 April 1938, Liddell Hart Papers, LH5/1. Also during April, Curtis and Salter, with the assistance

of Sir John Anderson, R.H. Brand, Major-General Sir Ernest Swinton, Lord Nuffield and Leo Amery, spearheaded the formation of an Air Defence League, later renamed the Civil Defence League. See correspondence in MSS. Curtis 12, fols. 89–90, 95–6, 101–3, 104, 126–8, 220.

72. Note by Allen to Members of the Foreign Affairs Group, n.d., Liddell Hart Papers, LH5/1; Allen to Curtis, 10 May 1938, MSS. Curtis 12, fol. 13b.

73. 'A Peace Policy for the Immediate Present', by Lord Allen of Hurtwood, with a covering note 'To Those Who Have Taken Part in the Discussion of Foreign Affairs at All Souls College', 10 May 1938, Liddell Hart Papers, LH5/1. Salter also attempted something along similar lines. See Salter to Allen, 4 May 1938, Allen Papers. Of related interest is a memorandum by Arnold-Forster, 'The Anglo–Italian Agreement', May 1938, Cecil ADD.MSS. 51140, fols. 97–105, British Library, London.

74. Entry of 15 May 1938, Nicolson Diaries.

75. Murray to Edwyn Robert Bevan, 1 June 1938, MSS. Murray 233, fol. 3.

76. Toynbee to Allen, 11 May 1938, Liddell Hart Papers, LH1/698. At the time Toynbee was consulting Liddell Hart about the Spanish civil war chapter for the 1937 edition of the Chatham House *Survey of International Affairs*. See further correspondence in the Liddell Hart Papers, LH1/698.

77. Liddell Hart to Toynbee, 25 May 1938, Liddell Hart Papers, LH1/698.

78. Allen to Toynbee, 17 May 1938, in Gilbert, *Plough My Own Furrow*, pp. 400–1.

79. Allen to Spender, 20 May 1938, Spender ADD.MSS. 46394, IX, fols. 103–6, British Library, London. This includes the only mention, in any record of the group, of H.A.L. Fisher as a participant.

80. See, for example, Allen to Curtis, 8 June 1938, MSS. Curtis 12, fol. 162; and the reply in Curtis to Allen, 10 June 1938, MSS. Curtis 12, fols. 163–4.

81. *The Times*, 30 May 1938; see also, Gilbert, *Plough My Own Furrow*, pp. 401–3. On Allen's relationship with *The Times* and its editors, see Marwick, *Clifford Allen*, pp. 176–7.

82. Murray to Wickham Steed, 10 June 1938, MSS. Murray 233, fol. 32. See also, Murray to Allen, 24 May 1938, MSS. Murray 232, fol. 197.

83. Murray to Edwyn Robert Bevan, 1 June 1938, MSS. Murray 233, fol. 3.

84. 'Memorandum on Czechoslovakia', 8 June 1938, and 'Memorandum by J.A. Spender', June 1938, Enclosures in Christina Hole to All Souls Group, 29 June 1938, Liddell Hart Papers, LH5/1. See also, J.A. Spender, *New Lamps and Ancient Lights* (London, 1940), and his *Between Two Wars* (London, 1943).

85. Curtis to Allen, 11 July 1938, MSS. Curtis, 12, fol. 219; Allen to Curtis, 13 July 1938, MSS. Curtis, 12, fol. 224.

86. Marwick, *Clifford Allen*, p. 178.

87. Allen to Nicolson, 20 July 1938, Liddell Hart Papers, LH5/1; Allen to Fisher, 20 July 1938, MSS. Fisher, 77, fol. 30, Bodleian Library, Oxford. Besides Salter and Allen, others invited to sign included Fisher, Lord Astor, Lord Cecil, Curtis, Hobson, Lord Lothian, Lord Lytton, Murray, Nicolson, Lord Noel-Buxton, Lord Samuel, Spender and Sir John Fischer Williams.

88. Allen to Halifax, 26 July, enclosing Letter to *The Times*; Minute by Strang, 27 July 1938; and Halifax to Allen, 29 July 1938, FO371/21730, C7766/1941/18.

89. Gilbert, *Plough My Own Furrow*, pp. 405–12; Marwick, *Clifford Allen*, pp. 178–85; Newton to Halifax, 13 Aug. 1938, FO371/21731, C8301/1941/18.

90. See, for example, Allen to Salter, 19 Oct. 1938, Allen Papers.

91. For some of the post-Munich thinking by participants, see, for example, Sir Arthur Salter, *Is It Peace? The Nettle and the Flower* (London, 1938); his *Security: Can We Retrieve It?* (London, 1939), which included 'A Draft Manifesto of British Policy', pp. 345–66; B.H. Liddell Hart, *The Defence of Britain* (London, 1939), pp. 8–125; E.L. Woodward, 'An Historian's Outlook on the Present State of Europe', 24 Oct. 1938, FO371/21627, C14420/95/62; and Murray to Halifax, 8 Nov. 1938, FO371/22512, W14847/3/98.

# German Bureaucrat or Nazified Ideologue? Ambassador Otto Abetz and Hitler's Anti-Jewish Policies 1940–44

## JOHN P. FOX

A detailed examination of the role of the Paris Embassy of Otto Abetz from 1940 to 1944, within the complex of the Nazi *Endlösung der Judenfrage in Europa* during the Second World War, contributes to a further understanding of the decision-making process involved in that deliberate policy of mass murder in at least two ways.[1]

First, it underlines the need for serious modification of Christopher Browning's main conclusions about the motivation of German 'diplomats' in promoting the Third Reich's persecution and extermination of European Jewry. Although many could hardly be described as career bureaucrats or diplomats in the accepted sense since they were members of the National Socialist Party (NSDAP) and had only lately entered the German Foreign Office, the Auswärtiges Amt, Browning has observed that 'they were primarily motivated by considerations of careerism, not racial ideology or fanatical and blind obedience to higher authority. The decisions which led to the original involvement of the Foreign Office in the Final Solution and later to pressing forward the Final Solution with increased urgency resulted from the pressures exerted upon the Foreign Office by virtue of the intense internal political rivalry which was the essence of the Nazi system of government'.[2]

Browning's contributions to the study of bureaucracy and the Nazi 'Final Solution of the Jewish Question' have generally thrown fresh light on aspects of the decision-making process in the Third Reich. Nevertheless, his main conclusions concerning an apparent lack of Nazi-style ideological anti-Jewish commitment on the part of 'diplomats' are very much open to question, especially when we consider the particular individuals who took the key policy decisions. In his 1980 review of Browning's book, Anthony Nicholls remarked that 'we should beware of creating artificial distinctions between careerism and political commitment. It is quite evident that anti-Semitic ideology was somewhere at work shaping the policies of the Third Reich, otherwise the fate of the Jews becomes quite inexplicable . . . the role of ideology in shaping government policies should not be treated too lightly'.[3] Virtually all the documents relevant to the part played by members of the German Embassy in Paris (and the Auswärtiges Amt in Berlin) in the Third Reich's anti-Jewish policies in wartime France confirm these key observations by Nicholls.[4]

Second, what may be referred to as the Abetz case – although the real *bête noire* was a subordinate in the Paris Embassy, Dr Karl-Theodor Zeitschel – underlines yet again the key role of Adolf Hitler in the decision-making process in the Third Reich, particularly on anti-Jewish policies. It does so by illustrating how, in terms of policy initiation and execution, all circles rounded out at the key focal point of the Third Reich, the Führer. Whether in a kind of false 'competition' with each other or in unison, State and Party offices always worked hard to achieve the anti-Jewish imperatives of Adolf Hitler they all believed in. This unity of purpose was based on the trinity of unquestioned belief in Nazi anti-Jewish ideological imperatives, unquestioned service to the State they served, and unquestioned emotional and ideological loyalty to the embodiment of the National Socialist movement and State, the Führer Adolf Hitler. As early as 16 August 1935, Reichsführer-SS Heinrich Himmler made this clear to SS personnel when forbidding individual actions against the Jews: 'the solution of the Jewish question, as of all other questions, is the business of the Führer and not of individuals'.[5]

There are other initial points to consider. First, the employment of Nazi-style language by some within the Auswärtiges Amt and diplomatic service when dealing with the Jewish question was often an indication of their own long association with the Party, and commitment to its ideals, because it was the one political movement which appeared to fulfil their hopes for Germany. Moreover, the use of such language by others in the diplomatic service who, initially in 1933 and for a short while afterwards, may have been less committed to the Nazi cause, shows the ease with which existing 'conservative' mores of anti-Semitism in the initially aristocratic-conservative dominated

Foreign Office[6] slid into Nazi ones, *because* of the 'enabling' or 'imperative' ideological and emotional conditions of Third Reich society.[7] Indeed, the years of peace between 1933 and 1939 are replete with sufficient evidence of Nazi-type anti-Jewish thinking and language in the Auswärtiges Amt to counter easily the Browning thesis of the non-ideologically motivated bureaucrat.[8] As early as 4 February 1934, Konstantin von Neurath, the German Foreign Minister, published an article entitled 'The Work of the Foreign Office in the First Year of the National Socialist Government' in the *Nationalsozialistische Beamtenzeitung*, which made it appear that the Auswärtiges Amt was completely imbued with National Socialist thinking about the tasks facing Germany.[9]

Second, Nazi mores on the racial issue also became German State ones after 30 January 1933 because anti-Jewish policy was central to the Third Reich and became a concern of most civil servants, including the diplomatic service.[10] It is difficult to accept, therefore, the blanket contention that 'the German Foreign Office played only a minor role in the formulation of Jewish policy before 1940'.[11] Its responsibility in holding the diplomatic ring for domestic anti-Jewish policies was paramount, while its advice to other government authorities from this experience could hardly be ignored in the uncertain international situation to 1938 and 1939. This was particularly true so far as its efforts to gain the substitution of 'Jew' for 'non-Aryan' in legislation and official ordinances was concerned.[12] Since the Auswärtiges Amt continued to play a key role in the wider European aspects of the Third Reich's Jewish policies during the war, Browning's conclusion that even then the Auswärtiges Amt, along with 'many other institutions in Germany' was successfully excluded 'from any effective role in Jewish affairs', needs to be read with great care since it views the situation from a wrong perspective.[13] It ignores the positive forms of Statist co-operation which necessarily developed between different Ministries in pursuit of common (Führer) goals.

Third, there was the steady and insidious influence of Party/SS authorities upon Auswärtiges Amt personnel from 1933, certainly after 1938 and 1939, and throughout the German civil service generally.[14] Until the end of 1937, only three out of seven departmental heads in the Auswärtiges Amt belonged to the NSDAP but none to the SS. By 1943 nine belonged to the NSDAP and six to the SS, a process undoubtedly speeded up after Joachim von Ribbentrop's appointment as Foreign Minister in February 1938. Naturally, this development had its effect upon political and ideological thinking within the Office.[15]

Fourth, and beyond legalistic and even social pressures upon civil servants to 'conform' because of the relentless series of 'non-Aryan' ordinances published from 1933 onwards,[16] there was the more significant step taken on 1 August 1934. On that date, a law was promulgated in which the offices of Reich President and Reich Chancellor were merged to form the new office of Führer and Reich Chancellor. Thereafter, especially following President von Hindenburg's death a few days later, Hitler's position of absolute power – embodying both State (constitutional) and Party (ideological) leadership forms – was justified throughout Germany 'in charismatic terms through his role as Leader of the German people, as the sole and exclusive representative of the nation's will and of its historical mission'.[17] As Adolf Eichmann later acknowledged to his Israeli interrogators, 'the extermination of the Jews was not provided for by Reich law. It was a Führer's order. . . . According to the then prevailing interpretation, which no one questioned, the Führer's orders had the force of law'.[18] This was to be of particular significance for the manner in which Executive (Hitlerian) orders were transmitted throughout the Statist chain of command.[19]

It is a mistake, therefore, to underestimate the political consequences of Hitler's constitutional position, or his charismatic effect on his followers, especially his circle of intimates. Even allowing for their propagandistic excesses, one cannot ignore the significance of Minister of the Interior Wilhelm Frick's statement in February 1933, that 'the name of Hitler is sufficient (National Socialist) programme',[20] or of Rudolf Hess's ringing declaration at the Nazi Party rally at Nuremberg in September 1934: 'Die Partei ist Hitler. Hitler aber ist Deutschland, wie Deutschland Hitler ist'. One of the most remarkable features of the National Socialist Party and the Third Reich was the stable web of personal loyalties with which Hitler surrounded himself. Another was his effect upon the German people (and civil servants), which Robert Koehl has likened to a practical application of the essential principles of feudalism.[21]

When, therefore, the leadership of the Third Reich decreed that its anti-Jewish policies should enter the stage of 'extermination' beyond that of 'extrusion', such 'servants of the State' as those in the diplomatic service, already duty bound to execute the policies decreed by the Executive of the State, found no moral difficulty in shifting gear and executing those new policies. And this, despite the constant refrain of 'diplomats' at the post-war trials that the Auswärtiges Amt 'could achieve nothing by open protests against Hitler's fundamental orders in the Jewish problem. Himmler and his experts . . . remained the masters when opposed by the representatives of the Foreign Office'.[22] But their intent then, of course, was to deny any responsibility for the Third Reich's anti-Jewish policies.

Among the many aspects of the Abetz case which directly contradict Browning's general line, the most important is the extent to which the individual loyalty to the Führer which permeated the whole Nazi system was complemented by the close co-operation and working arrangements – *not competition* – which operated at *all* levels of German State operations in wartime France in the name of Hitler. This was particularly true of the active working relationship – the importance of which cannot be emphasized enough – between Karl-Theodor Zeitschel of the embassy's Political Section (headed by Ernst Achenbach), responsible for Jewish and Freemasonry issues, and through whom all correspondence between the embassy and the Auswärtiges Amt passed,[23] and Adolf Eichmann's indefatigable *Judenreferat* in Paris, the fanatical Nazi and Jew-hater Theodor Dannecker, one-time Jewish expert in Reinhard Heydrich's *Reichssicherheitshauptamt* (RSHA) and, from September 1940 to September 1942, leader of the Jewish Section of the *Sicherheitspolizei-Sicherheitsdienst* (Sipo-SD) in France.[24] So highly did Zeitschel regard himself and his anti-Jewish tasks that he even had a special embassy section and notepaper with the heading, 'Pol.Ju', designating his fiefdom as that of the 'Politische Abteilung – Judenangelegenheiten'.[25] Abetz later described Zeitschel as 'a fanatical anti-Semite', and after the war absurdly tried to distance himself from his subordinate's anti-Jewish activities.[26]

Through these individuals (Zeitschel and Dannecker) and their respective chains of command, the circle was always rounded out in the personal embodiment of the National Socialist State, Adolf Hitler, to whom all owed allegiance and duty. On the one hand, to Ambassador Abetz and the Auswärtiges Amt, particularly its 'anti-Jewish' section, Abteilung Deutschland, once described as that 'absolutely alien body within the Foreign Office' and its fanatical head, Martin Luther.[27] His efforts at bureaucratic autonomy were underlined by siting his department in a different street from the main Wilhelmstrasse building. On the other, through local SS officers in France to Reichsführer-SS Heinrich Himmler, Chief of the Reich Security Head Office Reinhard Heydrich, and Adolf Eichmann. Eichmann and Dannecker were already long-standing colleagues before war in the West in 1940.[28]

These 'vertical' lines of authority were complemented by the 'horizontal' arrangements for liaison between Section D II of Abteilung Deutschland and the SS and Sipo-SD in Berlin, in addition to Franz Rademacher's usual contacts arising from his position as head of Section D III (see below). Moreover, the network of agency and personal relationships at the local level in France was underlined by those established between the Paris Embassy, the Sipo-SD offices, and the German military authorities in France.[29] Further, on 31 March 1941, Foreign Minister von Ribbentrop and Reichsführer-SS Himmler formally agreed to areas of responsibility and means of co-operation concerning the foreign policy and ideological repercussions of the Third Reich's *Volkstumsfragen*, in essence its racial policies. This not only reinforced the Auswärtiges Amt's claim to be consulted whenever those policies affected Germany's foreign policy situation, but tied that office more closely to all aspects of those policies.[30]

This practice of the *Führerprinzip* in the Third Reich was encapsulated in the person and role of Otto Abetz, whose memoirs actually admit to sympathy for members of the Sipo-SD in France.[31] Unlike many other ambassadors, Abetz, a former member of the Dienststelle Ribbentrop and active in pre-war France in the *Deutsch-Französischen Gesellschaft* (in France, the Comité France-Allemagne), married to a Frenchwoman, and named German Ambassador to France in August 1940 with a more substantive appointment announced in November,[32] had the rare privilege of sometimes attending Hitler in his meetings with other political leaders.[33] He was also granted a number of personal audiences with the Führer, which had an obvious effect on his personal feelings towards Hitler. In turn, Hitler seemed to be favourably impressed by Abetz compared with most of the diplomatic corps, a group he generally denigrated.[34] It is significant that when speaking with Benito Mussolini on 28 October 1940, Hitler confirmed what some historians are at pains to deny: that as Head of State he naturally received regular intelligence from the State Ministries of the Third Reich. He repeated to Mussolini what Abetz had reported to the Auswärtiges Amt about Jews and communists in France being the main supporters of General de Gaulle.[35]

For their part, many career diplomats such as State Secretary Ernst von Weizsäcker were extremely hostile towards Abetz,[36] as testimony at the post-war 'Ministry trials' of officials from the Auswärtiges Amt confirmed. Werner von Bargen, a junior Foreign Office official with wide experience in Western Europe from 1940 to 1944, including a short spell in Paris, told how Abetz's high opinion of himself led to his treating the Auswärtiges Amt as a *quantité negligeable*. Abetz preferred to pursue his seemingly exclusive relations with von Ribbentrop and the Führer, with whom he was undoubtedly *persona grata*.[37] Abetz thus deliberately ignored usual procedures at the Auswärtiges Amt: for example, appointing his own liaison officer, Hans Schwarzmann, to the office of the Foreign Minister.[38] Abetz himself confirmed this situation, testifying that after visiting von Ribbentrop in the Führer's Headquarters on about eight occasions, he 'interrupted [his] journey in Berlin in order to go to the Foreign Office and inform the various department chiefs of my discussions with Ribbentrop'. He also confirmed that when Schwarzmann was moved, from 1942 'telephone conversations between the German Embassy in Paris and the Foreign Office in Berlin' were conducted by Dr Strack.[39]

Many who manned the machinery of State in the Third Reich, be they established civil servants or more recent Party entrants, thus facilitated the Nazis' purpose because they firmly believed in the moral rectitude of those purposes within the framework of national, Party, and personal loyalty to the Führer and his ideological imperatives for Germany's regeneration in the post-1918 world. This is to suggest a far more positive *emotional and ideological* predisposition by 'diplomats' towards the range of Nazi anti-Jewish policies it was their responsibility to implement than the more prosaic power-struggle elements which Browning would impute.[40] German 'diplomats' could also fall under Norman Rich's strictures that 'the Nazis demonstrated how easy it is for man to find rational, even idealistic and moral, motives to carry out inhuman actions'.[41]

Finally, the Abetz case is relevant to the wider historical debate over whether emigration or extermination was the 'final' Nazi aim for the Jews since it touches upon what knowledge staff in the Paris Embassy and officials in other State agencies possessed, and when, about the exterminatory intentions and actions of the Nazi leadership.

The Franco-German war of May and June 1940 and its consequences intensified discussion in Berlin and then Paris of two important aspects of the Third Reich's *Judenpolitik*: how it affected France directly, and the French case within the pan-European resolution of the Jewish Question. When the French case was discussed at the Nuremberg war crimes trials, one exchange served to highlight just how far bureaucratic *Gleichshaltung* on the Jewish question had developed in the Third Reich. On 2 April 1946, M. Faure, French Prosecuting

Counsel, confronted von Ribbentrop with evidence concerning the anti-Jewish role of the German Embassy in Paris during the Second World War. Quoting from French evidential document number RF-1207, a report dated Paris, 1 July 1941 and entitled, *Judenfrage in Frankreich und ihre Behandlung* by Theodor Dannecker, Faure referred to Dannecker's conclusion: 'In this connection, I cannot speak of this matter without mentioning the genuinely friendly support which our work received from the German Ambassador [Otto] Abetz, his representative, the envoy [Rudolf] Schleier, and SS-Sturmbann-führer and Counsellor of Legation, Dr [Karl-Theodor] Zeitschel'.[42]

As everyone present in court was aware, Dannecker's report, in which he focused on France as the centre of Jewry's European and overseas networks, was written just over a week after the *Einsatzgruppen* of the SS and SD had begun to cut their murderous, anti-Judeo-Bolshevik swathe through Russia in the wake of Operation Barbarossa.[43] Even then, Nazi Germany's anti-Jewish policy in France and the rest of Europe was still one of non-murderous 'exclusion' – although by 22 June 1941 it was on the threshold of formally at least concluding the murder of Gentile Germans (in the main) in the euthanasia programme, following which the personnel of that exercise disposed of their expertise in the death camps in the east.[44] For France, anti-Jewish policy was not to become one of 'extermination' until the gassing in Auschwitz of Jews removed on the seventh transport on 19 July 1942.[45]

While von Ribbentrop had no alternative but to admit the 'collaboration' of Abetz and the Paris Embassy in anti-Jewish policy in France, he claimed that the ambassador, often acting on his own, always attempted 'to reach some kind of conciliatory settlement of this question'. Yet in the rest of his reply, the former Foreign Minister also acknowledged the degree to which 'the basic anti-Semitic tendency and policy of the German Government spread over all the departments . . . every Government office somehow or other came into contact with these matters'. Nevertheless, von Ribbentrop clearly lied, or at least dissembled, when he stated that 'the German Embassy was not responsible for any anti-Semitic measures of any description in France'.[46]

From a different perspective, Adolf Eichmann later complained of the extensive State apparatus necessarily involved in Germany's anti-Jewish operations, including that of the Auswärtiges Amt and the German railway system, the Reichsbahn:[47] 'it shows that evacuations were not so easy to carry out. No matter how large a German force was present, they couldn't just round up people, put them in freight cars, and ship them out. The whole evacuation process in the European countries required stubborn, long-drawn-out negotiations'.[48]

In France, where it was to have a special position in the Nazi European 'New Order',[49] the Auswärtiges Amt was determined it would not be treated by the SS/SD authorities over Jewish policy as it had been in Poland. There it had been entirely excluded, sharing its alienation with the Army which had been concerned about SS/SD atrocities against Poles and Jews.[50] A first effort to claim a significant position in the west for the Auswärtiges Amt was made by Franz Rademacher whose memorandum of 3 June 1940, written in unmistakably Nazi-style anti-Jewish terminology, sparked off the discussion about the so-called Madagascar Plan for the transfer of Jews to that French island possession within the general parameter of 'all Jews out of Europe'.[51] This is a notion taken seriously by some,[52] but justifiably dismissed by other historians: 'there is no indication that Hitler had ever intended it seriously'.[53] Apart from the intrinsic nonsense of the idea and the English naval blockade,[54] at the time of his victory over France, Hitler was already considering armed conflict against Russia.[55] This hardly promised an end to general conflict in Europe. Although the 'paper policy exercises' of Rademacher and others came to the notice of Hitler, he is alleged to have told Heinrich Himmler at the end of June 1940 that the Reichsführer-SS would have to 'undertake the progressive extermination of European Jewry'.[56]

More substantive developments in France originated with Otto Abetz and the German Embassy in Paris. Throughout the period of German domination, the embassy played an essential role in the anti-Jewish and deportation process in France. The fact that the Jewish 'specialists' on Abetz's staff, Rudolf Schleier and Karl-Theodor Zeitschel had been NSDAP members since 1931 and 1923 respectively, reinforces the point that for many of these 'officials' there was far more than a 'bureaucratic' predisposition towards ideological accommodation with Hitler's anti-Jewish norms. Zeitschel not only liaised with Fernand de Brinon, the Vichy government's representative in the Occupied Zone, but also worked closely with the 'non-extremist but realistic' leadership of the Gestapo and Sicherheistdienst in France, SS-Sturmbannführer Dr Helmut Knochen, Head of Security Police in France.[57] In particular, he developed a special relationship with its Jewish expert, Theodor Dannecker (who reported directly to Adolf Eichmann), and contacts with Karl Oberg, from June 1942 Himmler's SS representative in France.[58]

In further confirmation of von Ribbentrop's 1946 Nuremberg testimony, four other German government authorities were active in Jewish affairs in wartime France: the military government, *Militärbefehlshaber in Frankreich* (MBF); the Security Police with specialist divisions for Jewish affairs, a subdivision of the *Reichssicherheitshauptamt* (RSHA), members of which were quickly sent to France in July 1940 and which finally won its administrative autonomy there in May 1942;[59] the *Einsatzstab Rosenberg*, part of the fiefdom of Alfred Rosenberg and principally engaged in pillaging Jewish art; and the Armistice Commission at Wiesbaden, although its influence declined as the embassy became the principal contact with the Vichy government by 1941.[60] In France, these authorities acted as inter-connected extensions of complex bureaucratic relationships in Germany itself. Indeed, one individual who epitomized co-operative Statist anti-Jewish policy during the Second World War was Adolf Eichmann's railway Referat in the RSHA, SS-Obersturmführer Franz Novak. His function was to arrange transports for Jews due for deportation on specific dates to particular destinations, as and when the central 'demand' for Jews coincided with what 'local' offices in occupied Europe could supply. Novak arranged such transports directly with Amtsrat Otto Stange of Abteilung E II (211 – *Sonderzüge*) of the Reichsbahn.[61]

Abetz, ambitious to return to France in a senior position on the coat-tails of the victorious Wehrmacht, quickly made plain his Nazi-type sentiments on the Jewish question. On 24 May 1940 he delivered to the Army authorities a set of extreme proposals for German policy in the west. These included treating the French Jews (among others) as 'guilty' for the war.[62] His undoubted knowledge of how the power structure of the Third Reich really operated was shown by his appointment on 14 June as Auswärtiges Amt representative with the military authorities in France.[63] Six weeks later, on 30 July, he repeated his ideas of 24 May to von Ribbentrop in a document which has been taken as evidence of his personal 'super-Hitlerism'.[64]

In the summer of 1940, everything seemed to be going Abetz's way. On 3 August, he was received by Hitler at the Berghof.[65] Besides being named Ambassador to France and hearing the Führer's ideas about that country,[66] Abetz was told – in the deliberately vague manner which Hitler used time and again with many people – that it was his plan to 'evacuate all Jews from Europe after the war'.[67] That same day, von Ribbentrop informed Field Marshal Wilhelm Keitel, Chief of Oberkommando der Wehrmacht (OKW), of Abetz's responsibilities in France, the chief of which, on the Führer's express orders, was that he should be 'solely responsible for dealing with all political questions in occupied and unoccupied France'.[68] On 20 November, Hitler changed Abetz's status in Paris from 'Office of the Representative of the Foreign Office with the Military Commander in France' to that of Embassy, repeating the earlier point of his responsibility for political questions.[69] And nothing could be more 'political' for Hitler than the Jewish question, the 'resolution' of which in France concerned some 270,000 Jews by the end of 1939, supplemented by more than 40,000 from Belgium, Holland and Luxembourg in May 1940.[70]

Hitler's surprising gesture of confidence concerning his radical views on the Jewish question[71] undoubtedly impressed upon Abetz that he had been entrusted with the honour, indeed the duty, of personally executing a *Führerbefehl*, that essential linchpin of the *Führerprinzip* method of conducting business in the Third Reich.[72] On 17 August, and without orders from Berlin, he proposed that the MBF immediately prohibit the re-entry of Jews into the occupied zone; that preparations be made to expel all Jews from that zone; and consideration be given to the confiscation of Jewish property.[73] On 20 August, he requested von Ribbentrop's approval for four anti-Jewish measures which differed slightly from those of the 17th. He suggested these 'might serve as a basis for the later removal of Jews from unoccupied France as well' – a clear indication of Hitler's effect upon him on 3 August. Abetz now wished to prohibit the return of Jews across the demarcation line into the occupied zone; Jews in the occupied zone should be registered and Jewish stores clearly labelled; and trustees should be appointed for Jewish stores whose owners had departed.[74]

Of greater interest is the more lengthy Abetz Aufzeichnung of 'September 1940', undoubtedly written before the MBF issued its anti-Jewish ordinances of 27 September. Entitled 'Measures Against Jews in the Occupied Territory', it was a critique of the reluctant MBF stand and an attempt to 'ginger up' the military authorities. It also indicated something of the firm ideological anti-Jewish imperatives which motivated Abetz: 'the time has arrived to create in occupied France the basis for the attainment of the long-term aim of German policy in this matter. That aim is to bring about, unequivocally, in all spheres of public life, including the economy, the radical elimination of Jewish influence'. It could only be achieved in the whole of France 'if the French people themselves decide to free themselves from Jewry'.[75] So far did Abetz's anti-Jewish imperatives go that, on 1 October, he suggested to the Auswärtiges Amt the immediate denaturalization of German Jews found in France, a policy to be undertaken within the context of initiating 'the solution of the Jewish problem in the occupied territory of France'.[76]

None of this detail was allowed, of course, to besmirch the pages of Abetz's memoirs where an entirely different gloss was applied to events, or indeed his testimony for the post-war 'Ministry trials'.[77] Moreover, Rudolf Rahn, responsible for propaganda at the Paris Embassy until mid-1941, recorded in his memoirs how, at his first meeting with Abetz at the embassy, the ambassador had expressed concern about how Hitler's fanaticism had placed Germany in a conflict situation with other powers where time was not on its side. What Rahn's record confirms – disingenuously repeated by Abetz in his memoirs – is Abetz's fundamentally Nazi ideological position: 'today, Germany stands before a more or less united front of Catholicism, Protestantism, Jewry, Freemasonry, High Finance, Democracy, and Communism. The only chance of breaking this front, in his view [Abetz], was through a genuine and radical understanding with France'.[78]

Reluctantly, given their predominantly military objectives in France, the MBF authorities felt it necessary to consider the Abetz proposals,[79] especially since it was made plain to them that they accorded with the views of Hitler and were thus hallowed as a *Führerbefehl*.[80] While Abetz's initiatives led to desultory exchanges between the Auswärtiges Amt and Heydrich,[81] a clarification of sorts about early policy was signified by the anti-Jewish ordinances issued by the MBF on 27 September, following further contacts with Abetz, along the lines of Abetz's proposals of 20 August to Berlin.[82]

Although the MBF played an important role in setting the course of German anti-Jewish policy in the occupied zone in 1940 and 1941, it did so entirely in co-operation with the Auswärtiges Amt and the security forces.[83] Nevertheless, SS authority over Jewish policy in France was increasingly recognized, especially after Field Marshal Walther von Brauchitsch, Commander-in-Chief of the German Army, agreed in October 1940 that Himmler should assume responsibility for Jewish questions. Formalizing the steady infiltration of the SS into France since July, the Jewish section of the security forces, formally under the MBF but actually responsible to the RSHA, was led by Dannecker in Paris.[84] Significantly, Germany's unique position of occupying only half of France and maintaining official relations with the unoccupied part meant that the pursuit of Dannecker's and

Eichmann's goals there was impossible without the active co-operation and support of the Paris Embassy. That participation was extended without question because all concerned were imbued with the same ideological commitment to the anti-Jewish goals of the Führer. Yet for the diplomats, 'approval' necessarily constituted 'responsibility'.

This was clearly seen when Abetz appended his signature of approval to Dannecker's *Aufzeichnung* of 21 January 1941 recommending a *Zentraljudenamt* for France in Paris. Besides rationalizing a number of German approaches to the Jewish question in France, Dannecker saw his proposal as a further means of energizing the anti-Jewish activities of the French authorities. But the document Abetz approved contained these significant opening words:

In conformity with the will of the Führer, at the end of the war there should be brought about a final solution of the Jewish question within the European territories ruled or controlled by Germany. The Chief of the Security Police and the Sicherheitsdienst has already received orders from the Führer, through the Reichsführer-SS as well as the Reichsmarschall [Goering], to submit a project for a final solution. On the basis of the present extensive experience of the offices of the Chief of Security Police and the Sicherheitsdienst in handling Jewish issues, and thanks to the preparatory work carried out for so long, the project in all its essentials has been completed. It is now with the Führer and the Reichsmarschall. It is certain that its execution will involve a tremendous amount of work whose success can only be guaranteed through the most painstaking preparations. This will extend to the work preceding the wholesale deportation of Jews as well as to the planning to the last detail of a settlement action in a territory which has yet to be determined.[85]

Dannecker went on to explain that the objectives of the anti-Jewish policies in France and the rest of Europe were to mark out and separate Jews from all normal European life, as well as to establish centralized forms of control over them before deportation. Of particular significance, however, is this passage from the document concerning the urgency of establishing a *Zentraljudenamt*: 'otherwise, should the forthcoming deportation of the Jews become a reality, we shall be faced with an insuperable task'. This was a clear reference to two factors: the German experience in Poland in gathering together Polish Jews in urban ghettos through the destruction of suburban and rural settlements, so as to secure better German control over the Jews and the consequent creation of the *Judenräte*; and, in France, the necessity of organizing suitable internment premises for Jews in readiness for their expected transfer elsewhere.

Dannecker's opening remarks about an *Endlösungsprojekt*, and Abetz's personal commitment to the document, go to the heart of the historical debate about what constituted the Nazi 'final aim' on the Jewish question: emigration, transmigration (forcible removal) or extermination. Did his comments really refer to the Madagascar Plan which, although Eichmann told Bernhard Lösener of the Interior Ministry in December 1940 that the plan still awaited Heydrich's signature, was effectively dead after the failure to defeat Britain in September?[86] Or was this evidence in the post-September 1940 circumstances that other 'territorial solutions' for the Jews, as hinted at in Heydrich's letter of 24 June 1940 to von Ribbentrop, were being considered, further 'east', perhaps even in Russia? After all, Dannecker wrote in the period after 18 December 1940 when Hitler had issued Directive Number 21, Operation Barbarossa, in which he declared that 'the German Wehrmacht must be prepared to crush Soviet Russia in a quick campaign (Operation Barbarossa) even before the conclusion of the war against England'.[87] If so, was any solution there to the Jewish question really to be a 'territorial' one in the sense of 'transmigration'?

The question focuses attention upon the historiographical debate concerning the genesis and execution of the Nazi 'Final Solution of the Jewish Question' in the form of systematic physical extermination. As is well known, 'functionalist' historians argue that the nature of the Nazi *Endlösung* for the Jews of Europe changed and shifted *pari passu* as conditions altered, that early use of this term did not mean physical extermination, and that what developed was more or less a 'stumbling' radicalization of anti-Jewish policy from emigration, then transmigration (i.e. expulsions and ghettoization) when mass emigration became difficult or impossible, through to extermination.[88]

The opposing 'intentionalist' argument has it that Hitler knew entirely where he was headed on the Jewish question: extermination. There is valid evidence to suggest that he had conceived this policy as early as July and August 1920.[89] It was to start with the *real* Jewish enemy, the Judeo-Bolshevik element in Russia, a notion further derived from his 1922 conclusion that Germany's future territorial goal was to be Russia.[90]

The third part of the debate, encompassing the other two, concerns when, how, and by whom the decision was taken in 1941 to extend the policy of mass murder beyond that of Russian to non-Russian Jewry. However, the argument that extermination began in eastern Europe because local officials could no longer cope with the numbers of Jews deported to them, rather than that policy being in any way 'intended', must be rejected out of hand.[91]

The essential point, however, irrespective of the extent to which bureaucratic 'paper policy exercises' were pursued, often without initial reference to the Führer, is that it was Hitler's final policy decisions that mattered, resulting in the scrapping of irrelevant bureaucratic exercises. This perspective strengthens the view that the Madagascar notion was simply an irrelevant red herring. Certainly, one unsatisfactory study of the subject correctly places Hitler in the eye of the storm of extermination policy, as does Eichmann himself.[92] As Norman Rich has bravely put it, 'the point cannot be stressed too strongly: Hitler was master in the Third Reich . . . Deviationists among his supporters there might be, opponents might occasionally sidetrack or sabotage his programmes, but in all essential respects it was Hitler who determined German policy during the Nazi era'.[93]

Yet there are other matters to consider. Many observers argue that 'emigration' was the 'final aim' of the Nazis. That aim, so it is suggested, was only 'frustrated' into the path of 'extermination' by the restrictive immigration policies of the Western powers which, absurdly, are then made to 'share' the opprobrium for mass murder.[94] Such arguments are extrapolated from the trickle of Jewish emigration from *German* lands between 1939 and 1941, a line of reasoning which leads to the further unsubstantiated generalization that emigration *per se* was the Nazis' general policy for *all* Jews under their control after 1939.[95]

There are, however, a number of reasoned points which may be marshalled to counter those arguments. First, after 1 September 1939, Hitler had no intention that German anti-Jewish policy in Poland should consist of a 'normal and orderly' emigration process. In agreement with Reichsmarschall Goering, Hitler ordered 'shooting and extermination measures in Poland' to be carried out against 'mainly the Polish intelligentsia, the nobility, the clergy, and, of course, the Jews'.[96] Reinhard Heydrich also explained to Admiral Canaris on 8 September, 'we'll spare the common folk, but the aristocrats, priests and Jews must be killed'.[97] Moreover, in September and October 1939, Hitler gave orders for 300,000 Jews from Germany, Austria and Bohemia–Moravia to be packed off to Poland, although things did not turn out as he envisaged.[98]

Second, there is Adolf Eichmann's significant admission to his Israeli interrogators when confronted with Heydrich's *Schnellbrief* of 21 September 1939 on the Jewish question in occupied Poland, issued to the *Einsatzgruppen* leadership following the meeting that day with Heydrich, and which Eichmann attended.[99] While the protocol of 21 September dealt sparsely with the Jewish question, the *Schnellbrief* was exclusively devoted to the subject. In it, Heydrich emphasized that 'the planned total measures (the final aim – *Endziel*) are to be kept strictly secret [*streng geheim*]. Distinction must be made between: 1. the final aim [*dem Endziel*] (which will require extended periods of time) and, 2. the stages leading to the fulfilment of this final aim (which will be carried out in short periods)'.[100]

To his captors, Eichmann made this significant observation: 'to judge by this document, the order concerning the physical extermination of the Jews was not, as I formerly believed, issued or promulgated by Hitler at the outbreak of the German–Russian war. On the contrary, this, call it basic conception, was already firmly established at that [21 September 1939] date. I can think of no other interpretation for the words "the ultimate aim, which requires longer periods of time"'[101] – a point he repeated at his trial.[102] Here, Eichmann is referring to the term *Endziel*, the 'final aim', although in his previously composed memoirs he was at pains to deny the existence of a long-term plan for extermination.[103]

It is at this point that one confronts numerous difficulties in the debate, above all how historians are to 'read' – interpret – the language employed by the chief protagonists, let alone deal with the matter of translations. Some historians even suggest we should not take Hitler's words on the Jews seriously, even his death threat to the Jews on 30 January 1939,[104] or even read historical sources in a 'literal' manner.[105] Yet neither the *Schnellbrief* or Eichmann's response can be assessed correctly unless German sources are utilized. In the German edition of the Eichmann interrogations, unaccountably omitted from the English translation, is the additional phrase, 'in the senior and highest leadership' in connection with policies 'already firmly established' by 21 September 1939.[106] This additional information makes it clear, indubitably, certainly in Eichmann's view, if not in that of others,[107] that one has to impute to Heydrich's instructions the more sinister notion that 'extermination' of the Jews was by then a firm policy objective. Yet Jeremy Noakes and Geoffrey Pridham are not alone in finding it difficult to support such a view.[108] Their loose translation of the opening passage of the document considerably weakens its implied intent: 'die geplanten Gesamtmaßnahmen (also das Endziel)' becomes for them, 'the overall measures *envisaged* (i.e. the final goal)' [my italics].[109]

The more sinister meaning of the document would appear to be substantiated by the fact that this sentence is underlined – a significant point in German bureaucratic practice – and that the imperative of 'streng geheim' is included as an integral part of the message, not placed elsewhere on the document by hand or stamp. Moreover, only in Heydrich's *Schnellbrief* of 21 September 1939 do we read the term *Endziel*, while thereafter the more ambiguous phrase employed is *Endlösung der Judenfrage*. Signifying the means or 'solution' to achieve an aim already decided upon, the real meaning of the latter was entirely dependent upon what lay behind Heydrich's use of the term *Endziel* on 21 September 1939. While many historians juxtapose or interweave the meaning of the two terms (to the detriment of the former) by suggesting that what was meant by the 'final solution' changed or evolved, *pari passu* as practical conditions altered, this ignores Heydrich's unique and deliberate use of a special term to indicate that the 'final aim' had indeed been discussed and decided upon, the *Endziel* of extermination. If so, this makes a considerable difference how one evaluates other evidence, particularly if the subsequent omission of the term *Endziel* indicates an awareness that already too much had been given away on 21 September 1939.

Again, one must return to the special question of the language employed in documents. Interpretations of the 'stumbling towards a solution' kind are put upon many statements from the principals involved concerning 'emigration' or 'transmigration' before mass murder became a reality in the Russian campaign from 22 June 1941. Their general nature and vagueness are taken by some historians to represent forms of pragmatism in policy-making. Yet this is to miss something quite fundamental about Nazi intentionalism. From Poland in September 1939 to Russia in June 1941, the air was replete with the deliberate use of 'code words' and disguised language. Rather than these being taken to indicate pragmatism or uncertainty, there are any number of reasons why they should be taken more seriously as disguising firm intentions to annihilate the Jews.

Nasty and vicious as were the anti-Jewish practices and intentions of Hitler, Himmler and Heydrich, it is often forgotten, or deliberately ignored, that until Hitler's personally signed order for the euthanasia programme in October 1939 (significantly backdated to 1 September 1939 and, so far as we know, the only order he signed for mass murder), the Third Reich had not instituted any policy of mass murder. Until then the Third Reich was at peace, and mass murder would become possible only during a state of war.[110] From the onset of the euthanasia programme, however, the Nazi leadership was understandably uncertain how the German public and even the military authorities, whose loyalty Hitler desperately needed for his future plans, would react to even this tentative and limited step in the direction of mass murder. Just as it was incumbent upon the Party leadership and the professional operatives of that programme to keep it secret for as long as possible, so as to maximize its success, neither could any risk be taken of betraying ultimate intentions for the Jews through intemperate or precisely defined language, in conferences or in documents. Even during the euthanasia programme, SS and RSHA officials used the euphemism 'evacuation' for that killing process, and which from 1941 and 1942 was then used to cover the mass murder of European (non-Russian) Jewry.[111]

These considerations need to be related once more to the general emigration issue until the beginning of 1941. When Zionist reports collated a terrible catalogue of the persecution and murder of Polish Jews from September 1939,[112] just when the German authorities developed their *Judenräte* and ghettoization plans in the wake of Heydrich's orders of 21 September,[113] there was certainly no German intention to create a *Zentralstelle für jüdische Auswanderung* to arrange the so-called 'emigration' of millions of Polish Jews in a 'normal and orderly' fashion – apart from the limitations imposed upon such a concept by the naval blockade in a situation of war.

Yet even the Auswärtiges Amt in Berlin could hardly deny that Himmler's and Heydrich's offices were 'up to something' on the Jewish question in 1939 and 1940. The consistent nature of some communications it received from the security forces during 1940 indicated that something far-reaching, and which transcended any chimera of the Lublin or Madagascar notions, was afoot for the mass of Jews in Poland. In February 1940, the Reichsführer-SS placed a ban on Jewish emigration from Poland to Palestine, while an RSHA circular of 24 April 1940 imposed more controls on even the limited emigration permitted from the *Reichsgebiete*, particularly so far as this concerned the movement of Jews to other European nations. By September, Himmler's office informed Martin Luther of a more general prohibition on Jewish emigration from Poland: 'the emigration of Jews from the Generalgouvernement [of Poland] would adversely affect the possibility of the emigration of Jews from the *Altreich* [Germany], the *Ostmark* [Austria], and the Protectorate of Bohemia and Moravia. From this perspective and in view of the undoubted forthcoming final solution of the Jewish Question [*Endlösung der Judenfrage*], I am unable to accede to the request of the above-named.'[114] This latter injunction was repeated by the RSHA on 25 October 1940 to the General-gouvernement in occupied Cracow, which then made this directive known to its subordinate offices.[115] Furthermore, on 15 September 1940,

Richard Lichtheim, Head of the Jewish Agency in Geneva, reported to an unknown destination on a general ban on Jewish emigration from the German occupied territories of Holland, Belgium, Denmark, France and especially Poland.[116]

Theodor Dannecker's Paris Aufzeichnung of 21 January 1941 concerning anti-Jewish policy in France, above all its opening passage, thus takes on a special significance when placed in the wider context of 1940 and 1941. Dannecker betrayed in this document his awareness of trends of thought in Berlin concerning solutions to the wider European *Judenfrage*, if not elements of decided policy. Moreover, *pari passu* with the creation of the Dannecker document, more than straightforward military consequences were implicit in Hitler's Directive of 18 December 1940 for Operation Barbarossa against Russia. As Hitler's instructions to General Jodl of 3 March 1941 made clear, the forthcoming war with Russia 'would be more than one only of arms, it would be the clash of two *Weltanschauungen*' which would involve the necessary destruction of the 'Judeo-Bolshevik' leadership.[117] More specifically, orders from Field Marshal Keitel in 'Instructions on Special Matters attached to Directive No. 21 (Barbarossa)' of 13 March 1941, Paragraph 2(b), dictated by Hitler himself, read: 'in order to prepare the political and administrative organization the Reichsführer-SS has been given by the Führer certain special tasks within the operations zone of the army; these stem from the necessity finally to settle the conflict between two opposing political systems'.[118] The nature of those 'special tasks' was soon communicated to the squads of the *Einsatzgruppen* by their leaders.

If an implicit or even definite Berlin 'link' could be read into Dannecker's Aufzeichnung, that connection was 'extended' into France through subsequent discussions with the MBF and the Embassy on his proposals, all approved by Abetz. On 28 January 1941, for example, Helmut Knochen complained to the MBF about a lack of progress in anti-Jewish policies and proposed that concentration camps be established for foreign Jews.[119] Yet Dannecker's action in passing a copy of this letter to Zeitschel signified much more than confirmation of their working relationship.[120] It was meant to show the necessity of unified German action on the Jewish question, although Dannecker was of course preaching to the converted. Thereafter, pressure on the reluctant MBF was maintained by Knochen and an Sipo-SD colleague, SS-Sturmbannführer Kurt Lischka.[121]

The obvious urgency felt by those seeking a radical solution to the

Jewish question – indicative of an internalized psychological-ideological dimension to the problem – was thus fully shared by Ambassador Abetz and his officials. On 14 February, Abetz confirmed in writing to SS-Brigadeführer Dr Max Thomas in Paris his strong approval of Dannecker's proposals for a *Zentraljudenamt*. Given the urgency of its application in the unoccupied zone, he promised to raise the subject at his next meeting with Vichy representatives.[122] Zeitschel probably drafted this communication since a copy, together with the Dannecker document, was found in his files, confirming the closeness of their relationship by then.[123] Before Abetz's meeting with the French, it is significant that, on 28 February, Dannecker visited the embassy and discussed with Abetz, Zeitschel and Achenbach his proposals to extend German control over the Jews, especially the internment of foreign Jews, and to persuade the MBF to empower the Sipo-SD authorities to carry out the internment process.[124] Thereafter, Dannecker insti-tuted regular Tuesday meetings of the main German *Judenreferenten* in France.[125]

Since Dr Best of the MBF appeared not to have responded to Knochen's letter of 28 January it was, significantly enough, Zeitschel who proposed to Achenbach on 1 March that strong embassy pressure be exerted on the MBF to declare their position on internment procedures, above all on the Sipo-SD's claim to have executive powers in the matter. Zeitschel, who recommended that the embassy's letter be signed by Abetz, went so far as to state that it should be 'somewhat more emphatic' than the one from the SD of 28 January in order to persuade them 'to comply *immediately with the wish of the SD* [italics in original] by arranging a conference of the interested agencies in order to achieve clarity and co-operation in the Jewish question between the Military Administration, the SD, and the German Embassy'.[126] Clearly, Zeitschel acted at the behest of Dannecker, not of Abetz, and in a spirit of co-operation, not competition.[127]

Abetz, too, played his part by exerting pressure on Admiral Jean François Darlan, at that time (among other offices he held) Vice-President of the French Council of Ministers and Minister of Foreign Affairs, at their meeting on 5 March. He reported to the Auswärtiges Amt that:

despite this [vacillating] attitude of Pétain, which would suggest that a central office for Jewish affairs organized by the French Government would not proceed very vigorously, it would be advisable to have the French Government establish this office. The central office for Jewish affairs would thus have a valid legal foundation and its activity could then be stimulated through German influence in the occupied territory to such [an] extent that the unoccupied territory would be forced to join in the measures taken.[128]

Abetz, Zeitschel, Dannecker, Knochen and Lischka were at one in viewing the anti-Jewish policies to be pursued in France as an integral part of the pan-European *Endlösungprojekt* desired by the Führer to 'solve' the European Jewish question once and for all. All were convinced of the ideological rectitude of the intention to create a *judenfrei Europa*. Abetz's approval of the Dannecker Aufzeichnung, which showed how far those Leadership notions had progressed by then, indicated more than a 'bureaucratic' decision (namely, the Browning thesis) but a significant sharing of the Führer's anti-Jewish imperatives and acceptance of whatever forms they took. Indeed, the most recent research shows the extent to which plans for mass murder in Russia were then being developed in Berlin during January and February 1941.[129]

After its work during the first three months of 1941, the embassy, prodded by Dannecker, was well satisfied with one positive outcome of its pressure on the French authorities.[130] On 29 March 1941, the Vichy authorities established the Commissariat for Jewish Affairs under Xavier Vallat, a key function of which, as Abetz reported to the Auswärtiges Amt on 3 April after meeting him, would be the 'harmonizing of the laws regarding Jews passed by the French Government for all of France with the regulations regarding Jews passed by the Military Commander in France for the occupied area, as suggested by the Embassy'. These included the process of denaturalization, by which it was hoped to extend German regulations to even greater numbers of Jews in France. In formal recognition of the firmly established relationship between the embassy and Eichmann's Referat in Paris, Abetz reported that he had brought Vallat and Dannecker together, and had 'assigned Counsellor of Legation Zeitschel as liaison to the French Commissioner for Jews and [to] the specialist for Jews [Dannecker] of the Security Service in Paris'.[131]

A number of significant points of 'ideology' and 'bureaucracy' need to be made at this point. First, Dannecker's proposal of 21 January 1941 for thorough preparations in France for an eventual deportation of Jews, followed by Knochen's concentration camp proposals of seven days later, closely echoed Heydrich's policy document of 21 September 1939. That had initiated more efficient means of German control by attending to the 'concentration' and 'control' of Polish Jews.

Second, and bearing in mind the strong possibility that Dannecker's opening passage reflected advance thinking in Berlin, even about extermination, it is interesting that in a report to the Auswärtiges Amt on 24 March 1941, Counsellor of the Embassy Rudolf Schleier further underlined the imperatives involved in a definitive solution of the Jewish question intended by embassy and Sipo-SD staff in Paris when he commented on Berlin's plans to publish in America recent French anti-Jewish measures: 'I recommend therefore to publish only reports on measures already taken, but not on plans for the future'.[132]

Third, how far it is possible to make a direct connnection between Hitler's orders for Operation Barbarossa in March 1941 and when it is assumed he gave Heinrich Himmler orders for the extermination of the Russian Jews on the one hand; and an article that same month by Dr Walter Groß in the *Rassenpolitische Auslands-Korrespondenz*, the journal of the 'Enlightenment Office for Population Policy and Racial Development' he headed in the *Rassenpolitisches Amt der NSDAP* is difficult to tell. In view of what began on 22 June 1941, that publication and others reproducing speeches from the opening ceremony of the Institute for Research into the Jewish Question at Frankfurt am Main on 27 March 1941, deserves some consideration. Groß's article was entitled 'Racial Policy Prerequisites for a Total European Solution to the Jewish Question'. Among its conclusions was that 'an elimination' of the Jewish danger in Europe was only possible through [Jewry's] 'complete territorial removal'. Furthermore, 'on racial political grounds, there can be no question of a [Jewish] transfer to a European country nor to a territory outside Europe belonging to Arabs'. Finally, through a complete European solution to the Jewish question, this 'dangerous injury to the history and culture of Europe, and indeed the world, would be at an end'.[133]

Fourth, in his report of 3 April 1941, Abetz betrayed not only his own imperative on the anti-Jewish question, but demonstrated something further of the specifically Hitlerian nature of policy-making in the Third Reich. While the Führer always followed his own path, his decisions only became official German policy when they were ultimately translated into *known* orders to ministries and individuals, upon which occasion they immediately nullified all other 'paper exercises'. Until that happened, officials lower down the hierarchy operated on the basis of existing policy guidelines, if they existed, or even their own interpretations of what they perceived the Führer's wishes to be. On this occasion, Abetz stated: 'the laws still to be drawn up by Vallat are to force as large a portion as possible of the Jews residing in France from the remaining liberal professions, from industry and commerce as well, and prepare the way for their emigration'.

At one level, this indicates the general impression which some in the diplomatic service still perceived as constituting the ultimate intentions of Hitler, Himmler and Heydrich towards the Jews, an intention Abetz wholeheartedly agreed with on ideological and other grounds. Even on 12 August 1941, Zeitschel was obviously still guided by the chimera of emigration, although not for long. When commenting to Abetz about Darlan's notion of sending all Europe's Jews to Madagascar, Zeitschel wrote, 'in itself no bad thing'.[134] Nevertheless, especially if we take it that Dannecker, in January 1941, particularly through his contacts with Eichmann, was in some way familiar with unfolding developments in Berlin leading to a policy of extermination, were both Abetz and Zeitschel even then using 'emigration' as a euphemism?

Fifth, Dr Groß's article in March, together with a summary in the information sheet of the *Rassenpolitisches Amt der NSDAP* of 20 April, and similar arguments in his article, 'Zur Lösung der Judenfrage', in the May 1941 edition, of *Neues Volk*,[135] suggest that the German public was being 'softened up' for the *physical* extermination of Russian Jewry in connection with the planned attack on Russia. Hitler had in any case declined to approve reference to moving Jews to Madagascar in the speech Alfred Rosenberg was to make at the Frankfurt meeting on 28 March 1941.[136] Significantly, when the anti-Jewish operations of the *Einsatzgruppen* were under way in the summer and autumn of 1941, a series of Party circulars showed that the Leadership was at pains to ensure that the true nature of the 'either-or' fight between National Socialism and Judeo-Bolshevism was presented, at least to the Party faithful.[137]

Sixth, the general feeling of needing to resolve the Jewish question in France as part of a European *Gesamtlösung* was underlined by Dannecker's continuing anti-Jewish activities in Paris, and especially by his reference to 'future orders' expected from the RSHA in Berlin at an inter-agency meeting in Paris on 10 June, with Zeitschel representing the embassy. This gave added point to the weekly meetings he had organized of the respective German 'Jewish experts' so that RSHA orders might be complied with more expeditiously.[138] Quite possibly, Dannecker's revelation meant that for some time past, Eichmann's European Referenten had been instructed to organize things in readiness for when relevant orders came from headquarters in Berlin.[139]

Seventh, on 22 June 1941, a radically new departure in the Third Reich's anti-Jewish policies occurred, marking the beginning of the systematic annihilation of Russian Jewry in accordance with the Führer's long-held aims. These were the anti-Jewish *Einsatzgruppen* actions consequent upon the military operations of Operation Barbarossa, which themselves highlighted other questions which were to be of decisive importance in the subsequent pan-European anti-Jewish campaign, those of railway communications.[140] This was the 'war against the Jews', against the twin threat of *Weltjudentum* and the Judeo-Bolshevik leadership of Bolshevik Russia, which the Führer always had in mind and which he publicly threatened in the Reichstag on 30 January 1939.

The anti-Jewish exterminatory imperatives behind Hitler's action in attacking Russia in June 1941 were fully borne out by the pre-invasion orders and subsequent actions of the *Einsatzgruppen* in Russia.[141] And almost a month into the Russian war, at a conference on 16 July 1941 with Alfred Rosenberg, Wilhelm Keitel, Heinrich Lammers, and Reichsmarschall Goering, Hitler himself emphasized that there was no need to make public Germany's true aims in the war, otherwise this would complicate Germany's way forward. He also insisted that all means to achieve Germany's aims were permissible – shootings, deportations, and so on – especially since the Russian partisan war gave Germany the opportunity to 'exterminate everyone who opposed us'.[142] Hitler was thus directly responsible, in more ways than one, for the mass murder of Russian Jewry before that of European Jewry.

It has been concluded that the 'German invasion of Russia opened a new phase in France also ... the German authorities imposed sweeping new restrictions on Jews in the Occupied Zone'.[143] That new phase, including an intensification of internment policy – the roundups on 20 August were observed with some hostility by French public opinion[144] – was accompanied by no diminution in the ideological fervour of embassy officials. On 1 July 1941, for example, when Schleier emphasized to Dannecker the importance of allowing sufficient time for implementing anti-Jewish measures in France, he commented: 'it was not to be expected that what had to be set in motion step by step in Germany after the people had been made aware of the fourteen-year struggle of National Socialism with the Jewish problem, could now be immediately implemented in France without a corresponding period of preparation'. Significantly, he also urged immediate steps against non-French Jews in the occupied zone so as to induce the French authorities to proceed against their own Jews.[145]

This was followed on 21 and 22 August, by two Aufzeichnungen for Ambassador Abetz from Zeitschel who was obviously concerned to maintain the momentum and intensity of all anti-Jewish measures. It has been suggested that this was done at the behest of Dannecker, an entirely credible possibility.[146] In the first, Zeitschel countered the call by Theodore K. Kaufman, President of the American League for Peace, for the sterilization of all Germans by proposing that measure for the six or seven million Jews under German control. Zeitschel suggested that on his next visit to von Ribbentrop and the Führer, the ambassador should place this proposal before the two leaders.

The second Zeitschel *Aufzeichnung*, however, is the most intriguing from a number of perspectives: for what it may possibly reveal about the timing of the Leadership's decision to extend the anti-Jewish killing process from Russia to the European arena, particularly when taken in conjunction with Hitler's subsequent order to Himmler in September (see below); and the extent of 'knowledge' or 'guessing' about the new tendencies in anti-Jewish policy in various circles. At the very least, the document reveals something of current gossip in Paris and Berlin. Zeitschel declared that 'the progressive conquest and occupation of the extensive eastern territories enables us, in my opinion, to bring about in the shortest time a final and satisfactory solution to the Jewish problem in the whole of Europe'. The aim of making all Europe *judenfrei*, including clearing the Jewish ghettos in Warsaw, Lodz and Lublin, could be achieved by despatching all Jews to a territory in the east through mass transports, particularly since transporting some ten million to Madagascar by sea was now out of the question. While Zeitschel omitted to specify the fate of Jews when transported 'to the east', a sense of urgency was clearly evident since he linked this deportation process to the necessity of providing more internment space in France for even more Jews. He requested that Abetz submit his proposals to von Ribbentrop as a basis for discussions with Alfred Rosenberg, Heinrich Himmler, and Reichsmarschall Goering.

The fact and manner of Zeitschel's reference to Goering in this context betrays a great deal of how news spread through the German bureaucratic network. In proposing that Abetz communicate with the Reichsmarschall, Zeitschel commented how far Goering was receptive on the Jewish question and could, therefore, be expected to support strongly these ideas, especially in view of the Reichsmarschall's 'experiences of the war in the east'.[147]

Zeitschel was clearly aware of Goering's ostensible role as 'el supremo' in the Jewish question since 1938–39, as further evidenced by the Reichsmarschall's letter of 31 July 1941 to Heydrich, 'authorizing' him 'to undertake, by emigration or evacuation, a solution of the Jewish question . . . I hereby charge you with making all necessary organizational, functional, and material preparations for a complete solution of the Jewish question in the German sphere of influence in Europe. In so far as the jurisidiction of other central agencies may be touched thereby, they are to be involved. I charge you furthermore with submitting to me in the near future an overall plan of the organizational, functional, and material measures to be taken in preparing for the implementation of the aspired final solution of the Jewish question'.[148] Eichmann later claimed that Goering had only signed a letter taken to him by Heydrich, although it is not clear whether the document was dictated by or to, Eichmann.[149]

But there is more to consider about Zeitschel's actions in August and his circumspect language. Even though Zeitschel wrote at a time before *Einsatzgruppen* reports were officially circulated in the Auswärtiges Amt, it is evident from how he wrote on 22 August that his close contacts with Dannecker made him aware of the massive anti-Jewish killing operations of the *Einsatzgruppen* in Russia. It was, moreover, unlikely that Zeitschel was the only Auswärtiges Amt employee to have a close working or personal relationship with members of the security forces. This suggests the strong possibility that information about the extermination of Russian Jewry, and even hints at what else was planned, permeated through to the German Foreign Office earlier than some accounts would have it.[150]

If this is so, it must be concluded that Zeitschel was being patently disingenuous in hinting that there could be created a *Judenreservat* for European Jews in Russian territory, when he was obviously aware of such territories being made *judenfrei* through the mass destruction of Jews in Russia then taking place. Zeitschel's submission to Abetz concerning deporation eastwards, at the behest of Dannecker following information received from Berlin, may therefore be seen as part of a sophisticated ruse by RSHA authorities in Berlin to ensure the full co-operation, and indeed compliance, of such key local agencies as the Paris Embassy in the 'supply' of non-Russian Jews, as and when the green light was given to destroy European Jewry, by still disguising the exterminatory intention. Although during August 1941 Heydrich unsuccessfully tried to obtain Hitler's authorization to deport German Jews eastwards, two months later he and Eichmann were able to institute this policy in the Riga and Minsk regions.

There are other key points to consider about Zeitschel's notions concerning moving Jews 'to the east'. How and when was this to be done on a pan-European scale when, for many months in the autumn of 1941, the Germans were faced with the gigantic task of converting

the broader Russian railway gauge to the European standard?[151] And
what about continued military operations in Russia, or did Zeitschel
share the optimism of many in the leadership that victory over Russia
would be achieved 'by Christmas'? In the event, the logic of removing
the mass murder of European Jews from the gaze of German and
European eyes,[152] and the logistical realities of transporting millions of
human beings in a co-ordinated sweep by the only means possible,
railways, all within the context of ongoing military operations in the
east, dictated that there should be fixed extermination establishments
sited as far east as possible – but in Poland where the railway system
already shared the standard European gauge.

By the late summer and autumn of 1941 – with Himmler being
advised that the best means of mass extermination was the use of gas
chambers and his making suitable arrangements with Rudolf Höss at
Auschwitz;[153] with the Auswärtiges Amt receiving a number of communications from the RSHA during 1941 (as in 1940) extending
its prohibitions on Jewish emigration from Europe because of 'the
forthcoming final solution of the Jewish question';[154] and the August
1941 transfer of the euthanasia personnel and equipment to the east[155]
– there occurred a significant dovetailing of perceptions and policies in
Berlin with those of embassy and Sipo-SD personnel in Paris. This is
clear evidence of a general consensus about extending the Russian
killing operations to European Jewry. Important already, the
Zeitschel–Dannecker relationship became even more significant then
because of their place in the vertical chains of command.

Abetz obviously responded well to Zeitschel's submissions. On 2
September, the latter informed Dannecker that the ambassador
required precise details about the Jews already interned.[156]
Nevertheless, Zeitschel appeared uncertain. Shortly before Abetz's
departure to meet Hitler, he impressed upon him, on 10 September,
the urgency of his deportation proposals, the freeing of more camp
spaces in France for Jews, and the granting of full powers to the Sipo-
SD, urging him to take the memoranda with him.[157] Zeitschel's
nervousness was undoubtedly due to pressure from Dannecker.[158]

At their meeting on 16 September, Hitler told Abetz that the 'Asiatics
and Bolsheviks had to be driven out of Europe', and let slip the enig-
matic phrase, 'the Urals would be the boundary behind which Stalin and
his ilk could do whatever they pleased'.[159] Abetz also spoke to Himmler
about Zeitschel's deportation proposals and obtained his agreement,
subject to available transport.[160] Time and again, then, important personal links in the central and local chains of command were made.

Just as the Abetz–Zeitschel–Dannecker thrust made it clear to the Leadership that the 'local' level in France was prepared for whatever Berlin decided and when, it is more than likely that this information greatly assisted the Leadership in converting general ideas into firm policy decisions. That the dovetailing process did not always proceed in a downward direction is suggested by the fact that Abetz's communication of the Zeitschel–Dannecker proposals was followed, on 18 September, by a significant communication from Himmler to Arthur Greiser, the Gauleiter and Reichsstatthalter (Reich Governor) in Gau Wartheland: 'it is the Führer's wish that the Altreich and the Protectorates should be cleared of Jews from west to east. I am therefore doing all I can to see that the deportation of the Jews out of the Altreich and the Protectorates into the territories assimilated into the Reich during the past two years is completed during this year as a first stage, preparatory to their being sent *further east* [my italics] early in the new year'.[161] Only one month before, it had been 'the Führer's wish' *not* to accede to Heydrich's request to deport the Jews of the Altreich to the east.[162].

The Paris initiatives meshed neatly with current thinking in Berlin, since Himmler's 'combing out' policy could hardly be implemented were it not for the 'concentration' inititatives of authorities in territories such as France. But Zeitschel remained uncertain, for on 8 October he seemed to have doubts about Abetz's report on Himmler's positive response. Besides confirming to Dannecker his submissions to Abetz, Zeitschel wanted his friend to obtain confirmation from Berlin of Himmler's agreement so that 'the Jews in occupied France could be deported as soon as possible'.[163] This evidence of Zeitschel's frenetic urge to solve the Jewish question in France, together with his close working relationship with Dannecker, further weakens arguments about bureaucratic competition being the driving force of anti-Jewish policy in the Third Reich.

The dovetailing process continued during the final three months of 1941 and into 1942. Himmler's instruction of 18 September led to the transfer of some 20,000 Jews from the Altreich, Vienna and Prague to the Lodz ghetto in the Warthegau. From there, 50 per cent were exterminated the following year in the nearby extermination camp of Chelmno, which had begun to operate in December 1941. In addition, Heydrich finally succeeded in deporting German Jews. On 19 October, at a meeting over which Heydrich presided, Eichmann announced that *Einsatzgruppen* A and B, operating in the Riga and Minsk areas, were prepared to accept Jews deported directly into their 'zones of operation'

– obviously for extermination. On 24 October, an 'express letter' was issued by SS police authorities in Vienna for the transport of some 50,000 Jews from the Altreich, Vienna, and Prague to 'the zones of operation' in the period 1 November to December 4 1941.[164]

During October as well, correspondence between Dr Wetzel of the Ministry for the Occupied Eastern Territories and Reich Commissioner Heinrich Lohse for Ostland, confirmed the agreement of Viktor Brack of the Führer's Chancellery, in charge of the euthanasia operations, 'to collaborate in the manufacture of the necessary buildings and gas apparatus . . . on the spot'. Significantly, Wetzel referred to Eichmann's statement that camps for Jews would be established in Riga and Minsk, commenting further that 'in our present position we cannot afford to have scruples about taking advantage of Brack's facilities for the elimination of Jews who are not fit for work'.[165] This correspondence was further evidence of the extent of Himmler's preparations for mass extermination at fixed sites, following the emergent drawbacks of gas vans.[166] Similarly, experience in the field continued to show that if millions rather than thousands were to be exterminated, the practical and psychological inadequacies of mass shooting had to be replaced by other methods.[167].

In the West, Gestapo chief Heinrich Müller passed to SS headquarters in Belgium and France, on 23 October 1941, an order from Himmler that, apart from a few exceptions judged to be in the German interest, no more Jews were to emigrate from Germany or occupied Europe.[168] The real significance of this tightening of the European ring finally became clear when decisions about the fate of European Jews was immediately tied to other developments in Eastern Europe.

In France, meanwhile, further assassinations and sabotage against the Wehrmacht from October were a direct result of provocations by the SD because of its dissatisfaction with the MBF's anti-Jewish policies. Beyond leading to a fierce contretemps between these two forces, a number of interim military reprisal measures were promul-gated, supported by the Auswärtiges Amt and the Paris Embassy.[169] Finally, on 5 December 1941, the MBF drafted its full retaliatory proposals which Hitler approved on 12 December. These involved the shooting of hostages, imposing a billion-franc fine on Jews, and deporting a thousand Jews to the east, followed by extensive arrests.[170]

The satisfaction of the Paris Embassy with these developments was hardly surprising.[171] The notice issued by the MBF on 14 December, blaming 'young elements in the pay of Anglo-Saxons, Jews and

Bolsheviks', was influenced by Abetz, acting on the personal authority of
Hitler. The Führer had directed that 'the necessary public
announcements and propagandistic measures are to be prepared in
agreement with the German Ambassador in Paris'.[172] Significantly,
Abetz expressed his concern about the delicate state of the Franco-
German political relations unless the blame for anti-German actions was
put exclusively on 'Jews, Soviet and Secret-Service agents'. As he
informed Hans Heinrich Strack of the Auswärtiges Amt by telephone
on 12 December, Abetz also intended to pursue this line in the future 'as
it is not in our political interest to support the Anglo-Saxon and Russian
thesis that these outrages are the expression of a hostile attitude on the
part of the French population'.[173]

The key development which determined everything else in the Third
Reich's anti-Jewish policies for the whole of occupied Europe was the
eventual convening (after some delays) of the Wannsee Conference of
20 January 1942 and its practical consequences. Given concomitant
developments undertaken by Himmler and others in the autumn of
1941, this conference convened at a time when 'old' methods of
extermination in 'the zones of operation' of the eastern *Einsatzgruppen*
were in the process of being supplanted by extermination at fixed
gassing sites nearer at hand in the Warthegau, the Gouvernement-
General area of Poland, and Upper Silesia. The consequent overlap of
killing areas goes some way towards explaining the general use of, and
some confusion in, much of the correspondence concerning the term
'farther to the east'.

Significantly, Referat D III's 8 December 1941 submission to Martin
Luther, obviously at his behest, of an eight-point statement for the
conference originally proposed by Heydrich for 9 December, referred
to the deportation of Jews from Germany, the occupied areas, and other
territories 'to the east', terms and concepts long familiar to Dannecker
and Zeitschel.[174] In any case, by November and December 1941 both
von Ribbentrop and Luther were aware of the extermination of Jews in
Russia, behaving like everyone else in using euphemisms about all Jews
'having to leave Europe' at the end of the war within the framework of
the Führer's decision on this matter.[175]

From the winter of 1941–42, then, the language of Auswärtiges Amt
documents takes on added significance because of Wannsee,
particularly within the context of more widespread use of the coded
language used in official correspondence.[176] What may be said with some
certainty, therefore, is that denials by the diplomatic service of

knowledge of the policy of extermination fly in the face of evidence and commonsense.[177] Just as the German public became aware of the barbaric and anti-Jewish nature of the Russian campaign,[178] and, by the autumn of 1941, 'various members of the Foreign Office had learned of the massacres of the Russian Jews through unofficial sources',[179] so, from 30 October 1941, the first *Einsatzgruppen* reports from 31 July which referred in detail to the 'liquidation' of Jews and Bolsheviks, were regularly distributed to the Auswärtiges Amt and initialled by State Secretary Ernst von Weizsäcker.[180] Information about such liquidations was also picked up contemporaneously by Allied Intelligence facilities.[181] Luther's own knowledge of events in Russia gives added point to his statement on 4 December, in language reminiscent of Rademacher's memorandum of 3 July 1940, that 'the opportunity rendered by this war must be utilized to finally eliminate the Jewish question in Europe'.[182]

All this accorded with the line taken by Joseph Goebbels in *Das Reich* on 16 November 1941 in an article entitled, 'The Jews Are Guilty'. He declared that Hitler's prophecy of 30 January 1939 was being implemented since the Jews 'are now suffering a gradual process of extermination which they had intended for us and would have let loose against us without hesitation had they the power'.[183] Two days later, Alfred Rosenberg told members of the German press in the Reich Ministry for the Occupied Territories, that the Jewish question could only be resolved through 'a biological elimination of the entire Jewish population of Europe'.[184] And during 1942, privately and publicly, Hitler himself repeatedly drew attention to his 30 January 1939 threat to the Jews.[185]

When all this is added to the participation of the Auswärtiges Amt at the Wannsee Conference, upon which occasion Luther declared no problems would arise about deporting Jews from western Europe,[186] it is asking too much to accept the notion that when the 'diplomats' in France came to be 'sucked into' the Jewish deportation process organized by Eichmann and the Sipo-SD, they really did believe that Auschwitz was just a work camp, or even that it was a 'staging post' for their supposed 'deportation' further east. In official correspondence, the common expression used about transporting Jews from France to the extermination camp of Auschwitz was *Arbeitseinsatz*, for 'labour purposes'. In any case, Eichmann confirmed to his Israeli interrogators that despite all the tortuous language employed at Wannsee, the killing of Jews was the purpose of the discussion.[187] As it was, nine days after Wannsee, Himmler issued instructions to the Reichskommissariate

Ostland and Ukraine to proceed immediately with the annihilation of Jews in those territories.[188]

The term *Arbeitseinsatz*, as well as that also used at Wannsee, deportation 'farther to the east', were thus 'fictions' previously agreed upon by the SS/SD, the Auswärtiges Amt, and other government agencies to categorize the intended killing process at Auschwitz and other extermination camps. Nor do we need to rely on Eichmann's words alone to support this contention. On 18 December 1941, Otto Braütigam, Deputy Chief of the Political Division in the Reich Ministry for the Occupied Eastern Territories, replied to previous correspondence between Dr Leibbrandt of the RMBO and Heinrich Lohse, Reich Commissar for the conquered Baltic States and White Russia, concerning 'wild' executions of Jews and questions of their economic value. As Braütigam put it, economic considerations were to be disregarded while 'the Jewish question has in the meantime probably been *clarified by personal discussions*' [my italics].[189]

Furthermore, *Einsatzgruppen* Report Number 9 distributed in Berlin by the SS/SD on 27 February 1942 stated: 'it is our aim to cleanse the Eastern countries of Jews as completely as possible. Everywhere the executions are to be carried out in such a manner that they will hardly be noticed by the public. *Among the population, and even among the remaining Jews, the conviction is widespread that the Jews have merely been resettled*' [my italics].[190] On 13 May 1942, the military commander of the Greater Paris region passed on OKH orders concerning deportations, in which the phrase '*dispatch for forced labour*' [my italics] was to be substituted for 'dispatch to the East'.[191] On 15 June 1942, Dannecker also issued instructions that in order to avoid confusion with transports of French forced labour to Germany, the Jewish transports should be described as for 'Jewish settlement'. By giving the impression that this involved the movement of families, Dannecker believed this would facilitate the German aim of incorporating children under 16 in later transports.[192] Even the SS men who carried out gassing operations at Lublin on 18 July 1942 in the presence of Himmler were forced to sign a declaration of secrecy which referred to 'the process of the evacuation of Jews'.[193]

In Germany itself, because of widespread rumours 'about the position of the Jews in the east', the Party Chancellery felt it necessary to issue, on 9 October 1942, confidential instructions stating that Jews were being transported for 'labour purposes' and could even be transported 'farther to the east'. Nevertheless, neither Martin Bormann, Head of the Party Chancellery, nor Hitler himself, could prevent something of the real truth being admitted since the document continued: 'The nature of the matter makes it unavoidable that these very difficult problems, in the interest of a final security of our people, can only be solved with ruthless determination'.[194] A year later, even this imperative had to be revised. On 11 July 1943, Bormann issued a *Rundschreiben* containing Hitler's instructions that there was to be no public speculation on any 'future total solution' of the Jewish question. Instead, it was permitted to speak only about Jews being taken for 'appropriate labour purposes' (*zweckentsprechendem Arbeitseinsatz*).[195]

Given these developments, let alone the plethora of rumours and speculation, it is inconceivable that such diligent and loyal ideologues of the Third Reich as Abetz, Zeitschel and Dannecker could have been unaware of the ultimate fate which awaited Jews from France who were deported 'to the east', as a consequence of their joint efforts in Paris. Arguments to the contrary would imply that they believed there could be pursued in Russia and elsewhere in the occupied eastern territories a continuing and horrendous policy of exterminating Jews, conducted in a manner causing members of the *Einsatzgruppen* to have nervous breakdowns, only for the leadership to support European Jewry in supposed work camps or settlements somewhere in 'the east'. Or else, given the kind of language used by all participants in their correspondence and meetings, that words and phrases in German had lost all meaning.

As it was, Dannecker and Himmler themselves gave the lie to any such nonsense as this mythical 'twin-track' policy. On 20 July 1942, reporting on his journey through the unoccupied zone, Dannecker commented on efforts by Jewish organizations to arrange shipping space for Jews: 'this is an indication that world Jewry is fully aware that Jews in German-occupied territories face their entire extermination'.[196] Eight days later, Himmler informed his representative in the Reich Ministry for the Occupied Eastern Territories that 'the occupied territories will be purged of Jews. The Führer has charged me with the execution of this very difficult order'.[197] In his memoirs, even Abetz finally had to admit the truth: 'the pretext of labour purposes' was the cover applied to the deportation of Jews from France.[198]

How, then, did the 'diplomats' in France conduct themselves once extermination became the Third Reich's practice for the whole of Europe in the wake of Wannsee? Did their actions and the language they employed in official documents betray anything more than a case of 'getting on with the job', or even 'competing' with the SS and SD authorities? The short answer is that the ideological anti-Jewish imperatives of the 'diplomats', and therefore their personal commitment to the policies they helped implement, remained equal to that of their colleagues in the security forces at every stage. This is especially true if one discounts the fiction that the 'diplomats' believed the *Tarnspruch* everyone used to designate the deportation of Jews to Auschwitz. Besides which, participation at Wannsee and subsequent conferences bound those individuals and ministries irrevocably to the joint task of mass murder.[199]

The urgency manifested by the main characters in France remained undiminished. On 13 February 1942, for example, Zeitschel supported Sipo-SD complaints about the MBF 'protecting' Jewish informants. He suggested to Abetz that they be kept in a concentration camp, and the military authorities informed that 'in the long run, Jewish informants are anyway impossible since at the end of the war they would in any case have to leave Europe through the Final Solution of the Jewish Question'.[200] Two weeks later, Zeitschel accompanied Dannecker in a visit to the German Consul in Vichy, Krug von Nidda, to sound him out about Vichy's likely response to German demands that Jews be handed over for transportation to the east, in accordance with instructions Dannecker had received from Berlin.

Several important points emerge from Zeitschel's report on this visit. First, von Nidda felt Vichy would respond readily to firm German demands, even for between 1,000 and 5,000 Jews monthly, although whether these figures originated with Dannecker or his superiors in Berlin is not clear. Second, Dannecker felt it necessary that von Nidda provide Heydrich with intelligence about Vichy to enable the German authorities, when it came to occupying other territory in France, to proceed against the Jews. Third, the consul proposed a joint meeting of these three with Heydrich in Berlin to discuss transport facilities for deportation – but only after 'the beginning of the Spring offensive', an obvious reference to the forthcoming campaign against Russia and evidence of what kind of information spread easily throughout the diplomatic service. Fourth, Dannecker discussed with the press office of the consulate ways and means of co-ordinating, with the SD branch in Paris, anti-Jewish propaganda in the Vichy zone so as to intensify French animosity against the Jews.[201]

Thereafter, things moved quickly. On 4 March, Dannecker attended an RSHA meeting in Berlin where he was authorized to begin negotiations with the French government to deport 5,000 Jews to the east.[202] Five days later, Eichmann formally began the deportation process by requesting approval from the Auswärtiges Amt for the removal of 1,000 Jews.[203] That was a key point of bureaucratic procedure for which Luther had obtained Heydrich's agreement at Wannsee, and especially important given the numbers of foreign Jews likely to be involved in deportations, the diplomatic consequences of which that Office would have to handle.[204] Dannecker duly informed his Paris SS colleagues[205] and Zeitschel about the meeting of 4 March.

When Eichmann again approached the Auswärtiges Amt for further approval on 11 March, this time raising the figure by 5,000 in accordance with the decisions taken on 4 March,[206] Zeitschel unashamedly acted as Dannecker's *alter ego* in the embassy. He informed his embassy colleagues of the decisions of 4 March, and that Heydrich had promised transport on 23 March for the 1,000 Jews held in the camp at Compiègne, a process to be continued during 1942 and 1943. Jews would be transported, 'first to a reception camp in Silesia, and then taken farther east for labour purposes'. Zeitschel thus played his part in further spreading the 'fictions' all participants were agreed upon. And, learning from Dannecker (who had received the information from Heydrich) that, in Berlin, the Romanian, Slovakian and Croatian representatives had disowned Jews living beyond their boundaries, he asked that confirmation of this be obtained from the Auswärtiges Amt so that such Jews could be included in the Paris deportations.[207]

Not surprisingly, embassy 'approval' was always forthcoming.[208] In his post-war testimony, Abetz patently lied when he stated that 'as for the deportation of the 6,000 Jews, I do not recall that the Embassy was ever contacted in this matter', immediately contradicting himself in the same affidavit by declaring that he received from Zeitschel reports 'on the actions of the Security Service in connection with the Jewish question in France'. These reports he used as the basis of his own to the Auswärtiges Amt.[209]

Following the SD's unashamed bid in October and November 1941 to gain more control over the Jewish question against the MBF,[210] and just as the March 1942 programme got under way, on 9 March 1942 Hitler appointed a senior SS and Police Leader for France. Police powers were transferred from the MBF to the SD, but Karl Oberg's appointment – Himmler's 'ambassador'[211] – did not necessarily mean that 'the role of the Auswärtiges Amt and the Embassy was supplanted in the anti-Jewish policy', even though Oberg was to negotiate with Vichy on police matters, above all the implementation of *Endlösung*.[212]

Slipping into what was obviously familiar language, Zeitschel believed this development would 'have an especially favourable effect for the Final Solution of the Jewish question'.[213]

At the same time as the deportation began, attention also became focused upon another matter raised at the RSHA meeting on 4 March – Eichmann's proposal to make Jews in occupied Europe wear the star of David. That had been imposed since 1939 in Poland, and, following Goebbels' representations to Hitler on 20 August 1941, from 5 September 1941 in the Greater German Reich. That August decision had prompted Eichmann to ask the Auswärtiges Amt about the position of foreign Jews. This gave rise to much discussion since the Auswärtiges Amt's first reaction was that foreign Jews should be excluded from the measures.[214]

In France in 1942, where the intent was to 'mark' Jews before their deportation, several difficulties arose, not least because of what the embassy felt was the non-cooperative attitude of Vallat. Joint pressure by the principal German authorities in France, including the embassy, resulted in Admiral Darlan's dismissal of Vallat on 19 March and the appointment on 6 May of the more industrious Louis Darquier de Pellepoix, whom the embassy had long favoured and supported. Indeed, the embassy felt there would be no difficulty about extending a Jewish star policy to the Vichy region, so long as the MBF held off from issuing such an ordinance until de Pellepoix had asumed office.[215]

The embassy had two concerns about a Yellow Star policy: to agree to anything that would expedite German anti-Jewish policy without unduly disturbing that political relationship it had so assiduously worked to develop with the Vichy regime, and to avoid unnecessary foreign policy complications through marking the 'wrong' Jews. Although Abetz at first had doubts about the wisdom of such a policy, by 2 May he had abandoned them because of the number of attacks on German personnel which could be blamed on Jews and communists. Then, he considered that the political and psychological moment had arrived for this policy to be applied in France.[216] On 3 May he informed Knochen of his decision. The next day, Zeitschel again betrayed his own feelings of urgency when he exclaimed to Dannecker that 'publication of the [Jewish Star] order cannot come fast enough'.[217] On 5 May, and emphasizing Abetz's points to Berlin of 2 May, Zeitschel urged Dr Best of the MBF to take full advantage of the present 'politically favourable situation' to introduce forthwith a Yellow Star policy, particularly since the embassy had withdrawn its former objections.[218] While Zeitschel confirmed in writing to Knochen and

Dannecker the embassy decision,[219] the ambassador and other embassy officials co-operated with the MBF in the legal and propaganda preparations for the new policy, all of which duly emphasized, at the suggestion of the embassy, the responsibility of Jews for recent 'terror acts' against members of the Wehrmacht. Whether British and American Jews would be exempted from the new ordinances was an issue still to be decided.[220]

In Berlin, Rademacher suggested that the Paris Embassy impress upon the Vichy regime the need to apply a similar Yellow Star ordinance in their zone. Sensibly, Woermann of the Political Department advised that Abetz be consulted.[221] The ambassador, however, felt that a similar step in Vichy could hardly be expected without it first being fully implemented in the occupied zone, accompanied by circumspect diplomacy in the direction of Vichy. Included in his reply, the urgency of which entailed Zeitschel telephoning it through to Luther's office, was a request for an immediate response to the MBF's query about exceptions under the new ordinance. Luther's agreement was telegraphed to the Paris Embassy at half-past midnight in the morning of 22 May. Zeitschel straightaway informed the MBF and Oberg of this decision which enabled those authorities to complete yet another stage in the despatch of Jews in France to Auschwitz.[222] On 1 June, the MBF imposed the Jewish Star policy in the occupied zone, to come into force on 7 June, together with other restrictions on the daily life of Jews.[223] Initial targets were Jews from the Altreich, Belgium, Croatia, France, Holland, Poland, Romania and Slovakia.[224] Nevertheless, it remained a kind of half-measure in France since the Vichy regime always declined to issue a similar ordinance for their area. Even the Germans felt it more politic not to press the issue when they extended their occupation in November 1942.[225]

What did not remain a half-measure, however, were the activities of Heydrich, Eichmann and Dannecker throughout May and June in setting up the complicated process of moving tens of thousands of Jews from France across the continent of Europe to their destruction in Auschwitz. An essential element in that process was, of course, the provision of rolling stock and the slotting of deportation trains in complicated Reichsbahn timetables. Apart from the key responsibilities of Novak, the success of the plans of Eichmann and Dannecker also depended upon the head of the Wehrmacht's railway office in France, General Kohl. But since the general had declared himself 'an uncompromising enemy of the Jews, and agreed one hundred per cent with a final solution of the Jewish question which aimed at the complete annihilation of the enemy', the security forces could feel assured that in this direction, as with the embassy, their work of mass destruction could proceed unhindered.[226]

Five days after the second transport of Jews left France on 5 June, Eichmann emphasized at a meeting of his *Judenreferenten* from Belgium, France and Holland the need to expedite the deportation process from the west as a whole, as well as discussing how to involve the Vichy authorities. Significantly, given Eichmann and Heydrich's efforts from August to October 1941 to deport Altreich Jews to German-occupied Riga and Minsk for extermination by *Einsatzgruppen* in 'the zones of operation', the meeting began with the statement that 'on military grounds, the deportation of Jews from Germany to the eastern territories during the summer was no longer possible'.[227] This confirmed that for military and other reasons, the mass extermination of European Jewry would have to take place in the fixed gassing installations outside 'zones of operation', that is in Poland, although during 1942 deportations from the Reich to Riga and Minsk still occurred.[228] To ensure the 'supply' of Jews from France for this purpose, Dannecker was instructed to obtain assurances from Kohl that adequate transport facilities to deport 100,000 Jews from 13 July would be available.[229]

According to the proprieties of the German administrative system, Eichmann continued to feel obliged to obtain formal 'approval' from the Auswärtiges Amt for these steps. Yet the manner of his doing so on 22 June, when requesting Auswärtiges Amt authorization for the transportation of 40,000 Jews from the occupied zone in the period July to August for the purpose of 'labour in the Auschwitz camp', indicated that he felt his actions were not really dependent upon any reply he received.[230] In the event, Luther did not respond until the end of July, after he had communicated with Abetz in Paris.[231] Significantly, 22 June was the day the third transport departed, initiating the systematic deportation process from France until 1944,[232] a development which in France marked the apotheosis of Statist co-operation between the embassy, MBF and Sipo-SD authorities.

The sense of urgency spread everywhere. While Himmler issued orders that Jews should be deported from France as rapidly as possible,[233] Zeitschel expressed regret to the Sipo-SD at his enforced absence from Paris, just when Dannecker had told him that 50,000 Jews were required from the Vichy zone which necessitated the co-operation of the embassy in putting pressure on Pierre Laval, the French Prime Minister: '*in view of the urgency of the matter* [my italics] and since, *unfortunately* [my italics], I shall be away from Paris for eight days, I request that Hauptsturmführer Dannecker contact Counsellor Rahn directly on Monday 29 June or Tuesday 30 June, in order to learn from him about Laval's reply'.[234] Even more urgent and reflecting Eichmann's constant pressure on Dannecker – or was it the other way around? – was the tone of Zeitschel's report on this to Abetz on 27 June in which he mentioned Dannecker's 'ruthless' determination to remove 100,000 Jews from France that summer.[235]

In the crucial summer months of 1942, Abetz and other embassy officials betrayed no wavering of ideological commitment to the cause. Thus, the embassy briefed Knochen[236] for the important (and frustrating) negotiations which began on 2 July between Oberg, accompanied by Knochen, Lischka, Hagen and others, and René Bousquet, General Secretary of the French National Police, about which Jews (French, foreign, or stateless) were to be deported. Although one statement by Knochen at that meeting was designed to serve the immediate needs of the security services, it also indicated the ideological parameters within which the 'diplomats' co-operated wholeheartedly: 'in all his recent speeches, the Führer has emphasized nothing so clearly as the absolute necessity of a definitive solution to the Jewish Question. . . . Should the French government oppose the effective seizure [of the Jews], so undoubtedly the Führer will be unable to understand this'.[237] Thereafter, the Paris Embassy and the MBF were kept informed of the progress of these talks, undertaken in pursuance of Himmler's instructions to clear France in accordance with the dictates of *eine baldige Endlösung der Judenfrage in Westeuropa.*[238]

On the same day that Oberg began the difficult process of negotiating with the French, Abetz welcomed information he received from the Auswärtiges Amt that the Hungarian government agreed that Germany's anti-Jewish measures in France could be applied to Hungarian Jews. He considered this would incline the French to accept more readily new measures to include those foreign Jews hitherto exempt: 'the French working class would not understand it if Italian, Hungarian, Spanish, and Romanian Jews remained in France while Jews who had a long history in France were deported. This is understandable when one realizes that those responsible for a series of Jewish terror and sabotage acts have been foreign Jews'. But the ambassador went further in betraying his own sense of urgency about fulfilling the Führer's anti-Jewish policies. Abetz recognized that the Hungarian move underlined 'the urgent political interest' of ensuring that other allied and friendly nations acted similarly, especially Italy. But if Italy did not follow the Hungarian example, he was concerned that Italian Jews be recalled to Italy. Abetz viewed this matter seriously, given instructions he had received from the Auswärtiges Amt on 28 June about 'the massive evacuation measures concerning Jews for labour in the Auschwitz camp'. Above all, he was worried that Italy's attitude made it appear to the French as though 'the Axis does not appear to follow a unified policy'.[239]

Equally revealing were Abetz's other comments on 2 July to Luther's message of 28 June passing on the SS/SD's request for approval of further Jewish transports to Auschwitz.[240] Agreeing to 40,000 Jews being transported for 'labour in the Auschwitz camp', Abetz emphasized that it had always been the embassy's purpose in pursuing anti-Jewish measures to ensure they exacerbated anti-Semitic sentiment in France. That was especially strong against foreign Jews, just as similar feelings in Germany had previously been generated by the 'flood' of *Ostjuden* and other foreign Jews. Abetz felt it would have a positive psychological effect upon most Frenchmen if foreign Jews were deported first, and French Jews were drawn into the process only if foreign Jews did not fill the required quotas. But this would not, of course, mean giving French Jews a privileged position – they would 'likewise vanish in the course of liberating the European countries from Jewry'.[241]

Although Luther felt Abetz's suggestions were not then viable,[242] the early deportations from France contained only non-French Jews as the ambassador had proposed. Abetz, maintaining the close working relationship with the Sipo-SD authorities, informed Knochen and Dannecker, and then Heinz Röthke from July, about his current exchanges with the Auswärtiges Amt, including his agreement concerning the deportation of Hungarian Jews.[243] This was before Luther eventually wrote in the same sense to Eichmann on 29 July.[244]

The decision about Hungarian Jews also served to intensify Abetz's complaints about Italy's 'lax' treatment of the Jewish question in its territory, something Rademacher and others had long complained about.[245] On 4 July, he confronted General Gelich, General Secretary of the Italian Armistice Commission, about the matter, emphasizing that Arab opinion towards the European powers was conditioned by their treatment of the Jewish question.[246] Luther agreed with Abetz, and as a consequence of von Weizsäcker and von Ribbentrop lending their support to these complaints,[247] by 17 September the matter was being formally raised with the Italians.[248]

There was, then, for all German authorities in France, no cause for complacency about the progress of their anti-Jewish policies in that part of Europe. Although the Paris Embassy's efforts with other German authorities in the direction of Vichy appeared to be successful by early August since the deportation of stateless Jews from the unoccupied zone appeared secure, Luther's uncertainty was underlined by his request to be informed of developments.[249]

For his part, the ever-diligent anti-Jewish ideologue Abetz found other matters to occupy him. On 7 September, he observed that difficulties about applying German anti-Jewish measures to Jews of *all* nationalities in France, including the Jewish star one, apart from increasing French animosity towards foreign Jews and the Germans because of various exclusion provisions, also enabled 'enemy propaganda' to categorize the Third Reich's anti-Jewish actions simply as questions of 'nationality'. Abetz was offended that these policies were not seen in their true light, as a 'racial question'. To correct this unsatisfactory situation, Abetz, and on behalf of the Sipo-SD, proposed that if nothing was done by other governments by 31 December 1942, then from 1 January 1943 Germany's measures should automatically apply to all Jews found in France.[250] He continued to press for urgent action with the Italian, Romanian, Hungarian and Greek governments so that Germany's Jewish star regulations in France could be applied to their Jews, a 'softer' target than the French Jews in the unoccupied zone who for so long had been virtually 'protected' by the Pétain regime, much to the chagrin of Himmler.[251]

For his part, Zeitschel balanced Abetz's efforts towards the Auswärtiges Amt by reconstituting, on 15 September, the weekly Tuesday 'co-ordination' meetings of the Paris *Judenreferenten* which had fallen into abeyance because of Dannecker's transfer from France. Committed, like everyone else, to the goal of making France *judenfrei*, in effect to achieve their extermination in the east, Zeitschel found it 'especially regrettable' that difficulties had arisen in the unoccupied zone in meeting Sipo-SD deportation expectations, because the RSHA had confirmed that from 15 November at the latest until the following spring, no more transport facilities could be expected.[252] It has also been suggested that such was Zeitschel's influence on this occasion that, the following day, Röthke began serious preparations for new arrests of French Jews. Moreover, on 17 September, Zeitschel informed Knochen that the Auswärtiges Amt had stated that recent negotiations meant it was likely that Romanian Jews would be included in future deportations.[253]

By 19 September, however, Luther acknowledged the situation concerning foreign Jews in France to be serious enough to make it necessary to submit the matter to von Weizsäker and von Ribbentrop.[254] Since von Ribbentrop informed Luther on 24 September that 'the evacuation of Jews from the different European countries should be expedited as much as possible',[255] it is hardly surprising that, on 3 October, the Foreign Minister expressed his agreement with Luther's submission of 19 September containing Abetz's initiatives.[256] Copies of most of his correspondence found their way to the Sipo-SD authorities in Paris, courtesy of the ever-diligent Zeitschel.[257] Yet even before von Ribbentrop's agreement of 3 October, Romanian Jews had been rounded up in Paris on 24 September and transported east four days later. But as a report from Knochen to RSHA Headquarters in Berlin on 25 September made clear, the Germans were making sure they got their hands on as many foreign Jews in France as possible since the nature of relations with the Vichy regime meant that most French Jews escaped deportation, something which even Himmler was forced to accept for a time.[258]

Shortly afterwards, Germany's anti-Jewish policies in France took on a new dimension when the unoccupied zone was annexed on 11 November 1942, following the Anglo-American landings in North Africa three days before. Although the Paris Embassy was still responsible for resolving wider foreign policy problems arising from the large number of foreign Jews in France,[259] the occupation of the Vichy zone effectively removed a key *raison d'être* of its existence and functions. Subsequent anti-Jewish policy, in effect the incorporation of French Jews into the deportation process, really became the fiefdom of the SS/SD authorities. Despite the new situation, the Germans found it no easier dealing with Laval and other French authorities in their attempts to deport as many Jews as possible.[260] Since over two-thirds of Jews in France avoided deportation to Auschwitz and other extermination camps, it could be said that the Third Reich's anti-Jewish policies in France 'failed'. From the German point of view, that is, since the French authorities succeeded in saving French Jews at the expense of most non-French Jews in France.[261]

As the Abetz case reveals, Christopher Browning's main conclusions appear to require serious modification. There can be no doubt that beyond their normal bureaucratic duties and whatever conflicts these produced, the 'diplomats' who executed the Third Reich's anti-Jewish policies were completely motivated by authentic anti-Jewish feelings. Whether or not these pre-dated or were developed during the Nazi era in German history, within the wider parameter of Statist and Party loyalty to the Führer, the individuals concerned needed no alleged bureaucratic 'competition' to participate in an innovatory manner in the special nature of those policies. They did so because they shared a commitment to fulfil the anti-Jewish imperative of their charismatic leader, Adolf Hitler.

To understand the mainsprings of the genesis and execution of the Nazi extermination of the Jews, we have to achieve a greater understanding of what drove individuals such as Abetz, Schleier, Zeitschel, von Bülow-Schwante, Rademacher and Luther of the Auswärtiges Amt, to behave as they did. The answers lie in breaking with three somewhat conventional and, indeed, inadequate approaches. First, explanations based mainly upon 'anti-Semitism' as the panacea for all analytical problems, whatever that ill-defined and over-exposed term meant in practice, will hardly advance knowledge further.[262] As one authoritative source puts it, 'although historical anti-Semitism was clearly relevant to the Holocaust, it cannot be accepted as a primary cause'.[263] Second, it is also perfectly clear that 'no definitive understanding of the Holocaust can be drawn directly from the survivor literature'.[264] Third, viewing the issue through the lens of bureaucratic in-fighting provides what is essentially a one-dimensional explanation, and one which omits the primary human emotions of love and hate, at the centre of which for almost all Germans in the Third Reich was the Führer-figure of Adolf Hitler.

The essential trigger for mass murder in the Third Reich, and which may be seen as transcending most other explanations, was the political position and ideology of Adolf Hitler. Irrespective of what animosity or murderous feelings previously existed in Germany and Europe against Jews, Gypsies and other groups, without him neither the murderous operations of the *Einsatzgruppen* in Russia nor Auschwitz and the other extermination camps in occupied Poland would have been possible. He triggered the policy of extermination, and he was the motor force for its continuance because he was the 'sun king' of the Nazi court. The clues, then, lie more in the nature of the emotional and ideological commitment to Adolf Hitler of Abetz and the others, and less in explanations which stress objective bureaucratic professionalism.[265]

NOTES

The written completion of this chapter would have been impossible but for the additional opportunities provided by my appointment as the 1990–91 Maxwell Fellow in the Study and Teaching of the Holocaust at the Oxford Centre for Postgraduate Hebrew Studies, and the subsequent financial support of my wife, Martha Lucia. I am also extremely grateful to the staff of the following institutions for their unfailing assistance to me, directly and through correspondence: Bundesarchiv, Koblenz; Imperial War Museum, London; Library and Records Department, Foreign and Commonwealth Office, London; Politische Archiv, Auswärtiges Amt, Bonn; Public Record Office, Kew; The Wiener Library, London.

1. For the Third Reich's anti-Jewish policies, see Raul Hilberg, *The Destruction of the European Jews* (London, 1961); Helmut Krausnick, 'The Persecution of the Jews', pp. 1–124 in Helmut Krausnick, Hans Buchheim, Martin Broszat and Hans-Adolf Jacobsen, *Anatomy of the SS State* (London, 1968); Gerald Reitlinger, *The Final Solution. The Attempt to Exterminate the Jews of Europe 1939–1945* (London, 1968, 2nd revised augmented edition); Karl A. Schleunes, *The Twisted Road to Auschwitz. Nazi Policy Toward German Jews 1933–1939* (Illinois, 1970); Uwe Dietrich Adam, *Judenpolitik im Dritten Reich* (Düsseldorf, 1972); Lucy S. Dawidowicz, *The War Against the Jews* (London, 1975); Joseph Billig and Georges Wellers, *The Holocaust and the Neo-Nazi Mythomania* (New York: The Beate Klarsfeld Foundation, 1978). Detailed reference will not be made to the disingenuous and spurious arguments of Arno J. Mayer, *Why Did the Heavens Not Darken? The 'Final Solution' in History* (New York, 1988).

2. Christopher R. Browning, *The Final Solution and the German Foreign Office. A Study of Referat D III of Abteilung Deutschland 1940–43* (New York, 1978). p. 185. See also idem, 'Referat Deutschland, Jewish Policy and the German Foreign Office (1933–1940)', *Yad Vashem Studies*, XII (Jerusalem, 1977), pp. 37–73; idem, '*Unterstaatssekretaer* Martin Luther and the Ribbentrop Foreign Office', *Journal of Contemporary History*, Vol. XII, No. 2 (1977), pp. 313–44; idem, 'The Government Experts', pp. 183–97 in Henry Friedlander and Sybil Milton (eds), *The Holocaust: Ideology, Bureaucracy, and Genocide* (New York, 1982); idem, 'The Decision Concerning the Final Solution', pp. 8–38 in *Fateful Months. Essays on the Emergence of the Final Solution* (New York, 1985). For a slightly different version of the latter essay with the same title, cf. pp. 96–118 in François Furet (ed.), *Unanswered Questions. Nazi Germany and the Genocide of the Jews* (New York, 1989); idem, 'Nazi Resettlement Policy and the Search for a Solution to the Jewish Question, 1939–1941', *German Studies Review*, Vol. 9, No. 3 (Oct. 1986), pp. 497–519.

3. Cf. A.J. Nicholls' review in *The English Historical Review*, Vol. LXXXXV (April 1980), pp. 392–93.

4. For Germany and France during the Second World War, see Eberhard Jäckel, *Frankreich in Hitler's Europa. Die Deutsche Frankreichpolitik im Zweiten Weltkreig* (Stuttgart, 1966); Robert O. Paxton, *Vichy France. Old Guard and New Order 1940–1944* (London, 1972); David Pryce-Jones, *Paris and the Third Reich* (London, 1982); Michael R. Marrus and Robert O. Paxton, *Vichy France and the Jews* (New York, 1983); John F. Sweets, *Choices in Vichy France. The French Under Nazi Occupation* (Oxford University Press, 1986); Paul Webster, *Pétain's Crime. The Full Story of French Collaboration in the Holocaust* (London, 1990). More specifically on German anti-Jewish policies in France, see Joseph Billig, *La Solution Finale de la Question Juive. Essai sur ses principes dans le IIIe Reich et en France sous l'occupation* (Paris, 1977). Throughout this essay, references are to the German edition of Billig's study, *Die Endlösung der Judenfrage. Studie über Ihre Grundsätze im III. Reich und in Frankreich während der Besatzung* (New York: The Beate Klarsfeld Foundation: Frankfurt: The Jewish Young Leadership, 1979. The first and second parts appear in English as 'The Launching of the "Final Solution" ' in Billig and Wellers, pp. 1–104a. However, readers of that version should be warned about its appalling translation which is compounded by numerous inaccuracies of date); Serge Klarsfeld, *Die Endlösung der Judenfrage in Frankreich. Deutsche Dokumente 1941–1944* (Paris, 1977); idem, *Recueil de Documents des Dossiers des Autorités Allemandes Concernant la Persécution de la Population Juive en France (1940–1944)* (Paris, 1979); idem, *Vichy-Auschwitz. Die Zusammenarbeit der deutschen und*

*französischen Behörden bei der "Endlösung der Judenfrage" in Frankreich* (Nördlingen, 1989). See also the earlier selection of Auswärtiges Amt documents on the Jewish question throughout Nazi-occupied Europe published by Léon Poliakov and Josef Wulf, *Das Dritte Reich und seine Diener. Dokumente* (Berlin, 1956). Cf. idem, *Das Dritte Reich und die Juden* (Berlin, 1955; Munich, 1978). See also Hilberg, op. cit., pp. 389–421; Reitlinger, *The Final Solution*, pp. 327–51.

5. Hans Buchheim, 'Command and Compliance', pp. 303–96, esp. p. 351 in, Krausnick, Buchheim, Broszat and Jacobsen.

6. Cf. Hans-Jürgen Döscher, *Das Auswärtige Amt im Dritten Reich. Diplomatie im Schatten der 'Endlösung'* (Berlin, 1987), p. 77. For the social structure of the Auswärtiges Amt in the Weimar Republic, see ibid, pp. 35–50. For Auswärtiges Amt handling of Jewish issues during the Weimar Republic, see: John P. Fox, 'Weimar Germany and the *Ostjuden* 1918– 1923: Acceptance or Expulsion?', pp. 51–68 in. Anna C. Bramwell (ed.), *Refugees in the Age of Total War* (London, 1988); Trude Maurer, *Ostjuden in Deutschland 1918–1933* (Hamburg, 1986); Francis R. Nicosia, 'Jewish Affairs and German Foreign Policy during the Weimar Republic. Moritz Sobernheim and the Referat für jüdische Angelegenheiten', pp. 261–83 in *Leo Baeck Institute Year Book*, XXXIII (London, 1988) (henceforth LBYB); Reiner Pommerin, 'Die Ausweisung von "Ostjuden" aus Bayern 1923. Ein Beitrag zum Krisenjahr der Weimarer Republik', *Vierteljahrshefte für Zeitgeschichte*, 34 Jhg, Heft 3, July 1986, pp. 311–39 (henceforth VfZ).

7. Döscher, p. 122.

8. Cf. Filmed copies of German Foreign Office documents, Foreign and Commonwealth Office Library, London: 8787/E612192–96, Runderlaß, Berlin, 30 April 1933; idem, E612197, von Bülow-Schwante/Aschmann, Berlin, 3 May 1933 (Referat Deutschland. 42/4, 43/1, 2, 3. Po. adh. 6. Die Judenfrage. Allgemeines) (henceforth AA); AA 8789/ E612457–64, von Bülow-Schwante/Missionen, Berlin, 11 July 1933 (Referat Deutschland. 43/4,5. Judengesetzgebund); AA 8788/E612298–311, von Bülow-Schwante/Missionen mit Anlage, Berlin, 28 Feb. 1934 (Inland II A/B. 39/1, 2, 3. Das Judentum in Deutschland); AA 9450/E666822–23, Notiz Schumburg, Berlin, 30 Jan. 1935. See also idem, E666825, Aufzeichnung von Bülow-Schwante, Berlin, 25 Jan. 1935 (Inland II A/B. 26/2. Entjudung der Verwaltung und Judengesetzgebund); *Documents on German Foreign Policy 1918– 1945*, Series D, Vol. V, Document 664, Runderlaß, Berlin, 25 Jan. 1939 (London: Her Majesty's Stationery Office, 1966) (henceforth DGFP).

9. John P. Fox, *Germany and the Far Eastern Crisis 1931–1938. A Study in Diplomacy and Ideology* (Oxford University Press, 1982), pp. 25–6, and 347, n.13; Auswärtiges Amt, Bonn, Politische Archiv. Inland II A/B. Band 25/4. Runderlaß, von Bülow-Schwante/Missionen mit Anlage, Berlin, 5 March 1934 (henceforth PA). For other early Auswärtiges Amt reactions to the Nazi *Machtübernahme*, cf. Döscher, pp. 67–68.

10. For the Auswärtiges Amt's handling of the foreign policy consequences of the Third Reich's domestic anti-Jewish polices, see Eliahu Ben Elissar, *La Diplomatie du IIIe Reich et les Juifs (1933–1939)* (Paris, 1969). For two specific examples *vis-à-vis* Japan and Great Britain, see John P. Fox, 'Japanese Reactions to Nazi Germany's Racial Legislation', *The Wiener Library Bulletin*, Vol. XXIII, Nos. 1/2, New Series, Nos. 15 and 16 (October 1969), pp. 46–50; idem, 'Nazi Germany and German Emigration to Great Britain', pp. 29–62 in Gerhard Hirschfeld (ed.), *Exile in Great Britain. Refugees from Hitler's Germany* (Oxford: Berg Publishers, 1984), originally published as *Exil in Großbritannien. Zu Emigration aus dem Nationalsozialistischen Deutschland 1933–1945* (Stuttgart, 1983).

11. Browning, *Final Solution*, p. 11.

12. Cf. Fox, *Far Eastern Crisis, passim.*

13. Browning, *The Final Solution*, pp. 21–2.

14. Döscher, pp. 69–71, and in particular, Chapter IV, 'Anfänge personeller und institutioneller Einflußnahme der SS-Führung auf den Auswärtigen Dienst (1933–1938)', pp. 103–44, and Chapter VI, 'Progressive Einflußnahme der SS auf Personalstruktur und Politik des Auswärtigen Amtes (1938–1945)', pp. 157–305. For the position of German civil servants in modern history, see generally: Peter Diehl-Thiele, *Partei und Staat im Dritten Reich. Untersuchungen zum Verhältnis von NSDAP und allgemeiner innerer Staatsverwaltung* (Munich, 1969); Döscher, *passim*; Hans Fenske, *Bürokratie in Deutschland. Vom späten Kaiserreich*

*bis zur Gegenwart* (Berlin, 1985); Hans Mommsen, *Beamtentum im Dritten Reich. Mit ausgewählten Quellen zur nationalsozialistischen Beamtenpolitik* (Stuttgart, 1966); Dieter Rebentisch, *Führerstaat und Verwaltung im Zweiten Weltkrieg. Verfassungsentwicklung und Verwaltungspolitik 1939–1945* (Stuttgart, 1989); Marion Thielenhaus, *Zwischen Anpassung und Widerstand: Deutsche Diplomaten, 1938–1941* (Paderborn, 1985).

15. Döscher, pp. 192ff. Cf. Peter Longerich, *Propagandisten im Krieg. Die Presseabteilung des Auswärtigen Amtes unter Ribbentrop* (Munich, 1987), pp. 28–9. For a 'Ribbentrop-centric' view of German foreign policy, see the study by Wolfgang Michalka, *Ribbentrop und die Deutsche Weltpolitik 1933–1940. Außenpolitische Konzeptionen und Entscheidungsprozesse im Dritten Reich* (Munich, 1980).

16. Cf. Jeremy Noakes and Geoffrey Pridham (eds), *Nazism 1919–1945. Volume 2: State, Economy, and Society 1933–39. A Documentary Reader* (Exeter Studies in History No. 8, University of Exeter, 1984), Chapter 8: The 'Coordination of the Civil Service', pp. 220–32; Joseph Walk, *Das Sonderrecht für die Juden im NS-Staat* (Heidelberg/Karlsruhe, 1981).

17. Noakes and Pridham, pp. 198–200. See also PA. Inland II A/B. Band 25/4. Runderlaß, von Bülow-Schwante/Missionen mit Anlage einer Aufzeichnung über die Vereinigung der Ämter des Reichspräsidenten und des Reichskanzlers, Berlin, 19 Sept. 1934.

18. Jochen von Lang and Claus Sibyll, *Eichmann Interrogated. Transcripts from the Archives of the Israeli Police* (London, 1983), p. 124.

19. See the useful discussion on this key point by Billig, *Die Endlösung*, pp. 50–3, 60–1.

20. Seev Goshen, 'Eichmann und die Nisko-Aktion im Oktober 1939. Eine Fallstudie zur NS-Judenpolitik in der letzten Etappe vor der "Endlösung"', VfZ, 29 Jhg, Heft 1 (January 1981), pp. 74–96, esp. p. 74.

21. Robert Koehl, 'Feudal Aspects of National Socialism', pp. 151–74 in Henry A. Turner, Jr (ed.), *Nazism and the Third Reich* (New York, 1972). See also the essential study by Ian Kershaw, *The 'Hitler Myth'. Image and Reality in the Third Reich* (Oxford, 1987).

22. Imperial War Museum. Case XI. FO 646. Box 453, Weizsäcker Document Book 6, Document 249, Affidavit Dr Werner Best; idem, Box 453, Document 16, Affidavit Dr Wilhelm Melchers; idem, Box 455, Weizsäcker Supplementary Defence Documents, Document 473, Affidavit Rudolf Rahn (henceforth FO 646).

23. Cf. Billig, *Die Endlösung*, pp. 128–30; Klarsfeld, *Vichy-Auschwitz*, pp. 32–3.

24. Cf. Klarsfeld, *Vichy-Auschwitz*, pp. 36–40.

25. Billig, *Die Endlösung*, pp. 129, 140.

26. Robert M.W. Kempner, *Eichmann und Komplizen* (Zürich, 1961), p. 346; Billig, *Die Endlösung*, p. 129.

27. FO 646. Box 453, Weizsäcker Document Book VI, Document 336, Affidavit Dr Herbert Siegfried.

28. For two recent studies of Heinrich Himmler, see Peter Padfield, *Himmler. Reichsführer-SS* (London, 1990); Richard Breitman, *The Architect of Genocide. Himmler and the Final Solution* (London, 1991). For Himmler and the SS generally, see also Gerald Reitlinger, *The SS. Alibi of a Nation 1922–1945* (London, 1957); Heinz Höhne, *The Order of the Death's Head. The Story of Hitler's SS* (London, 1969). See also Hans Buchheim, 'The SS – Instrument of Domination', pp. 127–301 in Krausnick, Buchheim, Broszat and Jacobsen. For Heydrich, see Günther Deschner, *Reinhard Heydrich. A Biography* (New York, 1981). For Eichmann and Dannecker, see Billig, *Die Endlösung*, pp. 17, 22, 26–7, 35–7, 41–8.

29. A useful diagram of the German and French Offices and personnel concerned with the Jewish question in France is to be found in Klarsfeld, *Vichy-Auschwitz*, p. 87.

30. Cf. AA 1861/422929, Vereinbarung über die Zuständigkeit in Volkstumsfragen, Berlin, 31 March 1941 (Inland II g. Führer-Erlaß. Volkstumsfragen in der Partei).

31. Otto Abetz, *Das Offene Problem. Eine Rückblick auf Zwei Jahrzehnte Deutscher Frank-reichpolitik* (Cologne, 1951), pp. 324–5.

32. Jäckel, *Frankreich*, pp. 66–8, 135.

33. Cf. DGFP, D, XI, Document 564, Aufzeichnung Schmidt, Paris, 24 Dec. 1940; *Akten zur deutschen auswärtigen Politik 1918–1945*. Series E. Vol. IV. Document 314, Aufzeichnung Schmidt, Berlin, 24 Dec. 1942 (Göttingen, 1969–) (henceforth ADAP). These documents are also reproduced in Andreas Hillgruber (ed.), *Staatsmänner und Diplomaten bei Hitler. Vertrauliche Aufzeichnungen über Unterredungen mit Vertretern des Auslandes 1939–1941*.

Vol. I: 1939–41, Document 57; Vol. II: 1942–44, Document 23 (Frankfurt/am Main, 1967, 1970).

34. DGFP, D, XII, Document 584, Aufzeichnung Schmidt, Fuschl, 3 June 1941; Hillgruber, *Staatsmänner*, Vol. I, Document 79: Werner Jochmann (ed.), *Adolf Hitler. Monologe im Führer-Hauptquartier 1941–1944. Die Aufzeichnungen Heinrich Heims* (Munich, 1982), p. 254, Wolfsschanze, 2 Feb. 1942, midday. The standard English version of Hitler's 'table-talk', recently reissued, compresses the more extensive language of the Heims version: cf. H.R. Trevor-Roper (intro), *Hitler's Table Talk 1941–1944* (Oxford University Press, 1988), p. 278.

35. DGFP, D, XI, Document 246, Aufzeichnung Schmidt, Florenz, 28 Oct. 1940; Hillgruber, *Staatsmänner*, Vol. I, Document 40.

36. Cf. Leonidas E. Hill, *Die Weizsäcker-Papier 1933–1950* (Frankfurt/am Main, 1974), pp. 229–30, 261, 309–10.

37. FO 646. Box 418, Von Erdmannsdorff, Defence Document Book II, Document 89, Affidavit Werner von Bargen.

38. FO 646. Box 456, Woermann Document Book III, Document 91, Affidavit Hans Schwarzmann.

39. FO 646. Document Book 60-B, Document NG-1838, Affidavit Otto Abetz.

40. Browning, 'The Government Experts', p. 188; idem, *Final Solution*, p. 183.

41. Norman Rich, *Hitler's War Aims. Volume II: The Establishment of the New Order* (London, 1974), p. 422. For some recent historiographical debates about the nature of the Nazi State, see: John Hiden and John Farquharson, *Explaining Hitler's Germany. Historians and the Third Reich* (London, 1989, 2nd edn.); Ian Kershaw, *The Nazi Dictatorship. Problems and Perspectives of Interpretation* (London, 1989, 2nd edn.). For more recent discussions about Hitler's key role in the Third Reich, see the important contribution by Rebentisch, *passim*.

42. *Trial of the Major War Criminals Before the International Military Tribunal* (Nuremberg, 1947), Vol. X, 401–2 (henceforth IMT). For more lengthy extracts from this document, see idem, Vol. VII, pp. 29–35.

43. Cf. Helmut Krausnick, Hans-Heinrich Wilhelm, *Die Truppe des Weltanschauungskrieges. Die Einsatzgruppen Sicherheitspolizei und des SD 1938–1942* (Stuttgart, 1981).

44. Cf. Ernest Klee, *'Euthanasie' im NS-Staat. Die 'Vernichtung lebensunwerten Lebens'* (Frankfurt am Main, 1983); idem, *Dokumente zur 'Euthanasie'* (Frankfurt/am Main, 1985); Hans-Walter Schmuhl, *Rassenhygiene, Nationalsozialismus, Euthanasie* (Göttingen, 1987); Benno Müller-Hill, *Murderous Science. Elimination by Scientific Selection of Jews, Gypsies, and Others. Germany 1933–1945* (Oxford University Press, 1988); Robert Proctor, *Racial Hygiene. Medicine Under the Nazis* (Harvard University Press, 1988); Michael H. Kater, *Doctors Under Hitler* (University of North Carolina Press, 1989); Paul Weindling, *Health, Race, and German Politics Between National Unification and Nazism, 1870–1945* (Cambridge University Press, 1989).

45. Klarsfeld, *Vichy-Auschwitz*, p. 330.

46. IMT, Vol. X, pp. 402–3.

47. On this subject, see the short but informative study by Raul Hilberg, *Sonderzüge nach Auschwitz* (Mainz, 1981). See also Heiner Lichtenstein, *Mit der Reichsbahn in den Tod. Massentransporte in den Holocaust 1941 bis 1945* (Cologne, 1985).

48. Lang and Sibyll, pp. 99, 145–6. See also, Dr Rudolf Aschenauer (ed.), *Ich, Adolf Eichmann. Ein historischer Zeugenbericht* (Leoni am Starnberger See, 1980) pp. 309–22.

49. For the general position of the Auswärtiges Amt in Nazi-occupied Europe, see Browning, *Final Solution, passim*; Hilberg, *The Destruction*, pp. 349–55; Arnold Toynbee and Veronica M. Toynbee (eds), *Survey of International Affairs 1939–1946. Hitler's Europe* (Oxford University Press, 1954), pp. 108–12. For the German position generally in Belgium during the Second World War, see Wilfried Wagner, *Belgien in der deutschen Politik während des Zweiten Weltkrieges* (Boppard am Rhein, 1974).

50. Cf. Klaus A. Maier, Horst Rohde, Bernd Stegemann and Hans Umbreit, *Das Deutsche Reich und der Zweite Weltkrieg. Band 2. Die Errichtung der Hegemonie auf dem Europäischen Kontinent* (Stuttgart, 1979), p. 139ff (henceforth *Zweite Weltkrieg*); Bernhard R. Kroener, Rolf-Dieter Müller, Hans Umbreit, *Das Deutsche Reich und der Zweite Weltkrieg. Band 5: Erster Halbband. Organisation und Mobilisierung des Deutschen Machtbereichs. Kriegs-*

*verwaltung, Wirtschaft, und Personelle Ressourcen 1939–1941* (Stuttgart, 1988), p. 287.
Wehrmacht complaints against SS policies in Poland were epitomized by the 'daring
memorandum of February 8, 1940', written by General Johannes Blaskowitz, Supreme
Commander of the German Army in occupied Poland: cf. Nachman Blumental, 'Con-
cerning the Question: When Did the Idea of the "Final Solution" Originate in Hitler's
Germany?', *Yad Vashem Bulletin*, No. 20 (1967), pp. 6–10.

51.  Cf. Browning, *Final Solution*, pp. 35–43; Döscher, pp. 215–16; AA 1512/372108, Notiz
ohne Unterschrift, Berlin, 3 June 1940; (Abteilung Inland IIg. Endlösung der Judenfrage);
DGFP, D, IX, Document 527, von Weizsäcker/von Ribbentrop, Berlin, 22 June 1940;
AA 1512/372047. Heydrich/von Ribbentrop, Berlin, 24 June 1940; DGFP, D, X, Docu-
ment 23, von Ribbentrop/von Weizsäcker, 26 June 1940, and fn. 1; AA 1512/372104–05,
Aufzeichnung Rademacher, Berlin, 2 July 1940; idem, 372109–11, Aufzeichnung
Rademacher, Berlin, 3 July 1940; idem, 372053–71, Schreiben mit Anlage, Dannecker/
Rademacher, Berlin, 15 Aug. 1940; idem, 372050–52, Aufzeichnung Rademacher,
Berlin, 30 Aug. 1940.

52.  Cf. H.G. Adler, *Der Verwaltete Mensch. Studien zur Deportation der Juden aus Deutschland*
(Tübingen, 1974), p. 72.

53.  Eberhard Jäckel, *Hitler in History* (University Prerss of New England, 1984), p. 51;
Dawidowicz, pp. 118–19; Reitlinger, *The Final Solution*, p. 80. Cf. also, Philip Friedman,
'The Lublin Reservation and the Madagascar Plan: Two Aspects of Nazi Jewish Policy
during the Second World War', pp., 34–58 in Ada June Friedman (ed.), *Philip Friedman.
Roads to Extinction: Essays on the Holocaust* (New York/Philadelphia: Jewish Publication
Society of America, 1980). See also, Browning, *Final Solution*, pp. 35–43; Döscher,
pp. 215–20.

54.  Cf. W.N. Medlicott, *History of the Second World War. United Kingdom Civil Series: The
Economic Blockade* (London, 1952–59, 2 vols.).

55.  Cf. Andreas Hillgruber, *Hitler's Strategie. Politik und Kriegführung 1940–1941* (2. Auflage,
Munich, 1982), pp. 207ff.

56.  Reitlinger, *The Final Solution*, p. 81.

57.  Klarsfeld, *Vichy-Auschwitz*, pp. 47–8.

58.  For details on Achenbach and Zeitschel, see Billig, *Die Endlösung*, pp. 119–94.

59.  *Zweite Weltkrieg*, 5/1, pp. 118–19; Marrus and Paxton, p. 79.

60.  Marrus and Paxton, pp. 77–80, 373. For France and more generally in Europe, see also
Hilberg, pp. 389–421; *Zweite Weltkrieg*, 5/1, pp. 102–21.

61.  Lichtenstein, pp. 60–1, 111–12; Hilberg, *Sonderzüge*, pp. 59–60, 67.

62.  *Zweite Weltkrieg*, 2, p. 324; idem, 5/1, pp. 304–5.

63.  Abetz, p. 132; Jäckel, *Frankreich*, p. 66; DGFP, D, X, Document 170, Representative of the
Foreign Ministry with the Military Commander in France/Chief of the Military Administration in France, Paris, 15 July 1940.

64.  Billig, *Die Endlösung*, pp. 192–3.

65.  Abetz, pp. 141ff.

66.  Jäckel, *Frankreich*, p. 67; DGFP, D, X, Document 282, von Ribbentrop/Chief of the High
Command of the Wehrmacht, Fuschl, 3 Aug. 1940.

67.  DGFP, D, Vol. X, Document 345, Memorandum by Luther, 15 Aug. 1940; Hilberg, p. 393.
Döscher, p. 216, fn. 20, suggests that by this, Hitler could only mean conclusion of the war
against France. Yet by that date, Hitler's thinking was even more firmly set on 'war' against
Bolshevik Russia than before. Cf. Browning, 'Nazi Resettlement Policy', p. 509, for Hitler's
statements to Colin Ross on 12 March 1940 about wanting to resolve the Jewish question,
but complaining that it 'really was a space question which was difficult to solve, particularly
for him, since he had no space at his disposal'.

68.  DGFP, D, X, Document 282, von Ribbentrop/Keitel, Fuschl, 3 Aug. 1940.

69.  DGFP, D, XI, Document 368, Decision by the Führer, Vienna, 20 Nov. 1940.

70.  Hilberg, *The Destruction*, p. 392.

71.  Billig, *Die Endlösung*, p. 124.

72.  Cf. the discussion about the *Führerbefehl* question in Billig, *Die Endlösung*, pp. 50–3, 60–1.

73.  Klarsfeld, *Vichy-Auschwitz*, p. 356, Aufzeichnung Dr Best, Paris, 19 Aug. 1940; Hilberg,
*The Destruction*, p. 393.

74. DGFP, D, X, Document 368, Abetz/von Ribbentrop, Paris, 20 Aug. 1940.
75. Klarsfeld, *Vichy-Auschwitz*, pp. 358–9, Abetz Aufzeichnung, 'September 1940'.
76. FO 646. Document Book 60-B, Document EC-265/NG-2846, Abetz/Berlin, Paris, 1 Oct. 1940.
77. Abetz, pp. 318–19; FO 646. Document Book 60-B, Document NG-1838, Affidavit Otto Abetz.
78. Rudolf Rahn, *Ruheloses Leben. Aufzeichnungen und Erinnerungen* (Düsseldorf, 1949), p. 146; Abetz, p. 151.
79. Klarsfeld, *Vichy-Auschwitz*, pp. 356–8, Aufzeichnung Mahnke, Paris, 22 Aug. 1940.
80. Billig, *Die Endlösung*, p. 132; *Zweite Weltkrieg*, 5/1, p. 294, which refers to information in General Franz Halder's diary of 26 Aug. 1940. This point is omitted from the English version of the Halder diary: cf. Charles Burdick and Hans-Adolf Jacobsen, *The Halder War Diary 1939–1942* (London, 1988), pp. 250–1.
81. AA K773/K204573–74, Luther/Himmler, Goering, Berlin, 23 Aug. 1940; idem, K204571, Aufzeichnung Rademacher, Berlin, 31 Aug. 1940; idem, K204570, Luther/Himmler, Berlin, 10 Sept. 1940; idem, K204567–68, Heydrich/Luther, Berlin, 20 Sept. 1940; idem, K204565, Luther/Abetz, Berlin, 28 Sept. 1940 (Inland II. Geheim. 7/1); *Trials of the War Criminals Before the Nuremberg Military Tribunals Under Control Council Law No. 10* (Washington, 1952), Vol. XIII, The Ministries Case, pp. 156–9 (henceforth TWC); Poliakov and Wulf, *Das Dritte Reich und seine Diener*, pp. 104–6.
82. Billig, *Die Endlösung*, p. 133; AA K773/K204561, Schleier/Schwarzmann, Paris, 9 Oct. 1942; idem, K204562–63, Luther/Himmler, Berlin, 16 Oct. 1940; TWC, Vol. XIII, pp. 159–60; Poliakov and Wulf, *Das Dritte Reich und seine Diener*, pp. 106–7.
83. *Zweite Weltkrieg*, 5/1, p. 295; Billig, *Die Endlösung*, pp. 134–5; Hilberg, pp. 393–4; Jäckel, *Frankreich*, pp. 225–6.
84. Billig, *Die Endlösung*, p. 133; Hilberg, p. 391; Jäckel, *Frankreich*, pp. 65, 226; Marrus and Paxton, p. 79; *Zweite Weltkrieg*, 5/1, pp. 118–19.
85. Klarsfeld, *Vichy-Auschwitz*, pp. 361–3, Dannecker Aufzeichnung, Paris, 21 Jan. 1941.
86. Browning, *Final Solution*, p. 42.
87. DGFP, D, XI, Document 532, Führer Directive Number 21, 18 Dec. 1940.
88. This is the main burden of the account in Browning, 'Nazi Resettlement Policy', *passim*. See also Michael Marrus, *The Holocaust in History* (University Press of New England, 1987), pp. 31ff; Rich, Vol. II, p. 5.
89. Cf. Albrecht Tyrell, *Vom 'Trommler' zum 'Führer'. Der Wandel von Hitlers Selbstverständnis zwischen 1919 und 1924 und die Entwicklung der NSDAP* (Munich, 1975), pp. 214–15, fn. 273.
90. The classic summary of this part of the argument remains the contribution by Andreas Hillgruber, 'Die *Endlösung* und das deutsche Ostimperium als Kernstuck des rassen-ideologischen Programms des Nationalsozialismus', VfZ, 20 Jhg, Heft 2, April 1972, pp. 133–53. See further, idem, 'War in the East and the Extermination of the Jews', *Yad Vashem Studies*, XVIII (1987), pp. 103–32. See also, John P. Fox, 'Adolf Hitler's Impera- tives for War in September 1939: An Assessment of the Jewish Factor', pp. 135–54 in Sanford Pinsker and Jack Fischel (eds), *Holocaust Studies Annual 1990. General Essays* (New York, 1990); idem, 'Reichskristallnacht 9 November 1938 and the *Ostjuden* Perspective to the Nazi Search for a "Solution" to the Jewish Question', POLIN, *A Journal of Polish–Jewish Studies*, Vol. 5 (1990), pp. 74–102. The basic argument of the spurious Mayer study is a comprehensive rejection of the idea that Hitler attacked Russia in order to carry out the extermination of Russian Jewry. More generally on Hitler's ideology and policies, cf. Jäckel, *Hitler in History*; Robert Wistrich, *Hitler's Apocalypse. Jews and the Nazi Legacy* (London, 1985); Rainer Zitelmann, *Hitler. Selbstverständnis eines Revolutionärs* (Oxford, 1987); Philippe Burrin, *Hitler et les Juifs. Genèse d'un Génocide* (Paris, 1989); Marlis Steiner, *Hitler* (Paris, 1991).
91. This crucial debate is summarized in the well-known exchange between Martin Broszat and Christopher Browning, now reprinted from their original publications in the essential 15-volume collection of several hundred articles on the Holocaust in English, edited by Michael Marrus, *The Nazi Holocaust. Historical Articles on the Destruction of European Jews* (Westport/London, 1989): cf. Vol. 3, Part 1, *The 'Final Solution': The Implementation of*

*Mass Murder*; Martin Broszat, 'Hitler and the Genesis of the "Final Solution": An Assessment of David Irving's Theses', pp. 115–67; Christopher R. Browning, 'A Reply to Martin Broszat Regarding the Origins of the Final Solution', pp. 168–87. See also Wolfgang Scheffler, 'Wege zur "Endlösung"', 186–214 in Herbert A. Strauss and Norbert Kampe (eds), *Antisemitismus. Von der Judenfeindschaft zum Holocaust* (Frankfurt/am Main, 1985); Hans Mommsen, 'The Realisation of the Unthinkable: The "Final Solution of the Jewish Question"', pp. 97–144 in Gerhard Hirschfeld (ed.), *The Policies of Genocide. Jews and Soviet Prisoners of War in Nazi Germany* (London, 1986).

92. Cf. Gerald Fleming, *Hitler and the Final Solution* (London, 1985); *Ich, Adolf Eichmann*, pp. 178, 234; Lang and Sibyll, pp. 75, 81.

93. Norman Rich, *Hitler's War Aims. Volume I: Ideology, the Nazi State and the Course of Expansion* (London, 1973), p. 11.

94. Cf. Bernard Wasserstein, *Britain and the Jews of Europe 1939–1945* (Oxford, 1979), pp. vi, 42–5. See also my review of this book, apparently the only critical one world-wide, in *European Studies Review*, Vol. X (Jan. 1980), pp. 138–46, and the ensuing debate with Wasserstein in idem, October 1980, pp. 487–92; Monty Noam Penkower, *The Jews Were Expendable. Free World Diplomacy and the Holocaust* (University of Illinois Press, 1983), p. vii; David S. Wyman, *The Abandonment of the Jews. America and the Holocaust 1941–1945* (New York, 1985), pp. xiii, 5–6, 331. See also the eminently sensible critique of Wyman by Frank W. Brecher, 'David Wyman and the Historiography of America's Response to the Holocaust: Counter Considerations', *Holocaust and Genocide Studies*, Vol. 5, No. 4 (1990), pp. 423–46, and Wyman's distinctly unhelpful reply in idem, 485–6, 'Letter to the Editor'. Without considering any other evidence or arguments, Louise London uncritically follows the line of Penkower, Wasserstein, and Wyman: Louise London, 'British Government Policy and Jewish Refugees 1933–45', *Patterns of Prejudice*, Vol. 23, No. 4 (Winter 1989–90), pp. 26–43, esp. pp. 26, 32; idem, 'Jewish Refugees, Anglo–Jewry and British Government Policy, 1930–1940', pp. 163–90 in David Cesarani (ed.), *The Making of Modern Anglo–Jewry* (Oxford, 1990). See also, Norbert Kampe, '"Endlösung" durch Auswanderung? Zu den widersprüchlichen Zielvorstellungen antisemitischer Politik bis 1941', pp. 827–43 in Wolfgang Michalka (ed.), *Der Zweite Weltkrieg. Analysen, Grundzüge, Fordschungsbilanz* (Munich, 1989).

95. See in particular Marrus, pp. 27, 62–3, 123, 165. See also the more recent contribution by Browning, 'The Decision'.

96. IMT, Vol. II, pp. 447–8, evidence of General Erwin Lahousen, personal representative of Admiral Canaris. For a variation of this evidence, see Breitman, pp. 70–1, which is based on Lahousen's formal interrogations. See also, Heinz Höhne, *Canaris* (London, 1979), pp. 358, 364. Cf. also, Helmut Krausnick, 'Hitler und die Morde in Polen. Ein Beitrag zum Konflikt zwischen Heer und SS um die Verwaltung der besetzen Gebiete', VfZ, 1 Jhg, 2 Heft, April 1963, pp. 196–209.

97. Höhne, *Canaris*, p. 363; Krausnick and Wilhelm, pp. 63–4.

98. Cf. (in date order), Kurt Pätzold (ed.), *Verfolgung, Vertreibung, Vernichtung. Dokumente des faschistischen Antisemitismus 1933 bis 1942* (Frankfurt/am Main, 1984), p. 234: Vermerk über eine Amtschefbesprechung Reinhard Heydrichs am 7 September 1939, betr. die Aufgaben der Sicherheitspolizei im besetzten Teil Polens; idem, pp. 239–40: Vermerk über eine Besprechung Reinhard Heydrichs mit den Amtschefs und Einsatzgruppenleitern am 27 September 1939, betr. die Deportation jüdischer Deutscher und die Ghettoisierung der jüdischen Bevölkerung in Polen; Hans-Günther Seraphim, *Das politische Tagebuch Alfred Rosenbergs 1934/35 und 1939/40* (DTV Munich, 1964), pp. 98–100, Diary entry of 29 Sept. 1939; TWC, Vol. XIII, pp. 141–3, Nuremberg Document NO-3075: Decree of the Führer and Reich Chancellor for the Strengthening of Germanism, 7 Oct. 1939; Bundesarchiv Koblenz. Gestapo. R.70, Böhmen-Mähren-9: Vermerk, Mähr. Ostrau, Oct. 1939 (date obscured), concerning a conference on 9 Oct. 1939 which Adolf Eichmann attended and in which the following words are recorded: 'Der Führer hat vorerst die Umschichtung von 300.000 unbemittelten Juden aus dem Altreich und aus der Ostmark angeordnet' (henceforth BA); idem, Schreiben, RSHA, Zentralstelle Mähr-Ostrau/Transportkommandatur Oppeln, 13 Oct. 1939, concerning discussions with Gauleiter Wagner and others for the transport of Jews from Kattowitz: 'die jede Unterstützung zu sagten, damit der vom Führer

angeordnete Versuch der Umsiedlung von Juden durchgeführt werden kann'; Peter Longerich (ed.), *Die Ermordung der europäischen Juden. Eine umfassende Dokumentation des Holocaust 1941–1945* (Munich, 1989), pp. 52–3: Vermerk des Eichmann-Mitarbeiters Brunner: Umsiedlung aus der 'Ostmark' nach Polen, 18 Oct. 1939; Tatiana Berenstein, Artur Eisenbach, Bernard Mark, Adam Rutkowski (eds), *Faschismus-Getto-Massenmord. Dokumentation über Ausrottung und Widerstand der Juden in Polen während des zweiten Weltkrieges* (Frankfurt/am Main, n.d.), pp. 42–3: Anordnung Himmlers über die Deportation der polnischen und jüdischen Bevölkerung aus den polnischen, nunmehr aber ins Reich eingegliederten Gebieten ins Generalgouvernement, 30 October 1939. See also, H.G. Adler, pp. 124ff; Goshen, *passim*; Votjech Mastny, *The Czechs Under Nazi Rule* (New York, 1971), p. 112.

99. Goshen, pp. 79–81. A copy of the protocol of the 21 Sept. 1939 meeting used as prosecution document 983 in the Eichmann trial was kindly supplied to me some time ago by Dr Anton Hoch of the Institut für Zeitgeschichte, Munich. The collection of the 'Amtschef-Besprechungen' for 7 Sept. to 14 Oct. 1939 is available at the Bundesarchiv Koblenz, reference R 58/825.

100. Nuremberg document PS-3363. It has been published (among others) in the following: Yitzhak Arad, Yisrael Gutman and Abraham Margaliot (eds), *Documents on the Holocaust. Selected Sources on the Destruction of the Jews of Germany and Austria, Poland, and the Soviet Union* (Jerusalem, 1981), pp. 173–8; Berenstein *et al.*, *Faschismus*, pp. 37–41; Longerich, *Die Ermordung*, pp. 47–52; Pätzold, *Verfolgung*, pp. 236–9.

101. Lang and Sibyll, pp. 92–3.

102. Dawidowicz, p. 116. During the trials of the major war criminals at Nuremburg in 1946, Erich von dem Bach-Zelewski, Higher SS and Police Leader for Central Russia and SS Chief of Anti-Partisan Units in Nazi-occupied Soviet Russia, was asked by Dr Alfred Thoma, defence counsel for Alfred Rosenberg, for his opinion on a speech by Reichsführer-SS Heinrich Himmler at Wesselsburg at the beginning of 1941 before the start of the campaign against Soviet Russia: 'do you believe that Himmler's speech, in which he demanded the extermination of 30 million Slavs, expressed only his personal opinion; or do you consider that it corresponded to the National Socialist ideology?'. When Bach-Zelewski replied that 'today I believe that it was the logical consequence of our ideology', Thoma countered by referring to the testimony of SS General Otto Ohlendorf, Chief of Amt III of the Reich Security Main Office and leader of an Einsatzgruppe in Russia. Ohlendorf had been questioned by Major General I.T. Nikitchenko, the Russian member of the Nuremberg tribunal, about whether 'the annihilation of the Soviet people [was] in conformity with the policy of the German Government or the Nazi Party or was it against it?', and had replied: 'a policy amounts to a practice so that in this respect it was a policy laid down by the Führer. If you were to ask, whether this activity was in conformity with the idea of National Socialism, then I should say "no"'. Bach-Zelewski, however, maintained his own standpoint and emphasized to Thoma that, 'I am of a different opinion. If for years, for decades, a doctrine is preached to the effect that the Slav race is an inferior race, that the Jews are not even human beings, then an explosion of this sort is inevitable'. Cf. IMT, Vol. IV, pp. 338–9, 494.

103. *Ich, Adolf Eichmann*, p. 179.

104. Hans Mommsen's attempt to deny the reality of this death threat must be dismissed out of hand: cf. fn 36, pp. 134–5 of Mommsen, and my review in *German History*, Vol. 6, No. 1 (1988), pp. 106–9.

105. Cf. Kershaw, *The Nazi Dictatorship*, p. 91; Tim Mason, 'Intention and Explanation: A Current Controversy about the Interpretation of National Socialism', p. 31 in Gerhard Hirschfeld, Lothar Kettenacker (eds), *Der 'Führerstaat'. Mythos und Realität. Studies zur Struktur und Politik des Dritten Reiches* (Stuttgart, 1981); Hans Mommsen, 'Nationalsozialismus oder Hitlerismus?' in Michael Bosch (ed.), *Persönlichkeit und Struktur in der Geschichte. Historische Bestandsaufnahme und didaktische Implikationen* (Düsseldorf, 1977) pp. 65, 67. Christopher Browning follows this line of thought, formulating it somewhat differently: 'even if the Final Solution can be "logically" deduced from Hitler's *Weltanschauung*, it is improbable that Hitler made that deduction before 1941 and consciously pursued the systematic murder of the European Jews as a long-held goal', cf. Browning, 'The Decision', p. 100 in Furet – a viewpoint I strongly disagree with.

106. Jochen von Lang and Claus Sibyll, *Das Eichmann-Protokoll. Tonbandaufzeichnungen der israelischen Verhöre. Mit 66 faksimilierten Dokumenten* (Berlin, 1982), pp. 84–5.
107. Cf. Joseph Kermish, 'When and By Whom was the Order for "The Final Solution" Given', *Yad Vashem Bulletin*, No. 14 (March 1964) pp. 26–31, who concludes: 'in sum: the decision regarding the destruction of the Jews was taken on September 21, 1939'. Dawidowicz, p. 116, also believes that this document testifies to the fact that 'a master plan for annihilating the Jews had already been conceived, though only the preliminary stages were now to be implemented'. But see Blumental for the intriguing suggestion concerning the intended anti-Jewish use of massive anti-tank trenches built along part of the new German-Russian border.
108. Cf. Adler, p. 107.
109. Jeremy Noakes and Geoffrey Pridham, *Nazism 1919–1945. Volume 3. Foreign Policy, War, and Racial Extermination. A Documentary Reader* (Exeter Studies in History, No. 13, University of Exeter, 1988), p. 1051.
110. Cf. Billig, *Die Endlösung*, p. 60, who correctly observes that 'an organized bloodbath in peacetime would not have been possible'.
111. Breitman, p. 156.
112. Cf. Henry Friedlander and Sybil Milton (General Eds), *Archives of the Holocaust, A Facsimile Series of Key Documents and Photographs from International Archives*, 18 Vols. (New York London, 1990), Vol. 4: Francis R. Nicosia (ed.), *Central Zionist Archives, Jerusalem. 1939–1945*, pp. 5–6; Dina Porat, *The Blue and the Yellow Stars of David. The Zionist Leadership in Palestine and the Holocaust 1939–1945* (Harvard, 1990), pp. 8–10.
113. Cf. Isaiah Trunk, *Judenrat. The Jewish Councils in Eastern Europe Under Nazi Occupation* (New York, 1972).
114. AA K1507/K338585, Berlin, 7 Feb. 1940, Rödiger/German Embassy Rome (Quirinal) (Abteilung Inland II A.B. Judenauswanderung u.a); idem, K338852, Berlin, 25 Sept. 1940, Weintz, Office of Reichsführer-SS/Martin Luther, Head of Abteilung Deutschland, Auswärtiges Amt. For the circular of 24 April 1940, see Adler, p. 27.
115. Cf. Berenstein, *et al.*, p. 59, Document 18, Rundschreiben Eckhardt, Krakau, 23 Nov. 1940.
116. Nicosia, *Central Zionist Archives*, p. 19.
117. Horst Boog, Jürgen Förster, Joachim Hoffmann, Ernst Klink, Rolf-Dieter Müller, Gerd R. Ueberschär, *Das Deutsche Reich und der Zweite Weltkrieg. Band 4: Der Angriff auf die Sowjetunion* (Stuttgart, 1983), pp. 413–15.
118. *Zweite Weltkrieg*, 4, pp. 415; Helmut Krausnick, Hans Buchheim, Martin Broszat and Hans-Adolf Jacobsen. *Anatomy of the SS State* (London, 1968), p. 60.
119. Klarsfeld, *Vichy-Auschwitz*, pp. 363–4, Knochen/Chef der Militärverwaltung Frankreich, Paris, 28 Jan. 1941; idem, 364–5, Aufzeichnung Mahnke, Paris, 3 Feb 1941.
120. Klarsfeld, *Vichy-Auschwitz*, p. 366, Dannecker/Zeitschel, Paris, 28 Feb. 1941.
121. For a report on the Lischka trial in Cologne in 1979–80, see Rudolf Hirsch, *Um die Endlösung. Prozeßbericht über den Lischka-Prozeß in Köln und den Auschwitz-Prozeß im Frankfurt/M* (Rudolstadt, 1982); Klarsfeld, *Vichy-Auschwitz*, pp. 364–5, Aufzeichnung, Mahnke, Paris, 3 Feb. 1941. Cf. RF-1207, Dannecker's report of 1 July 1941 for mention of the MBF's lack of interest in the idea of a *Zentraljudenamt* at the end of Jan. 1941, as well as critical comments concerning Xavier Vallat.
122. Klarsfeld, *Vichy-Auschwitz*, p. 365, Abetz/Thomas, Paris, 14 Feb. 1941; DGFP, D, XII, Document 127, Abetz/von Ribbentrop, Paris, 6 March 1941.
123. Billig, *Die Endlösung*, p. 137.
124. Klarsfeld, *Vichy-Auschwitz*, pp. 365–6, Aufzeichnung ohne Unterschrift, Paris, 28 Feb. 1941.
125. Klarsfeld, *Vichy-Auschwitz*, pp. 371–3, Aufzeichnung Dannecker, Paris, 22 Feb. 1942; Marrus and Paxton, 81.
126. FO 646, Document Book 60–B, Document NG–4896, Zeitschel/Achenbach, Paris, 1 March 1941.
127. Billig, *Die Endlösung*, pp. 148–9.
128. DGFP, D, XII, Document 127, Report 763, Abetz/Berlin, Paris 6 March 1941.
129. Cf. Breitman, pp. 147ff.
130. Billig, *Die Endlösung*, pp. 138–9.
131. DGFP, D, XII, Document 198, Tel. 958, Schleier/AA, Paris, 24 March 1941; ibid,

Document 254, Tel. 1068, Abetz/AA, Paris, 3 April 1941; Billig, *Die Endlösung*, pp. 140–2; Marrus and Paxton, pp. 96 ff, 398 ff.

132. DGFP, D, XII, Document 198, Report 958, Schleier/AA, Paris 24 March 1941.
133. BA, R.57/894. Deutsches Ausland-Institut. Eur. 41/3/6.
134. Marrus and Paxton, p. 113.
135. BA, NSD 17. Drucksachen der NSDAP: NSD.17/15, 'Die Rassenpolitischen Voraussetzungen zur Lösung der Judenfrage', *Informationsdienst, Rassenpolitisches Amt der NSDAP, Reichsleitung*, 20 April 1941; idem, NSD.17/8, Dr Groß, 'Zur Lösung der Judenfrage', *Neues Volk*, May 1941, pp. 4–5.
136. Billig, *Die Endlösung*, p. 64. For the text of Rosenberg's approach to Hitler via Martin Bormann, see Billig and Wellers, p. 97a.
137. BA, NS 18. Reichspropaganda Leiter der NSDAP: NS.18/38, Berlin, 21 July 1941, *Deutschland zum Endkampf mit dem Jüdisch-Bolschewistischen Mordsystem Angetreten*; idem, NS.18/199, Berlin, 24 Sept. 1941, General Instructions on Propaganda, including the Jewish question.
138. Cf. RF-1207, Dannecker's report of 1 July 1941; Marrus and Paxton, p. 81 and fn. 12, p. 384.
139. Cf. Billig, *Die Endlösung*, p. 151: 'Ist aber nun die terrorisierende antijüdische Aktivität der Sipo-SD in Paris im Mai und August 1941 Dannecker von Eichmann aufgezwungen worden oder aber resultierte sie vielmehr aus der Furcht Danneckers und Lischkas, nicht für die Abtransporte gerüstet zu sein, wenn der entsprechende Befehl von Eichmann dazu erteilt würde?'.
140. Cf. Klaus Schüler, 'Der Ostfeldzug als Transport- und Versorgunsproblem', 203–20 in: Bernd Wegner (ed.), *Zwei Wege nach Moskau. Vom Hitler-Stalin-Pakt bis zum "Unternehmen Barbarossa"* (Munich, 1991). I am extremely grateful to Dr Jürgen Förster of the Militärgeschichtliches Forschungsamt, Freiburg, for having drawn my attention to this important publication. See also Alan Clark, *Barbarossa. The Russian-German Conflict 1941–1945* (London, 1965, 1985), p. 129.
141. Billig, *Die Endlösung*, pp. 65-8; Billig and Wellers, p. 98a; Krausnick, 'The Persecution of the Jews', pp. 62–3; Krausnick and Wilhelm, pp. 158–9.
142. DGFP, D, XIII, Document 114. Unsigned Memorandum, Führer's Headquarters, 16 July 1941; IMT. Vol. VII, pp. 167-8; idem, Vol. XXXVIII, pp. 86-94, Nuremburg Document 221–L, Aktenvermerk, Führerhauptquartier, 16 July 1941.
143. Marrus and Paxton, p. 223.
144. Cf. Billig, *Die Endlösung*, pp. 146–56; Klarsfeld, *Vichy-Auschwitz*, pp. 28–31; Marrus and Paxton, p. 223.
145. AA 3748/EO40486, Notiz Schleier, Paris, 1 July 1941 (Pariser Botschaft: Geheim Akten der Politischen Registratur. Juden und Freimaurer in Frankreich).
146. Billig, *Die Endlösung*, pp. 152–3.
147. Klarsfeld, *Vichy-Auschwitz*, pp. 367–8, Aufzeichnung, Zeitschel/Abetz, Paris, 21 Aug. 1941; idem, 22 Aug. 1941.
148. IMT, Vol. XXVI, 266–7. Billig, *Die Endlösung*, p. 70, incorrectly dates this document '31 January' 1941, a mistake repeated in the English version of Billig's account, viz., Billig and Wellers, p. 51.
149. *Ich, Adolf Eichmann*, p. 479. See also, Leni Yahil, ' "Memoirs" of Adolf Eichmann', *Yad Vashem Studies* Vol. XVIII (1987), pp. 133–62, esp. pp. 138–41.
150. Cf. Breitman, p. 223.
151. Cf. Schüler.
152. Cf. Breitman, p. 204, for the post-war statement by Erich von dem Bach-Zelewski, Higher SS and Police Leader for Central Russia and SS Chief of Anti-Partisan Units in Nazi-occupied Soviet Russia, who suggested that 'the extermination camps arose because Germans and Central Europeans were not suited to be mass executioners'.
153. Breitman, pp. 189–90; Buchheim, 'The SS', p. 224; Hilberg, *The Destruction*, p. 562.
154. Cf. AA K1648/K403725, Eichmann/AA, Berlin, 9 May 1941; PA. Inland II A/B. Band 5–I, Eichmann/AA, Berlin, 28 Aug. 1941 *et al.* For the 20 May 1941 directive issued by Schellenberg, see Adler, p. 29, and Billig, *Die Endlösung*, p. 69. For the letter of 12 March 1941, see Adler, p. 28.

155. Breitman, pp. 197–9.
156. Billig, *Die Endlösung*, p. 153.
157. Billig, *Die Endlösung*, p. 153; Klarsfeld, *Vichy-Auschwitz*, pp. 368–9, Notiz, Zeitschel/ Abetz, Paris, [10 Sept. 1941].
158. Cf. Kempner, p. 351.
159. DGFP, D, XIII, Document 327, Statement by the Führer to Ambassador Abetz on 16 Sept. 1941.
160. Klarsfeld, *Endlösung*, Document 10, Schreiben, Zeitschel/Dannecker, Paris, 8 Oct. 1941.
161. Krausnick, 'The Persecution of the Jews', pp. 69–70.
162. Billig, *Die Endlösung*, p. 73.
163. Klarsfeld, *Endlösung*, Document 10, Schreiben, Zeitschel/Dannecker, Paris, 8 Oct. 1941.
164. Billig. *Die Endlösung*, pp. 74–5; IMT, Vol. XXXIII pp. 534–6. For a list of these transports from Oct. to Dec. 1941, see Kempner, p. 116. Hilberg, *Sonderzüge*, pp. 130–8, reproduces the report of the police officer accompanying one such transport for Riga which left Düsseldorf on 11 Dec. 1941.
165. Krausnick, 'The Persecution of the Jews', pp. 97–8.
166. Cf. Breitman, pp. 197ff; Mathias Beer, 'Die Entwicklung der Gaswagen beim Mord an den Juden', VfZ, 35 Jhg. 3 Heft, July 1987, pp. 403–17.
167. Cf. Einsatzgruppe Operational Report 128 for Russia, distributed from Berlin on 3 Nov. 1941: TWC, Vol. IV, pp. 150–54, Document NO-3157.
168. Kempner, p. 181; Krausnick, 'The Persecution of the Jews', pp. 68–9; Marrus and Paxton, pp. 248.
169. Jäckel, p. 227; Kempner, pp. 112–13; Klarsfeld, *Vichy-Auschwitz*, pp. 33–4, 47; DGFP, D, XIII, Document 338, Tel. 4477, von Ribbentrop/Abetz, Westfalen, 19 Sept. 1941; idem, Document 422, Report 3325, Abetz/von Ribbentrop, Paris, 25 Oct. 1941.
170. *Ich, Adolf Eichmann*, p. 318; Hilberg, p. 404; Klarsfeld, *Vichy-Auschwitz*, pp. 34–5, 370; Marrus and Paxton, p. 81; Reitlinger, *The Final Solution*, pp. 330–31.
171. AA 3748/E040487, Aufzeichnung Zeitschel/Abetz, Paris, 9 Dec. 1941.
172. ADAP, E, I, Document 16, Freiherr von Welck/Auswärtiges Amt, Wiesbaden 16 Dec. 1941, and fn 1: and Ritter Aufzeichnung, 13 Dec. 1941 (AA 898/292072). See also, FO 646. Document Book 60-B, Document NG-3571, OKH, Wolfsschanze/Ritter (AA), 12 Dec. 1941; idem, Aufzeichnung Ritter/Ribbentrop, Berlin, 13 Dec. 1941. In his memoirs, Abetz is at pains to record his personal opposition to the shooting of hostages: Abetz, pp. 208–9, 278. See also Billig, *Die Endlösung*, pp. 158–9.
173. ADAP, E, I, Document 16, fn. 1, Abetz Aufzeichnung, 12 Dec. 1941 (AA 898/292074). See also FO 646. Document Book 60-B. Document NG-3571, Strack report of telephone message from Abetz, Berlin, 12 Dec. 1941.
174. AA 1512/372043-44, Heydrich/Luther, Berlin, 29 Nov. 1941; ADAP, E, I, Document 150, fn 10, Referat D III/Luther, Berlin, 8 Dec. 1941; AA 1512/372039, Heydrich/Luther, Berlin, 8 Jan. 1942.
175. Browning, *Final Solution*, pp. 72–6; Döscher, pp. 246–9; DGFP, D, XIII, Document 504. Aufzeichnung Rintelen (von Ribbentrop and Bulgarian Foreign Minister Popov), Berlin, 27 Nov. 1941; ADAP, E, I, Document 72, Aufzeichnung Luther, Berlin, 30 Dec. 1941.
176  Cf. Hilberg, pp. 649–62.
177. Cf. Döscher, pp. 243–55.
178. Cf. Hans-Heinrich Wilhelm, 'The Holocaust in National-Socialist Rhetoric and Writings. Some Evidence Against the Thesis that before 1945 Nothing was Known About the "Final Solution"', *Yad Vashem Studies*, XVI (Jerusalem 1984), pp. 95–127; David Bankier, 'The Germans and the Holocaust: What Did They Know?', *Yad Vashem Studies*, XX (Jerusalem, 1990), pp. 69–98; Ian Kershaw, 'The Persecution of the Jews and German Popular Opinion in the Third Reich', LBYB, XXVI (1981), pp. 261–89. See also idem, *Popular Opinion and Political Dissent in the Third Reich: Bavaria 1933–1945* (Oxford, 1983), *passim*; and Jörg Wollenberg (ed.), *"Niemand war dabei und keiner hat's gewußt". Die deutsche öffentlichkeit und die Judenverfolgung 1933–45* (Munich, 1989).
179. Browning, *Final Solution*, p. 72.
180. TWC, Vol. XIII, pp. 177–80, 185–8, 199–200, 207–8; Reitlinger, *The Final Solution*, pp. 213, 333.

181. Cf. F.H. Hinsley, *British Intelligence in the Second World War. Volume 2: Its Influence on Strategy and Operations* (London, 1981), Appendix 5, 'The German Police Cyphers', pp. 669–73. The British 'Postal and Telegraph Censorship Reports on Jewry 1941–42' contains examples of the intelligence which Allied authorities obtained through radio traffic about the anti-Jewish operations of the *Einsatzgruppen* in Russia: Public Record Office, Kew, Home Office Correspondence, HO 213. Vol. 953. GEN. 462/2/6. In the collection of information from Nazi-occupied Europe dated 22 Jan. 1942, one reads of anti-Jewish executions and *Aktionen* in the Ukraine that could only have come from such sources. For example, its report that the SS executed 546 Jews at Berditshev on 26 Aug. 1941 is confirmed by official German reports of the activity of *Einsatzgruppe* C. Although these Allied reports greatly underrate the number of Jews shot at Kamienietz Podolsk on 27 and 28 Aug. 1941, German reports do confirm massacres there at the time, but in far greater numbers: cf. Krausnick and Wilhelm, pp. 166 and fn 314, and 189.

182. TWC, XIII, pp. 195–6, Aufzeichnung Luther, Berling, 4 Dec. 1941.

183. A (differently) translated copy of the article was placed in the British Foreign Office files only three days later, on 19 Nov. 1941: FO 371, Vol. 26569. C12779/6362/18.

184. BA, R6/37, Bl. 15–30, esp. 11; Müller-Hill, p. 47.

185. For a discussion of Hitler's 'table talk' and public references in 1942 to the extermination of the Jews, see Billig, *Die Endlösung*, pp. 57–60; Max Domarus, *Hitler. Reden und Proklamationen 1932–1945* (Wiesbaden, 1973), *Band II, Zweiter Halbband 1941–1945*, pp. 1828–9; idem, pp. 1843–4; Hillgruber, 'War in the East', *passim*.

186. TWC, Vol. XIII, pp. 192–4, 198–9; Browning, *Final Solution*, pp. 76ff; ADAP, E, I, Document 150, Undated Protocol of the Wannsee Conference [20 Jan. 1942].

187. Hilberg, *Documents of Destruction*, p. 106; Lang and Sibyll, pp. 91–2; Fleming, p. 92. A more recent study also makes the same point, besides suggesting that one point of seeming ambivalence in the language of the Wannsee Conference Protocol indicates that 'other' forms of 'final solution', i.e. for groups other than Jews, may also have been discussed or intended: Götz Aly and Susanne Heim, *Vordenker der Vernichtung. Auschwitz und die deutschen Pläne für eine neue europäische Ordnung* (Hamburg, 1991), pp. 454, 466.

188. Yad Vashem 0–4/53–1, Document 295. I am extremely grateful to Dr Yitzhak Arad, Director of Yad Vashem, Jerusalem, for having supplied me some time ago with a copy of this document.

189. This correspondence is published in the following: Serge Lang and Ernst von Schenck (eds), *Portrait eines Menschheitsverbrechers nach den hinterlassenen Memoiren des ehemaligen Reichsministers Alfred Rosenberg* (St Gallen, 1947), pp. 130–1, and in an English translation (Chicago/New York, 1949), pp. 117–18; Poliakov and Wulf, *Das Dritte Reich und die Juden*, pp. 190–1. Cf. the entry by Yitzhak Arad, 'Reichskommissariat Ostland', pp. 1243–4 in Vol. 3 of Yisrael Gutman (ed.), *Encyclopedia of the Holocaust* (Oxford/New York, 1990).

190. IMT, Vol. XI, p. 372.

191. Nuremberg Document RF-1215, IMT, Vol. VII, p. 36; Klarsfeld, *Vichy-Auschwitz*, p. 379.

192. Klarsfeld, *Vichy-Auschwitz*, p. 380, Vermerk Dannecker/Knochen, Paris, 15 June 1942.

193. Arad, Gutman and Margaliot, pp. 274–5, show that the SS personnel concerned had to sign the document, whereas Breitman, p. 237, using the same source, states that 'each man was supposed to swear that Hauptsturmführer Höfle, Globocnik's chief of staff had thoroughly informed him . . .'. But 'swearing' to something is different from being forced to sign a document.

194. Billig, *Die Endlösung*, pp. 87–92; Longerich, pp. 433–4.

195. BA, NS.6/344. Partei-Kanzlei.

196. Klarsfeld. *Vichy-Auschwitz*, pp. 413–16, Vermerk Dannecker/Knochen, Lischka, Oberg, Paris, 20 July 1942.

197. TWC, XIII, 240–1, Himmler/Berger, Reval, 28 July 1942.

198. Abetz, p. 283.

199. Döscher, pp. 226, 237–9.

200. AA 4636/E208947, Zeitschel/Abetz, 13 Feb. 1942.

201. Klarsfeld, *Vichy-Auschwitz*, pp. 373–4, Zeitschel/Schleier, Paris, 28 Feb. 1942.

202. Billig, *Die Endlösung*, p. 103; Klarsfeld, *Vichy-Auschwitz*, pp. 42–3; idem, 374–5, Dannecker Bericht/Knochen, Lischka, Paris, 10 March 1942.

203. AA 702/261432, Eichmann/Rademacher, Berlin, 9 March 1942.
204. ADAP, E, 1, Document 150, Undated Protocol of the Wannsee Conference [20 Jan. 1942]; idem, Band III. Document 209. Luther/Feldquartier Feldmark, Berlin, 21 Aug. 1942.
205. Klarsfeld, *Vichy-Auschwitz*, pp. 374–5, Vermerk Dannecker/Knochen, Lischka, Paris, 10 March 1942.
206. AA 702/261430, Eichmann/Rademacher, Berlin, 11 March 1942.
207. Klarsfeld, *Vichy-Auschwitz*, p. 375, Aufzeichnung Zeitschel/Schleier, Achenbach, Rahn, Paris, 11 March 1942; AA 5499/E383395, Schleier/AA, Paris, 17 March 1942 (Pol. II. Richtlinien. 14/2. Material Allgemeines Judenfragen).
208. Cf. ADAP, E, II, Document 56, Rademacher/Eichmann, Berlin, 20 March 1942, and foot-note references concerning other AA correspondence with Eichmann, and with the Paris Embassy, in March 1942; idem, III, Document 298, Aufzeichnung Luther, Berlin, 19 Sept. 1942; Klarsfeld, *Endlösung*, Document 97, Vermerk Röthke, Paris, 30 Oct. 1942; ADAP, E, IV, Document 274, Schleier/AA, Paris, 11 Dec. 1942; idem, V, Document 64, Luther/ Gaus, Berlin, 20 Jan. 1943. See also Billig, *Die Endlösung*, pp. 164–6; Kempner, pp. 184–92.
209. FO 646, Document Book 60-B, Document NG-1838, Affidavit Otto Abetz.
210. Klarsfeld, *Vichy-Auschwitz*, pp. 369–70, Reinhard Heydrich/Generalquartiermeister, Berlin, 6 Nov. 1941.
211. Billig, *Die Endlösung*, p. 168; Klarsfeld, *Vichy-Auschwitz*, pp. 46–7.
212. Billig, *Die Endlösung*, p. 169.
213. Hilberg, *The Destruction*, p. 405; Klarsfeld, *Endlösung*, Document 32, Aufzeichnung ohne Unterschrift/Schleier, Achenbach, Quiring, Paris, 18 March 1942; idem, *Vichy-Auschwitz*, p. 46. Kempner, p, 352, mistakenly – because of whom the document of 18 March was sub-mitted to – credits Dannecker with this significant comment.
214. AA 4851/E247712–13, Aufzeichnung Rademacher/Luther, Berlin, 21 Aug. 1941; idem, E247713, Aufzeichnung Luther, Berlin, 22 Aug. 1941; idem, E247680, Vortragsnotiz Luther/Reichsaußenminister, 22 Aug. 1941; idem, E247693–95, Vortragsnotiz Luther, Berlin, 11 Sept. 1941; idem, E247688, Aufzeichnung Luther, Berlin, 19 Sept. 1941 (Inland II. Geheim. 52/6. Kennzeichnung der deutschen und ausländischen Juden). For the text of Goebbels' submission to Hitler on this subject, see Adler, pp. 50–1.
215. AA 3748/E040487, Aufzeichnung Zeitschel/Abetz, Paris, 9 Dec. 1941; AA 4636/E208948, Aufzeichnung Zeitschel/Achenbach, Paris, 28 Jan. 1942 (Botschaft Paris. 143/1. Juden und Freimauer in Frankreich); AA 3748/E040488, Aufzeichnung Zeitschel/Schleier, Paris, 25 Feb. 1942; AA 4636/E208949–50, Aufzeichnung ohne Unterschrift/Achenbach, Paris, 3 March 1942; idem, E208951, Aufzeichnung Zeitschel, Paris, 20 March 1942; idem, E208941–43, Schleier/Best, Paris, 21 March 1942; AA 3872/E046554–55, Abetz/AA, Paris, 2 May 1942 (Pol. II. Richtlinien, Material Allgemeines, 14/2, Judenfragen); Billig, *Die Endlösung*, p. 145; Marrus and Paxton, pp. 118, 283ff.
216. AA 3872/E046554–55, Abetz/AA, Paris, 2 May 1942.
217. Klarsfeld, *Endlösung*, Document 35, Vermerk Dannecker, Paris, 4 May 1942.
218. AA 3796/E042692, Zeitschel/Best, Paris, 5 May 1942 (Pariser Botschaft. 1125. Juden-fragen). The policy of despatching 'special' groups of Jews eastwards in reprisal for attacks on Wehrmacht personnel was a continuous one: cf. AA K1509/K345269, Achenbach/AA, Paris, 15 Feb. 1942 (Inland II A/B. Juden in Frankreich. Band 5).
219. AA 3796/E042691, Zeitschel/Hagen, Paris, 5 May 1942.
220. Cf AA 3796/E042690, Aufzeichnung Krüger/MBF, Paris, 13 May 1942; Klarsfeld, *Endlösung*, Document 40, Dr Ernst, MBF/Leitenden Feldpolizeidirektor beim MBF, Paris, 13 May 1942; AA 3796/E042687–89, Aufzeichnung Buscher, Paris, 14 May 1942; AA 4851/E247658, Aufzeichnung Rademacher/Luther, Berlin, 14 May 1942; AA 4851/ E247660, Abetz/AA, Paris, 15 May 1942 (Inland II g. 52/6. Kennzeichnung der deutschen ausl. Juden); AA 4851/E247655 and E247657, Aufzeichnung Rademacher/Luther, Gaus, Woermann, Weizsäcker, Berlin, 15 May 1942; Klarsfeld, *Endlösung*, Document 39, Aufzeichnung mit Anlage, Zeitschel/Abetz, Paris, 21 May 1942.
221. AA 4851/E247657 and E247656, Vermerk Rademacher, Berlin, 18 May 1942; idem, E247653–54, Aufzeichnung Woermann, Berlin, 19 May 1942.
222. AA 4851/E247645, Luther/Abetz, Berlin, 21 May 1942; idem, E247635, Abetz/AA, Paris, 21 May 1942; idem, E247644, AA record of Zeitschel communication of Abetz's telegram;

ADAP, E, II, Document 230, Luther/Paris, Berlin, 21 May 1942; FO 646, Document Book 60-B, Document NG-3668, Zeitschel/MBF, Oberg, Paris, 22 May 1942.

223. AA 4851/E247629–30, Abetz/AA, Paris, 5 June 1942; Marrus and Paxton, pp. 235–40; Reitlinger, pp. 334–5.
224. Hilberg, *The Destruction*, p. 405.
225. Marrus and Paxton, pp. 236–40.
226. Klarsfeld, *Vichy-Auschwitz*, p. 377, Dannecker Bericht/Knochen, Lischka, Paris, 13 May 1942. The manner in which General Kohl's statement is presented by Marrus and Paxton, p. 351, could be taken by some readers as having come from Dannecker; Klarsfeld, *Vichy-Auschwitz*, p. 378, Lischka/RSHA IV B 4, Paris, 15 May 1942.
227. Klarsfeld, *Vichy-Auschwitz*, pp. 62–3.
228. Billig, *Die Endlösung*, p. 81.
229. Klarsfeld, *Vichy-Auschwitz*, pp. 66–8, 379–80, Vermerk Dannecker/Knocken, Lischka, Paris, 15 June 1942; idem, p. 69, for the observations by Oberg and Knochen. See also idem, p. 380, for a further Vermerk by Dannecker on 15 June 1942 concerning the proposed transport schedules. A more wide-ranging meeting of Eichmann's *Judenreferenten*, both in terms of participants and subject matter, took place at RSHA headquarters in Berlin on 28 Aug. 1942: Klarsfeld, *Vichy-Auschwitz*, 447–48, Vermerk Ahnert, Paris, 1 Sept. 1942.
230. ADAP, E, III, Document 26, Eichmann/Rademacher, Berlin, 22 June 1942.
231. ADAP, E, III, Document 26, Eichmann/Rademacher, Berlin 22 June 1942; idem, fn 2, Luther/Paris, Berlin, 28 June 1942; idem, Document 141, Luther/Eichmann, Berlin [29 July 1942].
232. Cf. Hilbert, *The Destruction*, p. 406; Klarsfeld, *Vichy-Auschwitz*, pp. 330–2.
233. Klarsfeld, *Vichy-Auschwitz*, Vermerk Dannecker-Eichmann, Paris, 1 July 1942.
234. Klarsfeld, *Vichy-Auschwitz*, p. 388, Zeitschel/Sipo-SD, Paris, 27 June 1942; IMT. Vol. VII, 38–9.
235. Klarsfeld, *Vichy-Auschwitz*, p. 389, Zeitschel/Abetz, Paris, 27 June 1942.
236. Billig, *Die Endlösung*, pp. 172ff.
237. Billig, *Die Endlösung*, p. 172; Klarsfeld, *Vichy-Auschwitz*, pp. 393–7, Aktenvermerk Hagen/Oberg, Paris, 4 July 1942; Marrus and Paxton, pp. 233ff. The same 'Führer-imperative' was referred to in Röthke's record of his meeting on 1 Sept. 1942 with Leguay's Cabinet Chief, Kommandant Sauts: Klarsfeld, *Vichy-Auschwitz*, pp. 449–50, Vermerk Röthke/Knochen, Lischka, Hagen, Paris, 1 Sept. 1942: 'Im übrigen handele es sich nach wie vor um die Endlösung der Judenfrage in Europa, die vom Führer und Reichskanzler unbedingt erreicht werden würde'.
238. Klarsfeld, *Vichy-Auschwitz*, p. 400, Knochen/MBF, Kommandant von Groß-Paris, Deutsche Botschaft, Paris, 7 July 1942.
239. AA 5549/E387828–29, Tel. 2783, Abetz/AA, Paris, 2 July 1942 (Inland II Geheim. 55/4: Juden in Frankreich); Browning, *Final Solution*, p. 105.
240. ADAP, E, III, Document 26, Eichmann/Rademacher, Berlin, 22 June 1942, and fn 2: Luther/Paris, Berlin, 28 June 1942.
241. ADAP, E, III, Document 58, Tel. 2784, Abetz/AA, Paris, 2 July 1942. See also, TWC, XIII. 234–5, and Klarsfeld, *Vichy-Auschwitz*, p. 392. In his memoirs and post-war testimony, Abetz tried to put a completely different gloss on all such actions: Abetz, p. 319; FO 646. Document Book 60-B, Document NG-1838, Affidavit Otto Abetz.
242. ADAP, E, III, Document 58, fn 4, Luther/Paris, 10 July 1942.
243. Billig, *Die Endlösung*, pp. 172–3, 179; Klarsfeld, *Vichy-Auschwitz*, p. 86.
244. ADAP, E, III, Document 141, Luther/Eichmann, Berlin, [29 July 1942].
245. AA K810/K212130, Notiz Rademacher/Luther, Berlin, 10 Jan. 1942, and resubmitted on 10 July 1942 (Inland II Geheim. 56/1: Juden in Italien). See also Meir Michaelis, *Mussolini and the Jews. German–Italian Relations and the Jewish Question in Italy 1922–1945* (Oxford, 1978); Jonathan Steinberg, *All or Nothing. The Axis and the Holocaust 1941–1943* (London, 1990).
246. AA 702/261417–19, Tel. 2822, Abetz/AA, Paris, 4 July 1942 (Inland II Geheim. 52/4: Abbeförderung von Juden aus dem besetzten französischen Gebiet nach Oberschlesien [Auschwitz].
247. AA 5549/E387834–35, Vortragsnotiz Luther/Staatssekretär, Reichsaußenminister, Berlin,

24 July 1942; Browning, *Final Solution*, p. 105.

248.  AA 5549/E387809–10, Tel. 3727, Luther/Rom, Berlin, 17 Sept. 1942; idem, E387811, Tel. 4093, Luther/Paris, Berlin, 17 Sept. 1942.

249.  ADAP, E, III, Document 178, Feihl/AA, Paris, 11 Aug. 1942; idem, fn 3, Luther/Paris, Berlin, 22 Aug. 1942.

250.  AA 2257/478665–66, Bericht 1738, Abetz/AA, Paris, 7 Sept. 1942 (Inland II Geheim. 55: Juden in Frankreich).

251.  AA 5549/E387804–05, Tel. 4082, Abetz/AA, Paris, 15 Sept. 1942; idem, E387806–08, Tel. 4084, Abetz/AA, Paris, 16 Sept. 1942; idem, E387794, Tel. 4239, Abetz/AA, Paris, 24 Sept. 1942; Hilberg, *The Destruction*, pp. 410–11.

252.  Klarsfeld, *Vichy-Auschwitz*, p. 464, Aufzeichnung Zeitschel, Paris, 16 Sept. 1942. See also AA 5549/E387802–03, Tel. 4004, Schleier/AA, Paris, 11 Sept. 1942.

253.  Klarsfeld, *Vichy-Auschwitz*, p. 176.

254.  AA 5549/E387789–91, Vortragsnotiz Luther, Berlin, 19 Sept. 1942.

255.  ADAP, E, III, Document 307, Aufzeichnung Luther, Berlin, 24 Sept. 1942.

256.  AA 5549/E387788, Aufzeichnung Sonnleithner, Westfalen, 3 Oct. 1942.

257.  Billig, *Die Endlösung*, pp. 179–80.

258.  Klarsfeld, *Vichy-Auschwitz*, p. 468, Vermerk Röthke/Knochen, Lischka, Paris, 24 Sept. 1942; idem, p. 469, Knochen/RSHA Berlin, Paris, 25 Sept. 1942; idem, p. 469, details of transport number 38 of 28 Sept. 1942.

259.  ADAP, E, IV, Document 274, Bericht 5843, Schleier/AA, Paris, 11 Dec. 1942; Billig, *Die Endlösung*, pp. 180–1.

260.  Hilberg, *The Destruction*, pp. 413–19.

261.  Reitlinger, *The Final Solution*, pp. 327, 351.

262.  Cf. the erudite discussion in Gavin I. Langmuir, *Toward A Definition of Antisemitism* (University of California Press, 1990).

263.  George M. Kren and Leon Rappoport, *The Holocaust and the Crisis of Human Behaviour* (New York, 1980), p. 3.

264.  Kren and Rappoport, p. 128.

265.  For some of the other issues raised by the role of bureaucrats and the structures of modern political societies in such atrocities as the Holocaust, see Zygmunt Bauman, *Modernity and the Holocaust* (Cambridge, 1989).

# Beyond Intelligence: The Study of British Strategy and the Norway Campaign, 1940

## WESLEY K. WARK

### D.C. Watt and the Study of Intelligence

Ever since the *Sunday Times* 'Insight' team showed what could be done with mundane reference sources in reconstructing intelligence careers, notably that of H.A.R. 'Kim' Philby, reading about the ordered and formulaic lives of the British elite as depicted in *Who's Who* has taken on new interest. Harold Evans, the *Sunday Times* editor who launched the Philby investigation in 1967, recalled that the Insight team often had recourse to *Who's Who* in search of leads provided by gnomic references such as 'attached Foreign Office' or simply 'FO', and for telltale gaps in the recorded careers of British officials. 'One had a picture of these intelligence officers, for that is what they were, pausing over the career section of the entry when they filled in *Who's Who*. "Spying for HMG" hardly seemed right.'[1] The *Who's Who* entry for Professor Donald Cameron Watt has its own gap, one of interest to his students and readers, though hardly sinister or sensational. Unrecorded is the fact that Donald Watt had an early exposure to the world of intelligence that may well have been a formative experience for his later historical research and writing. Born in 1928, Donald Watt was too young for service in the Second World War, but instead experienced the Cold War from the front lines, doing his National Service in the British Army's Intelligence Corps in Austria in the late 1940s. His tasks included, among other things, interrogation of defectors, displaced persons and border-crossers from behind the Iron Curtain. He apparently displayed, in what has become a legendary story among his colleagues and friends, a skill and assiduousness in the clandestine collection of documents which was to serve him well when he took his first professional job in 1951 as assistant editor of the official series, *Documents on German Foreign Policy, 1918–1945*. More recently Donald Watt has become one of a remarkable cadre of British diplomatic and military historians who have turned their attention and academic training to the issue of the 'missing dimension' of intelligence, often using their own experience of service in the British intelligence community to intellectual advantage.[2] Watt has written widely on the subject and has helped to advance its academic status through his position on the editorial board of the journal *Intelligence and National Security*, and as an executive member and leading spirit of a study group in the UK which devotes its activities to the history of intelligence.

Donald Watt once remarked in conversation that he thought that historians and intelligence analysts had much in common. He added that he liked the spy novels of Anthony Price for just this reason: Price's characters (especially Major Audley) are often historians who have succumbed to the lure of the intelligence world, but who remain fundamentally and sometimes eccentrically scholarly in their demeanour and thinking. To be likened to spies, especially if one is spying on a (deceased) intelligence community, no doubt adds appeal to the research task, but the remark seems weightier than this. It is suggestive about the similarities of the historian's and the intelligence analyst's tasks in reconstructing a complex event from fragmentary and conflicting information, and equally suggestive about the nature of the rules of evidence and the sceptical frame of mind that must be employed in both intelligence assessment and historical research. Thinking about an enemy and thinking about the past would appear to be genuinely analogous activities: both require an effort to cross mentally into the world of another culture and people and consider their criteria for action. It is possible to speculate that this analogy, this border-crossing metaphor, first took hold in the mind of the young Intelligence Corps sergeant as he sifted his documents and weighed up the testimony of his sources; certainly it is displayed in his recent writings. A survey of Donald Watt's publications on intelligence reveals a working methodology and set of assumptions about the historian's task which, while never fully articulated in any single piece of writing, are impressive in the aggregate.[3] Their potential application to the case of British planning and intelligence for Norway will be developed later in this essay.

Watt's studies of intelligence and related issues cohere in the way in which he provides answers to three critical questions: what is the content of such studies; how is the historical performance of intelligence agencies to be assessed and how are intelligence failures, in particular, to be understood; and what kind of methodology can the historian apply to such matters? With respect to the content of intelligence studies, Watt uses what amounts to a working typology of the intelligence process, one that enjoys wide currency in recent studies. In this typology a threefold structure of intelligence is identified, for the purpose both of understanding the ways in which intelligence is generated and for approaching the special problems associated with each stage in the creation of an intelligence image. Thus we have a diagrammatic concept of an intelligence cycle incorporating (1) the collection of intelligence data, (2) the assessment of intelligence reports and bureaucratic communication of findings, and (3) the impact of intelligence on policy-making.[4] What is marked in Watt's approach is the relative attention that he gives to the historical and intellectual roots of the assessment and impact stages of the cycle, and his flexible handling of the typology itself.

Typically, Watt focuses on the ways in which misperceptions serve to mislead intelligence staffs and blunt the impact of intelligence assessments and warnings. In his essay surveying British intelligence before the outbreak of the Second World War, Watt stresses the importance, among other factors, of 'psychological and other barriers to the appreciation of such intelligence by the policy-makers'.[5] He goes on to discuss four such barriers, from the aptly named 'not made in Britain syndrome' (which prevented British intelligence from assessing correctly aspects of German military technology), to the exaggerated fear of a German knock-out blow from the air that so distorted British intelligence on the Luftwaffe.[6] There is in his work a tendency to ascribe major intelligence failures to a process of blinding imposed by misconceptions, rather than to lapses of geo-political attention, or lack of covert sources of information.[7] Thus in Watt's study of British intelligence regarding the diplomacy of the Nazi-Soviet pact in August 1939, he ascribes to Foreign Office officials a 'rigidity of assumption which underlies so many of the great intelligence surprises'.[8] In the conclusion to a more synoptic essay on British diplomacy in the 1930s, Watt identifies at least four principal areas of 'misconception' – over the German 'moderates', the prospects for an Eastern front in 1939, the American position, and Soviet policy – that affected policy and weakened Britain's ability to deter or deal effectively with the Third Reich.[9]

The significant question of how mistaken ideas emerge and take hold is treated by example in Donald Watt's essay on British military perceptions of Soviet power after 1945. Here he draws attention to the ways in which British officials read post-1945 Soviet actions in light of their understanding of German totalitarian policy in the pre-war period. This point is underlined by the general formula that 'past experience is of particular importance since it is in the remembered experience of the past that one may find the stereotypes by which current expectations may be judged or to which appeal will be made if these expectations are disappointed'.[10] Discussion of the function of misperceptions and the origins of mistaken thinking are the hallmarks of Donald Watt's investigation of intelligence. His approach stresses mentality over organizational history and bureaucratic policy. It may serve as a useful corrective in the burgeoning literature on intelligence, which has already discovered its schools, disciplinary fractures and national types.[11] While Donald Watt's typology of intelligence and his treatment of intelligence failures can be situated within mainstream approaches to the study of intelligence, he has been strongly critical of the lack of debate among historians about an appropriate methodology for the subject, and has called attention both to the repetitive and perhaps unrealistic nature of academic appeals for greater access to aged intelligence records.[12] Watt's own brand of methodology avowedly embraces the need for inference and speculation in studies of intelligence. Not only does he plead for such methods in the abstract, and is prepared to accuse other historians of 'defeatism' in the face of the inevitable archival gaps, but he has provided an example of the methodology put to practice in a thoughtful and indeed cunning and tenacious investigation of the role of a key Soviet agent in the 1930s. This essay stands as proof of the historian/intelligence agent analogy mentioned earlier. Watt finds the mole and, like some historical George Smiley, traces the intricate routes by which purloined British material may have reached Britain's enemies.[13]

Among possible case-studies, the Norway campaign of 1940 provides rich ground for further investigation of the sort that Donald Watt has given to other examples of intelligence failures. There is also a false sense of closure surrounding the literature on this campaign – a sense that it has been so closely studied that there could be little more of value to discover. Thinking about the role of misperception, its historical roots, and the uses of inference and speculation may help uncover some lost 'secrets' of British intelligence in the Norway campaign.

## Norway, 1940: The Historiography of Intelligence Failure

The magnitude of the intelligence failure which had been inflicted on the British by the German assault on Denmark and Norway in April 1940 was quickly grasped by contemporary observers. That the Phoney War had been brought to an abrupt end by a campaign which challenged the near mythological capabilities of both the British Secret Service and the Royal Navy was a painful lesson. One of the earliest published accounts of the Norwegian campaign, rushed into print even before the final evacuation of Narvik by Allied forces, attempted to explain how it was that so shocking and nasty a surprise had been engineered. Lord Strabolgi, the author of the account and a former senior naval officer, placed great emphasis on the formidable character of the Nazi fifth column in Norway and on the ruthless and unconventional tactics of Adolf Hitler. But in his very first chapter, entitled 'The Plot', Strabolgi did not hesitate to place the blame squarely on the intelligence services in London. In bringing his discussion of 'The Plot' to a close, Strabolgi asked: 'Why were the immense preparations for this invasion allowed to proceed for so many months without the knowledge of the Governments of London and Paris? Why could this underground burrowing, bribery, corruption, plotting and espionage be carried on in Norway without at least some of the facts being known? Whitehall was as astonished by the turn of events as were the Government circles in Oslo.'[14]

Strabolgi's question was, of course, purely rhetorical. The answer, he felt, was 'inescapable'. In what must have been the harshest public criticism meted out to the intelligence services of the government since the outbreak of the war, Strabolgi wrote:

Our Intelligence Service was inefficient. . . . True, the preparing of troop transports and landing forces in the German Baltic ports was known; but that they were being got ready for a descent upon Norway was apparently unexpected. The only way apparently open to us for finding out what forces lay in the vitally important port of Narvik was to allow a British flotilla of destroyers to enter the fiord to find out. . . . The conclusion that we were caught napping is inescapable.

Norway's trade, shipping, strategical situation, are all so important to us that the blame must be attached to our Secret Service, to our Foreign Office, to our Trade Intelligence Department, and to the Intelligence Services of the Army, Navy, and Air Force. Whatever else may be said about Herr Hitler and the present clique who dominate Germany, they are not orthodox. In waging war, as in everything else, they may be expected to adopt revolutionary methods. The old, gentlemanly, conventional means of counteraction are not sufficient. The whole technique of the aggression against Norway, with its undermining and burrowing, its treachery and cunning provide an object lesson for all the world to see.[15]

Castigation of the British intelligence services for failing to understand the true nature of Hitlerian aggression was fully warranted, even more so than Strabolgi, with only superficial evidence and an obsession with the Fifth Column, could have known. Behind closed doors in Whitehall, anxiety, and in some quarters, anger was expressed about the performance of British intelligence. Lord Hankey, Minister without Portfolio, was in the midst of a review of the secret services when the Norway campaign began.[16] He asked the chief of the SIS, Colonel Sir Stewart Menzies, for a report on the warnings that had been available to the government about German action. The SIS answer was contained in a five-page memorandum detailing the intelligence it had received and passed on to the service departments, dating back to May 1939. It was a careful exercise in self-defence, carried the whiff of a suggestion that other departments were to blame for the fiasco, and betrayed considerable complacency. The warnings that were catalogued were of a miscellaneous character, from ungraded sources, many apparently casual – the airplane passenger, for example, who had reported seeing on 8 April a force of German destroyers and merchantmen while flying between Copenhagen and Oslo. Like Strabolgi, the SIS pointed to the existence of a German plan, and claimed in hindsight to have seen it at work since December 1939. The final sentence in the memorandum passed the buck, albeit ambiguously: 'That it [the German plan] existed and that it could not be purely of academic interest is a matter of documentary evidence.'[17] Hankey was not entirely convinced. He felt that the SIS had exonerated itself in the business of receiving and passing along items of intelligence, but was concerned that no one had attempted any sustained assessment of the cumulative nature of the warnings received. Hankey blamed the service departments for this short-coming.[18] Correspondence on this issue reached the Prime Minister, and might have led to considerable early reforms in the intelligence community but for the fall of the Chamberlain government on 10 May and Hankey's own removal from the War Cabinet when Winston Churchill came to power.[19]

More visceral responses to the intelligence failure were also recorded in London. The Chief of the Imperial General Staff, General Sir Edmund Ironside, commented angrily in his diary on 10 April that secret intelligence had been 'deplorable' for failing to anticipate the German invasion, especially as Norway must have been 'stinking with Nazis'.[20] Ironside thought, rightly, that the military situation he now faced, to mount a combined operation to expel the German occupation forces, was a 'poisonous proposition'.[21] It was certainly one for which British planning was totally unprepared; it would poison certain careers, including those of Neville Chamberlain and Ironside himself.[22]

Subsequent investigations since 1940 have enlarged on the reasons behind the British intelligence failure, so that we now possess a full, and sometimes even microscopic, picture of the weaknesses in intelligence-gathering, organization, assessment and policy implementation that bedevilled the British during the Phoney War. These weaknesses, in the aggregate, were staggering and their cataloguing has tended to dominate the unfolding historiography of British intelligence on Norway. Some rehearsal of them may be useful.

Strabolgi's account was followed, in the course of time, by more dispassionate and scholarly work that considered the role of intelligence in the Norwegian débâcle. The campaign was deemed of sufficient merit to warrant a separate volume in the British official history of military operations in the Second World War. T.K. Derry's *The Campaign in Norway* appeared in 1952. While it did not devote a great deal of space to a recounting of British intelligence problems, it did pinpoint intelligence failure and the infliction of surprise as one of the three key lessons of the campaign. The author stated, in a concluding chapter on 'The Campaign in Retrospect', that 'deficiencies in our Intelligence work, including appreciation of intelligence, had cost us dear'.[23] Derry recognized that wishful thinking, particularly about the nature of the German response to British intervention in Norway, had clouded the minds of strategic planners. But beyond this the official historian writing in the early 1950s clearly found it difficult to go. The intelligence maze remained impenetrable, and any analysis of the nature of the British failure had to be largely conjectural. Derry ended on a note of puzzlement; he found it 'difficult to understand the lack of comprehensive and precise intelligence and the failure in evaluating what intelligence there was.'[24]

Captain Stephen Roskill, Derry's counterpart as official historian of naval operations, was equally critical of the poor quality of British intelligence as it affected British fleet actions off Norway. But Roskill, whose first volume of *The War at Sea* was published in 1954, came no nearer than Derry to a thorough-going analysis of the intelligence failure. He was content to rest his observations on the disadvantages of being forced to act on the defensive. Roskill stated: 'the correct assessment of intelligence will, however, always be difficult as long as the strategic initiative rests with the enemy, since he is able to strike in so many different directions'.[25] His detailed account of intelligence deficiencies as they affected fleet operations remained a catalogue of missed opportunities.[26] Donald McLachlan's semi-official *Room 39: British Naval Intelligence in Action*, had the benefit of access to the papers of Admiral Godfrey, the Director of Naval Intelligence (DNI). But despite its many insights into the conduct of the naval war, it added little to the story of the Norwegian débâcle.[27]

Any further advance in the historiography of intelligence for the Norway campaign had to await the outpouring of works that followed the introduction of the 30-year rule for the release of government records in 1967, coupled with a renewed attention devoted to intelligence. The decision to open up a part of the Second World War signals intelligence archive, and the publication, beginning in 1979, of successive volumes in the British official history of intelligence in the Second World War, were vital sources of inspiration and knowledge. F.H. Hinsley, in a section of his official history appropriately entitled 'In the Dark', provides the first detailed analysis of why British intelligence failed to predict, or react swiftly to, the German attack on Norway.[28] The answer is, as Strabolgi surmised some 39 years earlier, that British intelligence was incompetent in all its dimensions: collection of data, assessment, inter-agency co-ordination, and communication of its findings to the appropriate decision-makers. In the critical months of the winter and spring of 1940, as both German and British planning for their respective operations in Scandinavia reached a climax, British intelligence was forced to rely on traditional agent, attaché and diplomatic mission information, supplemented by the occasional warning and titbit from unofficial sources. This network had many geographic loopholes, one of which was Norway. Its communications were slow and its product difficult to assess, and, when inconvenient, correspondingly easy to dismiss. It may well have been an instrument played upon by the German secret service when it suited their purposes.[29] As a network it was prey to the gusts of news and rumours that swept through Europe during the 'war of nerves' that was the intelligence services' experience of the military 'sitzkrieg'. Such an intelligence network was, in a word, unreliable.

Such unreliability was a product of the perennial failings of human intelligence as a source. It was compounded by the fact that the British were still trying to make up for the locust years of the 1930s and the failure to exploit new, promising and more technologically orientated sources of intelligence before the outbreak of war. In fact, British intelligence was in the spring of 1940 on the brink of its near miraculous revolution in methods and achievement. But that revolution came too late to affect the outcome in Norway. The very first air photo coverage of Kiel harbour was completed by a long-range Spitfire (the brainchild of Sidney Cotton and his maverick SIS unit) on 7 April, only a day before the first German naval units sailed for the invasion of Norway.[30] This mission provided considerable evidence of German naval and air activity at the port, but was robbed of significance by the lack of any prior coverage of Kiel, and any standard by which to judge what was suddenly being observed.[31] Similarly, traffic analysis techniques, which the Government Code and Cypher School was slowly beginning to perfect, led one junior intelligence analyst at Bletchley (none other than F.H. Hinsley) to a remarkable and unsettling discovery about German naval activity in the Baltic on the night of 6–7 April, 1940. Again, unfamiliarity with the potential of such a source of intelligence, and lack of any previous traffic analysis findings of similar import, made it impossible to appreciate the true nature of the material available.[32] The most potent of all forms of intelligence in the Second World War, decrypted signals intelligence, was also just coming into the grasp of the British as the Norwegian campaign began. On 15 April, as the first contingent of hapless British troops made their way to Norway to try to undo the German surprise and eject German troops from Narvik, Bergen and Trondheim, the Government Code and Cypher School made its first significant breakthrough in the continuous reading of the German Enigma machine. The breakthrough involved cracking the Enigma 'Yellow' key, which provided a considerable quantity of operational intelligence for the British on German air and land operations in Norway.[33] But this material proved difficult to exploit, not least because the intelligence breakthrough was itself a major surprise. Channels of communication and methods for utilization of such precious intelligence scarcely yet existed.

In the end, it was the traditional sources of intelligence that provided the British with what warnings they had of German intentions and moves in Norway: diplomatic and SIS agent reports, air and fleet sightings, and prisoner of war intelligence.[34] In the fog of war that descended on 8 April, in particular, it took the British intelligence service a good 24 hours fully to uncover the nature of German operations. Not until noon on 9 April did it become clear that the Germans had managed to land troops at Narvik – the greatest of the suprises suffered.[35] Air photo reconnaissance, the 'Y' service's traffic analysis, and signals intelligence were intelligence tools for the future. The absence of such sources condemned British intelligence to a state of inefficiency and saddled it, inevitably, with a reputation for unreliability. But the lack of high quality sources was not the only ingredient in the British intelligence failure in the spring of 1940. What intelligence there was was poorly used by a system that suffered badly from lack of co-ordination and inter-service rivalry, miscomprehension and aloofness. The Joint Intelligence Committee (JIC), to serve later in the war as the central focus for strategic intelligence appreciations, was still in its infancy. It was busying itself with a host of miscellaneous projects and administrative matters.[36] The weakness of the JIC itself mirrored the larger problem – that the forces pulling in the direction of centralization of intelligence work in Whitehall, with all that this would eventually provide in the way of efficiency, were not yet strong enough to overcome the centrifugal strength of an established system of intelligence fragmentation and compartmentalization. This prevailing system in fact nurtured the final element in the story of the British intelligence failure over Norway. To the problems posed by the unreliability of intelligence data, and the fractured nature of the intelligence system that tried to assess it, was added the force of expectations about the outcome of the British–German confrontation over Norway. Here, the official historian handicaps himself with his much criticized formula of 'pas de monstres, et pas de héros'.[37] Even so, Hinsley does note that each department with a hand in intelligence assessment and the decision-making process had its own set of cherished beliefs about events on the Scandinavian front. The Admiralty is singled out as particularly prone to, or a victim of, such expectations. Hinsley comments that in the Admiralty, 'no intelligence section, until it was too late, dissented from the belief of Mr Churchill, the First Lord, that a landing in Scandinavia was beyond Germany's powers'.[38]

The dissection, under the official historian's knife, seems meticulous and complete. The British intelligence failure in Norway was a compound of poor quality sources, inadequate assessments, a faulty machinery for applying intelligence to strategy, and unrealistic expectations. To this account the recent gloss by Basil Collier adds little, beyond a beguiling (but partial) table of some 33 intelligence warnings that reached the British.[39] Patrick Beesly's biographical study of Admiral Godfrey is not altogether convincing in its effort to show that naval intelligence performed better than some of its critics allowed.[40] Beesly does demonstrate, however, that there were some dissenting spirits in the Admiralty who took the German threat to Norway more seriously than the First Lord.[41] But he does not overturn the official historian's conclusion that such dissent was too little, too late. Recent memoirs from female officers who served with air photo intelligence and the Y service provide a personal perspective on aspects of the story told by Hinsley and his team.[42] Olivier Desarzens' little-known but valuable book sets British intelligence in a comparative context wherein the relative German successes in intelligence work in Norway are contrasted with the Anglo-French failures.[43]

For brevity, it is difficult to imagine a more concise summing up than that provided by Hinsley at the close of his Norwegian discussion: the essential problem for British intelligence in the spring of 1940 was that no adequate machinery existed 'for confronting prevailing opinions and lazy assumptions with rigorous and authoritative assessments of the massive but miscellaneous information about the enemy that was nevertheless available'.[44] But this summary, while it surely completes the enquiry begun by Lord Strabolgi in public and by Lord Hankey in secret in 1940, introduces a methodological problem of considerable importance for the study of the Norway failure and, perhaps, for intelligence studies in general.[45] For, in any study of intelligence failure it is necessary to try and analyse not only the specific assessments drawn up by the responsible intelligence authorities, but also the 'prevailing opinions and lazy assumptions' held by decision-makers. To attempt to separate the professional intelligence judgement from the surrounding, contextual framework of ideas is surely artificial. Each penetrates and influences the other, to the extent that the boundaries between intelligence assessments and prevailing attitudes must necessarily be very blurred and, perhaps, for the purposes of studying failure, worthless.

This is especially relevant when one considers the Phoney War period of 1939–40, when the slow and unsatisfactory development of British intelligence created opportunities for decision-makers to act as their own best intelligence analysts. These opportunities were pronounced in the case of planning for operations in Scandinavia, owing to the many different guises through which such planning went, the secrecy involved, the sometimes fantastic nature of the schemes under consideration and, not least, the nature of the strong personalities who advocated offensive action in the north. One is drawn back, as Donald Watt would have it, to an appreciation of the uses of 'misconception' as a focus, a more inclusive phrase that naturally unites the realms of intelligence assessment and general climate of ideas. If we release ourselves from Hinsley's unwillingness to interrogate the role of individuals, 'whose misconception?' becomes a pertinent question and a fruitful line of enquiry. This is not because 'guilty men' is the issue, but rather because the exploration of the commixture of intelligence and assumption, where personal documentation survives, is an exercise in the possible. There are a number of candidates for study, including Neville Chamberlain, who had his own idiosyncratic complex of ideas about the Phoney War and who occasionally looked to intelligence reports for justification for his views, and Winston Churchill, the eager warrior and chief proponent of the Norway campaign.[46] Less well known is Churchill's partner in what critics labelled the 'crazy gang' – General Sir Edmund Ironside.

### Ironside, the War Office and Intelligence

The performance of General Sir Edmund Ironside, Chief of the Imperial General Staff during the Norwegian campaign, stands out as a perfect case-study in the overlapping roles of decision-maker and intelligence analyst, and in the impossibility of drawing hard-and-fast distinctions between intelligence, opinions and lazy assumptions at the highest levels of government. Ironside is an appropriate subject for three reasons: he was a senior army officer with an unusual attribute for his generation, namely a genuine appreciation of and taste for intelligence; he was one of the chief promoters of British schemes in Scandinavia and contributed to the intelligence failure suffered by the British by holding to an erroneous view of the probable outcome; and he has left behind a massive and revealing documentation of his thinking, in the shape of a private diary.[47]

At the very outset of his long army career, Ironside devilled in intelligence work; it was to become a lifelong interest. Shortly after the conclusion of the Boer War, Ironside volunteered for Secret Service duties in German South West Africa and managed to pose for a time as a Boer transport driver with the German columns that were operating against the Herero uprising. So valuable were his services to the German Army that he was pressed to enlist, an offer that he managed to refuse, and was subsequently awarded a German campaign medal.[48] John Buchan drew on his knowledge of Ironside's exploits and character to create his fictional hero, Richard Hannay.[49] Ironside's subsequent ambitions to become an intelligence officer on the Western Front in the First World War and to be posted as military attaché to Berlin after 1918 were never achieved. But while Ironside went on to bigger things, he never lost his early taste for intelligence work. On many later occasions, Ironside would pay special attention to intelligence tasks in his command. At Archangel (1918–19) and in Persia (1920) he established his own intelligence networks to operate against Bolshevik forces opposed to him. During the inter-war years he kept in close touch with MI5 and its chief, General Vernon Kell. His diaries reveal him to have possessed a huge appetite for political and military information, and to have been a thinker used to ranging over the strategic issues of the day.

When Ironside arrived at the War Office in September 1939 as CIGS, without previous experience of staff work in Whitehall, it was only natural that he would continue old habits. Ironside was well accustomed to acting as his own intelligence analyst. In any case, he tended to divide the army into 'men of action' and staff officers, and disliked and distrusted the latter. The Operations and Intelligence branch had been disrupted by the departure, against Ironside's wishes, of the incumbent director, General Sir Henry Pownall, who joined Lord Gort as Chief of Staff to the British Expeditionary Force in France. Moreover, Ironside was determined to give vigorous leadership to the war effort, and wanted to make the CIGS' post into a veritable commander-in-chief of British land forces. Ironside's ambitions were similar, though less exalted, to those of Churchill at the Admiralty.[50] To achieve them required centralization of decision-making in Whitehall and, of course, a good supply of intelligence to the CIGS. In the circumstances, it was only natural that when Ironside found that War Office intelligence was unavailable, or unsuitable to his purposes, that he should substitute his own thinking. The effort by Ironside to create a command post in Whitehall provided the first stimulus towards the confusion of intuition with intelligence that would mark British military planning for Scandinavia.

Correlation of Ironside's personal diary with the surviving intelligence record reveals that the CIGS was a careful consumer of military intelligence directorate reports. Not long after the first SIS information began to arrive in London about concentrations of shipping in the Baltic, Ironside noted in his diary the obvious implication that Germany was collecting an invasion fleet for operations in Scandinavia, probably against Sweden.[51] When such reports continued to come in in January, Ironside commented that they indicated that Germany might undertake some aggression in Scandinavia and was making preparations for landing troops.[52] This early intelligence was hot and timely. German planning for operations in Scandinavia was only approved by Hitler on 14 December, after entreaties from Admiral Eric Raeder and a series of meetings with the notorious Major Quisling.[53]

British and German planning for the northern theatre proceeded apace after December 1939.[54] The British looked to Scandinavia as an arena where they could tighten the conduct of economic warfare by strangling German supplies of iron ore, take the military initiative, utilize their seapower, and create a strategic diversion. German planning sought to deny the Scandinavian opening to the Allies by striking first. Neither side possessed hard intelligence about the full intentions of the other, though the Germans had the better indications, made better guesses and enjoyed much greater secrecy.[55]

Ironside appropriated and enlarged the military intelligence directorate's appreciations of the developing situation. He placed its often pedestrian and cautious reporting within the larger context of a set of individual assumptions about the military balance between Britain and Germany and about the nature of the Nazi regime. One example of this tendency occurred in January 1940. On 21 January, a military intelligence appreciation was circulated that discounted the possibility of reaching hard conclusions from the evidence coming in of a German military build-up in the Baltic ports.[56] MI3 (responsible for military intelligence on Germany) believed that these reports were both incomplete and susceptible to a number of interpretations. Six days later, Ironside added his own gloss, accepting the MI3 conclusion and explaining it by reference to two strongly-held beliefs. One was that intelligence arriving from Europe was a product of a war of nerves being waged deliberately by the Germans: consequently all such material was necessarily tainted and difficult to appreciate. The second belief was more pertinent yet: all intelligence concerning German preparations for action in Scandinavia had to be considered in the light of German capabilities, broadly defined. These assessments Ironside was perfectly prepared to make on his own, the more so as they fitted with the MI directorate's scepticism. Ironside, throughout the period of build-up towards the Norwegian campaign, refused to believe in the power of the German military to conduct a successful campaign in Scandinavia. He noted, for example, in his diary on 27 January 1940 that he doubted the Germans would go into Scandinavia, for they were not experts in overseas operations.[57] Similar comments abound in the diary.

The freedom that Ironside felt to apply his own thinking to northern front appreciations was a product of something more than egomania. His military experience, the responsibilities of his office, and his ambitions drove him on, but the gaps in War Office intelligence presented an irresistible vacuum. These gaps were of several kinds. First, War Office intelligence on future German intentions was, throughout the period of the Phoney War, quite sketchy. On one occasion Ironside complained directly about the lack of intelligence available about German activities with respect to Sweden and Scandinavia.[58] Second, military intelligence remained wedded, in this period, to a traditional and conservative view of the intelligence function. The bulk of its efforts were absorbed by the grinding task of producing order of battle intelligence, on the location, size, and disposition of German land forces.[59] In comparison with the concrete nature of this task, predictions of enemy intentions must have seemed a wildly abstract business. In addition, the military intelligence directorate, like its sister agencies in London, suffered from the highly compartmentalized intelligence structure which was another Whitehall tradition. In the War Office's case, this took the absurd form of a compartmentalization that restricted the intelligence interchange betweeen MI2, responsible for Scandinavia, and the more powerful MI3, with its German intelligence mandate.[60] In these conditions of fragmentation, when lines of communication were difficult even within a single service, it was only to be expected that a CIGS of the stature of Ironside, sure of his knowledge of European armies, would substitute his own wider judgements for an intelligence product that was hardly ever delivered to him.

Against these difficulties, it should be noted that the War Office intelligence system was, in relation to other service intelligence branches, relatively sophisticated in its handling of intelligence. As Hinsley has pointed out, the military intelligence branch was the only body in Whitehall in the 1939–40 period that even attempted to produce regular, integrated intelligence assessments, that would combine reports from more than one Whitehall department.[61] Its efforts in this direction were hindered by problems experienced with the Admiralty. But the War Office was routinely able to incorporate at least Foreign Office, SIS and air intelligence material, on a selective basis, into its appreciations.

War Office intelligence was thus, in many ways, in a state of transition. It continued to practise a relatively traditional and limited view of the nature and contribution of intelligence, yet it was alive to the importance of appreciations that took account of a broad range of evidence. It enjoyed a certain authority with the army high command on the basis of its apparently sound performance of a limited task. On this basis it provided an underpinning of data that was extremely susceptible to higher interpretation, for it was in no position, certainly, to challenge the broad judgements of an Ironside. The CIGS and his intelligence directorate thus lived in a mutually reinforcing world of hierarchical authority and delineated responsibilities. The CIGS supplied the framework of strategic vision into which the military intelligence people poured their findings. It was an arrangement that apparently suited both parties.

From 21 January 1940, the first occasion on which the MI branch attempted to assess German intentions towards Scandinavia, down to 8 April, as German troops were landing in Norway, War Office intelligence remained sceptical of the possibility of a German incursion into Scandinavia. This consistent judgement seems to have been derived, in part, from a dissatisfaction with the kinds of intelligence that reached the War Office pointing towards such a German attack. Much of it could easily be attributed to the rumour mill, which the War Office fought shy of after having experienced, and doubtless grown habituated to, its alarms since late 1938. The War Office may also have been waiting for the unattainable: a conclusive piece of evidence on which it could base certain judgement. Given the poor quality of British intelligence sources in the period, and the lengths which the German authorities went to retain their secrets, this was not only bad intelligence methodology, but impractical in the circumstances.

A further contributor to the War Office's failure to provide adequate warning about Norway derived from its work on order of battle intelligence, and from an apparently arbitrary assessment of the number of divisions that Germany would require in order to launch any Scandinavian adventure. This number was set at between 20 and 25 divisions.[62] At no time before April 1940 was the War Office able to discover more than twelve divisions concentrated in the Baltic and northern Germany; the usual number was between five and six divisions.[63] Germany, in fact, launched its assault on Norway with only six divisions. The War Office intelligence branch was thus looking for, and awaiting, an armada that was never to exist. Curiously, no special effort seems to have been made to watch the deployment of mountain divisions or of air-landing troops, though both types of units were understood to be vital to a German campaign in the region.

In the matter of providing a realistic warning of the dangers or imminence of a German attack on Norway, the War Office was as culpable as the Admiralty. The War Office's appreciation of 8 April 1940, written at a time when the German invasion was already under way, concluded that the available intelligence did not point definitively to a German attack.[64] This appreciation was the exact counterpart of the Naval intelligence division's better known blunder of 7 April. The Commander-in-Chief of the Home Fleet was sent a number of warnings about threatening German naval movements, including a precise warning about the German destroyer force that carried troops to Narvik, all blunted and robbed of urgency by the appended conclusion that 'all these reports are of doubtful value and may well be only a further move in the war of nerves'.[65]

Ironside noted in his diary on 8 April, that intelligence reports, especially air reconnaissance reports and warnings from Copenhagen, seemed to indicate that Germany was on the move against Norway. But he, like his directorate, was prepared to hedge the warnings, despite their abundance and clarity. He concluded that they would just have to wait and see, and that the apparent German reaction to the British mine-laying in Norwegian waters was a 'hullabaloo, probably'.[66]

It was not. Early on the morning of 9 April the Chiefs of Staff were woken by the astounding news that the Germans had pre-empted British plans for mine-laying and a protective occupation of selected Norwegian ports with a full-scale invasion. General Hastings Ismay (War Cabinet military secretary), the first recipient of the news, rather hilariously and unintelligibly delivered by a duty officer who had lost his false teeth in the dawn panic, afterwards recalled how he felt 'for the first time in my life, the devastating and demoralising effect of surprise'.[67]

That the British high command was taken so completely by surprise by German action in Norway may suggest that we are back in the realm of 'prevailing convictions and lazy assumptions' as the best available explanation. But in the case of Ironside and the Military Intelligence Directorate, convictions and assumptions, especially about the unlikelihood of a German assault, were embedded in the intelligence process and indistinguishable from it. The question of why the British were so certain that they could not be forestalled in Norway requires explanation from another direction.

### 'Not Made in Britain', Rigidity, Lessons of the Past and other Problems

The British failure of warning over Norway can be seen to rest, not on slack intelligence, but on the opposite, the construction of an unreal architecture of strategic ideas and supporting intelligence that was itself a product of Phoney War needs and pressures. A German pre-emptive strike against Norway was ruled out not because the British had any hard information one way or another about future German plans – they had not and appeared not to be bothered by this lacuna – but because such an attack ran counter to the whole edifice of British thinking. That Britain should, for once, enjoy the initiative in the Scandinavian theatre was a crucial prerequisite of British planning. If that initiative was lost, British plans, given the marginal forces on which they were based, could not succeed. And if the Scandinavian plan was unworkable, British strategists knew they were adrift on a sea of dangerous French *projets*, without an independent offensive option or anything approaching a war-winning strategy in the near future.[68] A powerful compulsion to believe thus was built up behind the idea of a blow struck in Scandinavia.

The need to believe in some plan of action simply because the alternatives are ghastly or unavailable, is far from a rare condition, for states or individuals. However, the British did not rest their planning merely on the comforting assumption that it would succeed because it had to, and because the Germans would do nothing to upset this necessity. Rather on this foundation a complex superstructure was laid. Load-bearing and ornamentation were both products of the strategic mentality of the Phoney War, as constructed in Britain. The search for a way to carry off a victorious short war that would avoid all parallels to the First World War, use maritime weapons of economic blockade and naval supremacy, and might hit the vulnerable German home front a paralysing or at least a weakening blow, all found justification in intelligence assessments and high command judgements.

The process by which the Scandinavian plan came to be invested with such high expectations – as the one blow that could end the war quickly – began with a Phoney War assumption of the primacy of economic warfare, and the related economic intelligence on the significance of Swedish iron ore to the German war industrial machine.[69] To this economic dimension were added more purely political and military rationales, which involved putting Germany on the defensive and waiting for the fissures to appear in the Nazi political and military structures.

The Admiralty's 'net assessment' was straightforward. Given the weaknesses of the German surface fleet, British seizure of the initiative in Scandinavian waters would rule out effective German counter-measures. The Air Ministry held to an opposite conclusion, and were all too aware of the Luftwaffe's relative advantages in Scandinavia over the RAF.[70] But throughout the planning for Scandinavia, the Air Ministry treated it as a 'sideshow', a distraction from the central business of the future strategic air offensive, and so failed to develop any effective dissent. For the War Office, the business of constructing a favourable intelligence assessment of the balance of forces in any putative Scandinavian campaign was more complex. It was recognised that a Scandinavian operation would require the projection of force across the North Sea and into difficult terrain, and would necessitate the use of under-equipped and under-trained soldiers, given the current state of British rearmament on land. The German Army had more than enough divisions and was much better placed to intervene in the region. The War Office assumed that Britain held the intitiative, on the grounds that the Third Reich would find it in its best interest to keep the iron ore flowing and Scandinavia peaceful for as long as possible.[71] German retaliation for a British strike at the iron ore routes was taken for granted but the issue of how and where was left dangerously unresolved.

In the end, and on the eve of the Norway campaign, it was felt that the most likely form of German retaliation would be an accelerated assault on the Western Front. Here the British may well have been reacting to German deception. Alternatively it was thought the Germans might mount an invasion of Sweden to occupy the iron ore mines directly and secure their supply routes across the Baltic.[72] The written instructions given to the commanders of the British forces for operation 'R4' that was mounted to secure a 'protective occupation' of the Norwegian ore terminus at Narvik, the more southerly ports of Bergen and Trondheim, and the important air base at Stavanger, provide telling evidence of British expectations. Only at Stavanger was it imagined that a British landing might be forestalled; the Bergen and Trondheim force commanders were given to understand that German pre-emption was judged most unlikely. The possibility was not even mentioned in the instructions to the Narvik commander, whose principal concern was to be how to handle incidents of Norwegian resistance.[73]

So the edifice of strategic assumption and supporting intelligence rose higher and higher. If the Germans chose to retaliate by an attack on the West, the prevailing opinion was that this would be an enormous gamble. If they retaliated by invading Sweden directly, the

Germans would face a campaign in difficult country and might not be
able to secure their objectives before the anticipated choke-hold on
iron-ore deliveries took effect. Even if they were successful on the
counter-attack, the Third Reich would have been forced into a
strategic diversion, which might raise political difficulties at home and
would keep the Wehrmacht away from more vulnerable fronts, either
in the West or in the Balkans or Middle East.

To these general lines of thought, Ironside added his own particular
convictions, more buttressing, about the benefits of a Scandinavian
campaign. From an early enthusiasm for Churchill's visionary plan of
action against the iron ore route from Norway, a spark that struck
Ironside's combustible soul in December 1939, Ironside developed a
set of ideas that moved the strategic argument well forward.[74] Whereas
the military intelligence directorate rested its case for the improbability
of German pre-emption in Norway largely on the grounds of an
absence of positive intelligence and on their own construction of
German rational thinking, Ironside brought the War Office closer into
line with insouciant Admiralty opinion by suggesting that Germany
would not simply be unlikely to resist British initial moves in Norway,
but unable. His arguments, revealed most thoroughly in his diary, were
based on his own reading of the military culture of the Third Reich. He
held a remarkably low opinion of German generalship in the Nazi era,
doubted the ability of Nazi planners to improvise or recover well from
shock, and assumed deep conflicts between the General Staff and
Hitler.[75] Ironside had his own ideas about Hitler too. He saw him as
unstable, profoundly unmilitary, and at bottom perhaps a coward.[76]

The more extravagant the judgements upon which British planning
was based, the more rigid did British thinking become, especially on
the all-important premises of the achievement of surprise and the
impossibility of German pre-emption. The sheer investment of time,
energy and hope in the Scandinavian project, as British planning
ground on through an unfriendly, cold winter, strengthened such
rigidity still further. Phoney War strategic assumptions and supporting
intelligence set hard in the shape of a single plan help explain why the
British would not take seriously the prospect of German interference.
Explaining why they could not take such an outcome seriously leads us
from rigidity to the 'not made in Britain' syndrome. The German
concept for Operation *Weserübung* (the occupation of Norway) was
certainly not made in Britain. The idea of gambling the existence of an
inferior surface fleet on operations in distant waters could not be
dreamed of by an Admiralty intent on preserving naval assets for the

nightmare possibility of a three-ocean war. Understanding that the Germans would count so completely on the achievement of surprise, and on the workings of an impenetrable security cover, required an almost impossible mental shift from the conditions of democratic to totalitarian war-making. While British willingness to respect the neutral rights of the Scandinavian states had worn very thin by April 1940, it was still an unimaginable step to the kind of political subversion, allied with all-out military assault where necessary that the Third Reich incorporated in *Weserübung*. The surprise and shock of a plan 'not made in Britain' carried over into the actual conduct of the campaign and set poorly equipped British forces in central Norway reeling. The speed of German offensive operations, the imaginative and daring use of air transport, the effectiveness of air power in a ground support role were all fresh lessons, glimpsed at second-hand perhaps in Poland, but learned directly in Norway and too soon after in France.

No two intelligence failures are precisely alike. This takes the sting somewhat from Richard Betts' now orthodox thesis that intelligence failures are inevitable.[77] The one that befell Britain over Norway in 1940 cannot be seen, so the argument goes here, as a function of failure understood simply within the confines of the intelligence 'cycle' of collection, assessment and reportage. Rather it was a product of the sorry combination of an intelligence system still in transition from pre-war weakness and methods with a set of strategic concepts for fighting a 'Phoney' War that were alluring in their promise to provide victory without the historical costs associated with total war. The ultimate irony of the Norway campaign was that an act of historical evasion raised so many ghosts. The memory of Gallipoli could not be shaken from the anxious deliberations about risking the British fleet and precious regular army units in a direct assault on Trondheim. Further north General Pat Mackesy, in charge of the land forces sent to expel the Germans from Narvik, refused to bow to pressure from his naval commander and, notoriously, from Winston Churchill, to attempt an opposed landing by his troops from open boats across snow-covered beaches against machine-guns and pillboxes. He wired that he would not be responsible for leading his Guards brigade into another Passchendaele.[78] The British were trying hard to avoid the past. The Germans were trying something simpler – to avoid having a flank turned and a major source of vital raw materials cut off. In this discrepancy of aims also lay the elements of intelligence failure. Misconception, in this case, was the adoption of a false angle on history.

NOTES

1. Harold Evans, *Good Times, Bad Times* (New York, 1984), p. 43.
2. The list would include Ralph Bennett, *Ultra in the West: The Normandy Campaign of 1944–45* (London, 1979) and *Ultra and Mediterranean Strategy* (New York, 1989); Robert Cecil, *A Divided Life: A Biography of Donald MacLean* (London, 1988); F.H. Hinsley *et al.*, *British Intelligence in the Second World War*, 4 vols. (London, 1979–90); and Hugh Trevor-Roper (Lord Dacre), *Hermit of Peking: The Hidden Life of Sir Edmund Backhouse* (London, 1978) and *The Philby Affair: Espionage, Treason and the Secret Services* (London, 1968). Bennett and Hinsley served in British signals intelligence with the Government Code and Cipher School at Bletchley Park; Cecil and Trevor-Roper worked for SIS.
3. The works consulted for this section include 'British Intelligence and the Coming of the Second World War in Europe', in Ernest R. May (ed.), *Knowing One's Enemies: Intelligence Assessments before the Two World Wars* (Princeton, 1984), pp. 237–70; 'British Military Perceptions of the Soviet Union as a Strategic Threat, 1945–1950', in Josef Becker and Franz Knipping (eds), *Power in Europe?: Great Britain, France, Italy and Germany in a Postwar World 1945–1950* (Berlin, 1986), pp. 325–36; 'Fall-Out from Treachery: Peter Wright and the Spycatcher Case', *The Political Quarterly*, 59, No. 2 (April–June 1988), pp. 206–18; 'Francis Herbert King: A Soviet Source in the Foreign Office', *Intelligence and National Security*, 3, No. 4 (Oct. 1988), pp. 62–82; 'Intelligence and the Historian', *Diplomatic History*, 14, No. 2 (Spring 1990), pp. 199–204 ; 'Intelligence Studies: The Emergence of a British School', *Intelligence and National Security*, 3, No. 2 (April 1988), pp. 338–41; 'An Intelligence Surprise: The Failure of the Foreign Office to Anticipate the Nazi-Soviet Pact', *Intelligence and National Security*, 4, No. 3 (July 1989), pp. 512–34; 'Misinformation, Misconception, Mistrust: Episodes in British Policy and the Approach of War, 1938–1939', in Michael Bentley and David Stevenson (eds), *High and Low Politics in Britain: Ten Studies* (Oxford, 1983), pp. 214–54.
4. This approach is displayed most fully in Watt, 'British Intelligence'.
5. Ibid., p. 261.
6. Ibid.
7. Here, Watt is in agreement with some classic texts in the genre, especially Roberta Wohlstetter, *Pearl Harbor, Warning and Decision* (Stanford, 1962), as well as with Richard K. Betts, 'Analysis, War and Decision-Making: Why Intelligence Failures are Inevitable', *World Politics*, 31 (1978), pp. 61–89; the Betts approach has recently been criticized as the 'no fault school' in Eliot A. Cohen and John Gooch, *Military Misfortunes: The Anatomy of Failure in War* (New York, 1990).
8. Watt, 'An Intelligence Surprise', p. 521.
9. Watt, 'Misinformation', p. 253.
10. Watt, 'British Military Perceptions', p. 326.
11. See Watt, 'Intelligence Studies', and the essays by Roy Godson and John Bruce Lockhart in K.G. Robertson (ed.), *British and American Approaches to Intelligence* (London, 1987).
12. Watt, 'Intelligence Studies'.
13. On defeatism, see Watt's reply to John Gaddis, 'Intelligence and the Historian'; the study of the Soviet agent is in 'Francis Herbert King'.
14. Lord Stabolgi, *Narvik and After: A Study of the Scandinavian Campaign* (London, 1940), p. 63.
15. Ibid., pp. 64–5.
16. Hankey's review is discussed in F.H. Hinsley, *et al.*, *British Intelligence in the Second World War*, Vol. 1 (London, 1979), pp. 91–2.
17. SIS, 'The Scandinavian Invasion', 14 April 1940, PREM 1/435. (Unless otherwise noted, all document references are to papers held in the Public Record Office, Kew, UK).
18. Hankey to Sir Horace Wilson, 29 April 1940, ibid.
19. Sir Horace Wilson to Neville Chamberlain, 30 April, 1940 and subsequent correspondence in ibid.
20. General Sir Edmund Ironside's unpublished manuscript diary, entry for 10 April 1940 (henceforth cited as Ironside diary). All quotations are by permission of Lord Ironside.
21. Ibid., 9 April 1940.

22. On the impact of the Norway campaign on Ironside's career, see Wesley K. Wark, 'Ironside: The Fate of Churchill's First General' in Brian Bond (ed.), *Fallen Stars* (London, 1992). For a somewhat different assessment of Ironside's career during 1939–40, see Brian Bond, 'Ironside', in John Keegan (ed.), *Churchill's Generals* (London, 1991).
23. T.K. Derry, *The Campaign in Norway* (London, 1952), p. 233.
24. Ibid.
25. Stephen Roskill, *The War at Sea 1939–1945. Vol. One: The Defensive* (London, 1954), p. 19.
26. Ibid., pp. 159-160. Roskill's extended post-war correspondence with British naval commanders provides much additional illumination on the conduct of operations in the Second World War. His papers are held at Churchill College, Cambridge.
27. Donald McLachlan, *Room 39: A Study in Naval Intelligence* (New York, 1968).
28. Hinsley, *British Intelligence*, I, Chs. 3–4.
29. This suggestion is advanced by Watt in his essay, 'British Intelligence', cited in note 3.
30. Hinsley, I, p. 124 and Appendix: 'The SIS Air Photographic Unit'.
31. Ibid.; Ursula Powys-Lybbe, *The Eye of Intelligence* (London, 1983), p. 28.
32. Hinsley, I, p. 123 and footnote.
33. Ibid., p. 137 ff.
34. Basil Collier, *Hidden Weapons: Allied Secret or Undercover Services in World War Two* (London, 1982), p. 69, contains a useful summary of the final spate of warnings received in London.
35. Martin Gilbert, *Finest Hour: Winston S. Churchill 1939–1941* (London, 1983), pp. 217–23 provides a detailed account of the flow of news from Norway and government reactions on 9 April.
36. Hinsley, I, p. 98.
37. Ibid., p. ix.
38. Ibid., p. 120.
39. Collier, pp. 65–9.
40. Patrick Beesly, *Very Special Admiral: The Life of Admiral J.H. Godfrey* (London, 1980), p. 156.
41. Beesly used, for this purpose, the diary of Captain Ralph Edwards, Director of Operations Division (Home Waters) in the Admiralty. The Edwards diary is now held at Churchill College Archives, Cambridge. See also Beesly's more general recounting of naval intelligence problems regarding Norway in his *Very Special Intelligence: The Story of the Admiralty's Operational Intelligence Centre in World War Two* (London, 1978).
42. Aileen Clayton, *The Enemy is Listening: The Story of the Y Service* (London, 1980); Powys-Lybbe, *The Eye of Intelligence*; the earlier memoir by Constance Babington-Smith, *Evidence in Camera; the Story of Photographic Intelligence in World War Two* (London, 1957) remains useful.
43. Olivier Desarzens, *Nachrichtendienstliche Aspeckte der 'Weserübung' 1940* (Osnabruck, 1988).
44. Hinsley, I, p. 125.
45. The best short analysis of intelligence failures is Betts, 'Analysis, War and Decision-Making'. The theoretical and historical literature on this phenomenon is surprisingly large. In addition to Betts, useful studies are Michael Handel, *The Diplomacy of Surprise* (Cambridge, MA, 1981) and Ephraim Kam, *Surprise Attack: The Victim's Perspective* (Cambridge, MA, 1989).
46. For Chamberlain's use of intelligence, his weekly missive to his sisters is a valuable source. See Neville Chamberlain papers, NC 18/1, University of Birmingham Library. Christopher Andrew, 'Churchill and Intelligence', *Intelligence and National Security*, 3, No. 3 (July 1988), pp. 181–93, reprinted in Michael Handel (ed.), *Leaders and Intelligence* (London, 1989), attempts to summarize Churchill's special place in the evolution of British intelligence.
47. A censored and partial selection of the Ironside diaries was published by his military assistant, Colonel Roderick Macleod, and Denis Kelly (eds), *The Ironside Diaries 1937–1940* (London, 1962). The author is at work on a biography of Ironside, based on the original manuscript diaries.
48. The story was written up by *Times'* journalist and former ADC to Ironside, Ralph Arnold, 'Two Assignments', *Blackwood's Magazine* (Nov. 1966), pp. 385–99. A manuscript account of Ironside's secret service work survives in the papers of Colonel R. Macleod (Macleod 2),

Liddell Hart Centre for Military Archives, King's College, London.

49. Geoffrey Powell, 'John Buchan's Richard Hannay', *History Today*, 37 (August 1987), pp. 32–9.

50. A critical view of Churchill's role as First Lord of the Admiralty is provided by Stephen Roskill, *Churchill and the Admirals* (London, 1977). In a similar vein is Corelli Barnett, *Engage the Enemy more Closely: The Royal Navy in the Second World War* (New York, 1991), Chs. 3–5.

51. MI3 appreciation, 11 Dec. 1939, W[ar] O[ffice] 190/885; Ironside diary, 13 Dec. 1939.

52. Hinsley, I, p. 116; Ironside diary, 5 Jan. 1940.

53. For the development of German planning, see Walter Hubatsch, *Die Deutsche Besetzung von Daenemark und Norwegen 1940* (Göttingen, 1960); François Kersuady, *Norway, 1940* (London, 1990); Klaus Maier *et al.*, *Germany and the Second World War, Vol. II: Germany's Initial Conquests in Europe* (Oxford, 1991); and E.F. Ziemke, *The German Northern Theatre of Operations* (Washington, 1959).

54. A useful summary of British planning is in J.R.M. Butler, *Grand Strategy, Vol. II* (London, 1957), Ch. V; also Kersaudy, Chs. 1 and 3.

55. Desarzens is a well-documented source on German intelligence.

56. WO 190/891, 21 Jan. 1940; Hinsley, I, pp. 117–18.

57. Ironside diary, 27 Jan. 1940.

58. Ibid., 15 Feb. 1940.

59. The pre-war doctrine of the military intelligence directorate is considered in Wesley K. Wark, *The Ultimate Enemy: British Intelligence and Nazi Germany 1933–1939* (Ithaca, New York, 1985), pp. 237–40.

60. Hinsley, I, p. 120.

61. Ibid., p. 111.

62. MI3 report, 11 Dec. 1939, WO 190/885.

63. The high figure of 12 was reported by the British military attaché in Copenhagen on the night of 4–5 April 1940, see Hinsley, I, p. 123; Collier, p. 67.

64. MI3 appreciation, 'The Possibilities of German Action against Scandinavia', WO 190/891, 8 April 1940.

65. Hinsley, I, pp. 122–3; Beesly, *Very Special Admiral*, argues that the interpretation placed on the intelligence was not the work of the NID, or Godfrey, but of the operations staff in the Admiralty. The evidence for this assertion is unclear, but if true would suggest a strong analogy between Norway and a similar intelligence failure, 24 years earlier, at Jutland.

66. Ironside diary, 8 April 1940.

67. Lord Ismay, *Memoirs* (London, 1960), p. 119.

68. Such fears were brought to the surface especially in successive Supreme War Council meetings during 1939 and 1940. British reaction to a French plan for the capture of Petsamo and Murmansk, as mooted at the Supreme War Council meeting on 5 February 1940, is typical: SWC (40) 1, 5 Feb. 1940, CAB 99/3.

69. The British government was highly impressed by reports of Germany's dependence on Swedish iron ore reports that came from the Ministry of Economic Warfare and from the émigré German industrialist, Fritz Thyssen. See the MEW report for the Cabinet in WP(G) (39) 162, 18 Dec. 1939, CAB 67/3. The Thyssen report was discussed at length at the Supreme War Council meeting on 19 December in Paris, SWC 4, CAB 99/3. On this issue see the valuable study by Thomas Munch-Petersen, *The Strategy of Phoney War: Britain, Sweden and the Iron Ore Question, 1939–1940* (Stockholm, 1981).

70. The principal air staff opponent of British intervention in Scandinavia was (then) Group Captain John Slessor, head of the plans branch of the Air Ministry and a member of the Joint Planning committee. In his memoir, Slessor wrote 'this whole Scandinavian idea was magnificent, but it was not war', Marshal of the Royal Air Force Sir John Slessor, *The Central Blue* (London, 1956), p. 275.

71. This assumption appears in a number of Chiefs of Staff studies and in Ironside's diary. It was first laid down in the major early study by the COS of Scandinavian strategy, COS (39) 181, 'Military Implications of a Policy Aimed at Stopping the Export of Swedish Iron Ore to Germany', 31 Dec. 1939, CAB 80/6. In this paper the COS were careful to draw the War Cabinet's attention to the assumption that Britain would hold the initiative and that Germany

would not wish to disrupt the status quo in the north.

72. COS(40) 276(S), 'Certain Operations, Memorandum by the CIGS', 3 April 1940 and COS(40) 279(S), 'Policy Regarding Forces for Scandinavia', 4 April, 1940, CAB 80/105.
73. COS(40) 268(JP)(S), 'Certain Operations in Norwegian Territorial Waters', 29 March 1939; COS revision of report, COS(40) 269(S), 31 March 1940, CAB 80/104; and COS(40) 277(S), 'Plan R.4: Instructions to Commanders', 4 April 1940, in CAB 80/105.
74. Although he rejected earlier plans for British intervention in Norway as 'sideshows', Ironside was very taken by Churchill's project, as revealed to him in mid-December 1939. Churchill, Ironside enthused, had wonderfully 'big ideas', Ironside diary, 18 Dec. 1939.
75. Ironside's views on the German army are discussed in Wark, 'Ironside: The Fate of Churchill's First General'. Evidence for these views is contained in numerous entries in the Ironside diary, the earliest being a remark on 14 Nov. 1939.
76. Ironside diary, entries for 30 Dec. 1939; 17, 24 Feb., 2 and 30 March 1940.
77. Betts, 'Analysis, War and Decision-Making'.
78. Mackesy stated that he would not agree to the 'snows of Narvik being turned into another version of the mud of Passchendaele', quoted in Derry, p. 152. The official history of the campaign hints obliquely at the near-mutinous state of the military commanders on the spot, ibid.

# Weizmann, Ben-Gurion and the 1946 Crisis in the Zionist Movement

## NORMAN ROSE

One of the conventional wisdoms of Zionist historiography runs – in a somewhat dramatic and colourful form – as follows. At the Zionist Congress in December 1946, Chaim Weizmann, the venerable leader of the World Zionist Organization, was rejected by the movement he had nursed to political maturity. Ousted from the presidency, his fall signalled the end of an era. Weizmann's reputation, once without equal, was no longer sufficient to ward off the barrage of criticism aimed against him. Old beyond his years, exhausted and in ill-health, Weizmann, the inveterate Anglophile, the compromiser and trimmer who had sold his Zionist soul for a mess of British pottage, was no longer suited to, or capable of, running the affairs of the movement. The age of 'activism' had arrived. A new leader was needed: young, dynamic, proud, rooted in the ethos of the Yishuv, in step with the prevailing currents in international affairs. And lo and behold, history had yielded its man of destiny: the new torchbearer of Zionism appeared in the imposing, heroic figure of Ben-Gurion. The demise of Weizmann and 'diplomatic Zionism' and the rise of 'fighting Zionism' and Ben-Gurion was the historic step that led, in May 1948, to the establishment of the State of Israel.

'Crisis' is a well-worn word in Zionist terminology. Ever since its inception as a political movement Zionism – at least in the eyes of the Zionists – has existed in a state of 'permanent crisis'. Still, the terrible circumstances that prevailed at the end of the Second World War gave special and awful meaning to that hackneyed expression. The decimation of European Jewry; the burning necessity of resolving the Jewish refugee problem; and the refusal of Britain – still the Mandatary power – to abrogate the hated May 1939 White Paper lent the term 'crisis' a stark and cruel reality. It was abundantly clear that Zionist affairs were moving towards a climax.

Two weeks after Germany surrendered, on 22 May 1945, Weizmann approached Winston Churchill. 'This is the hour to eliminate the White Paper,' he wrote, 'to open the doors of Palestine, and to proclaim the Jewish State.'[1] The Zionist demand for a state was unequivocal. But it was met by a hostile refusal on the part of the Palestine Arabs who insisted on a unitary Palestinian state with minority rights for Jews, a position tacitly upheld by the Labour government in their adherence to the White Paper. The British Cabinet and its military and political advisers – with few exceptions – believed that to surrender to Zionist demands would be contrary to British imperial interests, and could be fatal to Britain's world role.

Ernest Bevin, the British Foreign Secretary, told the Cabinet defence committee in 1946 that 'without the Middle East and its oil . . . I see no hope of our being able to achieve the standard of living at which we are aiming in Great Britain', and Attlee made much the same point in January 1947.[2] How to break up this Anglo-Arab alliance and persuade or cajole the British to adopt a pro-Zionist policy was the key question facing Zionist policy-makers in the post-war era.

For Weizmann, direct military confrontation with Britain was out of the question. It was not only foreign to his political outlook, it was also, in the given balance of power between the Zionist movement and Britain, totally impracticable. To have done so would have been to recklessly mortgage the future of Zionism, the Yishuv, and the Jewish people. But this did not exclude pressing Britain for increased immigration and Jewish land settlement. Weizmann's way to achieve Zionist goals was to reach a *modus vivendi* with the Great Powers, in particular with Britain, through negotiation. But the results of his diplomacy would be influenced by day-to-day events in Palestine.

Since the mid-1930s Weizmann had steadily grown disillusioned with the direction of British policy. At the beginning of 1938 he had considered an emergency, crash programme 'to buy more land, occupy it and hold it'. Later in the year he declared his 'uncompromising hostility to Britain [he meant, of course, British policy] – to work, silently at first, toward arming and preparation, which in time (he knew not how long) would enable Jewry to pursue its own policy in the Middle East.'[3] His statements do not indicate that Weizmann was planning a *coup d'état* against the Mandatary power, but they do reflect his resentment as British policy and his angry disenchantment with those who formulated it. By the end of the war he knew that a confrontation with Britain was inevitable, as his letter to Churchill and the answer it received plainly demonstrates. But the question remained: what kind of confrontation? Despite his feelings, Weizmann knew that there was no substitute for Britain as a negotiating partner, if a political solution were to be attained. Weizmann applied himself to this issue in the following months.

Matters were further complicated by the international situation. The Soviet Union was now a dominant force and was perceived to threaten not only western Europe, but also the Near and Middle East. With the Americans – to the chagrin of the British – thinking in terms of retreat from Europe,[4] Britain was forced into the position of acting as the main bulwark against Soviet encroachment. But it was in no position to do so effectively. Virtually bankrupt, dependent upon American aid, saddled with added responsibilities in Europe, its Empire rent by belligerent nationalisms, Britain had a Labour government that was committed to a far-reaching programme of economic and social reform.[5] It was equally committed to revolutionary changes in Britain's imperial structure, namely the retreat from India and Burma – by far the most momentous event in the post-war history of the British Empire. With India gone, would not Egypt, Palestine and other British possessions in the area attain even greater importance for Britain as it attempted to maintain its role as a Great Power? Britain sought to preserve its position in the Arab and Muslim world, a holding-action in view of its shrinking resources. No leading British politician envisaged, or would countenance, Britain falling into the ranks of the second-rate powers.

It was through these minefields that the Zionist leadership had to pick its way. For almost a generation Weizmann had led the Zionist movement. He had led it to its greatest political triumphs: the Balfour Declaration and the ratification of the mandate. He had established, virtually single-handed, the enlarged Jewish Agency. He had succeeded, after the disastrous Passfield episode, in obtaining the MacDonald letter that guaranteed the development of the Yishuv during the critical 1930s. Weizmann's reputation was high. Regarded as a Zionist statesman – and not merely as a hack politician – by those world leaders with whom he came into contact, he related to them on a basis of equality, confident of his past achievements and moral stature.

The reasons for his success are not difficult to discern. He was a spellbinder. Possessed of immense personal charm, he could with equal facility captivate an audience with a bewitching mixture of paradox and ironic wit, or drown opponents in a sea of withering scorn. Beware of Weizmann, Anthony Eden once warned, 'he would see ministers and turn them inside out'. In the words of Sir Isaiah Berlin, he was 'an irresistible political seducer'.[6] But charisma alone does not guarantee political success. A scientist by training, Weizmann also possessed an artist's sense of timing. Politics, he once explained, 'is a matter of *Fingerspitzengefühl* [instinct, intuition]'.[7] Without losing sight of his goals, Weizmann knew when to press his advantage and when to retreat with grace – hoping to make up for lost ground when conditions and circumstances changed. He often said that it was better to obtain 70 per cent of something than 100 per cent of nothing – much to the fury of his more forthright colleagues, to say nothing of his opponents. Like Bismarck, he firmly believed that 'politics is the art of the possible'.

Weizmann saw Zionism as a genuine movement of national redemption and liberation. 'Zion shall be redeemed with judgement, and her converts with righteousness,' he often proclaimed.[8] This was Weizmann's lodestar, his guiding philosophy. Morover, it was an outlook that fitted in with the Great Powers' conception of Zionism. This is crucial to understanding Weizmann's policy. His most substantial triumphs were obtained when Zionism – his brand of Zionism – marched in unison with the Powers. Co-operation blended with compromise was his recipe for success. Conditions did not always allow this formula to work itself out – as he had bitterly discovered ever since the crisis of 1929–31. But if confrontation could not be avoided, it would be spiced with Weizmann's special brand of pragmatic, humane and ethical Zionism.

Despite his record, by 1946 cynics might have claimed that Weizmann's best days were behind him. He was no longer the 'benevolent despot' of the 1920s whose word had been well-nigh law. Now his position was precarious, his policies questioned, his every act scrutinized. In his autocratic way he had neglected over the years to create a political machine to back his policies. Rather, he relied upon a group (his critics called it a 'court') of devoted advisers. Talented, inventive, proficient, they were 'super-bureaucrats', not policy-makers, who represented no challenge to Weizmann as leader.

Since the mid-1930s, Weizmann had relied mainly upon Mapai for support. Less a love affair than a marriage of convenience, the relationship was useful to both parties. London and Jerusalem were competing as centres of political power, with the balance moving visibly towards Jerusalem. Although they were in broad agreement over general principles of Zionist policy, Weizmann and Mapai viewed each other with mutual suspicion. Put briefly, Weizmann regarded most Mapai leaders as 'country bumpkins', particularly in the delicate field of *haute diplomatique*. For its part, Mapai never fully trusted Weizmann, believing that he was too wedded to the British view and too set in his ways to change.[9] Moreover, Mapai possessed in Ben-Gurion a young and dynamic leader, ambitious and ruthless, who was able and willing to challenge Weizmann for leadership of the movement.[10] Without Mapai, Weizmann was powerless. But Mapai began to feel that it could manage comfortably – even if with less panache – without Weizmann.

Weizmann had lost ground among the British as well. Attlee and Bevin, the current arbiters of British policy, were far removed from Weizmann's world of drawing-room politics. He did not have the rapport with them he had had with their predecessors. Attlee, taciturn and calculating, was a poor substitute compared with the enthusiastic and volatile Lloyd George. Nor could Bevin, a trade union boss, coarse of tongue and brutal in manner, match up to the sophisticated, philosophical Balfour. They were 'Pharaohs who know not Joseph'.[11] The environment of the post-war world was harsh, and Weizmann appeared in it as anachronistic and old-fashioned to some observers.

In 1946 Weizmann was 72 years old. His health was failing. Never physically robust, he was now more prone than ever to bouts of depression – his 'fogs' – and to periodic spells of long recuperation in rest-homes. In 1944 he had contracted glaucoma, which left him half-blind. The war had also taken a personal toll; Michael, his youngest and favourite son, was killed in action. His wife, Vera, never recovered from this blow and this, too, affected Weizmann. Vera's influence extended to other spheres and her presence did not always soothe Weizmann. These factors must have caused some to wonder whether Weizmann was still capable of guiding the fortunes of the Zionist movement at its moment of supreme crisis.

By the end of the war, Weizmann was no longer the master of Zionist policy but its servant. This became clear at the London conference of Zionists held in August 1945. Against Weizmann's wishes, a policy of active resistance to reinforce the diplomatic struggle was decided upon. Weizmann believed such a policy to be 'irresponsible'. But the delegates rebuffed his arguments. Subjected to a barrage of criticism, observers thought that he 'handled the Conference badly, pouring "iced water"' on the delegates' hopes for a

Jewish state when all they could stand was 'tepid water'.[12] By autumn
1945 the United Jewish Resistance movement was set up to implement
the new, tougher line.[13] Weizmann was being shunted aside. The
emphasis of Zionist policy was changing. But it was still, despite these
substantial deviations, a policy largely Weizmann's own invention.

The key political issue facing the Zionists was partition. All were
agreed upon the necessity of a Jewish state. But what kind of state?
Would it encompass all of Mandatary Palestine? Or would it be a
partition of Palestine, along, as they hoped, an improved Peel line?
Weizmann's attitude was unequivocal. He believed in partition
because he believed that, given the circumstances, to insist upon the
whole of Mandatary Palestine would not be practical – though as a
starting-point in negotiations, it could be a legitimate ploy – and might
fatally damage the Zionist interest. He had held this view ever since the
idea of partition was first put to him at the beginning of 1937.

Partition – indeed any political solution – implied continued
diplomatic contact with Britain. Again, Weizmann's stand was clear.
Britain was the responsible power and, therefore, any agreement had
to be negotiated with it, however difficult and humiliating the task.
There was no alternative. It was axiomatic to Weizmann that
diplomacy could not be conducted through boycott or by issuing
ultimatums or by crying 'No!' all the time. That had been the Arabs'
mistake. Here were shades of differences between Weizmann and Ben-
Gurion. After the Biltmore conference of May 1942, these issues had
exploded into a furious personal quarrel, with Ben-Gurion clearly out
to seize Weizmann's crown.

In terms of policy, this fierce debate turned on how both leaders saw
the future of the British Empire, the enlarged role of the United States,
and how to relate Zionist strategy to these developments. Convinced
that governments do not keep their promises, Ben-Gurion argued
for self-reliance, for an independent line, one to be implemented
immediately. The Jews, he claimed, could rely on no one but themselves. Ben-Gurion asserted that the British Empire was doomed and
that the United States would inherit its role as the greatest force in the
world. It was vital, therefore, to shift the emphasis of Zionist work to
America and to harness America's mighty resources to the Zionist cause.
A combination of American and Zionist pressure would bring the British
to their knees and hence to their senses. Only then would it reach an
acceptable accommodation with the Zionists. 'The aim of the war [against
Britain],' he wrote, 'will have to be to obtain England's support.'
'Fighting Zionism', as now propounded by Ben-Gurion, envisaged

mass immigration (two million Jews in a year or two), the establishment
of a Jewish defence force to fight either the Arabs or the British or both,
and not only to demand a Jewish state, but to create it if necessary.[14]

Weizmann had recognized America's rise since the days of the
Balfour Declaration. He also anticipated the demise of the British
Empire; in particular, he foresaw the loss of India. This would lead to a
restructuring of the British Empire and re-ordering of imperial
priorities. British imperial activity would henceforth concentrate on
Africa, and here 'The vicinity of Palestine, just across the Suez Canal,
may prove a great boon'.[15] But Weizmann admitted that he did not
know where the emphasis of Zionist activity should be concentrated.
Would the United States retreat into isolation after the Second World
War as it had in 1919? There were powerful forces in the United States
pulling in such a direction. But to promote Ben-Gurion's revolutionary
programme in 1942–43, with Britain engaged in a titanic struggle
against Nazi Germany, would be not only morally reprehensible but
also totally counter-productive. In these circumstances, it was
reasonable to argue, as Weizmann did, that it was vital to maintain
contacts on both sides of the Atlantic. His arguments, logical and
dispassionate, gained the assent of a majority of Zionist opinion.[16]

At the time, Ben-Gurion called for Weizmann's resignation,
claiming that Weizmann was too autocratic and not to be trusted when
talking to the British. He never could say '"no" to an Englishman',
Ben-Gurion claimed. When Weizmann acts alone he can do
'incalculable harm': when confronted with a new situation, 'he does
not always grasp realities . . . and may give an unexpected answer
without realizing what it means. He wants always to seem reasonable
and not only to be reasonable to an Englishman'. These remarks –
intentional or not – came close to suggesting that Weizmann was
approaching senility. Naturally, Weizmann rejected the accusations 'in
toto', turning Ben-Gurion's phrase, indicting his accuser of always
'seeming to be unreasonable'. Ben-Gurion's statements were no more
than the product of 'a sick imagination – the imagination of a man who
suffers from sleepless nights and is worried', and they amounted to 'an
act of political assassination'. But rest assured, Weizmann comforted
Ben-Gurion, 'the future corpse is not worried'.[17]

In the summer and autumn of 1946 Ben-Gurion returned to these
charges, if somewhat toned down. After the Zionist Congress of
December 1946 he told the British that Weizmann's defeat had
resulted from 'his blind trust in Britain'.[18] Whether Ben-Gurion
believed what he said is arguable. It is more likely that by damning

Weizmann's 'watered-down' version of Zionism he was boosting his own brand of 'fighting' Zionism. In January 1936, for example, Ben-Gurion had noted that Weizmann 'told the [High] Commissioner [Sir Arthur Wauchope] things no English ear has heard. I do not know if a representative of a larger, stronger, armed, and more forceful nation could have allowed himself to speak in such a manner to an English representative'. When tempers had cooled, Ben-Gurion wrote:

Weizmann's moderation was evident only when he spoke to us, to his brethren, to the Zionists, at our Congress, for he knew our limits. But Weizmann was neither moderate nor humble when he spoke to the non-Jewish world. I was often present when he spoke to Cabinet Ministers and to those in high places, and I was always astounded by the inner forcefulness, sometimes even aggressiveness, of his manner.[19]

Ben-Gurion stood alone in the controversy of 1942–43, an isolated and misunderstood figure. Even his closest colleagues and admirers found it difficult to justify his perverse behaviour, both on personal and political grounds. He returned to Palestine to consolidate his forces and prepare for the next round. Weizmann, reduced to a state of nervous exhaustion from the row, retired to a Jewish rest-home in the Catskills to recuperate.

But perhaps there were deeper reasons for Weizmann's rejection of Ben-Gurion's programme. For Ben-Gurion's independent Zionist policy, however clumsily and brutally put, implied an anti-British line. Could Weizmann himself lead the movement if ever the conditions should ripen for implementing it? Was it not too foreign to his political outlook for him to execute? Had he the necessary reserves of energy to see the programme through? He must have sensed that time was against him, that the war years had unleashed forces beyond his control, and that his long period of leadership was drawing to a close.

By 1946 these disputes had sharpened. Preparations were afoot for the coming war against the Arabs and the struggle with Britain. 'Illegal' immigration was mounting, new settlements were being established, all in defiance of British regulations. Relations with Britain had reached a crisis. Ben-Gurion's wild prophecies of 1942 had come home to roost, and Weizmann had to adapt himself to a situation in which he had lost a large measure of control. On one grave issue, the question of purported 'activism', he took an uncompromising stand. His opposition to this aspect of Zionist policy has been much misunderstood and earned him a great deal of abuse and vilification. It is therefore worthy of clarification.[20]

What did Weizmann mean by 'activism'? 'Political violence,' he wrote at the end of June 1946, 'is one and indivisible. It is a method; and it is both inconsistent and useless to condemn one single act unless the whole method is discarded.'[21] He was remonstrating against the escalation in violence that had swept Palestine with the establishment of the United Jewish Resistance Movement.[22] Weizmann was utterly opposed to any form of co-operation with the Irgun and the Stern Gang, whom he considered terrorists. On this point he would brook no compromise. He abhorred the anarchy of terrorism – an insidious, corrupting manifestation of the nationalism he upheld. If allowed to flourish, it would tear apart the moral and political fabric of Zionism. He declared:

Assassination, ambush, kidnapping, the murder of innocent men, are alien to the spirit of our movement. We came to Palestine to build, not to destroy; terror distorts the essence of Zionism. It insults our history; it mocks the ideals for which a Jewish society must stand; it sullies our banner; it compromises our appeal to the world's liberal conscience.[23]

Ultimately, he saw terror as acts of desperate, irresponsible men who brought their cause into disrepute. Above all, he regarded terror as morally corrupting and politically counter-productive, a suicidal combination. He never deviated from this view.

By August 1946 the United Jewish Resistance Movement had been disbanded. Weizmann, on the brink of despair, had issued an ultimatum that he would resign his office unless the Haganah ceased all further joint operations with the terrorists. His threat carried sufficient weight to convince a majority of his colleagues, some of whom had also concluded that their alliance with extremists was proving harmful. Weizmann had succeeded in imposing his moral authority on the Haganah and the Jewish Agency; the Irgun and the Stern Gang went their own way, dragging the movement down to the level of the Mufti and his cohorts.

Weizmann's 'activism' centred on illegal immigration and the continuation of Jewish settlement.[24] These actions stood at the centre of the Zionist endeavour. Moreover, by their scope and nature they revealed the character of a genuine national struggle. Weizmann was not opposed in principle to military action to aid directly immigration and settlement. But Weizmann knew this was treading dangerous ground, for the line between legitimate military action and gratuitous violence was thin. There were occasions when the Haganah stretched

Weizmann's meaning of 'activism' to breaking-point; but on the whole these were transgressions that he could live with.

In Weizmann's order of priorities activism was subordinate to the demands of the political situation. He would not allow the 'activist tail' to wag the 'political dog', particularly as political work in the post-war years did not ease. Quite the contrary, the Anglo-American Committee of Inquiry; the United Nations Special Committee on Palestine, on-going negotiations with the Americans and the British, and contacts at the United Nations, all gave an added fillip to the importance of Zionist diplomacy. In this sphere, no one was more suited than Weizmann to advance the Zionist cause. But the Jewish Agency Executive had to make up its mind. It could not conduct an undeclared war against British authorities in Palestine and at the same time negotiate a political settlement with the British government in London. In a national struggle, he told Yigal Allon, the young commander of the Palmach, 'it is permitted to act when necessary and also to refrain when necessary'.[25]

By July–August 1946 the 'activist' policy that combined military pressure in Palestine with intensive lobbying in the United States to persuade the Truman administration to wean the British away from their anti-Zionist policy had failed. The British were angered by these methods. Attlee had effectively killed the Committee of Inquiry's report by conditioning its implementation on the disarming of the Yishuv.[26] The British had taken severe umbrage at Truman for endorsing – without consulting them beforehand – the Committee's recommendation to admit immediately 100,000 Jewish refugees into Palestine, particularly as it was clear to the British that the Americans would play no part in enforcing the report, should it prove necessary. This sparked off Attlee's stinging response. But Anglo-American contacts continued, and between them they fashioned a new scheme, the so-called Morrison–Grady plan. It provided for the cantonization of Palestine into four provinces under British trusteeship, allowing Jews and Arabs a large measure of provincial autonomy, and also for the admission of the 100,000 refugees within a year. But it also left the political solution open: perhaps partition; perhaps a binational state; perhaps a federal state.[27] A Jewish state in the whole of western Palestine – the Biltmore programme was by now a chimera, a political anachronism.

When the Jewish Agency Executive met in Paris at the beginning of August 1946 the question of partition had merged imperceptibly into a debate on the issues posed by the Morrison–Grady scheme: whether

or not anything of substance could be squeezed out of it. Their
deliberations were overshadowed by dramatic events that had recently
shaken Palestine: the punitive British operation against the Yishuv
(known to the Zionists as 'Black Sabbath'); and the bombing of the
King David Hotel by the Irgun. The latter had shown the hideousness
and futility of terrorist activity. But 'Black Sabbath' proved something
of greater consequence: that the British were capable of crippling, if
not crushing, the Yishuv. Weizmann's immediate reaction was that
'the work of the Yishuv for fifty years can be destroyed in a week'.[28] As a
result, the Jewish Agency was in disarray, its leaders either interned at
Latrun or in virtual exile. This put an exorbitant premium on an
unrestrained activist policy, one that threatened the existence of the
movement. This crisis was not lost on a majority of the Executive.
Weizmann was not present at its sessions – he was in London
preparing for another eye operation – but the draconian British
measures strengthened his position, despite Baffy Dugdale's
prediction that his absence was 'equivalent to abdication'.[29]

The Executive sessions took place on 2–5 August 1946.[30] Ben-
Gurion laid down his guidelines: the preservation of the unity of the
movement and the Yishuv; the premise that 'our prime political
purpose is the Jewish state'; and the proposition that 'we cannot accept
any continuance of British rule'. Nahum Goldmann – whose views
were close to Weizmann's – concurred, adding that 'our aim is the
Jewish state now, this year or next'. But he challenged Ben-Gurion's
latest edition of 'fighting Zionism'.

He [Ben-Gurion] has completely written Great Britain off as a factor with
whom we will be able to settle the Palestine problem. Therefore, his
conclusion that we must orientate ourselves towards the small peoples of the
world, the suppressed minorities, and align ourselves with all those in the
Middle East and the world who want Great Britain out of the Middle East.

For Goldmann, these 'tactics' would not lead to a realization of 'our
aims'. He had not completely 'written off' obtaining 'an acceptable
compromise' with the British. Goldmann admitted that the chances of
reaching an agreement were 'very small'. But boycotting Britain
implied postponing the establishment of the Jewish State and closing
the doors of Palestine to Jewish immigration. It could also lead to
something far worse: 'a policy of fight, pure negativism, protest
meeting in America, and "activist" policy in Palestine', a policy that
would lead inevitably to the disintegration of the movement. 'As long
as there is any chance to pursue a policy of legality of political fight,'

Goldmann went on, 'we must use this chance and turn to the policy proposed by Ben-Gurion only if any other chance has been used and failed.'[31]

Goldmann argued for improvements in the Morrison–Grady plan as a basis for future negotiations. The minimum area would be the Peel boundaries together with the Negev. Second, the Jews must control immigration into their province and the 100,000 must be admitted immediately. Finally, to elicit a 'clear statement that this cantonization is the first step towards a Jewish State, with a time limit of one to two years until the State will be established'. With this shopping-list, Goldmann would go to Washington to canvass American support.

The Executive's decisions reflected the ambiguity of the Morrison–Grady proposals – but in reverse order. Ready to discuss 'the establishment of a viable Jewish state in an adequate area of Palestine', they did not exclude, as a first step, the granting of 'full administrative and economic autonomy' to the area of Palestine designated to become a Jewish state, though the actual Morrison–Grady proposals were found to be 'unacceptable'. This resolution was formulated by Goldmann and passed by an overwhelming majority.[32]

There was nothing in all this that Weizmann objected to – he had never damned the new scheme in its entirety. Indeed, on 2 August, as the Executive was due to convene in Paris, Weizmann met George Hall, the Colonial Secretary in London, and raised demands identical to Goldmann's, with the important proviso that there could be no conference until his colleagues, still interned at Latrun, were freed, or even 'put on bail'. Those who had eluded arrest (Ben-Gurion and Moshe Sneh) would be allowed to participate in the talks.[33] On this issue, nothing separated Weizmann from the majority of the Executive.

Ben-Gurion, Weizmann's fiercest critic, adopted an oracular position in Paris. As a matter of habit he declared his loss of faith in Weizmann's ability to negotiate on behalf of the movement. He dissociated himself entirely from Weizmann's talk with Hall: 'I have no share whatsoever in his going to the Government', noting that 'Under the circumstances, I will not resign until the Congress is held'. But he too argued for partition, then abstained on the vote, and finally refused to accompany Nahum Goldmann to Washington to put the Jewish Agency case to the Americans. Was he for or against? His position seemed unclear. Still, on 23 August, Ben-Gurion, then in New York, wrote to the sixth convention of Mapai:

To submit is to be a second Vichy. I do not speak of traitors and informers – I cannot conceive of anyone in the Yishuv so depraved – but of submissiveness under the urge of principles seemingly patriotic and earnest [a reference to Weizmann?], as they were with the elect in the original Vichy, of fatal compromise that would devour the soul of our Movement just as a stand against impossible odds, at another Massada, would consume its body. Either way is downfall.

He continued: 'Unless the end in view is a transitional stage that leads surely to a Jewish State, we must reject any attempt by whatever Power to gain control over the country. . . .'[34] 'Either way is downfall.' That left the middle way, a path already well mapped out by Weizmann.

There can be no doubt that Ben-Gurion, like Weizmann, favoured partition. Nor can there be any doubt that, again like Weizmann, he did not rule out some kind of compromise. Perhaps he was too caught up in his own ambition and rhetoric to state this unequivocally. In May 1946, Albert Hourani, of the Arab Office in Jerusalem, remarked that 'the [Zionist] "moderates" and "extremists" do not really differ in anything but tactics'.[35] He was inferring, in the wake of the actions of the United Jewish Resistance Movement, that the initiative had been grasped by the 'extremists'. He might well have voiced the same comment that August – but now the balance had tilted in the opposite direction. Ben-Gurion's 'activism' and Weizmann's 'moderation' were indistinguishable, useful only to those with a political axe to grind.

When the Zionist Congress convened at Basel in December 1946 there were no political issues of substance separating Weizmann from Ben-Gurion. In some ways, Weizmann had consolidated his position over the past months. Not only had he liberated the Jewish Agency from its pact with terrorism, but he had guided the Executive – including, it seems, a reluctant Ben-Gurion – back to an open commitment to partition.

Disagreement had surfaced in October over whether the Zionists should continue talking to the British. Although the Zionists, the Arabs, and the Americans themselves finally rejected the Morrison–Grady plan, the British persevered. In September, they had presented the scheme for autonomous provinces as a basis for discussion at the forthcoming London conference that met intermittently, in various guises and with different participants, between September 1946 and February 1947. The Jewish Agency's initial response to the British proposal – that 'under present circumstances' it would not go to conference – was extreme, and it put Weizmann in 'an awful state of mind'. He spoke, yet again, of resigning his position.[36] Despite his frayed emotions, he continued his diplomatic manoeuvring.

When Weizmann met Bevin on 1 October he was treated to an angry diatribe on the anti-British attitude of the Zionists. 'The feeling in Great Britain was that the Jews had declared war.'[37] The British did not want to abandon Palestine, Bevin clarified, but if a reasonable solution should prove to be beyond their collective wit, there would be no alternative but to hand the question back to the United Nations. Bevin spoke again of a bi-national state for a limited period, a temporary solution that Weizmann did not exclude, as 'statehood could not be reached in one day'. But Weizmann stood firm on partition.[38] For his part, Bevin, despite the caveat that he would not force partition on the Arabs with British bayonets, hinted that he was not indifferent to the idea.[39] He insisted, however, on a trial 'transitional period'. But no agreement was reached about the Zionists joining the London conference – the release of the Latrun detainees proving the major stumbling-block. In effect, the decision was put off until the Zionist Congress convened.

Ben-Gurion wanted nothing to do with a conference that placed at the centre of its deliberations the provincial autonomy scheme – and certainly not one where Weizmann led the Zionist team. He feared (as did others) that once negotiations had begun, Weizmann would be inveigled into accepting an improved autonomy scheme, the Jewish state slipping away among Weizmann's cloudy phrases. Ben-Gurion was not opposed to 'an enlightened compromise'. 'Our line,' he wrote to Weizmann, 'should be the Mandate [he meant the original mandate of 1922, not its distorted version of 1939] – or a State. . . . If Britain is unable or unwilling to carry out the Mandate, [it] should agree to the establishment of a Jewish State, even if not in the whole of Palestine, but at once.' Nevertheless, he favoured ostracizing the conference. In fact, Ben-Gurion was implying that the British should commit themselves in advance – even before the talks had begun – to a Jewish state. This was asking for the impossible. Ben-Gurion's position meant deadlock.

Once again, Weizmann's position was clear. He preferred to use the autonomy scheme as a lever to pry out a Jewish state. Even Bevin did not rule out such a solution. There was nothing to be gained, and indeed much to be lost, if contact was broken off. Weizmann voiced 'cordial agreement' with the general lines of Ben-Gurion's policy, but thought 'it would be wrong to abstain from the conference, even if our point of view is not accepted beforehand'. Once negotiations had begun, he believed, 'the inexorable logic of facts will drive them [Byrnes, the United States Secretary of State, and Bevin] towards partition'.[40]

What did the differences amount to in fact? Fundamental principles of high policy were not at stake between Ben-Gurion and Weizmann. But personal issues were. The crucial question was: who would lead the Zionist movement if it was to be engaged in a remorseless struggle against British rule? Ben-Gurion had no faith that Weizmann was suited for such a role. It was of small consequence that Weizmann was now as disillusioned with Britain as his critics. In July 1946, after the events of the 'Black Sabbath', he wrote:

Something has definitely snapped in the relationship between Jews and British in Palestine, and I, as a firm believer in, and champion of, that relationship, am forced to realize that what has been destroyed is so deep, so vital, and of such moral significance, that it cannot be restored by projects, resolutions, and kind words.

Trust, understanding, co-operation had been swept away. The British, bereft of moral authority, had forfeited the right to rule over the Jews. It was no longer possible to resurrect the historic Anglo-Zionist partnership. Only partition, he claimed, 'an independent Jewish State in treaty relations with Great Britain', could provide an honourable way out of this impasse and lead to a rapprochement between Arabs and Jews.[41] All this had little effect. Weizmann's proudly fostered image as a dyed-in-the-wool Anglophile, something that he had worked hard at throughout his career, led to his political downfall.

Commentators with a sense of the dramatic have built much out of the so-called ideological differences between Weizmann and Ben-Gurion. These two almost diametrically opposite personalities undoubtedly clashed. But it was a clash based more on a dissonance in temperaments, on personal rivalry and ambition, than on actual policy. It was the classic confrontation in politics: a young, abrasive leader, anxious to get on, confronted by an older statesman, blocking his path and reluctant to relinquish his grip. Ambition is an indispensable part of the make-up of every successful politician. Great men tend to think of themselves as 'men of destiny', as somehow preserved by fate to meet the needs of the hour. Such feelings sustain and inspire them. This was certainly true of Weizmann. But no less of Ben-Gurion. For Ben-Gurion, his hour had arrived, and he would not be denied it.

At the Zionist Congress at Basel there was little Weizmann could do to break the Ben-Gurion–Abba Silver[42] alliance that had been raised to pull him down. Weizmann's final peroration to the Zionist Congress was stirring. 'The greatest speech of his life,' wrote Baffy Dugdale, his friend and adviser, adding soberly, 'But speeches seldom change opinions.'[43] And so it was. Congress voted 171 to 154 against attending the London conference, and reiterated the Jews' claim to all of western Palestine – in the circumstances a sterile gesture of public relations. No president was nominated to replace Weizmann, nor was he elected to the Jewish Agency Executive. Instead, Silver led the movement from New York, Ben-Gurion from Jerusalem – not the happiest of marriages. Weizmann had been pushed aside.

Ben-Gurion had again adopted an oracular stand. Some observers found his behaviour puzzling. '[He] has made an extraordinary speech,' thought Baffy Dugdale, as he attempted to say two contradictory things at the same time: to hold to the Biltmore programme and yet to discuss partition, if proposed. Far from clarifying the picture, he muddled it. He gave no firm lead and left his audience bewildered.[44] Perhaps this was all to the good. By allowing himself room to manoeuvre he covered all options, a legitimate ploy for the professional diplomat. But it was hardly the mark of decisive political leadership.

Two other factors should be stressed when discussing Weizmann's fall from official Zionist grace. The poor state of his health clearly posed serious questions about his continued leadership of the movement. Was this issue decisive in the calculation of his opponents? It is impossible to give a categoric answer. Still, sound health and sound politics go hand-in-hand, and it was both reasonable and sensible to take stock of Weizmann's deteriorating physical condition.

There was also Weizmann's so-called infatuation with the British, what Ben-Gurion described as his 'blind trust' in Britain. Was Weizmann capable of standing up to the British, of negotiating a satisfactory partition settlement with them? Ben-Gurion clearly believed – or claimed to believe – that he was not, and he played this card for all it was worth. There is no evidence to support this contrived argument. Indeed, no Zionist politician or diplomat had a finer record or was more experienced than Weizmann. Was he not, in Ben-Gurion's generous words, 'the greatest Jewish emissary to the Gentile world . . . the most gifted and fascinating envoy the Jewish people ever produced'?[45] It is true that Weizmann was often indiscreet and autocratic in his ways; it is also true that he was unsystematic in his working habits, preferred acting alone in his diplomatic dealings, and was not averse to snubbing his colleagues. But to infer from all this that he would automatically collapse before British – and by extrapolation, American – pressure is to indulge in special pleading.[46]

Now that Weizmann had been shunted aside, were the policies he espoused to be shelved, or just the man and what he symbolized? The conclusion is inescapable. By one of the strange ironies of history, Ben-Gurion and his allies found themselves, after their triumph at Basel, impaled on the horns of the same dilemma that had plagued Weizmann: how to conduct their relations with Britain. Nor did they discover a magic elixir that had escaped Weizmann's notice. At the end of January 1947 they entered into negotiations with the British government, finding salvation in semantics, digging out the face-saving formula of 'informal talks'. The Zionist delegation – now deprived of Weizmann's experience – was led by Ben-Gurion, but these talks petered out without conclusion.[47] By the time they terminated, on 19 February, the British had already decided to take the problem to the United Nations. In the final analysis it was not the Zionists – neither Weizmann nor Ben-Gurion – who abandoned Britain, but Britain who abandoned Zionism.

Even with Weizmann gone, Zionist policy underwent no fundamental change. It still rested on smashing the White Paper and establishing a Jewish state based on partition. The alliance with the Irgun and the Stern Gang was not resurrected; and contacts with the British and American governments continued – primarily because there was no alternative. All along this had been Weizmann's policy. It is difficult to detect a 'historical crossroad' here. Weizmann was 'dead' but 'Weizmannism' lived on. Or to put it another way: the 'activism' of 1945–46 was dead, but not even its most enthusiastic advocates bothered to resuscitate it. For Weizmann it was a bitter, not to say curious, experience to see Ben-Gurion masquerading in his stolen clothes. In the event, after some minor alterations, they fitted him very well.

NOTES

This essay first appeared in *Studies in Zionism*, 11, 1 (1990), pp. 25–44.

1. Joseph Heller (ed.), *The Letters and Papers of Chaim Weizmann. Series A. Letters* (henceforth *Letters*, Vol. xxii, p. 11. His letter included a memorandum from the Jewish Agency (in Weizmann Archives (henceforth WA), Rehovoth, that spoke of settling one million Jewish immigrants 'in the shortest possible time', mainly in the Negev. It also hoped for 'a clear-cut' decision by Britain – supported by the United States and the Soviet Union – in favour of a Jewish state, eventually to be an independent member of the British Commonwealth. Churchill's answer left him empty-handed, for it put off any immediate solution until the 'victorious Allies are definitely seated at the Peace table'.
2. Alan Bullock, *Ernest Bevin. Foreign Secretary* (London, 1983), pp. 113, n1, 348.
3. For Weizmann's 'emergency' programme, see Victor Cazalet to Weizmann, 2 Feb. 1938, WA; Norman Rose, (ed.), *'Baffy', The Diaries of Blanche Dugdale 1936–1947* (London, 1973), 11 Feb. 1938; and Weizmann to Blanche Dugdale, 9 April 1938, Aaron Klieman (ed.), *Letters*,

Vol. xviii, pp. 359–62. For his 'uncompromising hostility' to Britain, see 'Notes of two Conversations with "B" ' [Malcolm MacDonald], 13–14 Sept. 1938, WA, and Rose, *Dugdale*, 19–21 Sept. 1938. See also Norman Rose, *Chaim Weizmann. A Biography* (New York, 1986), pp. 335–9.

4. D. Cameron Watt, *Succeeding John Bull, America in Britain's Place, 1900–1975* (Cambridge, 1948) pp. 106–10.
5. Public Record Office (henceforth PRO), CP (46)53 and CP(46)58, 8 Feb. 1946, papers by Hugh Dalton and Lord Keynes in PREM 8/195, that graphically illustrate Britain's catastrophic economic situation.
6. Rose, *Weizmann*, pp. 260–1.
7. Heller, *Letters*, Vol. xxii, p. 196.
8. His favourite verse from Isaiah 1:27.
9. Rose, *Weizmann*, pp. 306–9, 315–16.
10. According to Ben-Gurion's biographer, he hankered after Weizmann's position as early as 1920; and with the passing of time his ambition strengthened. See Shabtai Teveth, *Ben-Gurion, The Burning Ground, 1886–1948* (New York, 1987), pp. 160, 483–4, 626, 750, 764, 793, 818, 820, 830.
11. Heller, *Letters*, Vol. xviii, p. 321.
12. The conference also reaffirmed the Biltmore programme and demanded the annulment of the May 1939 White Paper. For a summary of its decisions, see Heller, *Letters*, xxii, xi, p. 35. For Weizmann's behaviour at the conference, see Rose, *Dugdale*, pp. 223–5.
13. The United Jewish Resistance movement was comprised of the Haganah, the military arm of the Jewish Agency, the Irgun Zvai Leumi (IZL), the military wing of the Revisionst movement; and the Stern Gang, a militant offshoot of the IZL.
14. For the post-Biltmore quarrel, see the two special meetings held on 27–28 June in Rabbi Stephen Wise's home in New York, minutes in WA; see also, Rose, *Weizmann*, pp. 376–83, and Teveth, *Ben-Gurion*, pp. 816–31, 841. Ben-Gurion had formulated his 'combative' or 'fighting' Zionism as early as January 1939 (Teveth, *Ben-Gurion*, pp. 666–7).
15. Michael J. Cohen (ed.), *Letters*, Vol. xx, p. 389. Hugh Dalton, *High Tide & After, Memoirs, 1945–1960* (London, 1962), p. 105.
16. In January 1938 Baffy Dugdale noted that 'Ben-Gurion over-estimates the importance of U.S.A. opinion on H.M.G.' Rose, *Dugdale*, p. 77.
17. From the minutes of the meeting, WA, 27–28 June 1942.
18. Wm. Roger Louis, *The British Empire in the Middle East, 1945–1951; Arab Nationalism in the United States and Posture Imperialism* (Oxford, 1985), p. 452.
19. See Teveth, *Ben-Gurion*, p. 520, and M. Weisgal and J. Carmichael (eds), *Chaim Weizmann, A Biography By Several Hands* (New York, 1963), pp. 2–3.
20. A leading historian of 'Appeasement', the late Professor W.N. Medlicott, wrote that 'Appeasement should now be added to imperialism on the list of words no scholar uses'. (See D.C. Watt, 'Appeasement. The Rise of a Revisionist School?' *Political Quarterly* (April–June 1965), p. 191. It would, I suggest (though I fear in vain), be equally profitable for historians of Zionism to add the word 'activism' to this list.
21. Heller (ed.), *Letters*, Vol. xxii, p. 231.
22. Weizmann was referring specifically to a joint operation on the night of 16–17 June 1946 when the Palmach had blown up ten of the eleven bridges connecting Palestine with its neighbouring countries; the Irgun had kidnapped six British officers as hostages for their comrades under sentence of execution, and the Stern Gang had attacked the railway workshops at Haifa.
23. Barnet Litvinoff, *The Letters and Papers of Chaim Weizmann, Series B. Papers* (henceforth *Papers*) (Jerusalem, 1984), p. 636.
24. Of course, by virtue of his position he was not involved in the day-to-day running of these activities; nor was he always informed of their operational details. But he gave them wholehearted support and defended them staunchly before the British.
25. Yigal Lossin, *Pillar of Fire* (Jerusalem, 1983), p. 443.
26. For a full discussion of the Committee's work, see Amikam Nachmani, *Great Power Discord in Palestine. The Anglo-American Committee of Inquiry into the Problems of European Jewry and Palestine, 1945–46* (London, 1987).

27. Herbert Morrison, Lord President of the Council, introduced the plan to the House of Commons on 31 July 1946. In the same connection, see also Louis, *The British Empire*, pp. 434–45; Zvi Ganin, *Truman, American Jewry, and Israel, 1945–1948* (New York, 1979), pp. 76–9, 80–5, 97–8; and Bullock, *Bevin*, pp. 296–8.

28. Rose, *Dugdale*, p. 237. The British Army in Palestine had in mind even more punishing measures, and was only held back by its political masters. See report of a conversation between Nahum Goldmann and Bevin, 14 Aug. 1946, Central Zionist Archives (henceforth CZA), Z6/21, Jerusalem; also Joseph Heller, 'From the "Black Sabbath" to Partition – Summer of 1946 as a Turning Point in the History of Zionist Policy' (Hebrew), *Zion*, Jerusalem (1978), nos. 3–4, p. 335.

29. Rose, *Dugdale*, p. 239.

30. The minutes of the meeting are in the CZA, S100/50b/v.49. Cf. Heller, 'From the "Black Sabbath" to Partition', op. cit. See also Nahum Goldmann, *Sixty Years of Jewish Life* (New York, 1969), pp. 232–3; and Michael J. Cohen, *Palestine and the Great Powers, 1945–1948* (Princeton, 1982), pp. 141–7.

31. CZA, S100/50b/v.49.

32. Ibid. The other resolution, put by Ben-Gurion and Moshe Sneh, was decisively beaten, only its sponsors voting for it. It proposed that the 'Morrison plan should not serve as a basis for negotiation; [and that] the Executive authorize a member of the Executive to try and influence the American Government to reject the division plan and propose instead a Jewish State in Palestine'.

33. See Berl Locker's report to the Executive, 4 Aug. 1946. CZA Z6/21 (Locker had accompanied Weizmann). The British account differs only in that Weizmann considered a transition period of 3–5 years (record in FO371/52550). See also Heller, *Letters*, Vol. xxii, pp. 178–84, and Rose, *Dugdale*, pp. 238–9.

34. David Ben-Gurion, *Rebirth and Destiny of Israel* (New York, 1954), pp. 176–89. See also Joseph Heller, ' "Neither Vichy nor Massada": Diplomacy and Resistance in Zionist Politics, 1945–47', *International History Review* (October, 1981), pp. 540–61.

35. Louis, *The British Empire*, p. 417.

36. Rose, *Dugdale*, p. 240, and Heller, *Letters*, xxii, pp. 195–7.

37. Minutes of meeting WA; the British version in FO371/52560, E10030/4/31, and report of Bevin and Creech-Jones to the Cabinet, 5 Oct. 1946, in CP 358(46), CAB 133/85, PRO. See also Litvinoff, *Papers*, ii, pp. 622–6, and Bullock, *Bevin*, pp. 303–4.

38. According to the British ambassador in Washington, Lord Inverchapel (Archibald Clark Kerr), the 'breeze' of partition had developed into a 'whirlwind'. Several members of the cabinet came round to the view that this would eventually prove the only practicable solution. See Cabinet meeting for 25 Oct. 1946, in CAB 128/6, PRO, cited by Louis, *The British Empire*, pp. 438–9; also Dalton, *Memoirs*, pp. 189–490.

39. Bevin had told Goldmann in mid-August that 'he did not rule out Partition', and went on to repeat this phrase twice for good effect (minutes in CZA Z6/21); and Rose, *Dugdale*, p. 239. He also told Ben-Gurion the same thing when they met on 29 Jan. 1947 (minutes in WA). Two years later, Bevin repeated to the Cabinet that the Foreign Office had not opposed in principle a Jewish State. See PRO, CAB 128/15, minutes of a meeting on 17 Jan. 1949.

40. Ben-Gurion's letter, 28 Oct. 1946, in WA. It was written in Hebrew, by hand, and in especially large letters to enable Weizmann to read it more easily, a gesture that touched Weizmann. For this exchange, see Weisgal and Carmichael, *Weizmann, A Biography by Several Hands*, pp. 287–9, and Rose, *Weizmann*, pp. 416–17.

41. Weizmann to the Chief Rabbi of Palestine, Isaac Herzog, 21 July 1946. Heller, *Letters*, Vol. xxii, pp. 169–73.

42. Rabbi Abba Hillel Silver, president of the Zionist Organization of America and chairman of the American sector of the Jewish Agency. Silver, in Weizmann's caustic phrase, 'the filibustering Rabbi from Cleveland', was yet another aspirant to Weizmann's crown.

43. Rose, *Dugdale*, p. 244.

44. Ibid, pp. 243–4.

45. Weisgal and Carmichael, *Weizmann, A Biography by Several Hands*, p. 2.

46. It might be noted that from 1947 to 1949 Weizmann, even when out of office, was no less active and successful in the field of Zionist diplomacy than he had been in previous years.

But that is another story.

47. The discussions began on 29 Jan. 1947. There were six sessions in all, but the negotiations proved abortive. The British put forward a revamped version of the autonomy scheme, known as 'Bevin's Plan', as a basis for a permanent settlement. Ben-Gurion's final proposals excluded the establishment of Palestine as a Jewish state – so much for Biltmore! – and an independent Palestine as a unitary state, but plumped instead for partition, for 'the establishment of two States, one Jewish and the other Arab (or the Arab area might be joined to Transjordan)'. Transcripts of meetings in WA; for the British record, see CAB 133/85, PRO; also Ben-Gurion to Bevin, 14 Feb. 1947, WA.

# Sterling Balances and Claims Negotiations: Britain and Israel 1947–52

## URI BIALER

After the United Nations recommendation of November 1947 to terminate the Mandate and establish an Arab and a Jewish state in Palestine, the British government faced three financial problems which took nearly four years to solve.[1] First, would either or both new states remain in the sterling area; second, what would be done about the Palestine sterling balances; and, finally, what comprehensive financial settlement covering complicated problems of appraising assets and liabilities should be worked for? While the last issue had to wait until clarification of the overall political situation in Palestine, the first questions posed immediate subjects for decision from late 1947. The fundamental features of membership in the sterling area were that members used sterling as the normal means of external settlements, and that they held the major part of their reserves in sterling. They also looked to the United Kingdom as a major source of external capital and, finally, they co-operated to maintain the strength of sterling. The British aim concerning the bloc was defined late in 1947 by Sir Wilfrid Eady, a Treasury official who had been deeply involved in formulating British financial policies as 'to have some measure of [economic] control over the outlying parts [of the Empire] except in the case of the Dominions where we look for voluntary co-operation'. Fully conscious of this, officials in London thought it very difficult to keep Arab Palestine in the sterling bloc. They could not rely on a local exchange control administered by the Arabs to prevent a flight of capital out of that area. Moreover the freedom with which capital would flow into Arab Palestine from any other part of the sterling bloc might have proved 'an intolerable loophole'. On the other hand, there were some advantages as well as risks in keeping a Jewish state within the sterling area. British officials believed in December 1947 that a Jewish Palestine would prefer to remain in the sterling bloc and would accordingly be prepared to give all sorts of pledges about surrendering dollars (which the Jewish community in Palestine had accumulated), restricting imports, and managing exchange control generally. Still, it was assumed in those circles that the new state was likely to be under considerable American influence and might consequently be unwilling to comply with the sterling standard of austerity. Moreover, 'it might sooner or later – currently or retroactively – even seek to insist on a dollar ratio equivalent to Palestine's full dollar earnings'.

Although the two cases differed, the political considerations which dictated giving identical treatment to both Arabs and Jews overshadowed the dissimilarities and even before the termination of the Mandate encouraged a decision to exclude Palestine from the sterling area. Furthermore, although the prospects for the implementation of the UN plan for an Arab state in Palestine seemed very slight (not least because it was opposed by both the Jews and the Jordanians) the working hypothesis which had to govern British formal plans late in 1947 was the handing over of Palestine's administration to a special UN commission which would prepare for the establishment of the two states. The British government could not, however, rely on such a body to co-operate with them effectively on financial matters: 'The United Nations Commission knows nothing of exchange control administration on sterling area lines, and is most unlikely to see eye to eye on policy: even if it did its administrative machinery will be inadequate'. Grand strategy lay behind that formal justification, as Britain preferred an enlarged Trans-Jordan to the emergence of an Arab state in Palestine. Attention was thus turned mainly to relations with Abdullah. But the removal of Palestine from the sterling area forced the British to take an identical albeit much more difficult action against the kingdom. Since Jordan used Palestine currency there seemed no choice but to exclude it too from the sterling bloc, at least temporarily. As had been the case with Sudan when Egypt left the sterling area, the dangers of leakage if one of the two adjacent territories using the same currency was within and the other outside the area had been considered too great.

Many of the above considerations made it obvious why Britain had felt it also necessary to freeze the Palestine sterling balances. These balances came about because London˙was the financial centre for Palestine in the pre-war period, an arrangement that reflected the confidence placed in Britain's financial institutions. By 1939 these balances amounted to £20 million. After the outbreak of the Second World War and the imposition of currency regulations the holding of balances also became compulsory. Furthermore, although Palestine's imports declined during the war the volume of goods and services sold to the British Army more than compensated for the deficit in merchandise trade which Palestine maintained during the war. This, combined with the continuing inflow of Jewish capital and transfers, explains the accumulation of large sterling balances (held as frozen reserves in London by the Palestine Currency Board and by Palestine banks) which reached £80 million in December 1943, £115 million by December 1945 and £120 million twelve months later.[2] However, less than a year later, they had diminished by £20 million. This drastic fall worried the British government. It sought to slow down the process, and not only in Palestine, so as to prevent inflationary pressures and undesired fluctuation in the sterling exchange rate. Treasury officials realized that if they did not take steps to this effect, Palestine would be able to spend all its pounds freely in any part of the sterling bloc, including the UK, or even move balances to South Africa.[3] The prevalent opinion in London was that the general unrest during the transitional period was likely to reduce Palestine's exports drastically. Palestine would also be deprived of large amounts of sterling brought by British troops, and, as a result, might run a considerable deficit with the UK, which it might seek to make good by quickly drawing down its sterling balances. These considerations notwithstanding, British officials had to consider arguments which militated against this course of action. Freezing the funds before any orderly arrangements had been made for the transfer of power could make Britain vulnerable to dangerous criticism.

Looked at from the American point of view, hasty action of this nature can far too easily be represented as a master stroke to wreck any solution of the Palestine problem which does not conform to the wishes of His Majesty's Government. . . . If at the very moment when Congress is discussing the European Emergency Programme we present this propaganda weapon to the Jewish organizations in America (who collectively constitute probably the most powerful lobby in Washington) we shall place in jeopardy . . . our share of Marshall Aid.[4]

The Foreign Office, including Ernest Bevin the Foreign Secretary, had serious misgivings. The Treasury, however, could not be persuaded. Urging the Cabinet to 'have regard first to our interests', it viewed the current quick drawing of the sterling balances by the Jews as an ominous sign. In such circumstances, it was argued, Britain would have to block these balances sooner or later, by agreement or unilaterally. Waiting for a stable administration could mean a considerable financial loss, whereas action at a later stage might be interpreted as a hostile step. As Eady put it, 'we shall be accused in either event and had better play for safety by acting early'. Moreover, the balances were a significant bargaining counter and security to cover British claims against the new state in any overall financial agreement to be concluded. As was to happen later, after many internal debates on these subjects, Treasury's opinion prevailed. Consequently, on 22 February 1948 the British government announced its decision to exclude Palestine from the sterling area and to block its by then swiftly diminishing balances. In an effort to justify these actions the British took pains to emphasize to the Arabs, and mainly to the Americans, the economic and financial logic which had necessitated similar action in India, Egypt and Iraq.

These decisions should have solved the issue until the political situation in Palestine stabilized. As in India, this would have facilitated negotiations for an overall financial agreement, including other important issues.[5] But stabilization – at least as viewed from London – was not to happen until early 1949. Implementation of the decisions taken in February 1948 did, however, raise basic problems even earlier. When Palestine's sterling balances were blocked arrangements were made for £7 million to be released to supplement current accruals of sterling, and enable essential needs to be met during the period before the termination of the Mandate on 15 May 1948.[6] When this date arrived, without what British officials regarded as 'effective central control authority' in Palestine, they decided to make no further releases of a fixed amount. Nevertheless, they also decided to consider applications from individual banks, submitted through their correspondents in the United Kingdom to the Bank of England, for release from blocked accounts 'of reasonable sums required to make essential payments in sterling'. Instructions were laid down that before any such application 'HMG will require to be satisfied that the payment is for the purpose for which it is proper that release should be made'. Further releases thus seemed to become, in the words of a Foreign Office official, a 'technical matter'. Subsequently claims were quick to arrive. Moreover, Israel officials made enquiries about the possible release of sterling balances to be used to purchase desperately needed foodstuffs. They also offered to negotiate on an overall financial settlement. These became much more than 'technical matters' in the eyes of the Foreign Office. Britain's normal practice in similar cases had been to enter into an agreement with the country concerned providing for a reasonable rate of sterling release according to local earnings and obligations. But there was absolutely no question throughout 1948 of the British government making such arrangements with the Jewish authorities since it consistently refused to recognize the State of Israel, which was formally established on 15 May. From that date, Bevin showed a marked determination not to be manoeuvred into a position favouring recognition,[7] a rigid position stemming from his deep-rooted conviction that the Arabs had long been denied justice. It was not only a normative consideration which militated against recognizing Israel, but also the political conviction that support for Israel through recognition would seriously undermine highly important plans for Anglo-Arab co-operation. The British were thus forced to perform some legalistic acrobatics developing the theory of *res nullius* in order to justify their stand.

It is thus clear why late in August 1948 the basic policy concerning Palestine finances was reapproved.[8] Bevin refused to negotiate with Israel on these matters not only because it was not clear whether 'they (Jewish leaders) succeeded in establishing their state' but also

because any sign of a more forthcoming attitude on our part towards the Jews would convince the Arabs that they have no more hope from the Western Powers and induce in them a dangerous mood of desperation in which the most unwise counsels would prevail.[9]

The Cabinet concurred on 30 August, and implementation followed accordingly. There were to be no general financial discussions with 'the Jewish authorities' and no releases from the Palestine accounts without prior approval of all the departments concerned.[10] In this way the Foreign Office made certain that no change in the previous line would be made, and that not even small releases of sterling balances to firms and banks would be authorized without its explicit approval. The policy was duly implemented. When Israel asked in mid-September (on a bank to bank basis) for a release of £8 million from its sterling reserves, which should have covered the country's 'essential requirements' up to the end of the year, the British government took many weeks to approve the defreezing of a quarter of that sum. Moreover, the Bank of England's formal approval to transfer the money to the Anglo-Palestine Bank in Israel was made only after an indirect approach on behalf of Israel was made by some of its supporters in Britain. They made it clear to Sir Stafford Cripps, the Chancellor of the Exchequer, that what could easily be portrayed in the United States as economic sanctions against Israel would have grave consequences for British exports to the US. Cripps, who had been criticizing Bevin's policy of non-recognition since May, blaming him for not giving due weight to the importance of retaining American good will, thus became a useful target for the apparently well-informed Israelis. As a result, Bevin's veto was partly overruled.

A basic change in the situation depended nevertheless on a reorientation in the British policy of non-recognition of Israel. This happened early in 1949. Bevin was very reluctantly forced to change his stance because of public and parliamentary criticism of government policy, a back-bench revolt within his own party, and American demands. All these explain why Britain finally granted Israel *de facto* recognition on 30 January.[11] The change was not an easy one for Bevin to digest. It certainly needed time to be tested and implemented; tradition would not evaporate with a signature appended to recognition of Israel. However, it made it possible to start a long process of financial negotiations between Israel and Britain, which for both sides involved a mixture of political and economic considerations, influenced by the legacy of the past and future expectations.

As early as February the British began planning for such negotiations. The complexities became apparent almost immediately.[12] When Britain ceased to be responsible for the administration of Palestine, it left behind a number of assets and liabilities, those appertaining to Britain as such and those appertaining to the Mandatary Government of Palestine. Where Britain itself was concerned, the assets (mostly in the form of land, buildings and installations owned by the Service Departments) exceeded the liabilities. Britain's object was therefore to persuade the Israeli authorities to purchase the assets and to assume the liabilities. According to calculations made in London, the liabilities of the Mandatary Government of Palestine, on the other hand, greatly exceeded the assets. It was clear that persuading Israel to assume these liabilities would be extremely difficult. British officials expected Israel to be little affected by legal claims, strong as they might have been, since almost all the fixed assets were already within the grasp of the new state, and there was nothing to prevent it from expropriating them and repudiating the liabilities. Furthermore, the amount Israel should have paid in a general settlement was assumed to be between £25-30 million, an enormous sum in proportion to the real resources of the

Israeli government. Even on what the British considered to be the very unlikely supposition that Israel would observe an agreement in principle and with goodwill, it could not be expected to pay except by instalments over a considerable period. Moreover, 'at the most', wrote a Foreign Office official, 'we may hope to obtain from them something between 5 and 10 million pounds'. The only means of preventing a deadlock seemed to be to reinforce legal arguments by hard bargaining over Israel sterling balances, and to show willingness to scale down drastically British claims so as to bring them within the range of what the Israelis could reasonably be expected to pay. Time was a crucial element; the longer it took to reach an agreement the smaller the Israeli sterling balances remaining in London. Moreover, if better relations with Israel were established early on by the financial agreement, there was hope for a revival of British export trade and for profitable participation in Israeli reconstruction and capital development programmes. There was, however, one basic problem which the British had to solve before starting the negotiations: the precise relations between the sterling balances and the other questions. This proved to be a thorny issue throughout the following year, especially because different departmental perspectives prevented a coherent policy from being pursued.

The Foreign, Colonial, and War Offices firmly believed that negotiations on the release of Israeli sterling balances should not be separated from negotiations on Britain's assets in Israel and on the liabilities and assets of the old Mandatary Government in Palestine. They concurred that the beginning and completion of the two sets of negotiations should be synchronized as 'there was little hope of getting the Israelis to pay any substantial portion of Britain's claims unless the sterling balances could be employed as a bargaining counter'. The Treasury, however, rejected the clear-cut application of this prognosis. Realizing the complexities involved in the claims negotiations and, consequently, the time required to complete them, and the immediate need to facilitate trade between Israel and Britain by releasing sterling balances, it took independent action. Without consulting the other Departments, the Treasury informed an Israeli diplomat in London of Britain's desire to open talks in London on sterling releases which would later be complemented by claims negotiations in Tel Aviv. But the Foreign Office proved very reluctant to approve this course of action. Consequently, a compromise was reached late in March 1949 between the two conflicting approaches: immediate negotiations in London were authorized to arrange sterling releases for an interim period of no more than six months, while the claims negotiations were expected to begin in Tel Aviv in May, after the arrival in Israel of Britain's first ambassador, Alexander Knox Helm. Full synchronization between the two negotiations was nevertheless not achieved. This goes far to explain why the Foreign Secretary used his power to delay the arrival of the Israeli legation to London. There was another reason for this action. The Israeli government was then negotiating a cease-fire agreement with Jordan and pressure could thus be applied on Israel from London. 'I have decided,' wrote Bevin to the British consul-general in Haifa on 25 March, 'that in view of the present crisis in the relations between Israel and Transjordan it would be impolite for HMG to receive an Israeli delegation for formal talks in London.' Bevin did agree to release 'a small amount' of sterling to the Israelis 'to keep them going until talks can begin', provided that 'this is done without publicity'. Because of difficulties in establishing a British mission in Tel Aviv, the claims discussions in Israel began only during the first week of July, by which time an agreement had already been reached in London on limited sterling releases. Accordingly, during a six-month period ending in October, Israel was permitted to draw £950,000 per month, £250,000 of which were earmarked for the purchase of petroleum products. When the agreement was concluded it was decided that consideration of any subsequent agreement on sterling releases should be related to progress made in the Tel Aviv negotiations.

Several remarks are in order here to clarify the Israeli perspective.[13] From its very establishment, Israel faced overwhelming economic problems. The most acute was the total inadequacy of foreign currency reserves which were badly needed to finance the war effort, absorb hundreds of thousands of new immigrants, buy necessary foodstuffs, and, especially, buy oil. Israel's removal from the sterling area had certainly not improved the situation. The British action had been anticipated in Tel Aviv; its timing, before 15 May 1948 was not. However, it had not been considered crucially significant at the time and, accordingly, no efforts had been made by Israel since February 1948 to persuade the British to reverse their decision. Return to the sterling bloc had several recognized advantages for Israel. It would help release blocked accounts in London and make it easier to transfer Zionist funds and investment capital from sterling countries. It would facilitate purchases from European satellites of the sterling bloc, like France, Italy, Scandinavia and the Benelux countries (as Britain had trade agreements with these countries through which Israel might have utilized sterling more easily and thus saved hard currency). Finally, it would have assisted the diamond industry, since Israel had to get allocations of raw diamonds mainly from South Africa. But the disadvantages of returning to the sterling bloc appeared to carry more weight. It would have made Israel's desire to retain full control of the disposal of its dollar and hard currency reserves difficult to realize. Moreover, it would have turned away capital investment from the US which was essential for Israel's development. A return to sterling meant parity with the pound sterling which would have made dollar investments in Israel wholly uneconomic. Finally, as a memorandum on the subject put it:

There were psychological factors – the desire to build up closest relations with USA and particularly American Jewry, and on the other hand, reluctance to enter into any financial dependence on London.[14]

The £30 million Palestine sterling reserves in London were, unquestionably, of the utmost importance in the eyes of Israel's leadership, all the more so because it was money which the government could use without inflationary side-effects. The seemingly insoluble problem was the poverty of the weapons in Israel's arsenal to strike a deal with the British, although it had used several arguments in demanding special treatment. First, Israel claimed that unlike the sources of Britain's debts to India and Egypt, which were connected to the war effort, the balances were partly a result of the transfer of funds from the dollar bloc to Palestine. Second, Palestine was removed from the sterling bloc and did not opt for exclusion. And third, Israel's economic situation made Britain's release of funds an urgent necessity. But although legalistic and moral arguments were heavily employed by the Israelis, their real guiding lines were clearly those of *Realpolitik*. Thus, while openly denying Britain's legal right to freeze the sterling balances, in internal correspondence they typically accepted reality where 'possession is nine tenths of the law'. It was in fact a double-edged sword because the British government's property was in Israel's hands, and Israel had from the beginning stubbornly refused to compensate London for it, legal rights notwithstanding. Furthermore, although Israel later made much of the revival and development of bilateral trade connections with Britain as an important argument for the release of the sterling balances, it did not realy seem to regard that trade as critically significant. Nor was much help expected from the Americans after Israel had been recognized by Britain. Deadlock was thus almost inevitable in the opinion of Israel's leaders. The only viable option appeared to play for time. This view stemmed from a guarded hope that, under the cover of deliberately prolonged claims negotiations, the British would find it impossible to keep a total freeze on the sterling balances and would be gradually deprived of the only effective bargaining counter they had. In immediate operational terms, what Israel aimed at was the dissociation of the claims negotiations from the sterling balances negotiations. By mid-1949, it seemed to have gained at least a tactical temporary victory. On the other hand, Israel was in principle genuinely anxious to get the claims negotiations out of the way, first because it was simply impossible to postpone them indefinitely, and, second, because a successful conclusion of the negotiations would add another significant indication of Britain's recognition of Israel. During the second half of 1949 Israel's preferred order of priority was the issue of the sterling balances and then the claims problem.

The original instructions to the British delegation which conducted the claims negotiations in Tel Aviv from early July 1949 had been that the question of succession and the obligations to be assumed by the Government of Israel were primarily a matter for negotiation.[15] At the same time they laid down that the Government of Israel should be required to take over the liabilities of the former Palestine government in the same proportion as they took over its assets. They further recommended that the Israeli government be asked to make a substantial payment towards its share of the liabilities. Shortly after the negotiations started in Tel Aviv, it became obvious that no settlement was possible on the basis of these instructions. Israel unequivocally rejected Britain's demands, and insistence on them would have made a break inevitable. Theoretically, Israel could approach the negotiations in one of two ways. Israel could have admitted it was a successor state, but argue over every item, finally asking for generous treatment both for the sake of good relations and, more importantly, because it simply could not pay. Alternatively, Israel could deny either any obligation to meet the liabilities of the Mandatary Government or that it was a successor in law to that government. Several factors seem to have determined the adoption of this latter line. First, there was very deep-seated and bitter resentment at Britain's refusal to implement the UN resolution of November 1947. The Israelis felt that, had Britain carried out that resolution and had there been an orderly handing over of power, they would have been spared, perhaps, the expenditure of lives and money in the war and they would have been recognized as a successor government in every sense. They reminded the British of their offers to do so, which had been transmitted to the British delegation at the United Nations. The failure to accept those offers, they maintained, released Israel from any responsibility in this regard. Second, the negotiations were far more important to Israel than to the United Kingdom. Therefore, the terms of any agreement were going to be scrutinized clause by clause in the Knesset and in the press, and an unfavourable agreement might have created a political stir. Third, Israel did not have the money to pay Britain even moderate sums at that time, nor was it in a position to mortgage its future to pay London. According to British information, for the eleven months ending 31 May 1949, Israel's imports totalled 52 million Israeli pounds, and exports, 8 million Israeli pounds. The country was literally living on gifts and loan dollars from the United States, and even these were being mortgaged in advance. Economically, therefore, Israel could not afford to pay anything; and morally and politically, it felt under no obligation to pay anything.

The British government thus concluded that the most promising way of breaking the deadlock was to extract from the Israelis the admission that the Government of Israel had succeeded 'in time and space' to the Government of Palestine. This statement suggested that the two governments should, without prejudice to the view of either party on the question of succession, undertake to examine each of the liabilities of the Government of Palestine with a view to reaching an agreement on financial settlement. Tactically, the British delegation in Tel Aviv was authorized to accept Israel's suggestion for the order of priorities in which discussions of the individual liabilities of the former Mandatary Government should take place. At first Jerusalem seemed to accept this; however, as soon as the first item was broached (pensions of former Palestine Government officials) Israel's delegation re-introduced the question of succession. Deadlock occurred, making it necessary for the British to reconsider the connection between the claims negotiations and the release of the Palestine sterling balances. As a Foreign Office official phrased it:

> If a more co-operative attitude is to be inspired in the Israelis, a sharp jolt will be needed. The only really effective method at our disposal for inflicting this jolt is a straightforward threat that unless the Israelis change their attitude, no further sterling releases will be available to them.[16]

Logical as this prognosis may have sounded, it proved to be highly controversial within the British government. The Eastern Department of the Foreign Office strongly recommended that the threat of withholding further sterling releases should be used in order to bring Israel to a 'more reasonable frame of mind'. Furthermore, from the general political point of view, it was regarded as a mistake to allow Israel to 'put a fast one over on us'. The Colonial Office, which wanted to ensure that Israel took over Britain's liabilities in respect of pensions and government loans, and the War Office, which wanted to get some return on the extensive fixed assets in former Palestine, shared this view. The Treasury, on the other hand, was not in favour of using the threat. As on former occasions, the Treasury claimed that it would be hard to justify Britain's use of the reserves of independent banks, that is to say, private property, as a weapon in an inter-governmental dispute. The Treasury also felt that if sterling releases were stopped in this case and in this manner, it would seriously affect the confidence of many other countries who held sterling balances in London. Israel would no doubt also stop buying British goods. The Treasury was backed on this issue by the Economic Relations Department of the Foreign Office. Its officials felt that a threat to sterling releases was not as indefensible as the Treasury suggested, but it was likely to be ineffective; 'we would not make Israel budge, but at the same time, we would cut off our trade with her'. Britain's minister in Israel also warned against the adverse and 'very serious' political effect of a threat to withhold sterling balances, and suggested that, so long as these balances were kept in the background, 'we obtain the advantage without running into dangers which open use of them as a threat would undoubtedly incur'. The result of this divergence of opinions was an instruction to Helm to indicate to the Israelis that Britain would inevitably make decisions concerning sterling releases in the light of the results of the Tel Aviv negotiations: 'Both the outcome of the [sterling release] talks, and indeed the utility of holding them, may depend on the progress of the Tel Aviv talks.' Muted somewhat, the course of action recommended by the Eastern Department at the Foreign Office was generally accepted. Accordingly, although Helm insisted later in Tel Aviv that the British communication was not a threat, he admitted that it was indeed a 'warning'. In any case Israel was expected 'to play ball', especially in view of the pending expiry of the interim sterling release agreement on 31 October 1949.

And, indeed, although according to Helm's information the Israelis 'did not like the medicine I gave them' they decided eventually to 'take it'.[17] Israel declared itself ready to work towards a 'broad settlement across the table' which, when translated into operational terms, marked a definite advance on its part. The Israelis for the first time admitted that they should make some payments while withdrawing their counter-claims for loss of life on various occasions connected with the termination of the Mandate. They openly pleaded for 'fresh understanding and sympathy' in view of the country's acute financial problems and its poor capacity to pay. Presenting the Israeli case to Helm, the Director-General of the Israeli Treasury, David Horowitz, spoke of the yardstick applied to Germany in the 1920s; 'but,' he added, 'Germany was punished by reparations and whatever her faults he did not think we were out to punish Israel.' Although the Israeli proposals were unacceptable to the British, mainly because of a substantial gap between their financial calculations and those presented by Israel, they did, in the opinion of the Eastern Department and of the Economic Department of the Foreign Office, represent a fundamental change of attitude which made it possible to reopen the claims negotiations. Nevertheless, they declined to recommend fixing a date for the sterling release talks so long as these negotiations continued. The basic considerations were the vital importance, especially after the devaluation of the pound sterling early in October, of restricting all forms of sterling expenditure and the effect which any generosity to Israel might have upon other countries such as Egypt and Iraq who held sterling balances. They also pointed out that an invitation to further talks on sterling releases, which would result in a stringent rate of release, might have a more detrimental effect on the claims negotiations than the fixing of an arbitrary rate on a monthly basis. At this stage both sides of the Treasury were opposed to the issuing of an invitation – the imperial and foreign side because they considered the Israeli proposals unsatisfactory, the overseas finance side because it felt that, once negotiations had started, the merits of the Israeli case would compel generosity, while the claims negotiations remained inconclusive. The Overseas Negotiations Committee, which was called upon to decide the issue recommended therefore, with only the Board of Trade dissenting, that no invitation be issued to the Israelis for sterling release talks.

Surprisingly, however, this recommendation was not accepted. At a meeting of the Cabinet's Economic Policy Committee on 18 November 1949, the Chancellor of the Exchequer said he did not agree with the recommendation. The committee eventually decided that an invitation should be issued.[18] In reaching this decision, Cripps appeared to have been swayed by the consideration that if Britain adopted a restrictive policy in the matter of releases, Britain's commercial interests would be placed in jeopardy in Israel. Moreover, the Federation of British Industries had apparently convinced him that Israel was the base from which the United Kingdom's commercial activities could radiate throughout the Middle East, and that, if that base should be weakened, trade with the region generally would suffer. The Foreign Office's vehement objections to the Chancellor's prognosis – and more so to his diagnosis – notwithstanding, the gates were opened for sterling release negotiations in London. More significantly, the connection between these releases and the claims negotiations was blurred. The actual adoption of the formula that sterling releases should not be conditional upon the progress of the claims negotiations was to play into Israel's hands.

While the British were duly preparing themselves for the next round of separate negotiations on sterling releases and on the claims issue, the Israelis substantially changed their basic approach to these matters.[19] It should be recalled that the separation of the two seemed to serve Israel well. Indeed, only such separation could make it possible to extract sterling releases without paying too much in the way of concessions in the claims negotiations. However, early in December 1949 Israel decided to change tactics and to try to conclude one comprehensive agreement in London, rather than continue working on parallel tracks. There were several reasons for this change. First, the British reaction to Israel's offer in the claims negotiations of 'a genuine attempt to settle the matter' and the maximum to which the Cabinet and the Treasury could agree was an obvious disappointment. Britain's reply indicated that 'it was simply regarded as an opening bid and made no real impact on people in London'. Moreover, Israeli negotiators saw little chance of achieving a breakthrough through the Tel Aviv talks, described as 'a game of chess by correspondence' where 'one is not face to face with one's opposite number and Helm merely acts as a post office for transmitting our offers'. Finally, and most important, was the realization that time was not on Israel's side. Financial experts in Jerusalem became extremely worried about the effects of what was perceived as a growing economic crisis in Britain, of the forthcoming elections in those circumstances, and the diminishing value of the sterling balances as a result of devaluations of the British pound on the prospects of securing the funds so crucial for Israel's economy. Thus at the end of 1949 marking time became a very dubious tactic. The idea that it was better to make concerted efforts in the London negotiations to secure a compromise on the dual issue of claims and sterling releases gained the upper hand. This course of action could result in two distinct and clear-cut solutions: an agreement, or a complete and highly significant breakdown. The Israelis were certainly gambling on the former.

In London the question had been considered by the Overseas Negotiations Committee Working Party on Israel, on which the Treasury, the Colonial, War and Foreign Offices were all represented. There was general agreement that refusing the Israeli request would put Britain in a false position: 'it might then seem that we were not anxious to reach an early settlement'. More important was the realization that Israel's offer was made in such circumstances that a settlement on British terms was really possible. As a Foreign Office official later put it:

[The Israelis] may well imagine that if a breakdown occurs, we shall be correspondingly strict with them over sterling releases. They may even fear that we shall stop releases altogether. They will certainly imagine that they would lose the benefit of large investment by this country in Israel; and there are other minor advantages deriving from potential good relations between the two countries to which they would have to bid farewell. Moreover there is the by no means negligible factor that Mr Horowitz is himself extremely anxious to avoid a breakdown. He has stated more than once that he has never yet failed in negotiations. Mr Sharett [Israel's Foreign Minister] recently failed in the eyes of the Israelis at New York [in December 1949 when the UN General Assembly confirmed the recommendation to internationalize Jerusalem] and the Israeli Government are probably anxious to avoid a similar failure in London.[20]

An invitation was therefore issued to Horowitz to come to London on the understanding that 'he will not be committed to the Israel Government's present attitude'.

Although the negotiations were clearly aimed at reaching a general financial agreement between the two states, they developed in two parallel lanes; the one relating to sterling releases proved to be the less problematic. However, it took hard bargaining and the resolution of several deadlocks to reach agreement. The Israeli delegation first asked that a straight release be made on the same basis as that in the six months' agreement ending on 31 October 1949, that is £700,000 a month for 14 months from 31 October 1949 to 31 December 1950, a total of about £10 million.[16] At the same time they asked that oil releases and charitable remittances be continued at the same rate as under the previous agreement. The British delegation offered a straight release of up to £2 million for the year to 31 December 1950, a working balance of a maximum of £4 million, release for oil up to a maximum of

£375,000 per month and charitable remittances to a maximum of £3 million. The Israelis did not accept the offer claiming that the increase in the population in Israel, the additional two months from 31 October to 31 December 1949, and Israel's anticipated large adverse balance of payment for 1950 were factors which should make for an improvement of the British offer. Nevertheless they found it possible to make a counter-proposal: a straight release of £5 million and, if necessary, the offer of a working balance reduced from £4 million to £3 million. The Israelis claimed that this was an irreducible minimum below which they could not go, implying that if it were refused they would have to accept the British offer. They would portray the offer in Israel and in the United States not as an agreement but simply as a British dictate. As on other occasions departmental differences of opinion manifested itself in Whitehall with regard to the best tactics to employ to avert the impending deadlock. The Eastern Department of the Foreign Office rejected the Israeli proposal on the grounds that it would affect adversely Arab opinion (particularly in Egypt and Iraq which held sterling balances in London and had been engaged in similar negotiations with the British). The Treasury, on the other hand, had clearly been impressed with the Israeli case and were initially ready to raise the straight releases to £4 million and to reduce the working balance to £3 million. It found an ally in the Economic Department of the Foreign Office which suggested that the effect of the Treasury's proposal on the Egyptian sterling negotiations could be discounted. The outcome of this divergence of opinions was a proposal to offer the straight release of £3 million, a working balance of £4 million and allowances for oil together with permission to effect charitable remittances of £2.5 million. After some hard bargaining the Israelis decided to accept. The compromise was equidistant from the actual desiderata of each side. The British did not concede much, while the unmistakable internal enthusiasm in the Israeli camp after the finalization of the agreement attests to the considerable gap between Israel's initial demands and its real expectations. The fact that there was no explicit effort on the British side to link the sterling balances issue with the other financial questions – which in fact had become a distinct policy option late in 1949 – puzzled the Israeli delegation but certainly played into their hands. One of them, informing Tel Aviv of the impending signature of the agreement on the sterling balances wrote:

This may perhaps look a little surprising, coming before there is much progress with the financial talks. It may, of course, be pure altruism, or there may be some other explanation. For [the forthcoming] election purposes ... a settlement on the sterling balances might be sufficient for them ... secondly, once the British have come to an agreement with us on the sterling balances, the moral pressure on us to come to an agreement with them on claims and counter claims is obviously greater and they know that this is a difficult proposition for us.[21]

The crux of the financial negotiations had long been recognized by British officials also to lie there. And, indeed, solution of the claims problem proved to be much harder to achieve.[22] Shortly after these negotiations opened during the last week of January 1950 it became apparent to the British that although the Israelis were prepared to make advances and to be conciliatory on secondary issues, they had hardly moved from the position adopted in their October 1949 memorandum on the question of the main liabilities of the Mandatary Government. Britain's total demand was for Israel to accept obligations of £22 million while Israel's offer was £8 million; breakdown seemed almost inevitable. That the negotiations ended differently was mainly the result of a reassessment within the British government at that point, as the Foreign Office tried to examine the various implications. Although financially serious a breakdown was not considered disastrous. According to Whitehall's calculations (which like most others pertaining to these negotiations are not detailed in the documents at the Public Record Office) the amount Britain might expect under the best settlement possible along the lines suggested by the Israeli delegation was £11.6 million, while the amount Britain would obtain or save in the event of a breakdown was £5.1 million. It could be argued, therefore, that non-agreement was financially worse than agreement on British lines, but not very much worse than the best result of generally conceding to Israel.

What worried British officials more, however, was the damage liable to be incurred from Jewish propaganda in the United States:

The Israelis have already dropped one or two hints during the negotiations to the effect that American public opinion is not fully informed of the fact of the situation between HMG and Israel.[23]

It was therefore argued in internal deliberations that the figures used to calculate British losses and gains in various outcomes of the negotiations made it worth while for Britain to secure any improvement upon the Israel offer. Similar estimates in London suggested that the

Israeli offer left Israel slightly worse off than if a breakdown occurred. There was thus evidence of a disposition to come some way to meet the British position. Furthermore, British officials were convinced that if a complete breakdown occurred the chances of a more favourable opportunity for a settlement in the future seemed remote. Overshadowing all these considerations was the common conviction that Israel's desperate economic situation made it really impossible for it to accept anything approaching the British demands. As one Foreign Office official put it, 'they simply cannot afford to pay us much on the nail'. Pressure on Israel could have extracted a settlement favourable to the British; however, 'the continuing bad feeling which would accompany it would hardly contribute in the long run to the advantage of HMG'. Thus neither a breakdown nor a settlement on Britain's terms seemed to Britain's advantage politically. The only viable solution was to scale down British demands. The figures suggested and finally accepted were remarkable. It was decided to ask Israel to assume an obligation to Britain of £11 million. The British were actually ready to compromise on a lower sum, the Chancellor of the Exchequer feeling that 'we should be fortunate if we agreed and were paid 10 million'. Compared with the initial desiderata this was indeed a drastic change. However, in absolute terms viewed from the Treasury the sacrifice was not an enormous one. Likewise the Foreign Office recommended it on political grounds: 'it would mean a great deal in terms of goodwill with the Israelis and properly used, could do much to enhance the reputation of HMG both in Israel and the United States'. The first round was thus clearly won by the Israelis.

This, however, was not the final stage of the negotiations. The Israelis let the British know at this point that they could not pay more than £6,177,000. Hard bargaining followed, in which British officials tried to convince the Israelis to 'throw in another couple of million and make a deal of it'. They were countered with arguments that put forward the different financial perspectives of the two sides. As Horowitz noted, 'a million pounds for Great Britain and a million pounds for us were very different things. Even on a population basis, a million pounds for Israel would be equivalent to between forty and forty-five million for Great Britain'. Israeli documents show no readiness to compromise. The impression gained by British officials concerning Israel's very poor capacity to pay clearly reflected the true state of affairs. Once again the Foreign Office and the Treasury in London had to consider the thorny question of what would be gained from a settlement compared with a continuation of the impasse. A purely financial comparison made at that time in London indicated that accepting Israel's proposal would result in a balanced outcome or possibly a loss of about £1 million than if there was no settlement at all. While British officials considered the political advantages of removing the remaining source of bitterness between the two states, a settlement too favourable towards Israel might provoke 'undesirable reactions in the minds of the Arab States'. Lastly, Israel's financial future had to be considered: 'whether we should ever be likely to get paid . . . we might well make an agreement with her and have to whistle for subsequent instalments'. Thus the agreement held little attraction. But the British set a final minimum as far as their desiderata was concerned – to split the difference between £11.5 million and £6.2 million at around £9 million. Foreign Office and Treasury officials felt that they could not recommend a settlement at anything below this figure.

However, when the Israeli delegation proved unmovable the Chancellor of the Exchequer – without consulting his department – told Horowitz privately that if the Israeli government were to offer about £7 million he would submit it to his colleagues with a favourable recommendation. To cite a Foreign Office official's understatement, this undertaking 'a little worried' Treasury officials. It is clear that a personal initiative rather than a departmental line facilitated the conclusion of the agreement. In his memoirs Horowitz claimed that his personal touch accounted for Cripps's action although there is little British documentary evidence to substantiate this claim. To the Foreign Office two reasons seemed to have prompted the Chancellor's behaviour then and, indeed, throughout the negotiations: he appeared to feel that there was a future for Israel as a Middle Eastern trade centre, and he believed that too much sterling was circulating in the Middle East, much of it finding its way to the free markets in Syria and Lebanon. Israel could be regarded as a closed economy since it had no trade with Arab states. Whatever the motives, faced with a *fait accompli*, the Foreign Office reluctantly concurred. One of its officials minuted:

It may be that the suggested settlement is the best we can reasonably hope for . . . and it will certainly be worth our while to get the tiresome problem out of the way. Nevertheless it cannot be denied that such a settlement is a poor one from the point of view of His Majesty's Government.[24]

The Israeli delegation accepted the proposal and on 30 March 1950 the claims agreement was duly signed in London. In contrast to the prevalent feeling within the Foreign Office and on the part of some Treasury officials the agreement was defined as 'excellent' in

Treasury officials the agreement was defined as 'excellent' in Horowitz's letter to Sharett. Apart from its content it assured the future orderly and quick transfer of the sterling balances to Israel, to be completed in three years.[25] This in turn marked the final financial disengagement of Britain from the mandatary legacy in Jewish Palestine. Economic contacts between the two states were to develop thereafter in a way which was at least formally disconnected from the imperial past.

Viewed from a political perspective, the negotiations between Britain and Israel have two implications. First, as has already been established, urgent economic needs greatly determined Israel's basic approaches to contacts with the outside world during its early history.[26] Second, the successful conclusion of the claims and sterling release negotiations was crucial for the subsequent development of relations between the two states.[27] Britain granted Israel *de jure* recognition in April 1950. Three months later it decided to offer training facilities in Britain for the Israeli defence forces. A few weeks later, the Defence Committee authorized the Foreign Office to inform the Israelis that they could put forward their request for arms. Two months, after that, the British military for the first time inquired about the possibility of British bases in Israel. With the exception of the first initiative, very little came out of all of these decisions. It is, however, highly unlikely that they could have been made had they not been preceded by the elimination of the financial link to the Mandate from the political agenda between the two states. The claims and sterling release negotiations were therefore a *sine qua non* for the normalization of bilateral relations.

### NOTES

This essay was first published in *Middle Eastern Studies*, 28, 1 (January 1992), pp. 157–77.

1. The following account is based upon and excerpts are taken from documents in the British Foreign Office files (henceforth FO) – FO371/61965, FO371/61887, FO371/68604, FO371/68605, and FO371/68606, and memorandum on the Sterling Area submitted by the Treasury to the Radcliffe Committee in R. Conan, *The Rationale of the Sterling Area* (London, 1961), pp. 33–47. For the issue of the sterling balances see A. Hinds, 'Sterling and Imperial Policy 1945–1951', *Journal of Imperial and Commonwealth History*, 15, 2 (1987), pp. 148–70, and idem, 'Imperial Policy and Colonial Sterling Balances 1943–1956', *Journal of Imperial and Commonwealth History*, 19, 1 (1991), pp. 24–44.
2. H. Shannon, 'The Sterling Balances of the Sterling Area 1939–1949', *The Economic Journal*, 329, LX (September 1950), pp. 531–51. For economic policy in Palestine see N. Gross, 'The Economic Policy of the Mandatary Government in Palestine', *Research in Economic History*, 9 (1984), pp. 143–85, and N. Gross and J. Metzer, 'Palestine in World War II: Some Economic Aspects', Discussion Paper No. 87.01, the Maurice Falk Institute, Jerusalem, 1987.
3. See note 1.

4. Minutes of 18 Dec. 1947, FO371/61965 E/2692/G.
5. B. Tomlinson, 'Indo-British Relations in the Post-Colonial Era: The Sterling Balances Negotiations, 1947–1950', *The Journal of Imperial and Commonwealth History*, 13, I (1985), pp. 142–62.
6. The following account is based upon and excerpts are taken from FO371/68606, FO371/68607, FO371/68608, and FO371/68609.
7. On this subject see Wm. Roger Louis, *The British Empire in the Middle East* (Oxford, 1984), pp. 383–573, A. Bullock, *Ernest Bevin Foreign Secretary 1945–51* (London, 1983), pp. 219–58, 559–65, I. Pappé, 'British Foreign Policy towards the Middle East 1948–1951: Britain and the Arab–Israeli Conflict' (D.Phil dissertation, Oxford University 1984), pp. 1–111, 360–430, and K. Pattison 'The Delayed British Recognition of Israel', *The Middle East Journal*, 37, III (1983), pp. 412–28.
8. The following is based on correspondence in FO371/68608.
9. 25 Aug. 1948, C.P. (48)208, CAB 129/29.
10. See correspondence in FO371/68610, and FO371/68611, unsigned letter to 'Reuven', 23 Oct. 1948, Israeli Foreign Minister Files (henceforth ISA) ISA2421/3, and minutes of discussions on sterling balances held at the Israeli Foreign Ministry on 7 Feb. 1949, and 22 March 1949, ISA2601/1, and Israeli Ministry of Justice Files (henceforth IMJ) IMJ1845/8.
11. Pattison, 'The Delayed British Recognition'.
12. The following account is based upon and excerpts are taken from correspondence in FO371/75395, FO371/75220, FO371/75221, FO371/75222, FO371/75223, and FO371/75229.
13. D. Horowitz, *In the Heart of Events*, (Tel Aviv, 1975), pp. 32–67. (Hebrew), correspondence in Israel Treasury Files, 5626/C 16/75/1/4, ISA2457/7, ISA2601/1, and IMJ1845/8 and Instructions to Israel's Missions Abroad No. 9, 13 Dec. 1949, ISA2421/3. For Israel's economy during that time see H. Barkai, *The Beginnings of the Israeli Economy* (Jerusalem, 1983) (Hebrew), N. Gross, 'Laying the Foundations of Israel's Economic System 1948–1951', Discussion Paper No. 88.07, The Falk Institute, Jerusalem 1988, N. Halevy (ed.), *A Banker to a Restored Nation* (Tel Aviv, 1977) (Hebrew), and R. Ottensooser, *The Palestine Pound and the Israeli Pound*, (Geneva, 1955).
14. Undated memorandum (1949) ISA2601/1.
15. The following account is based upon and excerpts are taken from FO371/75223, FO371/75225, FO371/75233, FO371/75235, FO371/75237, and FO371/75238.
16. Brenchley's minutes, 26 Aug. 1949, FO371/75238.
17. The following account is based upon and excerpts are taken from FO371/75228, FO371/75238, FO371/75239, and FO371/75240.
18. The following account is based upon FO371/75240.
19. The following is based upon and excerpts are taken from ibid, and U. Bialer, 'The Road to the Capital; The Establishment of Jerusalem as the Official Seat of the Israeli Government in 1949', *Studies in Zionism*, 5, II (1985), pp.273–96. See also note 10.
20. Brinson's minutes, 31 Jan. 1950, FO371/82554.
21. Linton's letter to Comay, 1 Feb. 1950, ISA2601/2.
22. The following is based on correspondence in FO371/82554 and ISA2601/1–2.
23. Brinson's minutes, 31 Jan. 1950, FO371/82554.
24. Unsigned memorandum, 6 March 1950, FO371/8255.
25. British Treasury Papers (henceforth T) T220/171, FO371/82554, FO371/82555, FO371/82556, and ISA2601/2. For later negotiations concerning sterling releases which ended in 1952 see FO371/82563, T220/171, FO371/91722, FO371/98805, and ISA2421/3. On Israel's foreign policy in the early 1950s and its strategic contacts with Britain see U. Bialer, *Between East and West: Israel's Foreign Policy Orientation 1948–1956* (Cambridge, 1990).
26. Bialer, op. cit. pp. 197–202.
27. Pappé, 'British Foreign Policy', pp.410–17.

# The Writings of Donald Cameron Watt

## BOOKS

*Britain Looks to Germany: A Study of British Policy and Opinion towards Germany since 1945* (London: Oswald Wolff, 1965).

*England blickt nach Deutschland* (Tübingen: Rainer Wunderlich Verlag, 1965) (German translation of *Britain Looks to Germany*).

*Personalities and Policies: Studies in the Formulation of British Foreign Policy in the Twentieth Century* (London: Longmans, Green & Co.; South Bend, Indiana: University of Notre Dame Press, 1965).

(With F. Spencer and N. Brown) *A History of the World in the Twentieth Century* (London: Hodder & Stoughton, 1967; New York: Morrow, 1968).

*Too Serious a Business. European Armed Forces and the Approach of the Second World War* (London: Temple Smith; Berkeley CA: University of California Press, 1975; reprint New York and London: Norton, 1992).

*Succeeding John Bull: America in Britain's Place, 1900–1975* (Cambridge University Press, 1984).

*Personalities and Policies. Studies in the Formulation of British Foreign Policy in the Twentieth Century* (Reprint of original 1965 edition; Westport, CT: Greenwood Press, 1976).

*How War Came. The Immediate Origins of the Second World War* (London: Heinemann; New York: Pantheon, 1989. Paperback, London: Mandarin, 1990).

Italian edition: *1939: Come Scoppio la Guerra*, translated by Sergio Manzini (Milan: Leonardo, 1989).

## PAMPHLETS

*Britain and the Suez Canal* (Royal Institute of International Affairs, August 1956).

*The Rome-Berlin Axis, 1936–1940: Myth and Reality* (Bobbs-Merrill

Reprint Series in European History, 1967, No. E-227; reprinted from *Review of Politics*, Vol. 22, 1960).

*The Impact of the Second World War on South and South East Asia* (Open University Course on War and Society, Unit 27. Milton Keynes: Open University Press, 1973).

*The Future Governance of the Seas*, inaugural lecture for the inauguration of the M.Sc. course in Sea-Use: Law, Economics and Policy-Making (The London School of Economics and Political Science, 1979).

*What About the People? Abstraction and Reality in History and the Social Sciences* (The London School of Economics and Political Science, 1983).

*Personalities and Appeasement*, lecture delivered to the Faculty Seminar on British Studies, University of Texas at Austin (Austin, Texas: Harry Ransom Humanities Research Center, 1991).

## BOOKS EDITED

(With J.B. Donne) *Oxford Poetry 1950* (Oxford: Blackwell, 1951).

(Editor with K. Bourne) *Studies in International History. Essays Presented to W.N. Medlicott* (London: Longmans Green, 1967).

*Survey of International Affairs 1961* (Oxford University Press, 1965).

*Survey of International Affairs, 1962* (Oxford University Press for the Royal Institute of International Affairs, 1970).

(Editor of and Introduction to) *Hitler's Mein Kampf* (London: Hutchinson, 1969; 2nd edn with enlarged Introduction, 1992).

(Editor) *Contemporary History in Europe* (London: Allen & Unwin, 1969).

*Survey of International Affairs, 1963* (Oxford University Press, 1977).

(Editor) *The North Sea: A New International Regime*. Records of an International Conference at the Royal Naval College, Greenwich, 2, 3 and 4 May 1979 (International Publishing Corporation Science and Technology Press, 1981).

(With Guido di Tella) *Argentina and the Great Powers, 1939–1945* (London: Macmillan; Pittsburgh, PA: University of Pittsburgh Press, 1989).

## HISTORIOGRAPHICAL, SOURCE MATERIALS

### (a) Historiographical

'Sir Lewis Namier and Contemporary European History', *Cambridge Review*, July 1954.

'Some Post-war British Memoirs and Pre-war Foreign Policy', *International Relations*, Vol. I, No. 3, April 1955.

'The Air Force View of History', *Quarterly Review*, October 1962.

'American Isolationism in the 1920s – is it a useful Concept?', *Bulletin of the British Association of American Studies*, New Series, No. 6, Summer 1963.

'Appeasement Reconsidered – Some Neglected Factors', *The Round Table*, No. 212, Sept. 1963.

'Appeasement. The Rise of a Revisionist School?', *Political Quarterly*, Vol. 36, No. 2, April 1965.

'Teaching and Research in Contemporary International History in Britain; Opportunities and Openings' in D.C. Watt (ed.), *Contemporary History in Europe* (London: Allen & Unwin, 1969).

'Contemporary History, Problems and Perspectives', *Journal of the Society of Archivists*, Summer 1969.

'Twentieth Century History' in M. Ballard (ed.), *New Movements in the Study and Teaching of History* (London: Temple Smith, 1970).

(Review article) 'Does "Europe" Really Exist?', *New Middle East*, August 1970.

'What is This World that We Must Teach the History of it?', *The World and the Teacher*, January 1971.

'Contemporary History and the *Survey of International Affairs*', in R. Morgan (ed.), *The Study of International Affairs. Essays in Honour of Kenneth Younger* (Oxford University Press for Royal Institute of International Affairs, 1972).

'The Historiography of Appeasement' in Alan Sked and Chris Cook (eds), *Crisis and Controversy. Essays in Honour of A.J.P. Taylor* (London: Macmillan, 1976).

(Review article) 'The Historiography of Nuclear Diplomacy', *Science*, October 1975.

'Some Aspects of A.J.P. Taylor's Work as Diplomatic Historian', *Journal of Modern History*, Vol. 49, No. 1, March 1977.

'Rethinking the Cold War. A Letter to a British Historian', *Political Quarterly*, Vol. 48, 1977.

'The Political Misuse of History' in *Trends in Historical Revisionism: History as Political Device* (London: Centre for Contemporary Studies, May 1985).

'The Debate over Hitler's Foreign Policy – Problems of Reality or *Faux Problèmes*?' in Klaus Hildebrand and Reiner Pommern (eds), *Deutsche Frage und Europäisches Gleichgewicht. Festschrift für Andreas Hillgruber zum 60. Geburtstag* (Cologne: Bohlau Verlag, 1985).

'Britain and the Historiography of Yalta', *Diplomatic History*, Vol. 13, No. 1, 1989.

(b) **Documentary Publications**

*Documents on the Suez Crisis. Selected with an Introduction* , London Royal Institute of International Affairs, January 1957.

'An Earlier Model for the Pact of Steel', *International Affairs,* April 1957.

(Editor) 'Documents, German Ideas on Iraq, 1937–38', *Middle East Journal*, Vol. 12, No. 2, Spring 1958.

(Assistant editor) 'The Third Reich: First Phase, 30 January–14 October 1933; 15 October 1933–13 June 1934; 14 June 1934–31 March 1935' in *Documents on German Foreign Policy 1918–1945* (London: Her Majesty's Stationery Office. In progress: Series C. Volumes I, II and III).

'Soviet Military Aid to Spanish Republicans, 1936–1938' *(Slavonic and East European Review*, Summer 1960), reprinted in Appendix to Hugh Thomas *The Spanish Civil War* (London, 1961).

'The Secret Laval–Mussolini Agreement of January 7, 1935 on Abyssinia' *Middle East Journal*, Vol. 15, No. 1, Winter 1961.

'Document: The Secret Laval–Mussolini Agreements of 1935 on Ethiopia' in E. Robertson (ed.), *The Origins of the Second World War* (London: Macmillan, 1970; reprinted from *Middle East Journal*, Winter 1962).

'Soviet Military Aid to the Spanish Republic in the Civil War 1936–1938' in Wolfgang Schieder and Christof Dipper (eds), *Der Spanische Burgerkrieg in der internationalen Politik (1936–39)* (Munich: Nymphenburgener Verlag, 1976).

(Editor) *Documents on German Foreign Policy, 1918–1945* Series C, *The Third Reich: First Phase*, Vol. V, *March 5–October 31, 1936* (London: HMSO, 1966).

(Editor) *Documents on German Foreign Policy*, Series D, Vol. XIII, *The War Years June 1941–December 11, 1941.* (London: HMSO, Government Printing Office, Washington, DC 1964).

(Editor with Geoffrey Warner, John Major and Richard Gott) *Documents on International Affairs, 1961* (Oxford: Oxford University Press for Royal Institute of International Affairs, 1965).

(Editor with J.B.L. Mayall and C. Navari) *Documents on International Affairs 1962* (Oxford University Press for Royal Institute of International Affairs, 1971).

(Editor with J.B.L. Mayall) *Current British Foreign Policy 1970.*

*Documents, Statements, Speeches, 1970* (London: Temple Smith, 1971).

(Editor with J. Mayall) *Current British Foreign Policy 1971* (London: Temple Smith, 1972).

(Editor with J. Mayall and C. Navari) *Documents on International Affairs, 1963* (Oxford University Press for Royal Institute of International Affairs, 1973).

(Editor with J. Mayall) *Current British Foreign Policy 1972* (London: Temple Smith, 1975).

(General Editor with K. Bourne) *British Documents on Foreign Affairs: Reports and Papers from the Foreign Office Confidential Print* (University Publications of America, 1984: Part I, Series A, D. Lieven (ed.), *Russia, 1859–1914.* Vols. 1–6, 1983).

(General Editor with K. Bourne) *British Documents on Foreign Affairs: Reports and Papers from the Foreign Office Confidential Print*: Part I, Series B, D. Gillard (ed.), *The Near and Middle East 1856–1914,* Vols. 1–10; Part II, Series A, D. Cameron Watt (ed.), *The Soviet Union, 1917–1939,* Vols. 1–3, Part II, Series A, D. Lieven (ed.), *The Soviet Union, 1917–1939,* Vols. 4–5 (University Publications of America, 1984).

(General Editor with K. Bourne) *British Documents on Foreign Affairs: Reports and Papers from the Foreign Office Confidential Print*: Part I, Series B, D. Gillard (ed.), *The Near and Middle East, 1856–1914,* Vols. 11–20; Part II, Series A, D. Lieven (ed.), *The Soviet Union, 1917–1939,* Vols. 6–10; Part II, Series B, R. Bidwell (ed.), *Turkey, Iran and the Middle East,* Vols. 1–15 (University Publications of America, 1985).

(General Editor with K. Bourne) *British Documents on Foreign Affairs: Report and Papers from the Foreign Office Confidential Print,* University Publications of America, Part II, Series D: *Latin America,* Vols. 1–5 (1989); Part II, Series H: *The First World War,* Vols. 1–12 (1989); Part I, Series F: *Europe,* Vols. 9–16 (1989) and 17–22 (1990); Part II, Series I: *Paris Peace Conference,* Vols. 1–7 (1989) 8–15 (1990); Part I, Series E: *Asia,* Vols. 1–9 (1990); Part II, Series B: *Turkey, Iran and the Middle East,* Vols. 14–15 (1989) and 16–20 (1990).

(General Editor with K. Bourne) *British Documents on Foreign Affairs. Reports and Papers from the Foreign Office Confidential Print. From the mid-Nineteenth Century to the First World War* (University Publications of America): Part I, Series D: *Latin America* (eds George Philip and Harold Blakemore), Vols. 1–5; Series F: *Europe* (ed. John F.V. Keiger), Vols. 23–35. Part II, Series B: *Middle East* (Robin Bidwell), Vols. 21–25; Series C: *North America* (ed. D.K. Adams), Vols. 7–15; Series D: *Latin America* (ed. George Philip), Vols. 6–15; Series E: *Asia* (ed. Ann Trotter), *Japan* Vols. 1–10; Series I: *The Paris Peace Conference, 1919* (ed. M. Dockrill), Vols. 8–15.

## (c) Sources

'United States Documentary Sources for the Study of British Foreign Policy, 1919–39'. *International Affairs*, Vol. 38, No. I, January 1962.

'Foreign Affairs, the Public Interest and the Right to Know', *Political Quarterly*, Vol. 34, No. 2, 1963.

'Restrictions on Research. The 50 Years Rule and British Foreign Policy'. *International Affairs*, January 1965.

'Sources for Contemporary History: The Press Library of the Royal Institute of International Affairs', *Vierteljahresheft für Zeitgeschichte*, 16 Jahrgang, Heft 1, January 1968).

'Congestion in the Public Record Office'. *Social Science Research Council Newsletter*, No. 8, February 1968.

'Sources for the History of the European Movement in the United Kingdom (1945–1955)' in Walter Lipgens (ed.), *Sources for the History of European Integration (1945–1955), A Guide to Archives in the Countries of the Community* (London: Sijthoff; Brussels: Bruylent; Leyden: Sijthoff; Stuttgart: Klett-Cotta; Florence: Le Monnier, 1980).

'The Publication of British Official Documents' in K.J. Kooijmans, Th. S.H. Bos and A.E. Kersten *et al.* (eds), *Bron en publikatie, Voordrachten en opstellen* (The Hague: Bureau den Rijkscommissie voor Vadenlandse Geschiednis, 1985).

## (d) Films and the Historian

'History on the Public Screen' in Paul Smith (ed.), *The Historian and Film* (Cambridge University Press, 1976).

'Film and the Historian', *History*, Vol. 55, 1970.

(Review Article, Film Section) 'Old and New Hitlers', *History*, Vol. 58, No. 194, October 1973.

## (e) Entries in Dictionaries, Encyclopaedias etc.

'British Politics 1955–1956', *Chambers Yearbook for 1956*.

'British Politics 1956–57', *Chambers Yearbook for 1957*.

International Relations' and 'Public Opinion' entries in J.S. Gould and
W.L. Kolb (eds), *A Dictionary of the Social Sciences* (London:
Tavistock Press for UNESCO, 1964).

Numerous entries (195 in all) in Alan Bullock and Oliver Stalleybrass
(eds), *The Fontana Dictionary of Modern Thought* (London:
Fontana, 1977; 2nd edn 1988).

'European Political Problems 1919–1934', 'The Approach of the
Second World War, 1931–1941', 'The War in Asia and the Pacific
1941–1945', 'The War in the West 1941–1945', 'Retreat from
Empire, 1939–1977' in Geoffrey Barraclough (ed.), *The Times Atlas
of World History* (London: Times Books, 1978).

'Towards the Second World War', 'Germany, Poland and Russia',
'The Second World War', 'The Post-War World', 'The Red East',
'The Non-Aligned World', 'The Middle East and the Arab World'
in *The Encyclopaedia of World History* (London: Hamlyn, 1979).

Numerous entries in Alan Bullock and R.B. Woodings, *The Fontana
Biographical Companion to Modern Thought* (London: Fontana,
1983).

Entries on 'Appeasement', 'Co-existence', 'The Cold War', 'Isolationism' in M.A. Riff (ed.), *Dictionary of Modern Political Ideologies*
(Manchester University Press 1987).

## HISTORICAL WORKS

### 1. International History

(a) CONTRIBUTIONS TO BOOKS

'Germany' in Evan Luard (ed.), *The Cold War: A Reappraisal* (London:
Thames and Hudson, 1964).

'Europe and the Marshall Plan' in R.H. Ferrell and J.N. Hess (eds),
*Conference of Scholars on the European Recovery Programme*, 20–21
March 1964 (President Harry S. Truman Library Institute for
National and International Affairs, Independence, Missouri, 1965).

'South African Attempts to Mediate Between Britain and Germany,
1935–1938' in K. Bourne and D.C. Watt (eds), *Studies in International History, Essays Presented to W.N. Medlicott* (London:
Longmans Green, 1967).

'Diplomatic History, 1930–1939' in C.L. Mowat (ed.), *The Shifting
Balance of World Forces, 1895–1945,* New Cambridge Modern
History, Vol. XII (2nd edn., Cambridge University Press, 1968).

'The First Moroccan Crisis' in J.M. Roberts (ed.), *Readings in Twentieth*

*Century History, Europe in the Twentieth Century, Vol. I, 1900–1918* (London: Macdonald, 1970).

'American Anti-colonist Policies and the End of the European Colonial Empires, 1941–1962' in A.N.J. den Hollander (ed.), *Contagious Conflict: The Impact of American Dissent on European Life* (Leiden: E.J. Brill, 1973).

'The Initiation of Negotiations leading to the Nazi-Soviet Pact. An Historical Problem' in Chimen Abramsky and Beryl J. Williams (eds), *Essays in Honour of E.H. Carr* (London: Macmillan, 1974).

Preface to Lawrence R. Pratt, *East of Malta, West of Suez. Britain's Mediterranean Crisis 1935–1939* (Cambridge University Press, 1975).

'Britain, France and the Italian Problem, 1937–1939' and 'British Domestic Politics and the Onset of War. Notes for a Discussion' in *Les Relations Franco–Britanniques de 1935 à 1939* (Paris: Centre Nationale de la Recherche Scientifique, 1975).

'Britain and the Cold War in the Far East, 1945–1951' in *Papers presented to the International Symposium of the International Environment in Postwar Asia, Kyoto, Japan* (Tokyo Institute of Technology, Basic Studies on the International Environment, 27–30 November 1975).

'The Breakdown of the European Security System 1930–1939' in *Papers Presented to the XIVth International Congress of Historical Sciences, San Francisco, 22–29 August 1975* (Comité Internationale des Sciences Historiques/American Historical Association, San Francisco, 1975).

'Nazi Political Warfare, Persuasion and Subversion' in Robert Cecil (ed.), *Hitler's War Machine* (London: Salamander Press, 1976).

Introduction to J.T. Emmerson, *The Rhineland Crisis, 7 March 1936* (London: Temple Smith, 1977).

'Imperial Defence Policy and Imperial Foreign Policy, 1911–1939. A Neglected Paradox' in Henry R. Winkler (ed.), *Twentieth Century Britain. National Power and Social Welfare (Journal of Commonwealth Studies*, 1963, reprinted *New Viewpoints*, New York: Franklin Watts, 1976).

'Introduction. The Historian's Tasks and Responsibilities' and 'Britain and the Cold War in the Far East, 1945–1958' in Yonosuke Nagai and Akira Iriye (eds), *The Origins of the Cold War in Asia* (University of Tokyo Press, 1977).

'Die Verhandlungsinitiativen zum deutsch-sowjetischen Nichtangriffspakt vom 24 August 1939: Ein historisches Problem' in Wolfgang Michalka (ed.), *Nationalsozialistische Aussenpolitik*

(Darmstadt: Wissenschaftliche Buchgesellschaft, 1978).

'Hauptprobleme der Britischen Deutschlandpolitik 1945–49' in Claus Scharf and Hans-Jurgen Schroeder (eds), *Die Deutschlandpolitik Grossbritanniens und die Britische Zone 1945–1949* (Wiesbaden: Franz Steiner Verlag, 1979).

'Historical Introduction' to R. John Pritchard and Sonia Magbuana Zaide, *The Tokyo War Crimes Trials, Transcript and Indexes* (New York: Garland, 1982).

'Work completed and Work as yet Unborn: Some Reflections on the Conference from the British Side' in Ian Nish (ed.), *Anglo-Japanese Alienation 1919–1952, Papers of the Anglo-Japanese Conference on the History of the Second World War* (CUP, 1982).

'The European Civil War' in Wolfgang J. Mommsen and Lothar Ketternacker, *The Fascist Challenge and the Policy of Appeasement* (London: Allen & Unwin, 1983).

'Misinformation, Misconception, Mistrust, Episodes in British Policy and the Approach of War, 1938–1939' in Michael Bentley and John Stevenson (eds), *High and Low Politics in Modern Britain* (Oxford: Clarendon Press, 1983).

'Setting the Scene' in Roy Douglas (ed.), *1939: A Retrospect Forty Years After. Proceedings of a Conference held at the University of Surrey* 27 October 1979 (London: Macmillan, 1983).

'Die Sowjetunion im Urteil der Britischen Foreign Office 1945–1949' in Gottfried Niedhart (ed.), *Der Western und die Sowjetunion, Einstellungen und Politik gegenüber der USSR in Europa und in den USA seit 1917* (Paderborn: Schöningh, 1983).

'Les Perceptions Européennes de la Puissance Militaire avant 1939' in René Girault and Robert Frank, *La Puissance en Europe, 1938–1940* (Paris: Publications de la Sorbonne, 1984).

'Senso kaihi wa kano de atta ka: Kure-gi-hokokhu to seisaku kettei eri – to no hanno' (Could War in the Far East have been prevented in November 1941? Sir Robert Craigie's Final Report on his Embassy to Japan and the reactions of the British Foreign Policy Making Elite) in A. Iriye and T. Aruga (eds), *Senkanki no Nihon gaiko* (University of Tokyo Press, 1984).

'Perceptions of German History Among the British Policy-Making Elite, 1930–1945, and the Role of the German Emigré Historians in its Formation' in Henning Kohler (ed.), *Deutschland und der Westen; Vorträge und Diskussionsbeiträge des Symposiums zu Ehren von Gordon Craig* (Berlin: Colloquium Verlag, 1984).

'Britain, the United States and the Opening of the Cold War' in Ritchie

Ovendale (ed.), *The Foreign Policies of the Labour Governments 1945–1951* (Leicester University Press, 1984).

'Britain and the Neutral Powers 1939–1945; Some General Considerations' in Louis-Edouard Roulet and Roland Blättler (eds), *Les Etats neutres Européens et la Seconde Guerre Mondiale* (Neuchatel: Editions de la Baconnière, 1985).

'Foreign Secretaries as Diplomatists' in Roger Bullen (ed.), *The Foreign Office 1782–1982* (University Publications of America, 1985).

Historical Introduction to R.J. Pritchard and Sonia Maguana Zaida (eds), *The Tokyo War Crimes Trial. A Comprehensive Index and Guide* (New York: Garland, 1987–1988, 5 vols).

'British Military Perceptions of the Soviet Union and the Strategic Threat 1945–1980' in J. Becker and Franz Knipping (eds), *Power in Europe. Great Britain, France, Italy and Germany* (New York: de Gruyter, 1986).

'The European Invasion and Withdrawal from the Far East, 1494–1986' in *International Affairs in Asia and the Pacific. Their Past, Present and Future*, Thirteenth Anniversary International Conference of Japan Association of International Relations, Tokyo 1986.

'Grossbritannien, die Vereinigte Staaten und Deutschland', in Joseph Forschepoth and Rolf Steininger (eds), *Britische-Deutschland und Basatzungspolitik, 1945–1949* (Paderborn: Schöningh 1985).

'Britain and the Historiography of the Yalta Conference with an Appendix: Select Bibliography of British Historical Work on the Opening of the Cold War' in Paolo Brundu Olla, *Yalta: Un Mito che resiste* (Rome: Edizioni dell'Atlantica, 1989).

Introduction to D. Cameron Watt and Guido di Tella, *Argentina and the Great Powers* (London: Macmillan, 1989).

'Alliance Negotiations on the Eve of the Second World War' in *Grands Thèmes Methodologie: Sections Chronologiques 1, Rapports et abrégés*, 17th International Congress of Historical Sciences, Madrid, 1990, International Committee of the Historical Sciences. Paper presented.

'Mitä oman ajan historiä on?' (What is contemporary history?) in Sappo Hentila and Timo Turja (eds), *Poliittinen Historia, Suomi ja Muut*, Festschrift for Professor J. Nevakivi (Oulussa, Finland, Pokjoinen, 1991).

'New Developments in the Conduct of Foreign Relations: The Influencing of Opinion against Governments in the Interwar Years. A New Field of Study' in Alessandra Nigliazze and Enrica Decleva (eds), *Diplomazia e Storia delle relazioni internationali, studio in*

*onore di Enrico Serra* (Milan: Giuffre Editori, 1991).
Foreword to B.J. McKercher (ed.), *Anglo-American Relations in the 1920s. The Struggle For Supremacy* (London: Macmillan, 1991).

(b) ARTICLES

'Uneasy Balance, German-Soviet Relations, 1917–1941', *Wiener Library Bulletin*, Vol. VIII, Nos. 5–6, September–December 1954.
'The Reoccupation of the Rhineland', *History Today*, Vol. VI, April 1956.
'The Anglo-German Naval Agreement of 1935: An Interim Judgement', *Journal of Modern History*, Vol. XXVIII, No. 2, June 1956.
'Some reflections on Austrian Foreign Policy, 1945–55', *International Relations*, October 1956.
'Anglo-German Naval Negotiations on the Eve of the Second World War', Article in two parts, *Journal of the Royal United Services Institute* (hereafter R.U.S.I. Journal), Vol. 103, Nos. 610–11, May and July 1958.
'Gli accordi mediterranei anglo-italiani del 1938', *Rivista di Studi Politici Internazionali*, XXVI, No. 1, January–March 1959.
'Les Alliés et la Résistance Allemande (1939–1944)' *Revue d'Histoire de la deuxième Guerre Mondiale*, December 1959.
'Der Einfluss der Dominions auf die Britische Aussenpolitik vor München, 1938', *Vierteljahresheft für Zeitgeschichte*, 8te Jahrgang, Heft 1, January 1960.
'Christian Essay in Appeasement', *Wiener Library Bulletin*, Vol. XIV, No. 2, August 1960.
'Pirow's Berlin Mission of November 1938', *Wiener Library Bulletin*, Vol. XII, Nos. 5–6, 1958.
'Japan in the Anti-Comintern Pact-Dilemmas and Hesitations', *Wiener Library Bulletin*, Vol. XIII, Nos. 5–6, 1959.
'The Rome-Berlin Axis, 1936–1940 – Myth and Reality', *Review of Politics*, Vol. 22, No. 4, October 1960.
'America and the British Foreign Policy-Making Elite, 1895–1956', *Review of Politics*, Vol. 25, No. 1, January 1963.
'Imperial Defence and Imperial Foreign Policy, 1911–1939', *Journal of Commonwealth Political Studies*, Vol. I, No. 4, May 1963.
'The Week-end Crisis of May 1938. A Rejoinder to Mr Wallace', *Slavonic and East European Review*, Vol. XLIV, No. 102, July 1966.
'German Military Plans for the Reoccupation of the Rhineland: A Note', *Journal of Contemporary History*, October 1966.

'British Reactions to the Assassination at Sarajevo', *European Studies Review*, Vol. I, No. 3, 1971.

'"The Week" That Was', *Encounter*, May 1972.

'Chamberlain and Roosevelt: Two Appeasers', *International Journal*, March 1973.

'The Secret Communications Between Chamberlain and Roosevelt', *Interplay*, January 1971.

'Hitler's Visit to Rome and the May Weekend Crisis: A Study in Hitler's Response to External Stimuli', *Journal of Contemporary History*, Vol. 9, No. 1, 1974.

'Bledne Informacje, Bledne Koncepje, Brak Zaufania z dziejow brytysjkiej polityki zagranieznaj w latach 1938–1939 (Misinformation, Misconception and Mistake. Some Aspects of British Foreign Policy 1938–1939)', Kwartalnik Historyczny, *Recznik* LXXXV, No. 4, Warsaw 1978.

'Every War Must End: Planning for Post-war Security in Britain and America in the Wars of 1914–18 and 1939–45. The Roles of Historical Example and of Professional Historians', *Transactions of the Royal Historical Society*, 5th series, Vol. 28, 1978.

'Gross Britannien und Europa, 1951–1959', *Vierteljahreshaft für Zeitgeschichte*, Vol. IV, 1986.

'Britain and Russia in 1939', *Britain – USSR*, No. 57, Spring 1980; Part I of an article in 2 parts.

'Britain and Russia in 1939', *Britain – USSR*, No. 58, Spring 1981; Part II of an article in 2 parts.

'Churchill und die Kalte Krieg', text of the 14th Annual Swiss Winston Churchill Memorial Foundation Lecture, *Schweizer Monatshefte*, 61 Jahr/Heft 11, Sonderbeilage, November 1981.

'Ideology in British Foreign Policy', *Jerusalem Journal of International Affairs*, Vol. 9, No. 1, March 1987.

'Those were the Weeks that Were – Claud Cockburn's Noises Off', *Encounter*, Vol. LXVI, No. 5, May 1986.

'1939 Revisited: On Theories of the Origins of Wars', *International Affairs*, Vol. 65, No. 4, Autumn 1989.

'How War Came', *R.U.S.I. Journal*, Vol. 134, No. 4, Winter 1989.

'Britain and German Security, 1944–1955' in Foreign and Commonwealth Office Historical Branch, *Occasional Papers No. 3*, November 1989.

(Review article) 'A.P. Young. Die x-Dokumente. Die geheime Kontakte Carl Goerdelers mit der britischen Regiering 1938/1939. Hrsg. von Sidney Aster. Betrauung der deutschen Ausgebe und Nachwort: Helmut Krausnick, München 1939', *Vierteljahresheft für*

*Zeitgeschichte*, 38 Jahrgang, 3 Heft, July 1990.
'La Guerra del dopoguerra' (The wars of the post-war years), *Relazioni Internazionali*, Vol. LV, December 1991.
Reply to Robert Marshall, 'The Atomic Bomb – and the Lag in Historical Understanding', *Intelligence and National Security*, Vol. 6, No. 2, April 1991.
'Who Plotted Against Whom? Stalin's Purge of the Soviet High Command Revisited', *Journal of Soviet Military Studies*, Vol. 3, No. 1, March 1990.
'Soviet Foreign Policy and the Molotov–Ribbentrop Pact', *Storia Delle Relazioni Internazionali*, Anno VII, 1991/2.

## 2. History of American Foreign Policy

(a) CONTRIBUTIONS TO BOOKS

'Demythologising the Eisenhower Era' in Wm. Roger Louis and Hedley Bull, *The 'Special Relationship': Anglo-American Relations since 1945* (Oxford: Clarendon, 1986).

(b) ARTICLES

'American Aid to Britain and the Problem of Socialism, 1945–1951', *American Review*, April 1963.
'American Strategic Interests and Anxieties in the West Indies, 1917–1940' *R.U.S.I. Journal*, Vol. 108, No. 3, August 1963.
'America and Russia: the Rise of the Super Powers', *International Affairs*, Vol. 46, November 1970.
(Review article) 'American Diplomatic History', *Review of Politics*, Vol. 27, No. 4, October 1966.

## 3. Middle Eastern History

(a) CONTRIBUTIONS TO BOOKS

'The High Dam at Aswan and the Politics of Control' in N. Rubin and W.M. Warren (eds), *Dams in Africa* (London: Frank Cass, 1968).
'The Saadabad Pact of 8 July 1937' in Urien Dann (ed.), *The Great Powers in the Middle East, 1919–1939* (New York and London: Holmes & Meier, 1988).

(b) ARTICLES

'The Foreign Policy of Ibn Saud, 1936–1939', *Journal of the Royal Central Asian Society*, Vol. 1, Part II, April 1963.
'Egypt as a Nation', *New Middle East*, June 1969.

## 4. German History, Anglo-German Relations

(a) CONTRIBUTIONS TO BOOKS

'Germany at War, 1939–1945' in E.J. Passant (ed.), *A Short History of Germany 1815–1945* (Cambridge University Press, 1959).

(b) ARTICLES

'Hitler and Nadolny', *Contemporary Review*, July 1959.

'New Light on Hitler's Youth', *History*, No. 1 (New York: Meridian Books Inc., September 1959, reprinted from *History Today*, Vol. VIII, No. 1, January 1958).

'Deutschland im Zwiespalt britischen Politik' in W. Höfer (ed.), *Europa und die Einheit Deutschlands, Eine Bialanz nach 100 Jahren* (Cologne: Verlag Wissenschaft und Politik, 1970).

'New Light on Hitler's Apprenticeship' in R.F. Hopwood (ed.), *Germany, People and Politics, 1750–1945* (Edinburgh: Oliver and Boyd, 1968; reprinted from *History Today*).

'New Light on Hitler's Youth', *History Today*, Vol. VIII, No. 1, January 1958.

'Die Bayerische Bemühungen um die Ausweisung Hitlers 1924', *Vierteljahresheft für Zeitgeschichte*, 6 Jahrgang, Heft 3, 1958.

'Hitler Comes to Power – Thirty Years After', *History Today*, Vol XIII, March 1963.

'British Opinion and the Oder-Neisse Line', *Survey*, October 1966.

## 5. Military History

(a) CONTRIBUTIONS TO BOOKS

'European Military Leadership and the Breakdown of Europe, 1919–1939' in Adrian Preston (ed.) *General Staffs and Diplomacy before the Second World War* (London: Croom Helm, 1978).

'Restraints on War in the Air before 1945' in Michael Howard (ed.) *Restraints on War, Studies in the Limitation of Armed Conflict* (Oxford University Press, 1979).

'Die Konservative Regierung und die EWG, 1950–1957' in Hans-Erich Volkmann and Walter Schwengler (eds), *Die Europäische Verteidigungsgemeinschaft Stand und Probleme der Forschung* (Boppard am Rhein: Boldt Verlag for the Militärgeschichtliches Forschungsamt, 1985).

'Schlussbetrachtung: Bemerkungen mit dem Ziel einer Synthese' in Norbert Wiggershaus and Roland G. Foerster, *Die Westliche Sicher-*

*heitsgemeinschaft 1948–1950: Gemeinsame Probleme und gegensät-liche Nationalinteressen in der Gründungsphase der Nordatlantischen Allianz* (Boppard am Rhein: Harald Boldt Verlag, 1988).

(b) ARTICLES

'German strategic planning and Spain, 1938–1939', *The Army Quarterly and Defence Journal*, Vol. LXXX, No. 2, July 1960.

'Die Ende der britischen Schlachtflotte' *Wehrwissenschaftliche Rundschau*, Jahrgang Heft 6, June 1962.

'Stalin's First Bid for Seapower', *Proceedings of the US Naval Institute*, 1964.

'Das Seminar für militarische Verwaltungsfragen der Universität London (LSE) 1930–1931', *Wehrwissenschaftliche Rundschau*, 1965.

'The London University Class for Military Administrators, 1906–1931: A Study in the British Approach to Civil-Military Relations', *LSE Quarterly*, Vol. 2, No. 2, Summer 1988.

## 6. Intelligence and International Relations

(a) CONTRIBUTIONS TO BOOKS

Introduction to D. Irving (ed.), *Breach of Security, The German Intelligence File on Britain* (London: William Kimber, 1968).

'British Intelligence and the Coming of the Second World War in Europe' in Ernest R. May (ed.), *Knowing One's Enemies: Intelligence Assessment Before the World Wars* (Princeton University Press, 1985).

'Le moral de l'armée française tel que se le représentaient les Britanniques en 1939 et 1940; une faillite des services de renseignements?' in *Français et Britanniques dans la drôle de guerre* (Paris: Editions Nationale de la Recherche Scientifique, 1979).

'Critical Afterthoughts and Alternative Historico-Literary Theories' in Wesley K. Wark (ed.), *Spy Fiction, Spy Films and Real Intelligence* (London: Frank Cass, 1991).

(b) ARTICLES

'Intelligence Studies: the Emergence of the British School' (review article), *Intelligence and National Security*, Vol. 3, No. 2, April 1988.

'Fall-out from Treachery: Peter Wright and *Spycatcher*', *Political Quarterly*, Vol. 59, No. 2, April–June 1988.

'Francis Herbert King: A Soviet Source in the Foreign Office',

*Intelligence and National Security*, Vol. 3, No. 4, October 1988.
'Learning from Peter Wright: A Reply', *Political Quarterly*, Vol. 60, No. 2, April–June 1989.
'The Foreign Office Failure to Anticipate the Nazi-Soviet Pact', *Intelligence and National Security*, Vol. 4, No. 2, April 1989.
'Intelligence and the Historian', *Diplomatic History*, Vol. 14, No. 2, Spring 1990.
'The *Sender der deutschen Freiheitspartie*: A First Step in the British Radio War Against Nazi Germany?', *Intelligence and National Security*, Vol. 6, No. 3, July 1991.


## 7. Diplomatic Theory and Practice

(a) CONTRIBUTIONS TO BOOKS

'Diplomacy and International Relations' in N.J. den Hollander (ed.), *Diverging Parallels. A Comparison of American and European Thought and Action* (Leiden: E.J. Brill, 1971).

(b) ARTICLES

'Nazi Leaders and German Diplomats', *Journal of Central European Studies*, July 1955.
'Sir Nevile Henderson Reappraised', *Contemporary Review*, March 1962.
'Hitler's Foreign Policy Apparat' (review article), *Government and Opposition*, Winter 1969–1970.


## 8. General History

(a) ARTICLES

'The Decembrists – Russia 1825, Ethiopia 1960: Two Revolutions Compared', *International Relations*, Vol. II, No. 7, 1963.
'Britain and America: the Last Quarter of a Century', *The World and the School*, No. 7, Summer 1966.
'Grande Bretagne et Les États Unis depuis 1941', *Le Monde et l'Ecole*, No. 7, Summer 1966.
'Revolution: An Historical Assessment', *The World and the School*, September 1972.
'The Veneti: A Pre-Roman Atlantic Sea Power', *Naval History*, Vol. 3, No. 2, Spring 1989.

## 9. Popularizations

(a) CONTRIBUTIONS TO BOOKS

'After Munich', 'Before the Blitzkrieg' and 'The Formation of the Triple Alliance' in B.M. Pitt (ed.), *History of the Second World War* (London: Purnell 1967).

'Après Munich', and 'La Veille de la Guerre' (Paris: *Histoire*, Nos. 2 and 3); 'Dopo Monaco' and 'Premesia della Blitzkrieg' (Rome: *Storia della Secundo Guerro Mondiale*, Nos. 2 and 3).

'The Nazi-Soviet Pact', *History of the Twentieth Century*, No. 60.

'Britain Swings to Labour, 1945', *History of the Second World War* Vol. VIII, No. 1.

'Indonesia 1945–1949', ibid., Vol. VIII, No. 10.

'Britain Swings to Labour, 1945', *History of the Second World War* No. 97.

'The First Moroccan Crisis', *History of the Twentieth Century*, No. 5, 1968.

## GOVERNMENT, POLITICS, WAR STUDIES, INTERNATIONAL RELATIONS

### 1. International Relations

(a) ARTICLES

'The Possibility of a Multilateral Arms Race – a Note', *International Relations*, Vol. II, No. 6, October 1962.

'Summits and Summitry Reconsidered', *International Relations*, Vol. II, No. 8, October 1963.

'Disarmament and Civil-Military Relations among the Smaller Powers', *International Relations*, Vol. II, No. 10, November 1964.

'The 1968 Elections in Baden-Wurtemberg', *World Today*, June 1968.

(b) CONTRIBUTIONS TO BOOKS

'Deutsche-britische Beziehungen heute und morgen' in K. Kaiser and R. Morgan (eds), *Strukturwandlungen der Aussenpolitik in Grossbritannien und in der Bundesrepublik* (Munich/Vienna: R. Oldenbourg Verlag, 1970); English original ms.

'Anglo-German Relations Today and Tomorrow' in K. Kaiser and R. Morgan (eds), *Britain and West Germany: Changing Societies and the Future of Foreign Policy* (Oxford University Press for Royal Institute of International Affairs, 1971).

'Implications for Canada–UK Relations in the 1990s' in D.K. Adams (ed.), *Britain and Canada in the 1990s*, Proceedings of a UK/Canada Colloquium, Leeds Castle, Kent (Aldershot, Hants: Dartmouth Publishing for Canadian Institute for Research on Public Policy, 1992).

## 2. War Studies, Military Policy

(a) ARTICLES

'American Strategy in the Western Pacific', *British Survey*, No. 175, October 1963.

'British Intervention in East Africa: An Essay in Strategic Mobility', *Revue Militaire Général*, Vol. 5, May 1966.

'The Role of the Aircraft Carrier in some Recent British Military Operations', *R.U.S.I. Journal*, Vol. 111, No. 641, May 1966.

'The Continuing Strategic Importance of Simonstown', *Proceedings of the US Naval Institute*, October 1969.

'Balanced Force Reductions and the American Military Withdrawal from Europe', *R.U.S.I. Journal*, Vol. 115, June 1970.

'Piracy on the High Seas. A New Kind of Warfare', *New Middle East*, January 1972.

'Lessons of the American Defeat in Vietnam' *R.U.S.I. Journal,* Vol. 118, January 1973.

## 3. British Foreign Policy

(a) ARTICLES

'Das Labour-partei und Deutschland', *Europa-Archiv*, Vol. 79, No. 22, November 1965.

'Great Britain and Germany: the Last Three Years', *International Journal*, Autumn 1968.

'The Decision to Withdraw from the Gulf: A Study in Political Irrelevancy', *Political Quarterly*, Vol. 39, No. 3, 1968.

'Britain and the Indian Ocean: Diplomacy before Defence', *Political Quarterly*, Vol. 42, June 1971.

'Britain and a European Security Conference', *R.U.S.I. Journal,* Vol. 116, June 1971.

'External Affairs in the 1990s' in *Looking Back, Looking Forward*, Essays by members of the Editorial Board to mark the Fiftieth Anniversary of the journal, *Political Quarterly*, Vol. 51, No. 1, January 1980.

## 4. Diplomatic Services

(a) ARTICLES

'The Home Civil Service and the New Diplomacy', *Political Quarterly*, Vol. 40, October–December 1969.

'The Future of British Foreign Policy', *Political Quarterly*, Vol. 41, January 1970.

'The Reform of the West German Foreign Service: The Herwath Report', *The World Today*, July 1970.

'The Reform of the West German Foreign Service: the Herwath and the Duncan Reports Compared', *The World Today*, July 1970.

'The Diplomatic Service. Reform or Abolition. Commentary', *Political Quarterly*, Vol. 48, No. 4, October–December 1977.

## 5. The Middle East

(a) CONTRIBUTIONS TO BOOKS

*British Interests in the Mediterranean and Middle East* (Oxford University Press for Royal Institute of International Affairs, 1958).

(b) ARTICLES

'Grossbritannien und Suez', *Europa-Archiv*, 11 Jahrgang, No. 24, 20 December 1956.

'Les rélations franco-anglaises au Moyen Orient', *Politique Etrangère*, Vol. 22, No. 1, 1957.

'Gross-Britannien und die Mittelost-Krise', *Europa-Archiv*, Vol. 13 Nos. 22–23, 20 November–5 December 1958.

'The Future of the Gulf States', *The World Today*, November 1964.

'The Postponement of the Arab Summit', *The World Today*, September 1966.

'Labour and Trade Unionism in Aden, 1952–60', *Middle East Journal*, Winter 1966.

'Soviet Presence in the Mediterranean. A Study in the Application of Political Influence', *New Middle East*, October 1968.

'Soviet Demands for Middle Eastern Oil', *New Middle East*, December 1968.

'No Commercial Future for the Suez Canal. New Trends in Maritime Trading', *New Middle East*, January 1969; reprinted in *Survival*, April 1969.

'A New Sarajevo in the Middle East?' *New Middle East*, January 1970.

'Death of the "Arab Nation" – End of a Myth', *New Middle East*, October 1970.
'The Proposed New Arab Union' (Note), *The World Today*, December 1970.
'The Arabs, the Heath Government and the Future of the Gulf', *New Middle East*, March 1971.
'Can the Union of Arab Emirates Survive?' *The World Today*, April 1971.
Contributor to *Britain's Future Role East of Suez*, Report of a Seminar held at the Royal United Service Institute, 3 February 1971.
'Ventures in Soviet Diplomacy, III: The Persian Gulf – Cradle of Conflict?', *Problems of Communism*, May–June 1972.
'El Golfo Persico', *Problemas Internacionales*, August 1972.
'The Soviet Union and the Middle East: Unfruitful Involvement', *Soviet Analyst*, August 1972.
'Towards a Middle Eastern Settlement? The Politics of Ambiguity', *Political Quarterly*, Vol. 49, No. 1, January–March 1978.

## 6.  US Foreign Policy

(a)  ARTICLES

'American Foreign Policy and Vietnam', *Political Quarterly*, Vol. 43, January–March 1972.
'American Foreign Policy after Vietnam', *Political Quarterly*, Vol. 44, July 1973.
'A Return to Americanism? The Foreign Policy of President Carter', *Political Quarterly*, Vol. 48, No. 4, October–December 1977.
(Review Article) 'Where is the World? – American Foreign Policy', *Encounter*, January 1977.
'Henry Kissinger; an interim judgment', *Political Quarterly*, Vol. 48, 1977.

## 7.  Education

(a)  CONTRIBUTIONS TO BOOKS

'Expansion at the London School of Economics', in C.B. Cox and A.B. Dyson (eds), *Fight for Education: A Black Paper* (1969), reprinted in C.B. Cox and A.E. Dyson (eds), *The Black Paper on Education* (London, 1971).
'The Freedom of the Universities: Illusion and Reality 1962–1969' in C.B. Cox and A.B. Dyson (eds), *Black Paper Two* (London, 1976).

(b) ARTICLES

'The Security of British Universities': *Top Security*, 216, 1976.
'European Students Strike for Academic Reforms', *The Reporter*, Vol. 33, No. 11, 16 December 1965.

## SEA USE

(a) CONTRIBUTIONS TO BOOKS

'Great Britain, the North Sea and the Greenwich Forum' in Hans R. Kramer (ed.), *Die Wirtschaftliche Nutzung der Nordsee und die Europäische Gemeinschaft* (Baden-Baden: Schriftenreihe des Arbeitskreis Europäische Intregration e.t. Bd. 6, Minos-Verlag, 1979).
(Editor) *Britain and the Sea. The 200-mile Zone and its Implications*, Institute of Marine Engineers.
'Introduction' and 'Offshore Policies and Policy-Making in the United Kingdom' in D.C. Watt (ed.), *The North Sea: A New International Regime* (International Publishing Corporation, Science and Technology Press, 1981).
'Conclusions' in M.B.F. Ranken (ed.), *Greenwich Forum VI: World Shipping in the 1990s Record of a Conference at the Royal Naval College Greenwich 23-25 April 1980* (International Publishing Corporation Science and Technology Press, 1981).
'British Sea Policy. Past Achievements and Future Prospects', in M.B.F. Ranken (ed.), *Greenwich Forum IX. Britain and the Sea. Future Dependence: Future Opportunities* (Edinburgh: Scottish Academic Press, 1984).

(b) ARTICLES

'Security of North Sea Oil Rigs' in *Papers Presented to Offshore Europe 1975* (London: Spearhead Publications, 1975).
'The Security Problems with North Sea Oil Installations', *Top Security*, Vol. I, No. 10, February 1976.
'Britain and North Sea Oil: Policies Past and Present' *Political Quarterly*, Vol. 47, No. 4, October 1976.
'The E.E.C. and Fishing. New Venture into Unknown Seas', *Political Quarterly*, Vol. 48, No. 3, July 1977.
'The Security of Offshore Resources', *R.U.S.I. Journal*, Vol. 123, No. 2, June 1978.
'Into Deeper Waters: The Royal Society Conference on Moving into Deeper Waters, June 1977', *Marine Policy*, Vol. I, No. 4, 1977.

'First Steps in the Enclosure of the Oceans. The Origins of Truman's proclamation on the resources of the continental shelf, 28 September 1945', *Marine Policy*, Vol. III, July 1979.

'Offshore Britain: Today and Tomorrow', *International Affairs*, Vol. 56, No. 2, April 1980.

'Who in Government should Co-ordinate and Direct, and What Arms of Government should undertake the Task Afloat – the Royal Navy, H.M. Coastguard, and Police, or Some New Body, perhaps of the E.E.C.?' in *The 200 Mile Exclusive Fisheries Limit. How is Government to meet its Extended Obligations Afloat? Report of a Meeting at the House of Lords, 29 November 1976* (London: Greenwich Forum, January 1977.)

'Ocean Resources; the Need for Agreement', *International Affairs*, Vol. 58, No. 4, Winter 1981–1982.

'Towards a New Order for the World's Oceans?', *Round Table*, 285, January 1983.

'ISBA – The Realistic Option', *Sea Trade*, Vol. 13, No. 8, August 1983.

'To Sign or Not to Sign: the Debate in Britain on the Law of the Sea Convention', *International Journal*, Vol. XXXVIII, No. 3, Summer 1983.

## OTHER

(a) CONTRIBUTIONS TO BOOKS

'A Failure of Imagination' in *Race and Riots 1981. A New Society Social Studies Reader* (London: New Society, 1981).

(b) ARTICLES

'The Public Interest in Question. Industry as Clients and Constituents of Government Departments', *Political Quarterly*, Vol. 59, No. 1, January–March 1988.

# Index